My pen calluses!

高橋和希

THERE'S ONE PROBLEM WHEN TRYING TO EXPRESS THE FUN OF CARD GAMES IN MANGA FORM. IN A REAL CARD GAME, THE CLOSER THE PLAYERS' SKILL LEVELS ARE, THE MORE FUN IT IS...BUT IN A MANGA, YOU NEED TO TIP THE POWER BALANCE TO SHOW HOW THE MAIN CHARACTER CAN BEAT OVERWHELMINGLY POWERFUL OPPONENTS. SO DON'T BE MAD IF THE SCORES OR EFFECTS OF THE CARDS IN THE MANGA ARE A BIT DIFFERENT FROM THE OFFICIAL CARD GAME VERSION!

KAZUKI TAKAHASHI, 2000

Artist/author Kazuki Takahashi first tried to break into the manga business in 1982, but success eluded him until **Yu-Gi-Oh!** debuted in the Japanese **Weekly Shonen Jump** magazine in 1996. **Yu-Gi-Oh!**'s themes of friendship and fighting, together with Takahashi's weird and wonderful art, soon became enormously successful, spawning a real-world card game, video games, and two anime series. A lifelong gamer, Takahashi enjoys Shogi (Japanese chess), Mahjong, card games, and tabletop RPGs, among other games.

YU-GI-OH!: DUELIST VOL. 12
The SHONEN JUMP Graphic Novel Edition

STORY AND ART BY
KAZUKI TAKAHASHI

Translation & English Adaptation/Joe Yamazaki
Touch-up Art & Lettering/Eric Erbes
Design/Andrea Rice
Editor/Jason Thompson

Managing Editor/Elizabeth Kawasaki
Director of Production/Noboru Watanabe
Vice President of Publishing/Alvin Lu
Vice President & Editor in Chief/Yumi Hoashi
Sr. Director of Acquisitions/Rika Inouye
Vice President of Sales & Marketing/Liza Coppola
Publisher/ Hyoe Narita

In the original Japanese edition, YU-GI-OH!, YU-GI-OH!: DUELIST and
YU-GI-OH!: MILLENNIUM WORLD are known collectively as YU-GI-OH!.
The English YU-GI-OH!: DUELIST was originally volumes 8-31
of the Japanese YU-GI-OH!.

Printed in the U.S.A.

Published by VIZ Media, LLC
P.O. Box 77010
San Francisco, CA 94107

SHONEN JUMP Graphic Novel Edition
10 9 8 7 6 5 4 3 2 1
First printing, December 2005

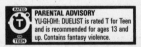

PARENTAL ADVISORY
YU-GI-OH!: DUELIST is rated T for Teen
and is recommended for ages 13 and
up. Contains fantasy violence.

THE WORLD'S
MOST POPULAR MANGA

GRAPHIC NOVEL

www.viz.com

www.shonenjump.com

SHONEN JUMP GRAPHIC NOVEL

Vol. 12

MAGICIAN VS. MAGICIAN

STORY AND ART BY
KAZUKI TAKAHASHI

THE STORY SO FAR...

YUGI MUTOU/ YU-GI-OH

When 10th grader Yugi solved the Millennium Puzzle, another spirit took up residence in his body...Yu-Gi-Oh, the King of Games, a dark avenger who challenges evildoers to "Shadow Games" of life and death!

YUGI FACES DEADLY ENEMIES!

Using his gaming skills, Yugi fights ruthless adversaries like Maximillion Pegasus, multimillionaire creator of the collectible card game "Duel Monsters," and Ryo Bakura, whose friendly personality turns evil when he is possessed by the spirit of the Millennium Ring. But Yugi's greatest rival is Seto Kaiba, the world's second-greatest gamer—and the ruthless teenage president of Kaiba Corporation. At first, Kaiba and Yugi are bitter enemies, but after fighting against a common adversary—Pegasus—they come to respect one another. But for all his powers, there is one thing Yu-Gi-Oh cannot do: remember who he is and where he came from.

HIROTO
HONDA

ANZU
MAZAKI

KATSUYA
JONOUCHI

MARIK

ISHIZU ISHTAR

SETO KAIBA

THE TABLET OF THE PHARAOH'S MEMORIES

Then one day, when an Egyptian museum exhibit comes to Japan, Yugi sees an ancient carving of himself as an Egyptian pharaoh! The curator of the exhibit, Ishizu Ishtar, explains that there are seven Millennium Items, which were made to fit into a stone tablet in a hidden shrine in Egypt. According to the legend, when the seven Items are brought together, the pharaoh will regain his memories of his past life.

THE EGYPTIAN GOD CARDS

But Ishizu has a message for Kaiba as well. Ishizu needs Kaiba's help to win back two of three Egyptian God Cards—the rarest cards on Earth—from the clutches of the "Rare Hunters," an evil criminal syndicate led by the mysterious Marik. In order to draw out the thieves, Kaiba announces "Battle City," an enormous "Duel Monsters" tournament. Now, while Jonouchi and Kaiba fight their way through the tournament, the Rare Hunters send their agent Pandora to take Yugi out of the running...permanently!

YU-GI-OH! DUELIST

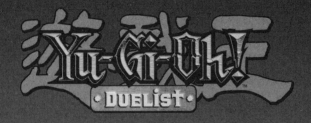

Vol. 12

CONTENTS

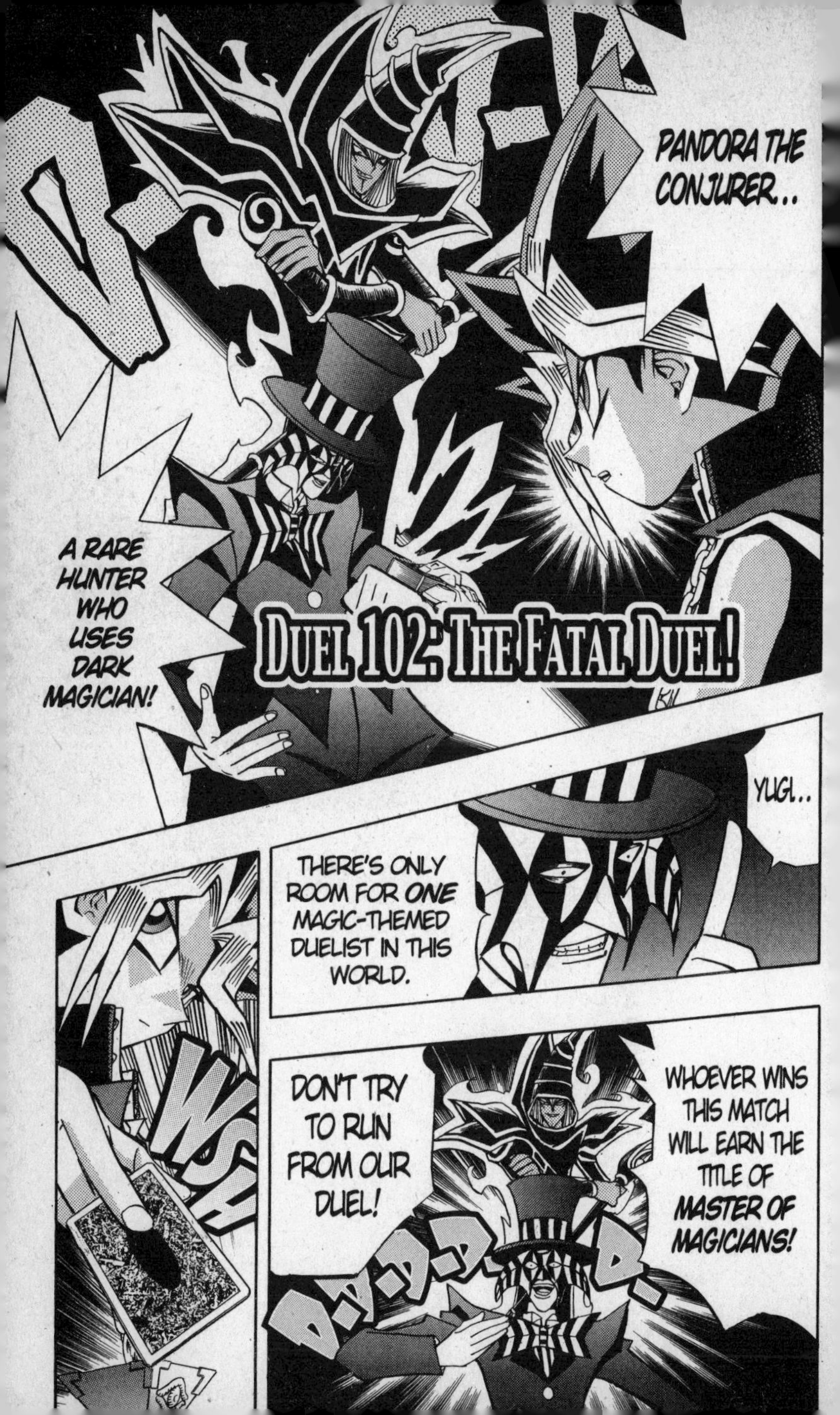
PANDORA THE CONJURER...
A RARE HUNTER WHO USES DARK MAGICIAN!
DUEL 102: THE FATAL DUEL!
YUGI...
THERE'S ONLY ROOM FOR ONE MAGIC-THEMED DUELIST IN THIS WORLD.
WHOEVER WINS THIS MATCH WILL EARN THE TITLE OF MASTER OF MAGICIANS!
DON'T TRY TO RUN FROM OUR DUEL!

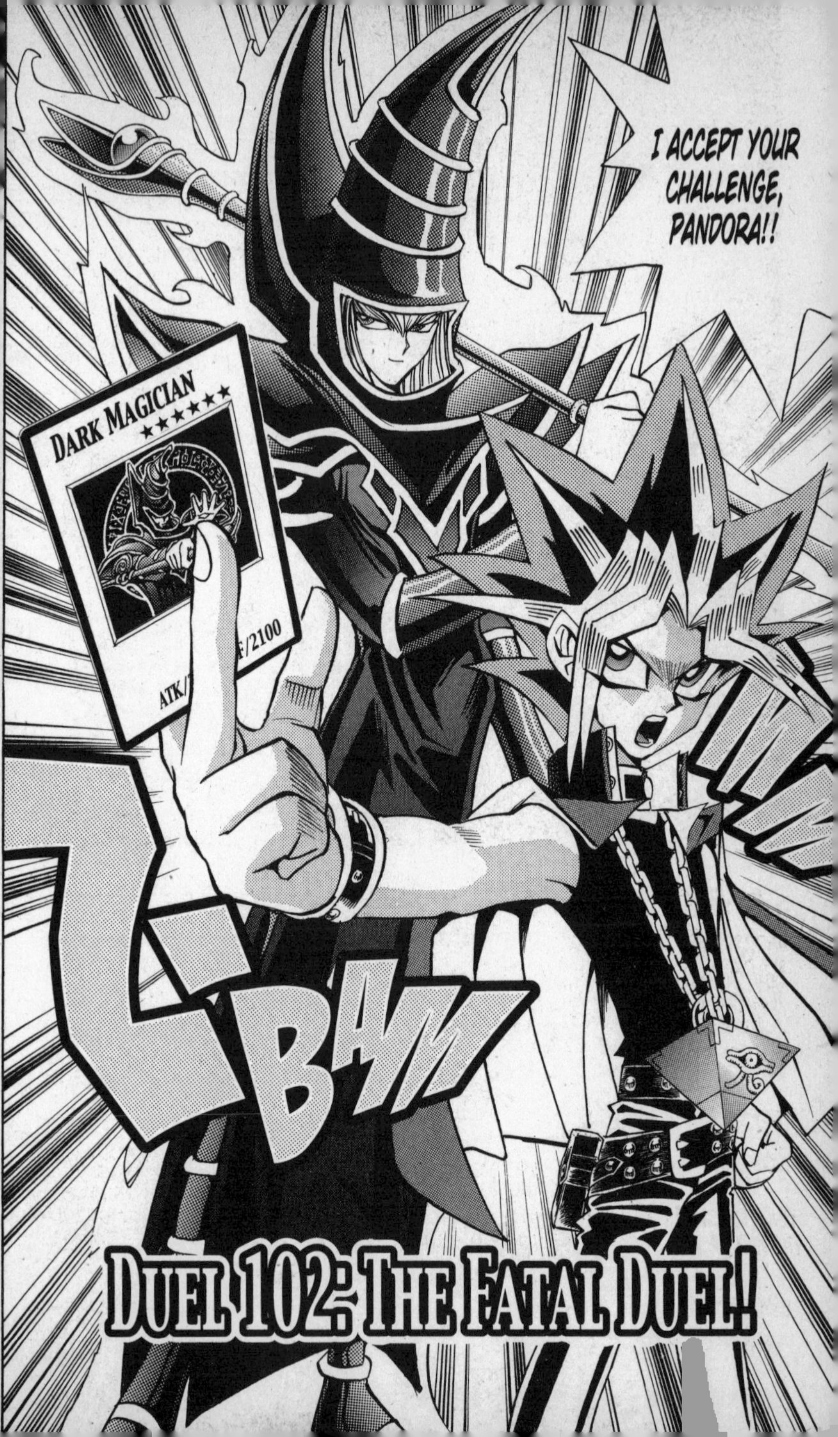
I ACCEPT YOUR CHALLENGE, PANDORA!!
DARK MAGICIAN
ATK/
/2100
BAM

Duel 102: The Fatal Duel!

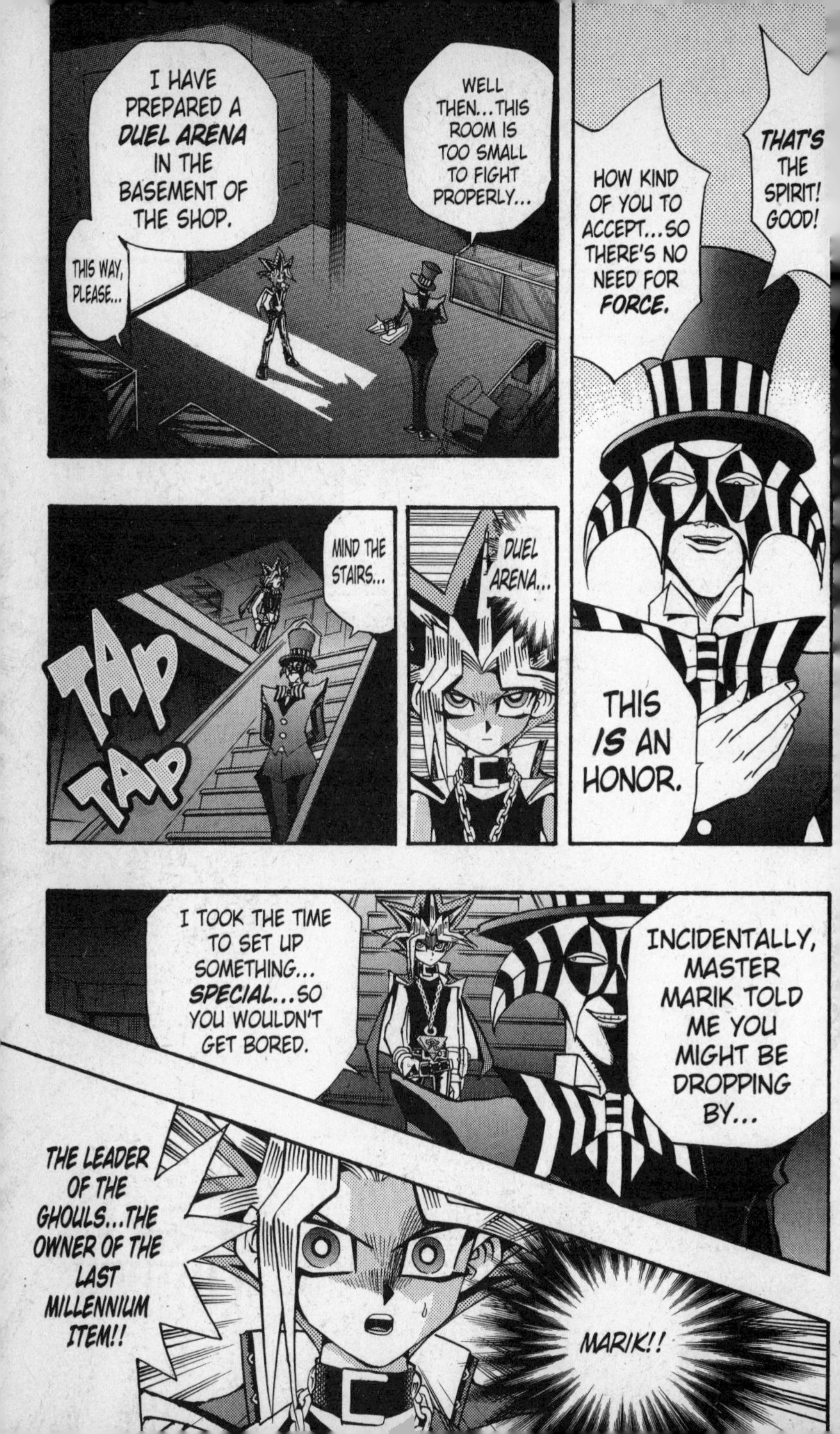
THAT'S THE SPIRIT! GOOD!
HOW KIND OF YOU TO ACCEPT...SO THERE'S NO NEED FOR FORCE.
THIS IS AN HONOR.
WELL THEN...THIS ROOM IS TOO SMALL TO FIGHT PROPERLY...
I HAVE PREPARED A DUEL ARENA IN THE BASEMENT OF THE SHOP.
THIS WAY, PLEASE...
DUEL ARENA...
MIND THE STAIRS...
TAP TAP
INCIDENTALLY, MASTER MARIK TOLD ME YOU MIGHT BE DROPPING BY...
I TOOK THE TIME TO SET UP SOMETHING... SPECIAL...SO YOU WOULDN'T GET BORED.
MARIK!!
THE LEADER OF THE GHOULS...THE OWNER OF THE LAST MILLENNIUM ITEM!!

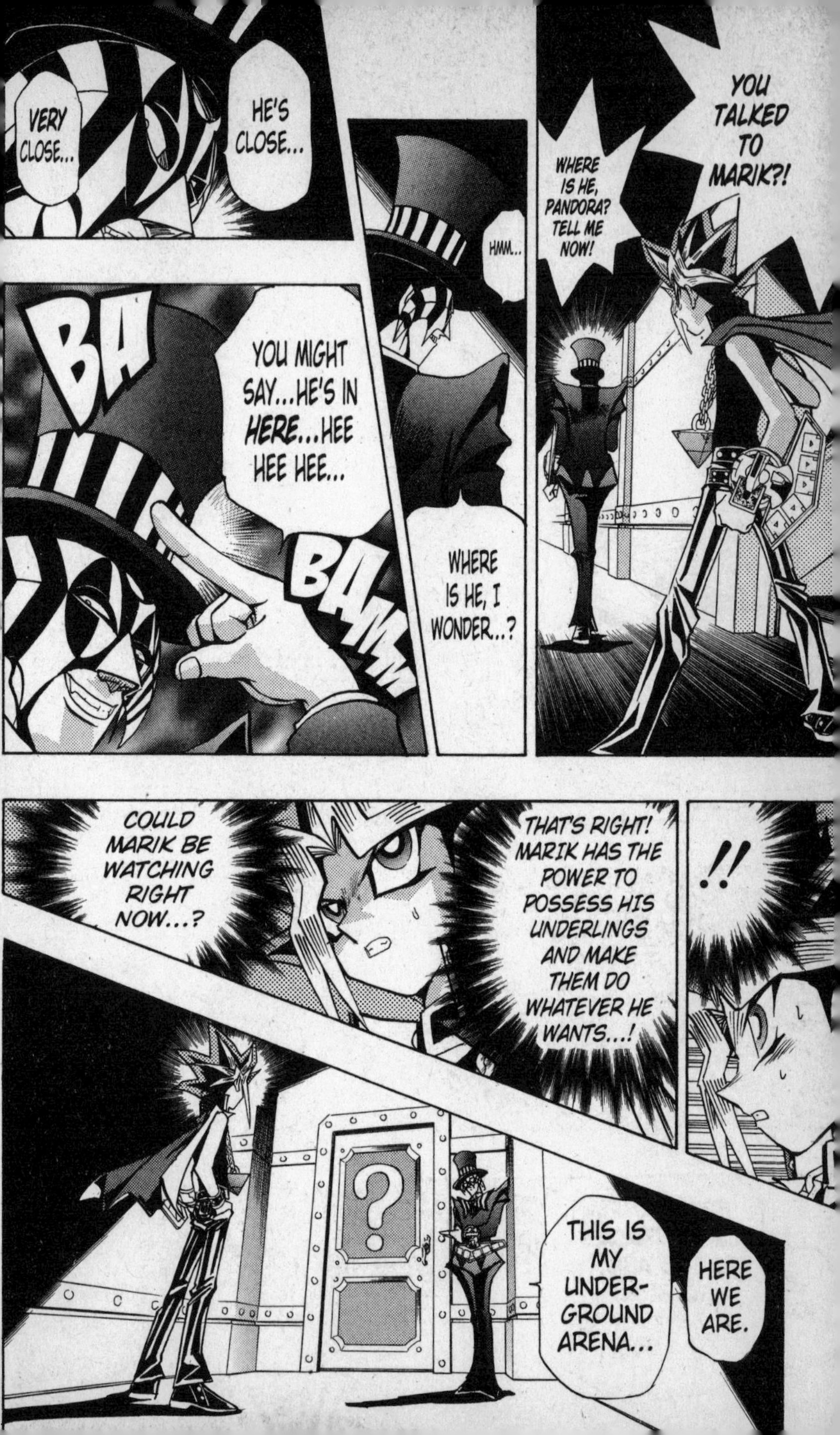
YOU TALKED TO MARIK?!
WHERE IS HE, PANDORA? TELL ME NOW!
HMM...
WHERE IS HE, I WONDER...?
HE'S CLOSE...
VERY CLOSE...
BA
YOU MIGHT SAY...HE'S IN HERE...HEE HEE HEE...
BAMM
!!
THAT'S RIGHT! MARIK HAS THE POWER TO POSSESS HIS UNDERLINGS AND MAKE THEM DO WHATEVER HE WANTS...!
COULD MARIK BE WATCHING RIGHT NOW...?
HERE WE ARE.
THIS IS MY UNDERGROUND ARENA...

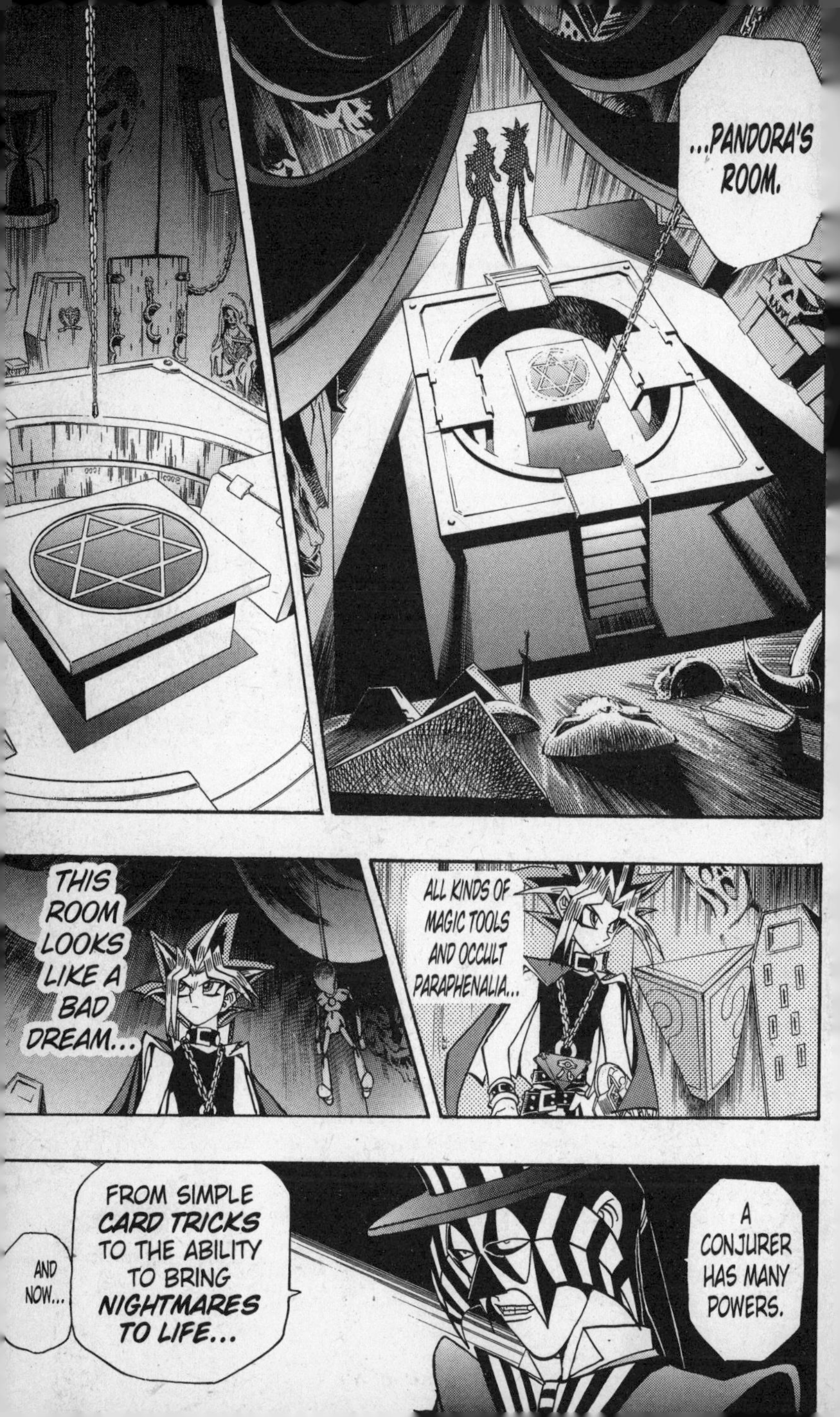
...PANDORA'S ROOM.
ALL KINDS OF MAGIC TOOLS AND OCCULT PARAPHENALIA...
THIS ROOM LOOKS LIKE A BAD DREAM...
A CONJURER HAS MANY POWERS.
FROM SIMPLE CARD TRICKS TO THE ABILITY TO BRING NIGHTMARES TO LIFE...
AND NOW...

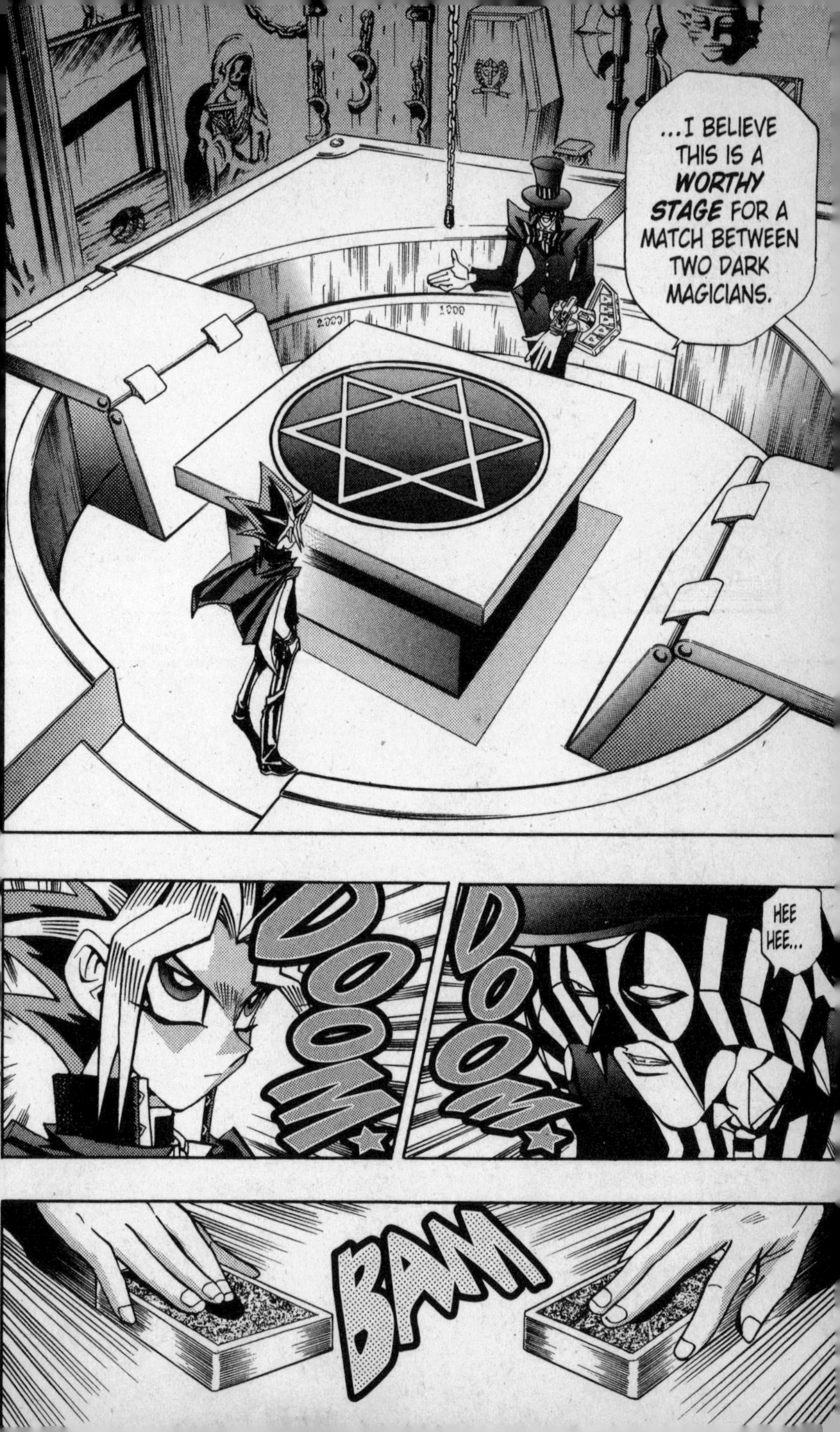
...I BELIEVE THIS IS A WORTHY STAGE FOR A MATCH BETWEEN TWO DARK MAGICIANS.
HEE HEE...
DOOOM
DOOOM
BAM

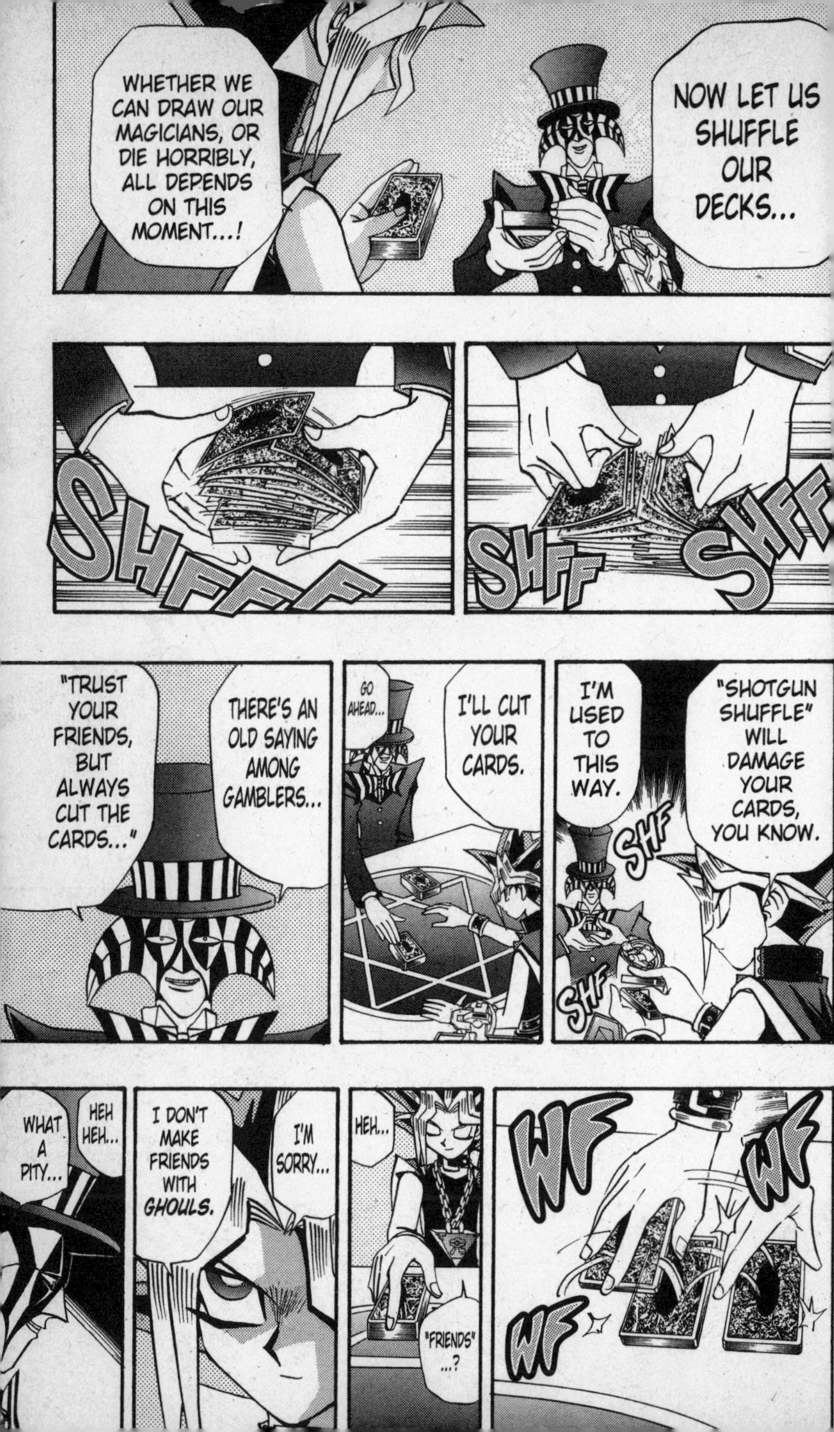

NOW LET US SHUFFLE OUR DECKS...
WHETHER WE CAN DRAW OUR MAGICIANS, OR DIE HORRIBLY, ALL DEPENDS ON THIS MOMENT...!
SHFF
SHFF
SHFFFF
"SHOTGUN SHUFFLE" WILL DAMAGE YOUR CARDS, YOU KNOW.
I'M USED TO THIS WAY.
SHF
SHF
I'LL CUT YOUR CARDS.
GO AHEAD...
THERE'S AN OLD SAYING AMONG GAMBLERS...
"TRUST YOUR FRIENDS, BUT ALWAYS CUT THE CARDS..."
WF
WF
WF
HEH...
"FRIENDS" ...?
I'M SORRY...
I DON'T MAKE FRIENDS WITH GHOULS.
HEH HEH...
WHAT A PITY...

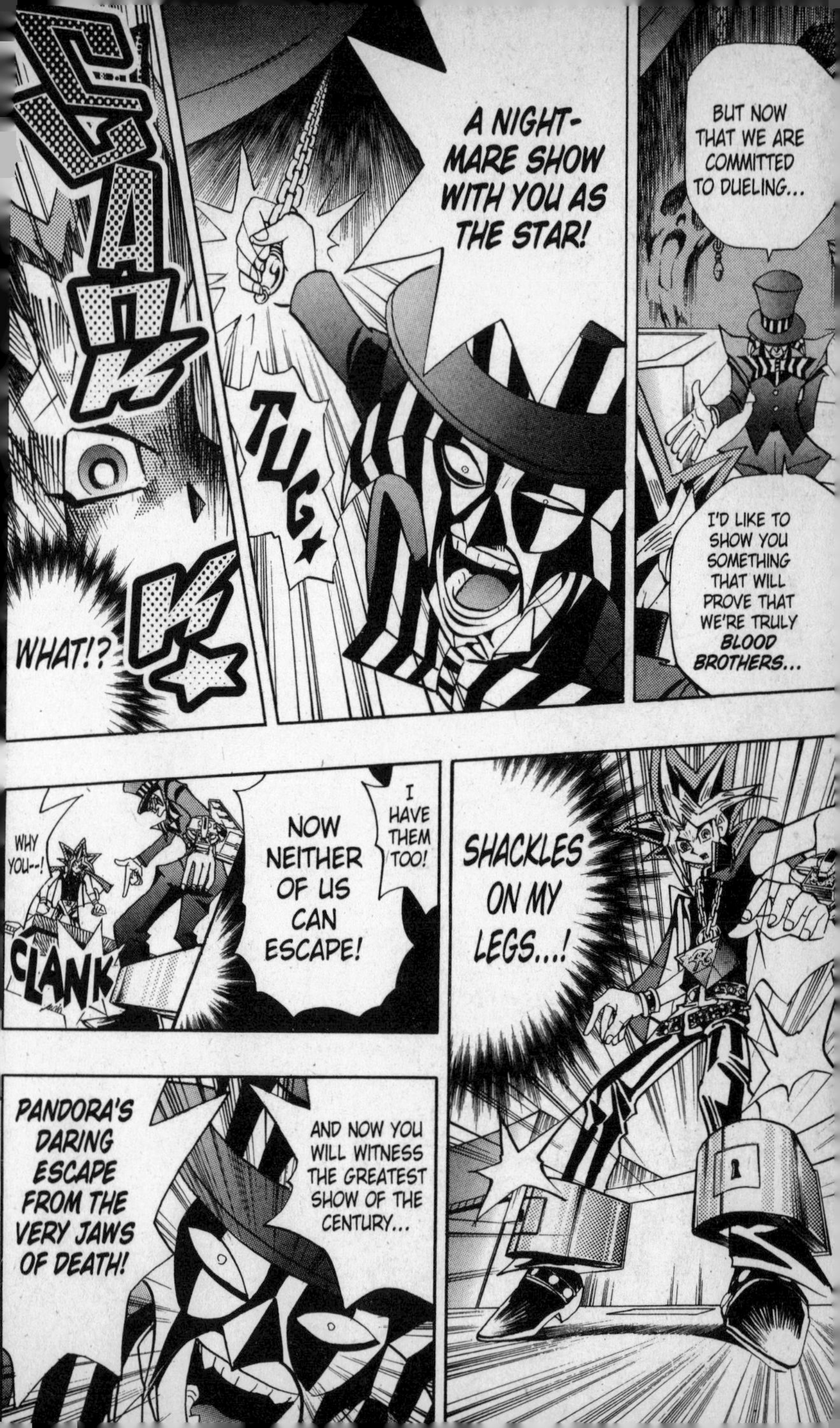
BUT NOW THAT WE ARE COMMITTED TO DUELING...
I'D LIKE TO SHOW YOU SOMETHING THAT WILL PROVE THAT WE'RE TRULY *BLOOD BROTHERS*...
A NIGHT-MARE SHOW WITH YOU AS THE STAR!
TUG
CLANK
WHAT!?
SHACKLES ON MY LEGS...!
I HAVE THEM TOO!
NOW NEITHER OF US CAN ESCAPE!
WHY YOU--!
CLANK
AND NOW YOU WILL WITNESS THE GREATEST SHOW OF THE CENTURY...
PANDORA'S DARING ESCAPE FROM THE VERY JAWS OF DEATH!

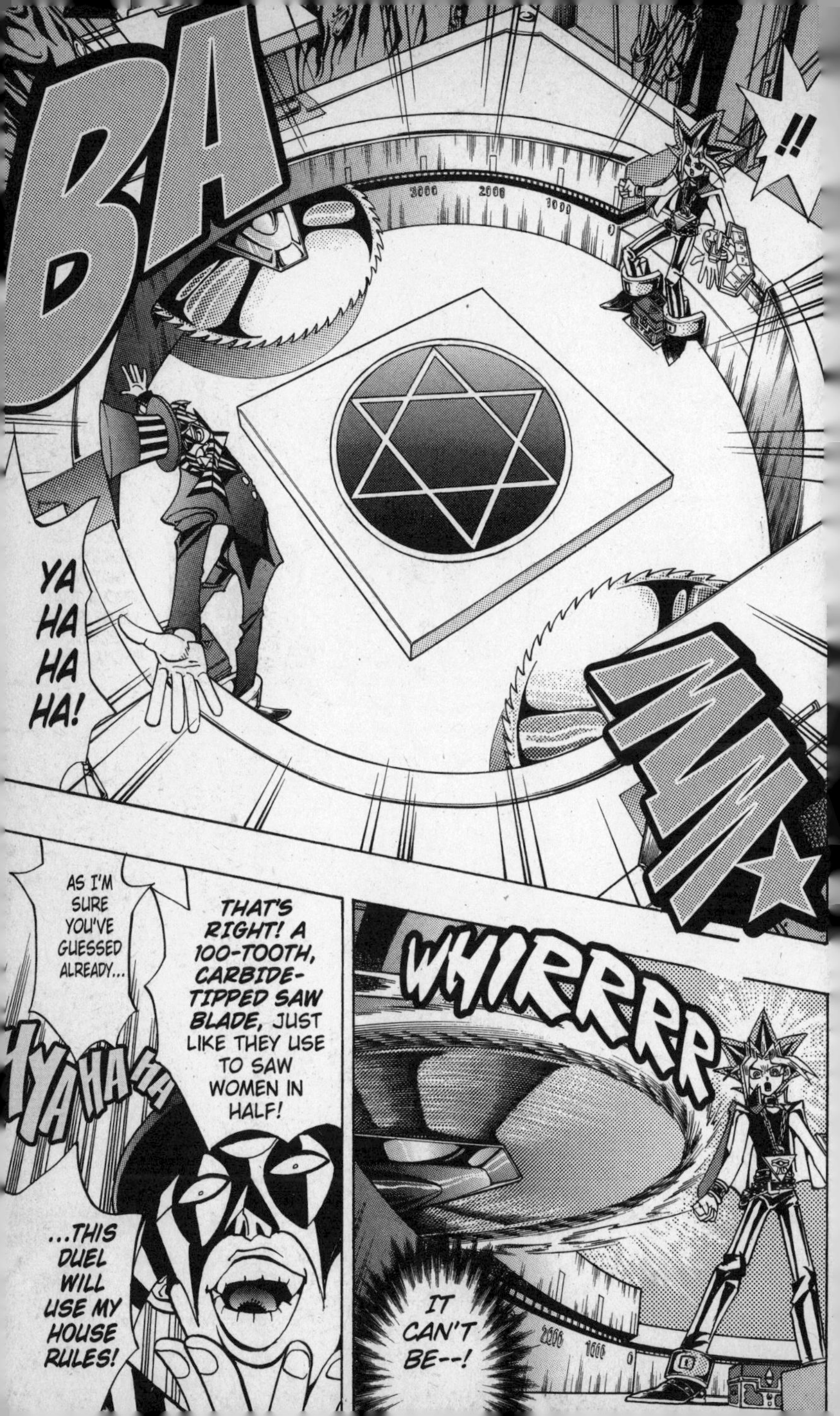
BA
!!
YA HA HA HA!
WHIRRRR
IT CAN'T BE--!
AS I'M SURE YOU'VE GUESSED ALREADY...
...THIS DUEL WILL USE MY HOUSE RULES!
THAT'S RIGHT! A 100-TOOTH, CARBIDE-TIPPED SAW BLADE, JUST LIKE THEY USE TO SAW WOMEN IN HALF!
HYA HA HA

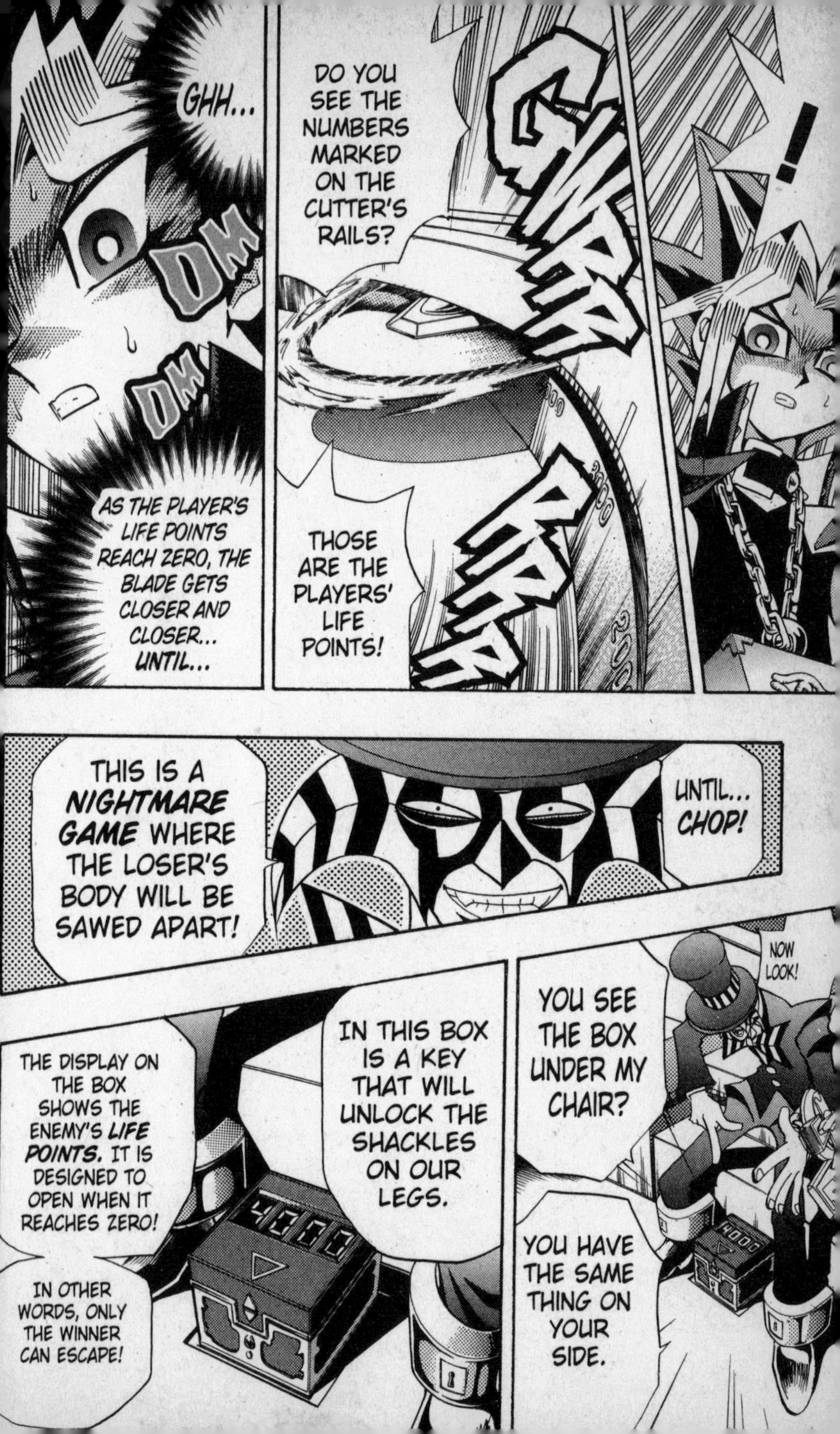
!
DO YOU SEE THE NUMBERS MARKED ON THE CUTTER'S RAILS?
THOSE ARE THE PLAYERS' LIFE POINTS!
GHH...
DM
DM
AS THE PLAYER'S LIFE POINTS REACH ZERO, THE BLADE GETS CLOSER AND CLOSER... UNTIL...
UNTIL... CHOP!
THIS IS A NIGHTMARE GAME WHERE THE LOSER'S BODY WILL BE SAWED APART!
NOW LOOK!
YOU SEE THE BOX UNDER MY CHAIR?
YOU HAVE THE SAME THING ON YOUR SIDE.
IN THIS BOX IS A KEY THAT WILL UNLOCK THE SHACKLES ON OUR LEGS.
THE DISPLAY ON THE BOX SHOWS THE ENEMY'S LIFE POINTS. IT IS DESIGNED TO OPEN WHEN IT REACHES ZERO!
IN OTHER WORDS, ONLY THE WINNER CAN ESCAPE!

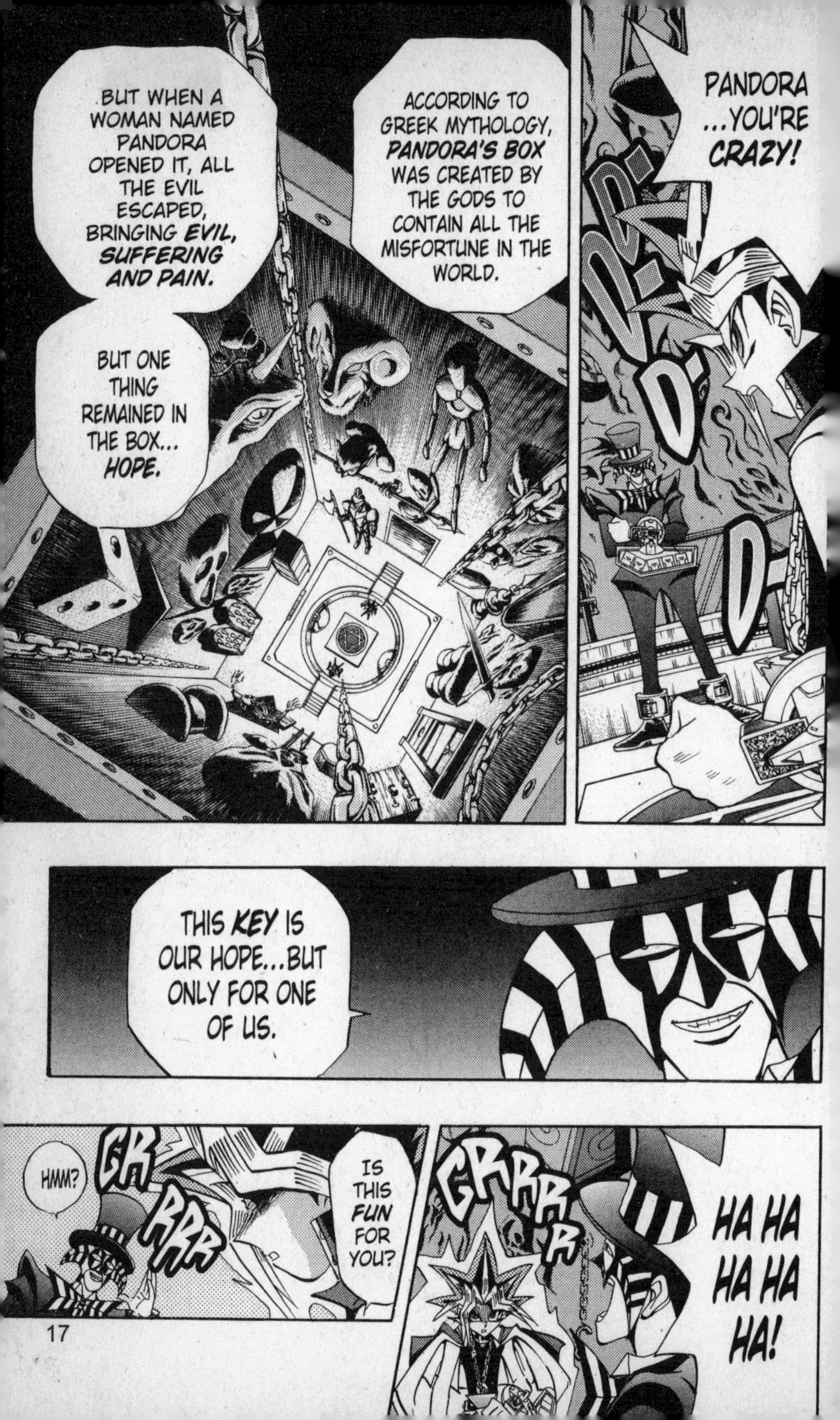
PANDORA ...YOU'RE CRAZY!
ACCORDING TO GREEK MYTHOLOGY, PANDORA'S BOX WAS CREATED BY THE GODS TO CONTAIN ALL THE MISFORTUNE IN THE WORLD.
BUT WHEN A WOMAN NAMED PANDORA OPENED IT, ALL THE EVIL ESCAPED, BRINGING EVIL, SUFFERING AND PAIN.
BUT ONE THING REMAINED IN THE BOX... HOPE.
THIS KEY IS OUR HOPE...BUT ONLY FOR ONE OF US.
GRRRR
HA HA HA HA HA!
IS THIS FUN FOR YOU?
GR RRR
HMM?

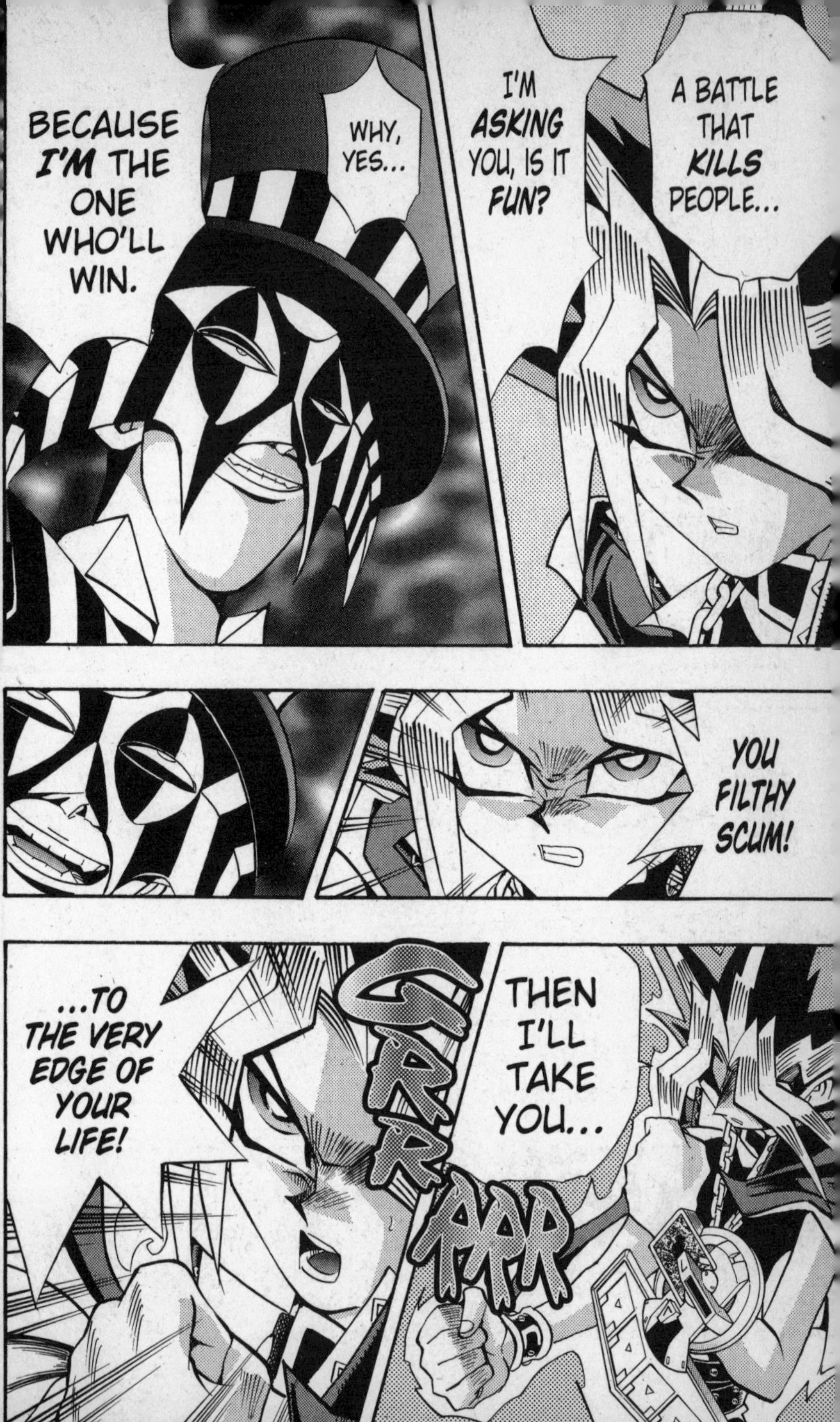
A BATTLE THAT KILLS PEOPLE...
I'M ASKING YOU, IS IT FUN?
WHY, YES...
BECAUSE I'M THE ONE WHO'LL WIN.
YOU FILTHY SCUM!
THEN I'LL TAKE YOU...
GRRAAR
...TO THE VERY EDGE OF YOUR LIFE!

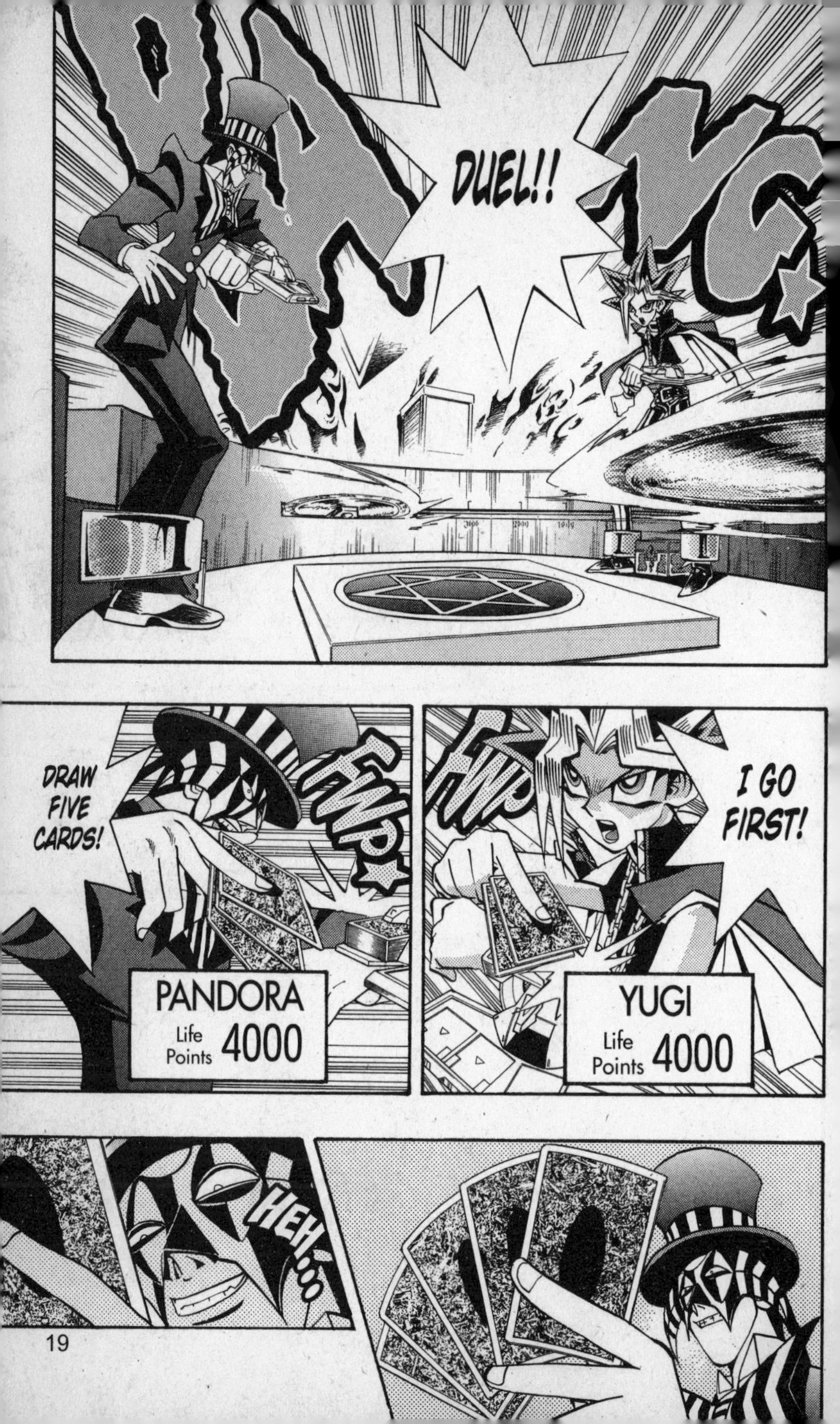
DUEL!!
I GO FIRST!
FWP
YUGI Life Points 4000
DRAW FIVE CARDS!
FWIP
PANDORA Life Points 4000
HEH...

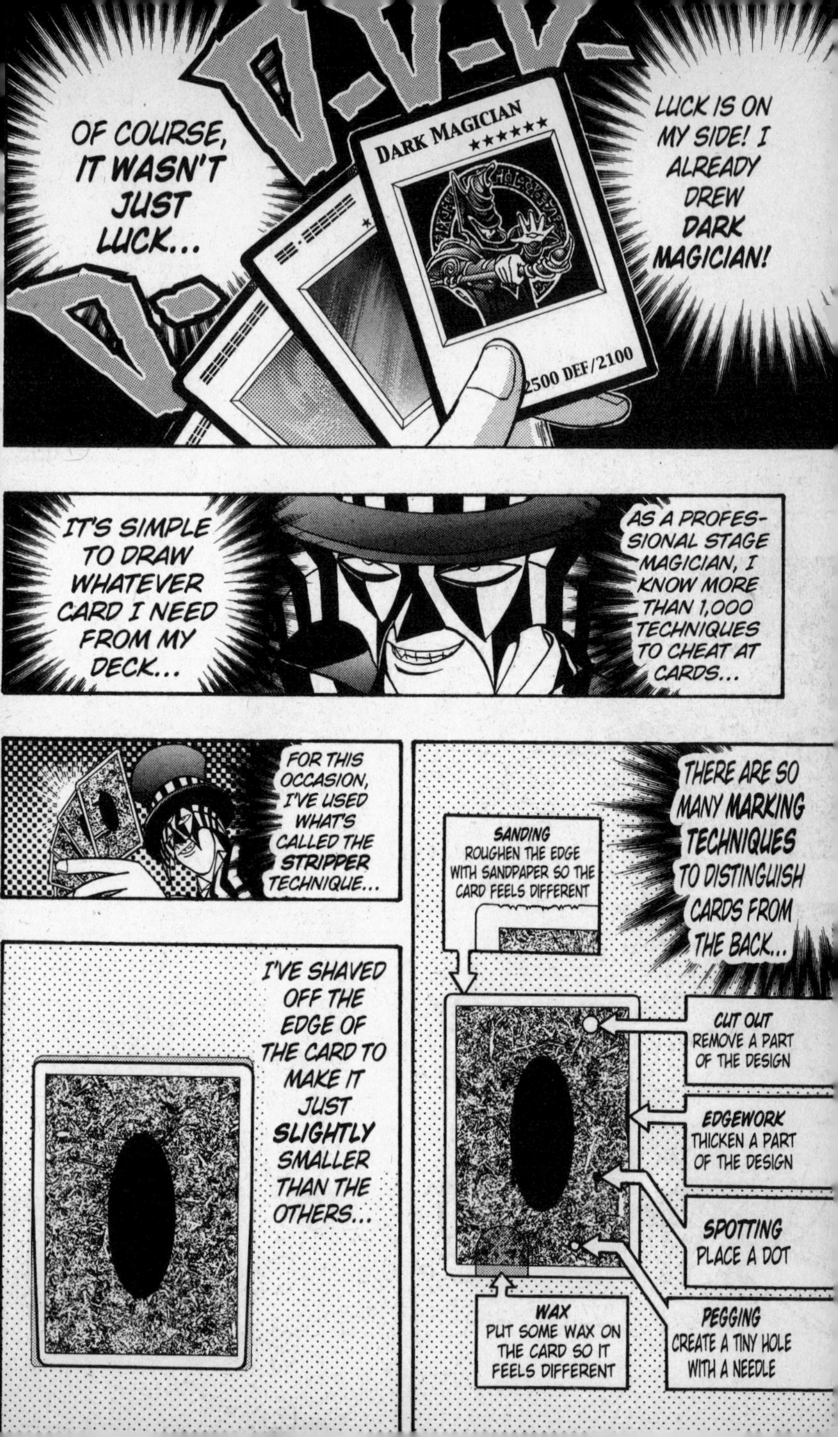
D-D-D-
DARK MAGICIAN
2500 DEF/2100
LUCK IS ON MY SIDE! I ALREADY DREW DARK MAGICIAN!
OF COURSE, IT WASN'T JUST LUCK...
AS A PROFES-SIONAL STAGE MAGICIAN, I KNOW MORE THAN 1,000 TECHNIQUES TO CHEAT AT CARDS...
IT'S SIMPLE TO DRAW WHATEVER CARD I NEED FROM MY DECK...
THERE ARE SO MANY MARKING TECHNIQUES TO DISTINGUISH CARDS FROM THE BACK...
SANDING ROUGHEN THE EDGE WITH SANDPAPER SO THE CARD FEELS DIFFERENT
CUT OUT REMOVE A PART OF THE DESIGN
EDGEWORK THICKEN A PART OF THE DESIGN
SPOTTING PLACE A DOT
PEGGING CREATE A TINY HOLE WITH A NEEDLE
WAX PUT SOME WAX ON THE CARD SO IT FEELS DIFFERENT
FOR THIS OCCASION, I'VE USED WHAT'S CALLED THE STRIPPER TECHNIQUE...
I'VE SHAVED OFF THE EDGE OF THE CARD TO MAKE IT JUST SLIGHTLY SMALLER THAN THE OTHERS...

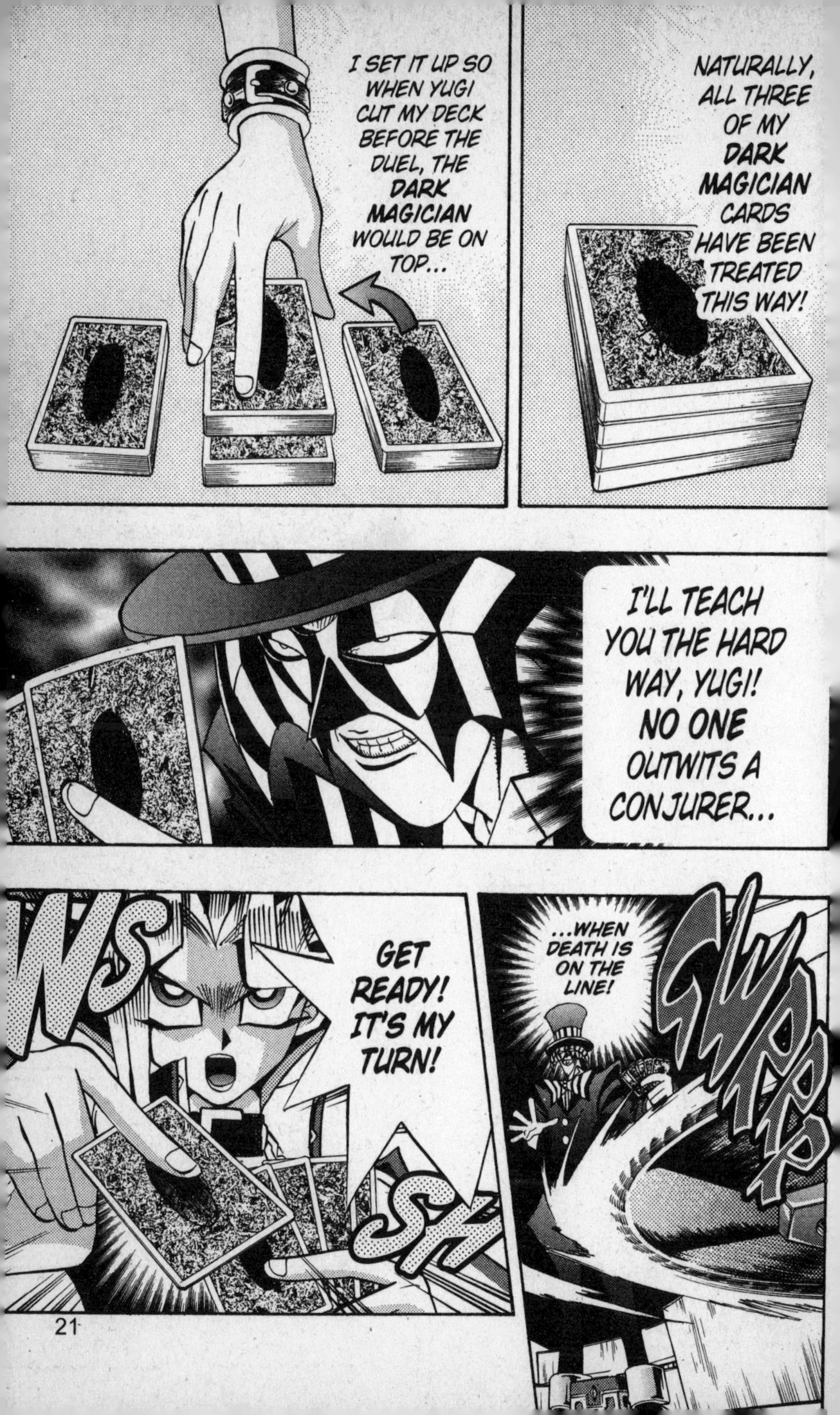

NATURALLY, ALL THREE OF MY **DARK MAGICIAN** CARDS HAVE BEEN TREATED THIS WAY!
I SET IT UP SO WHEN YUGI CUT MY DECK BEFORE THE DUEL, THE **DARK MAGICIAN** WOULD BE ON TOP...
I'LL TEACH YOU THE HARD WAY, YUGI! **NO ONE** OUTWITS A CONJURER...
...WHEN DEATH IS ON THE LINE!
GET READY! IT'S MY TURN!
SH

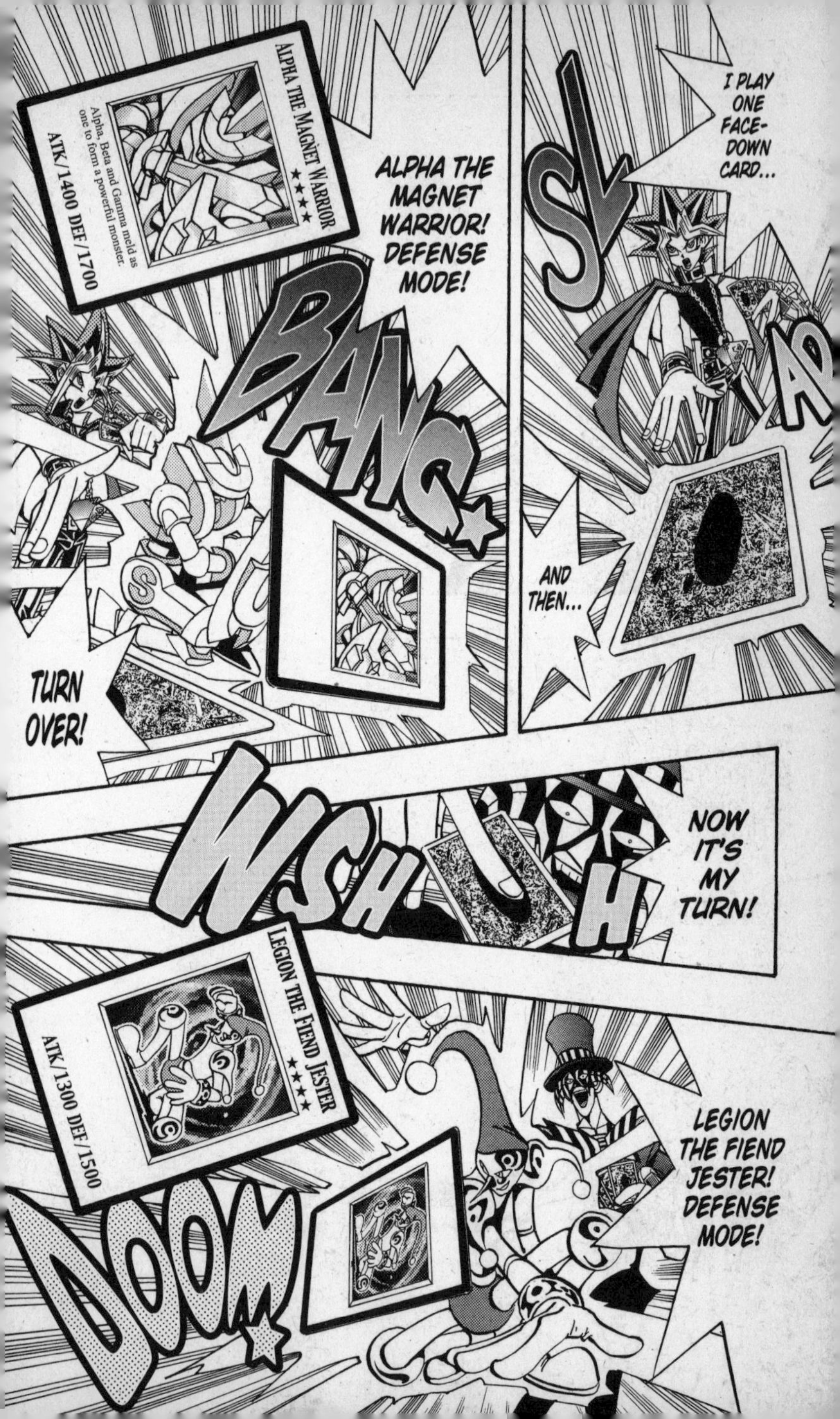
I PLAY ONE FACE-DOWN CARD...
SL
AP
AND THEN...
ALPHA THE MAGNET WARRIOR! DEFENSE MODE!
ALPHA THE MAGNET WARRIOR
★★★★
Alpha, Beta and Gamma meld as one to form a powerful monster.
ATK/1400 DEF/1700
BANG
S
U
TURN OVER!
NOW IT'S MY TURN!
WSH
H
LEGION THE FIEND JESTER! DEFENSE MODE!
LEGION THE FIEND JESTER
★★★
ATK/1300 DEF/1500
DOOOM

READ THIS WAY

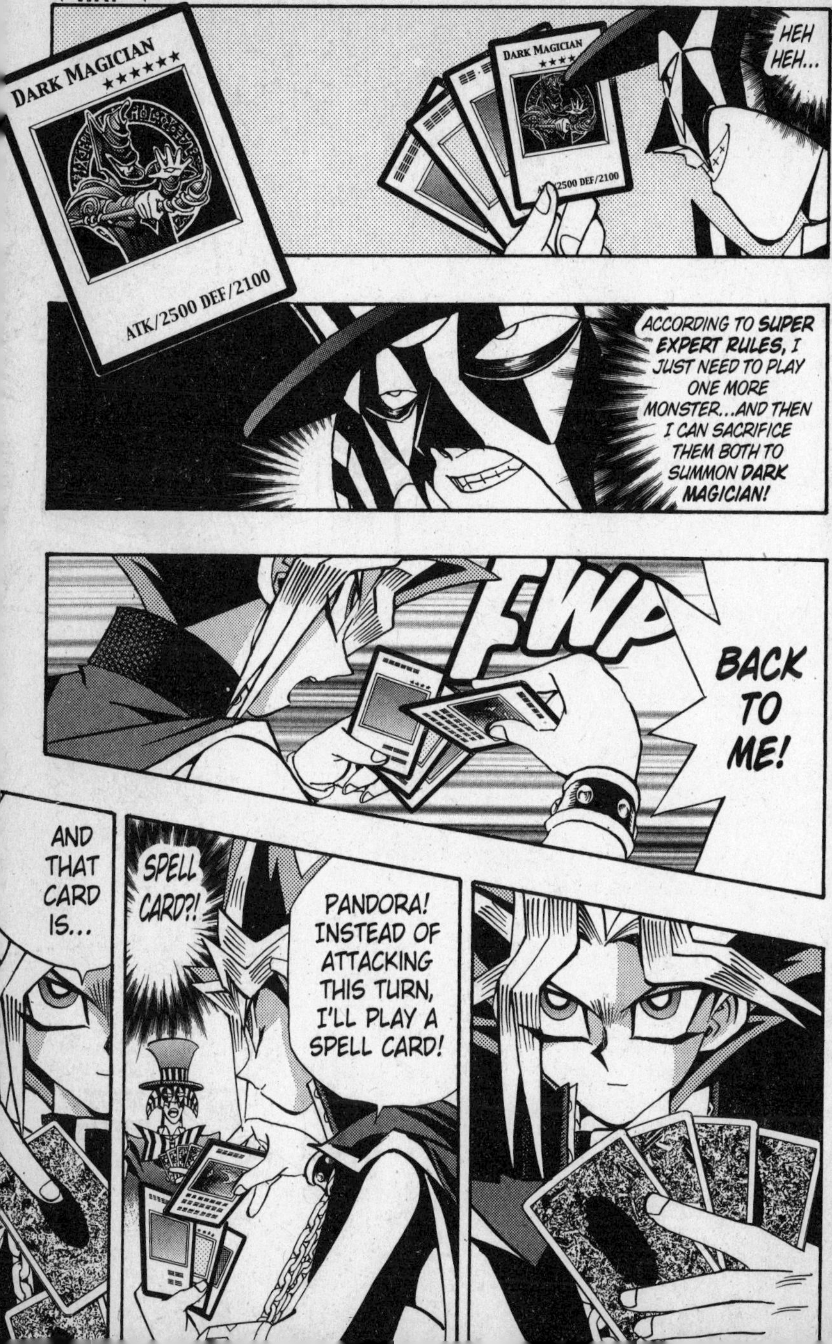
HEH HEH...
DARK MAGICIAN
ATK/2500 DEF/2100
DARK MAGICIAN
ATK/2500 DEF/2100
ACCORDING TO SUPER EXPERT RULES, I JUST NEED TO PLAY ONE MORE MONSTER...AND THEN I CAN SACRIFICE THEM BOTH TO SUMMON DARK MAGICIAN!
FWP
BACK TO ME!
PANDORA! INSTEAD OF ATTACKING THIS TURN, I'LL PLAY A SPELL CARD!
SPELL CARD?!
AND THAT CARD IS...

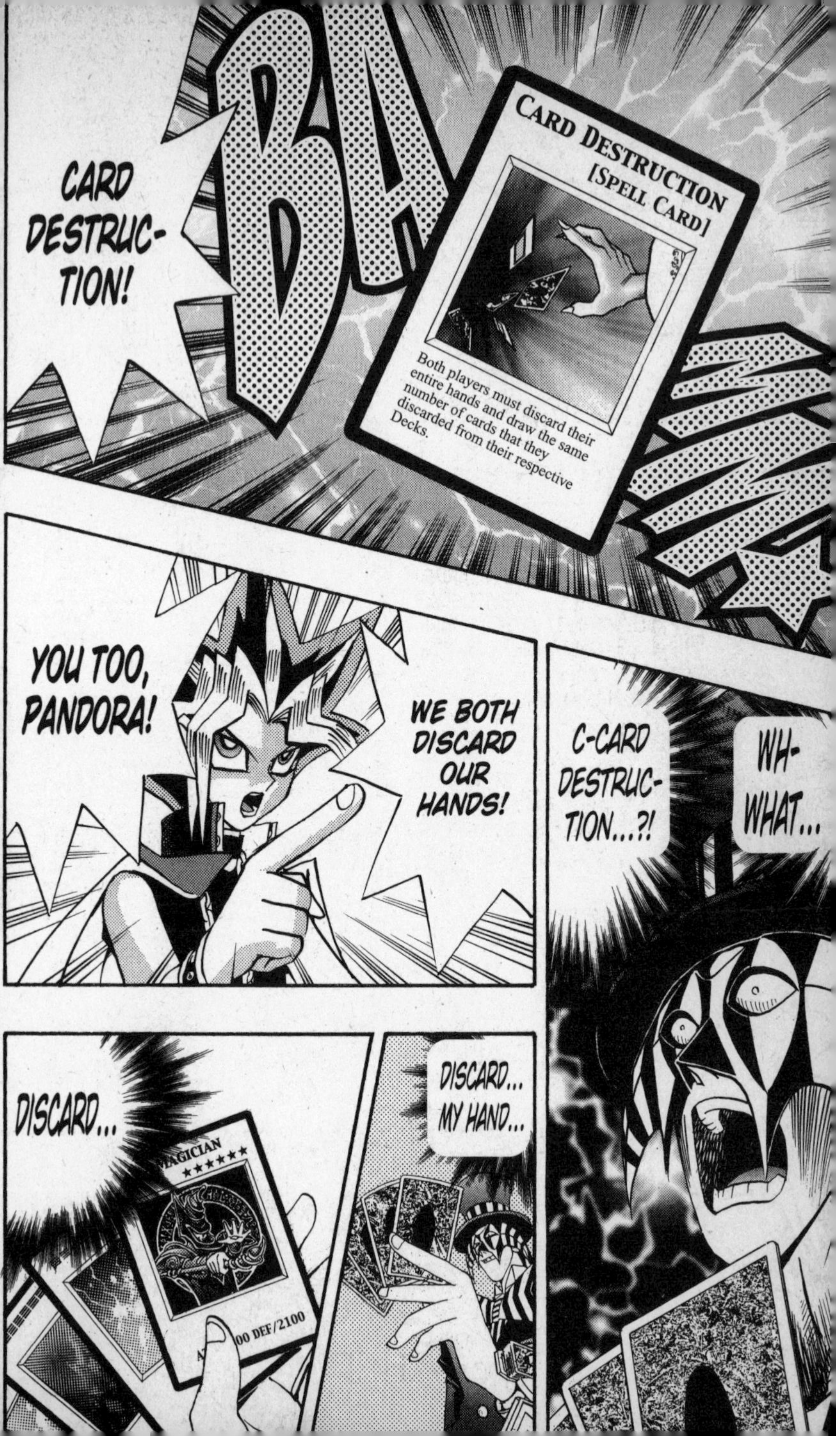
CARD DESTRUCTION!
BA
CARD DESTRUCTION
[SPELL CARD]
Both players must discard their entire hands and draw the same number of cards that they discarded from their respective Decks.
WH- WHAT...
C-CARD DESTRUCTION...?!
YOU TOO, PANDORA!
WE BOTH DISCARD OUR HANDS!
DISCARD... MY HAND...
DISCARD...
MAGICIAN

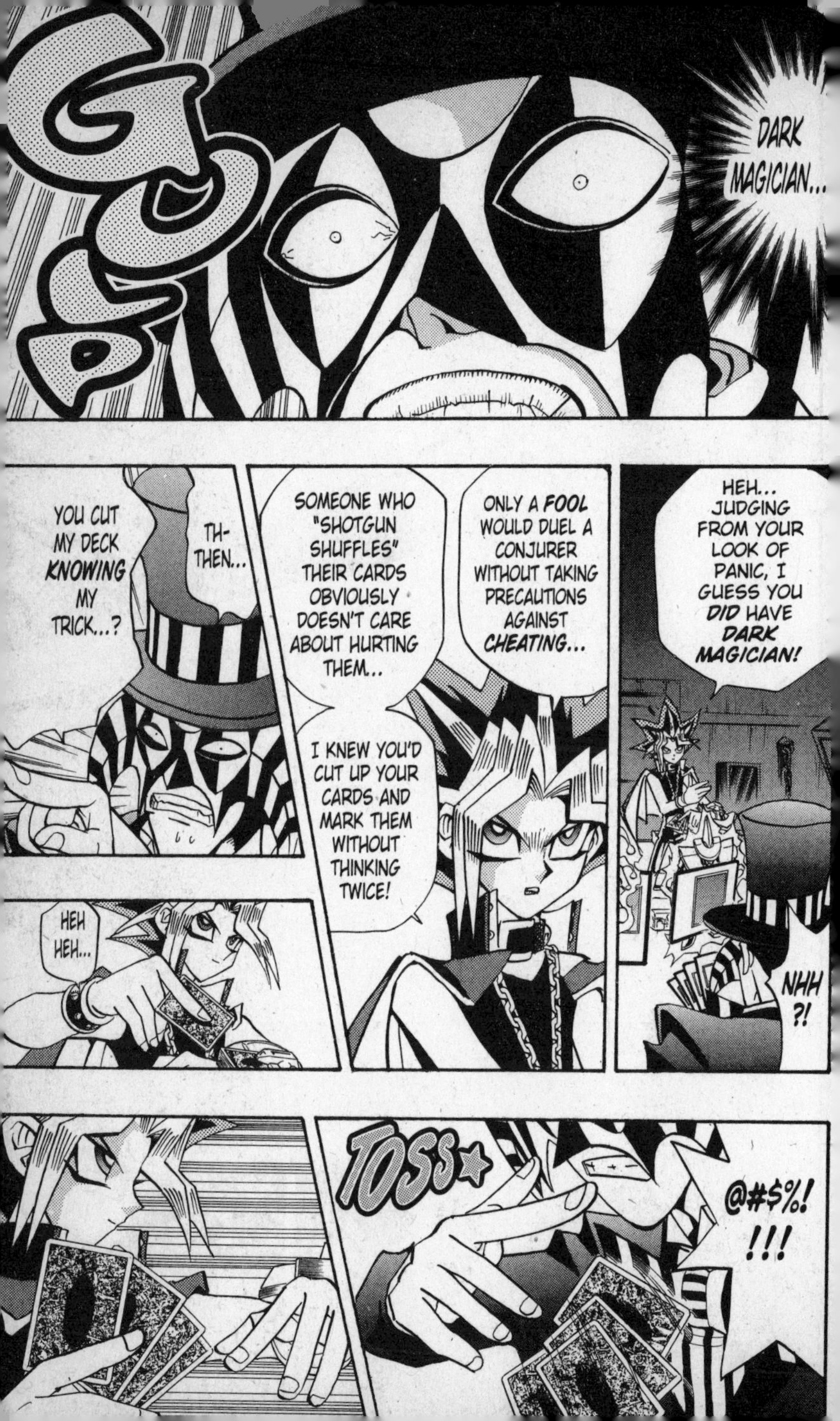
DARK MAGICIAN...
HEH... JUDGING FROM YOUR LOOK OF PANIC, I GUESS YOU DID HAVE DARK MAGICIAN!
NHH ?!
ONLY A FOOL WOULD DUEL A CONJURER WITHOUT TAKING PRECAUTIONS AGAINST CHEATING...
SOMEONE WHO "SHOTGUN SHUFFLES" THEIR CARDS OBVIOUSLY DOESN'T CARE ABOUT HURTING THEM...
I KNEW YOU'D CUT UP YOUR CARDS AND MARK THEM WITHOUT THINKING TWICE!
TH- THEN...
YOU CUT MY DECK KNOWING MY TRICK...?
HEH HEH...
TOSS
@#$%! !!!

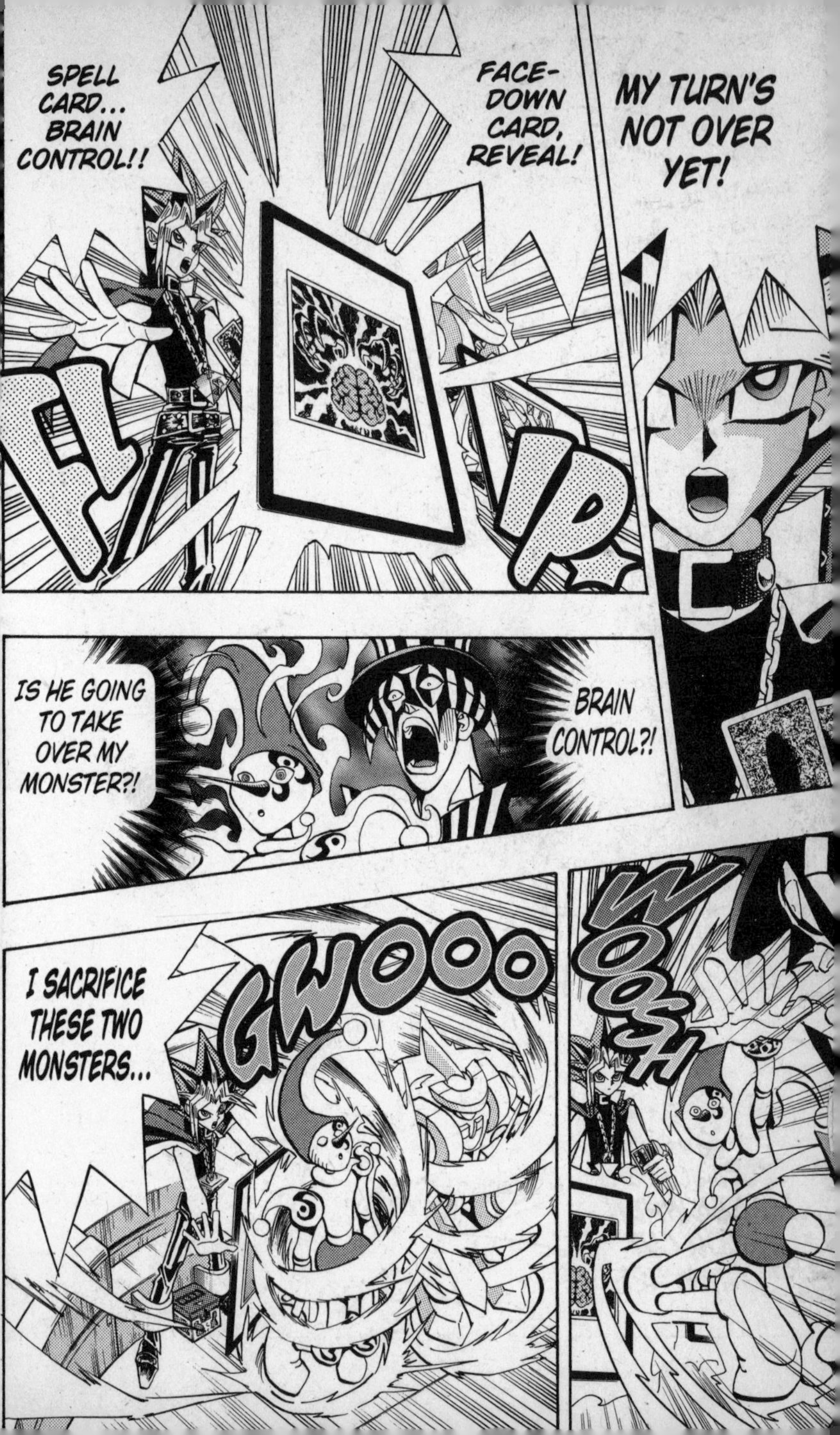
MY TURN'S NOT OVER YET!
FACE-DOWN CARD, REVEAL!
SPELL CARD... BRAIN CONTROL!!
BRAIN CONTROL?!
IS HE GOING TO TAKE OVER MY MONSTER?!
WOOSH
GWOOO
I SACRIFICE THESE TWO MONSTERS...

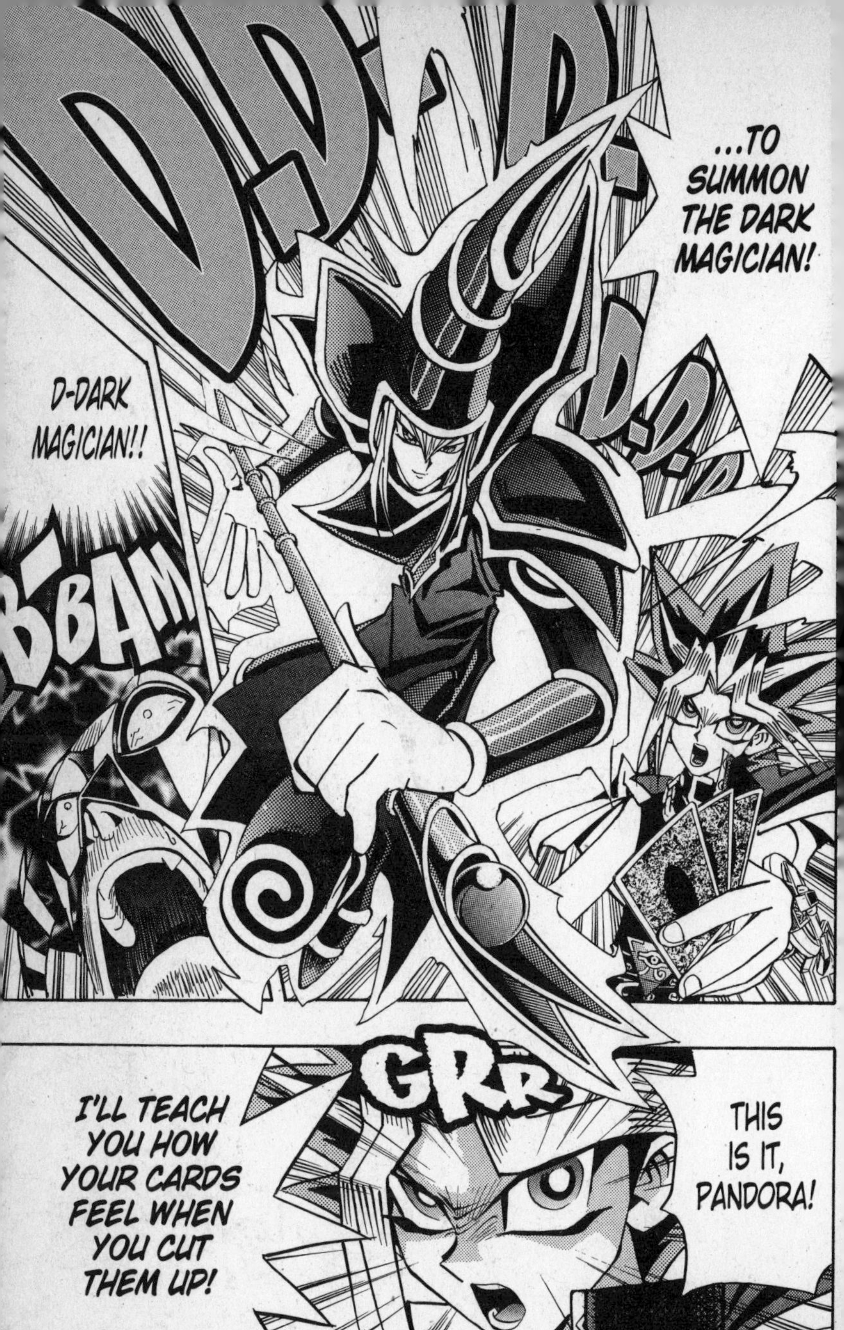
...TO SUMMON THE DARK MAGICIAN!
D-DARK MAGICIAN!!
BAM
THIS IS IT, PANDORA!
GRR
I'LL TEACH YOU HOW YOUR CARDS FEEL WHEN YOU CUT THEM UP!

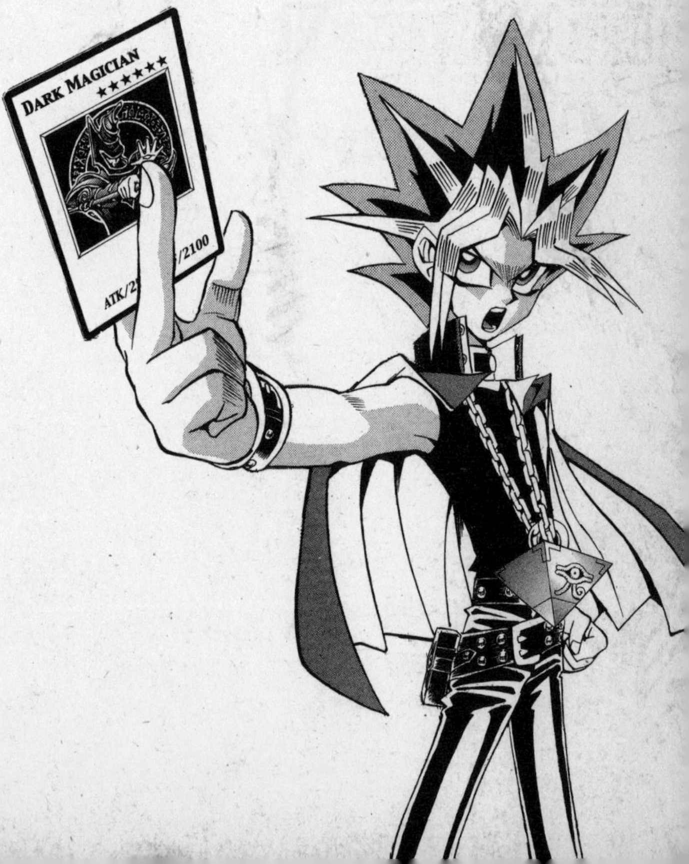
DARK MAGICIAN

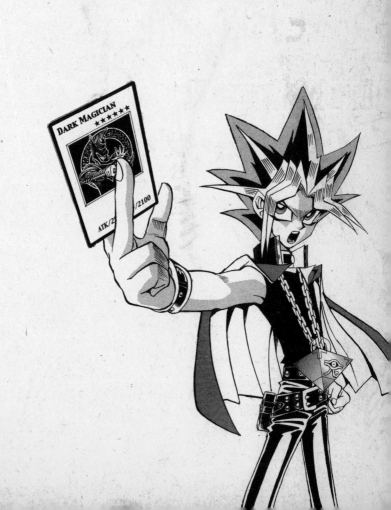

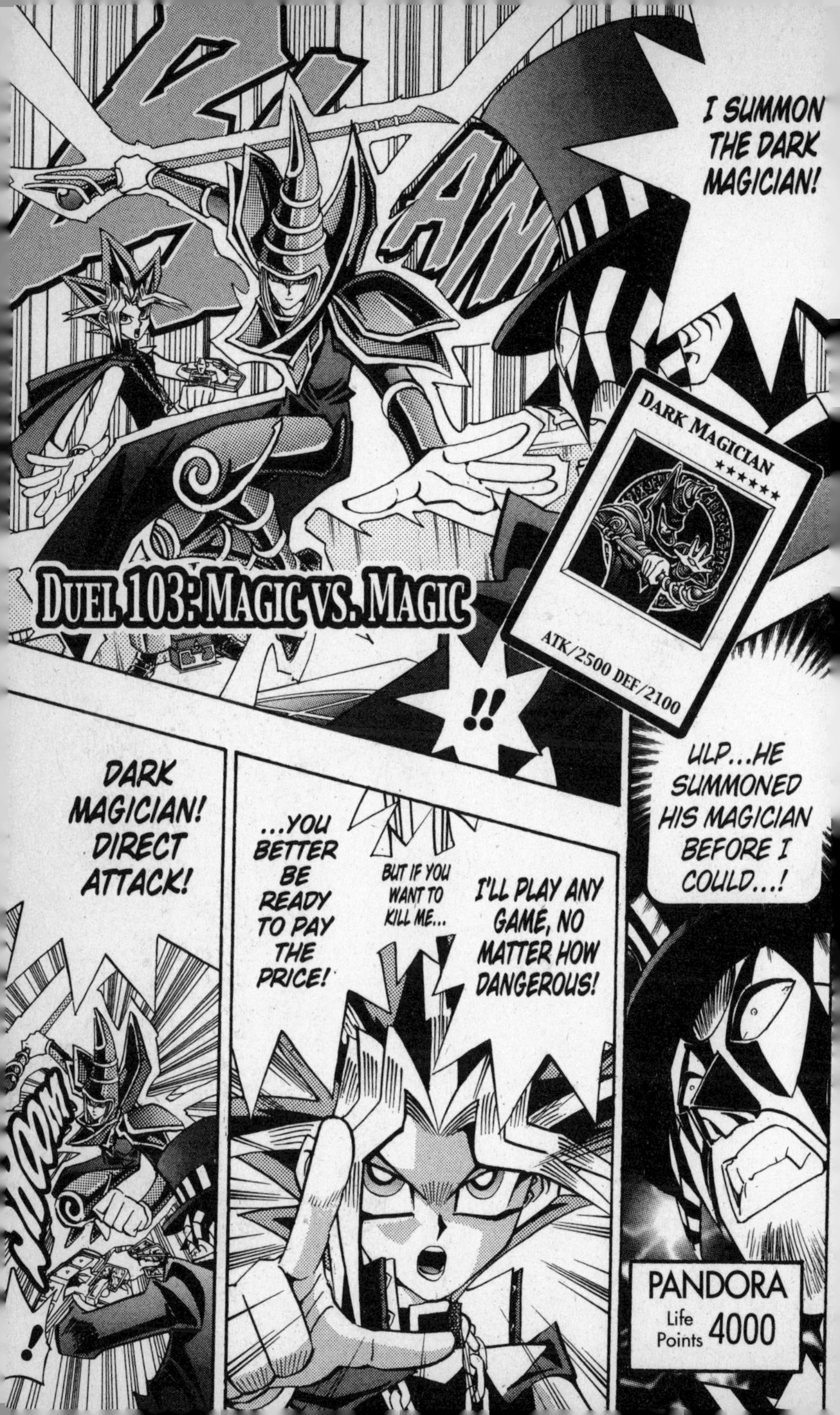
I SUMMON THE DARK MAGICIAN!
Duel 103: Magic vs. Magic
DARK MAGICIAN
ATK/2500 DEF/2100
!!
ULP...HE SUMMONED HIS MAGICIAN BEFORE I COULD...!
PANDORA
Life Points 4000
I'LL PLAY ANY GAME, NO MATTER HOW DANGEROUS!
BUT IF YOU WANT TO KILL ME...
...YOU BETTER BE READY TO PAY THE PRICE!
DARK MAGICIAN! DIRECT ATTACK!
!

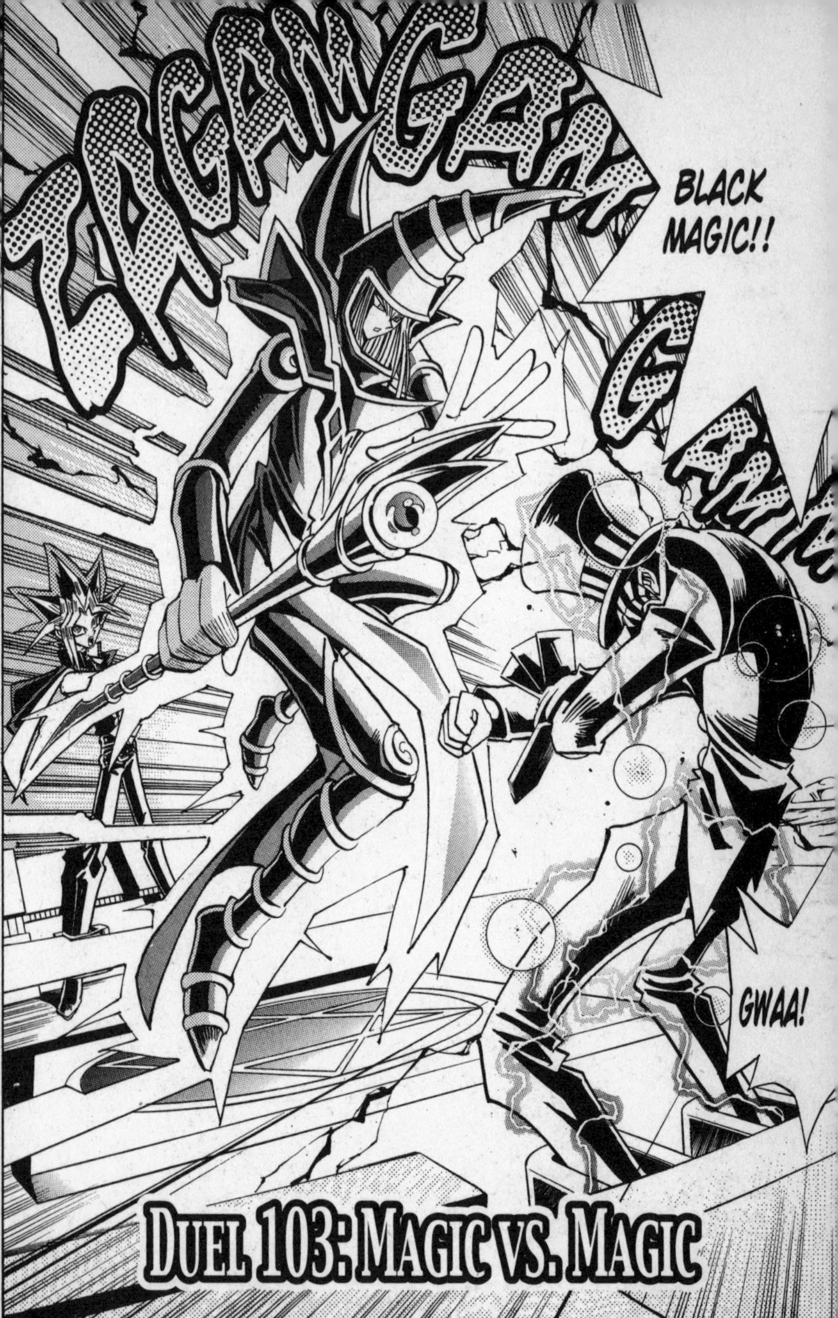
BLACK MAGIC!!
GWAA!
DUEL 103: MAGIC VS. MAGIC

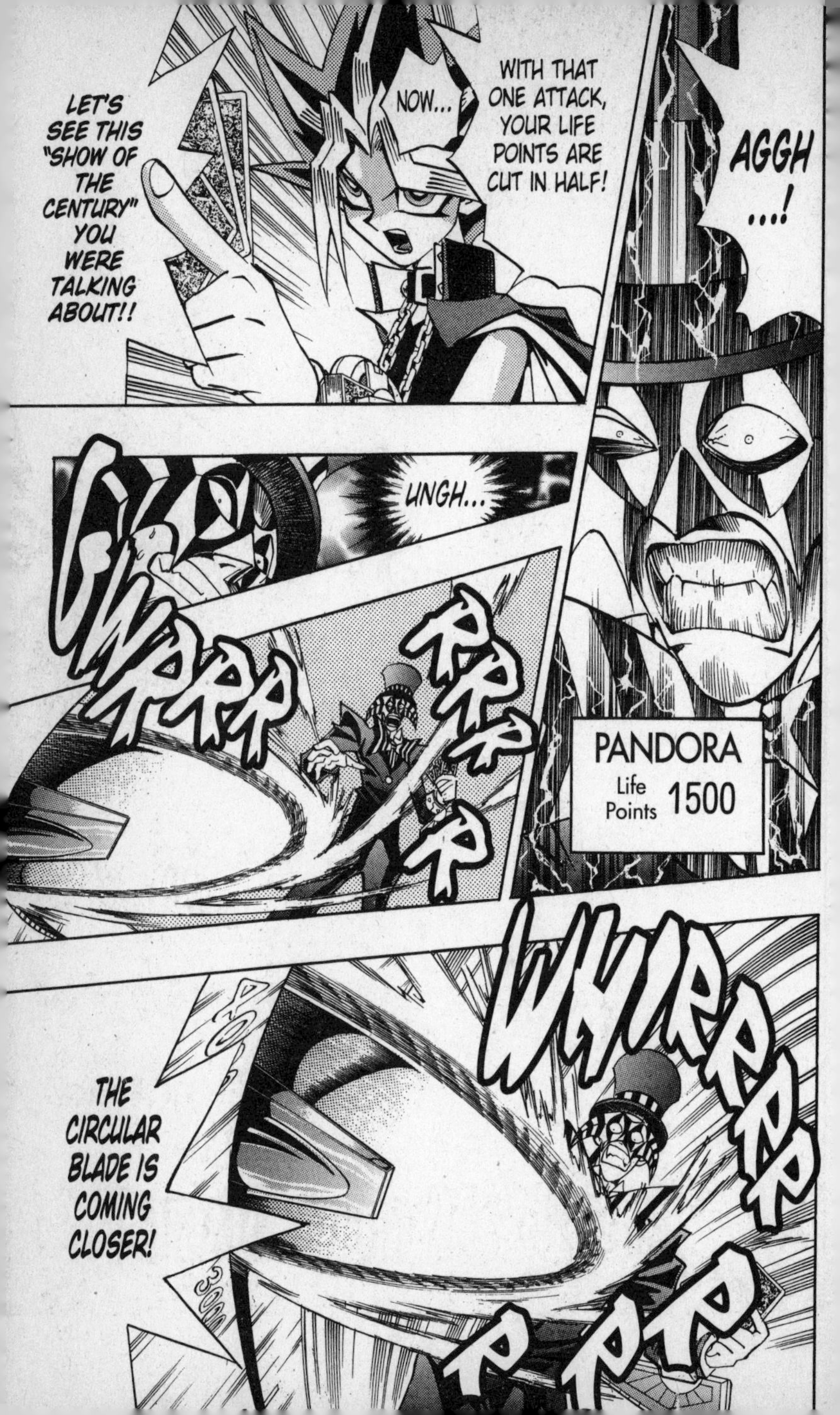
AGGH ...!
PANDORA
Life Points 1500
NOW...
WITH THAT ONE ATTACK, YOUR LIFE POINTS ARE CUT IN HALF!
LET'S SEE THIS "SHOW OF THE CENTURY" YOU WERE TALKING ABOUT!!
UNGH...
WHRRR
RRRR
WHIRRRR
RRRR
THE CIRCULAR BLADE IS COMING CLOSER!

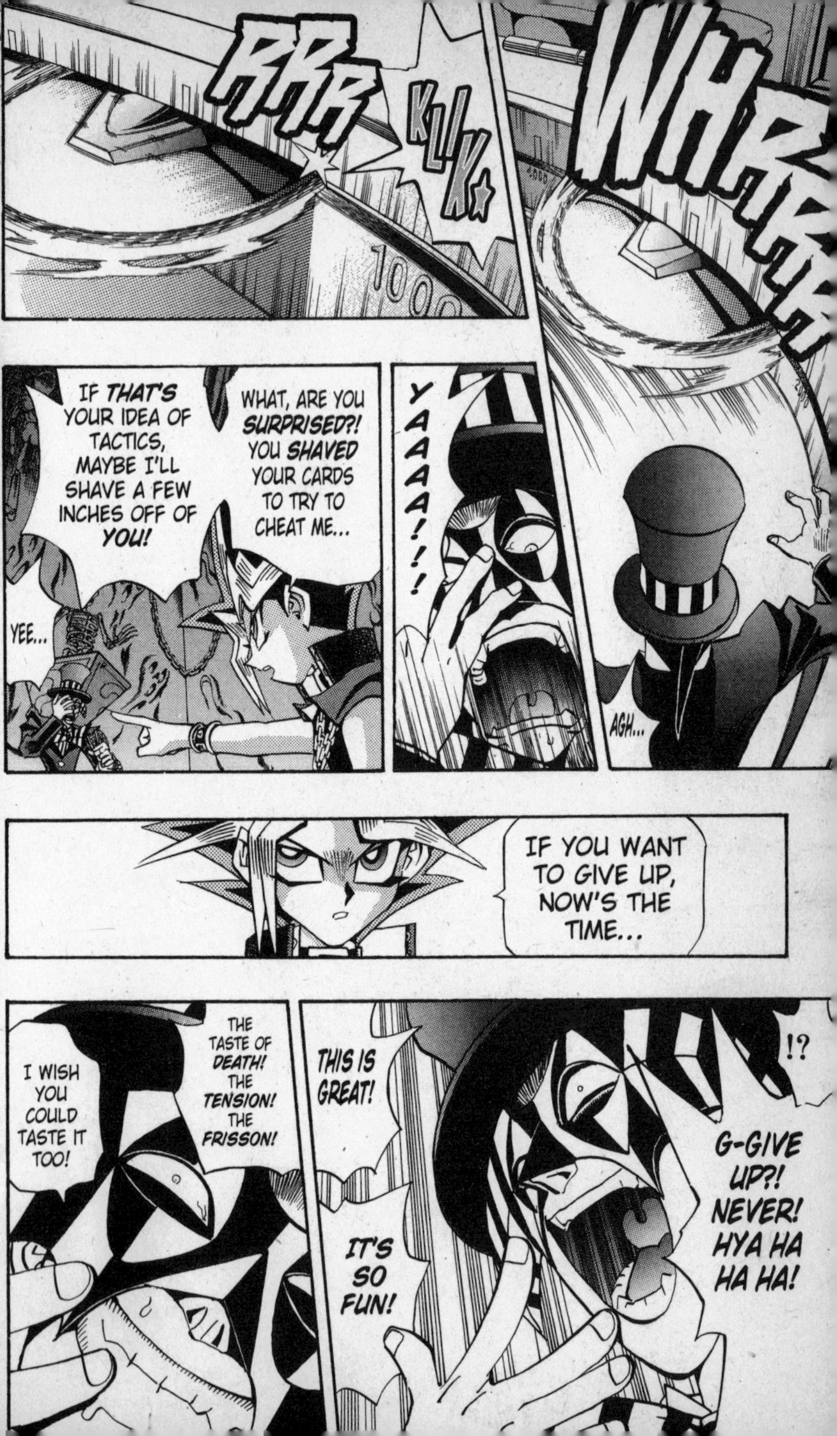

WHR
AGH...
BRR
KLIK
YAAAA!!!
WHAT, ARE YOU SURPRISED?! YOU SHAVED YOUR CARDS TO TRY TO CHEAT ME...
IF THAT'S YOUR IDEA OF TACTICS, MAYBE I'LL SHAVE A FEW INCHES OFF OF YOU!
YEE...
IF YOU WANT TO GIVE UP, NOW'S THE TIME...
!?
G-GIVE UP?! NEVER! HYA HA HA HA!
THIS IS GREAT!
IT'S SO FUN!
THE TASTE OF DEATH! THE TENSION! THE FRISSON!
I WISH YOU COULD TASTE IT TOO!

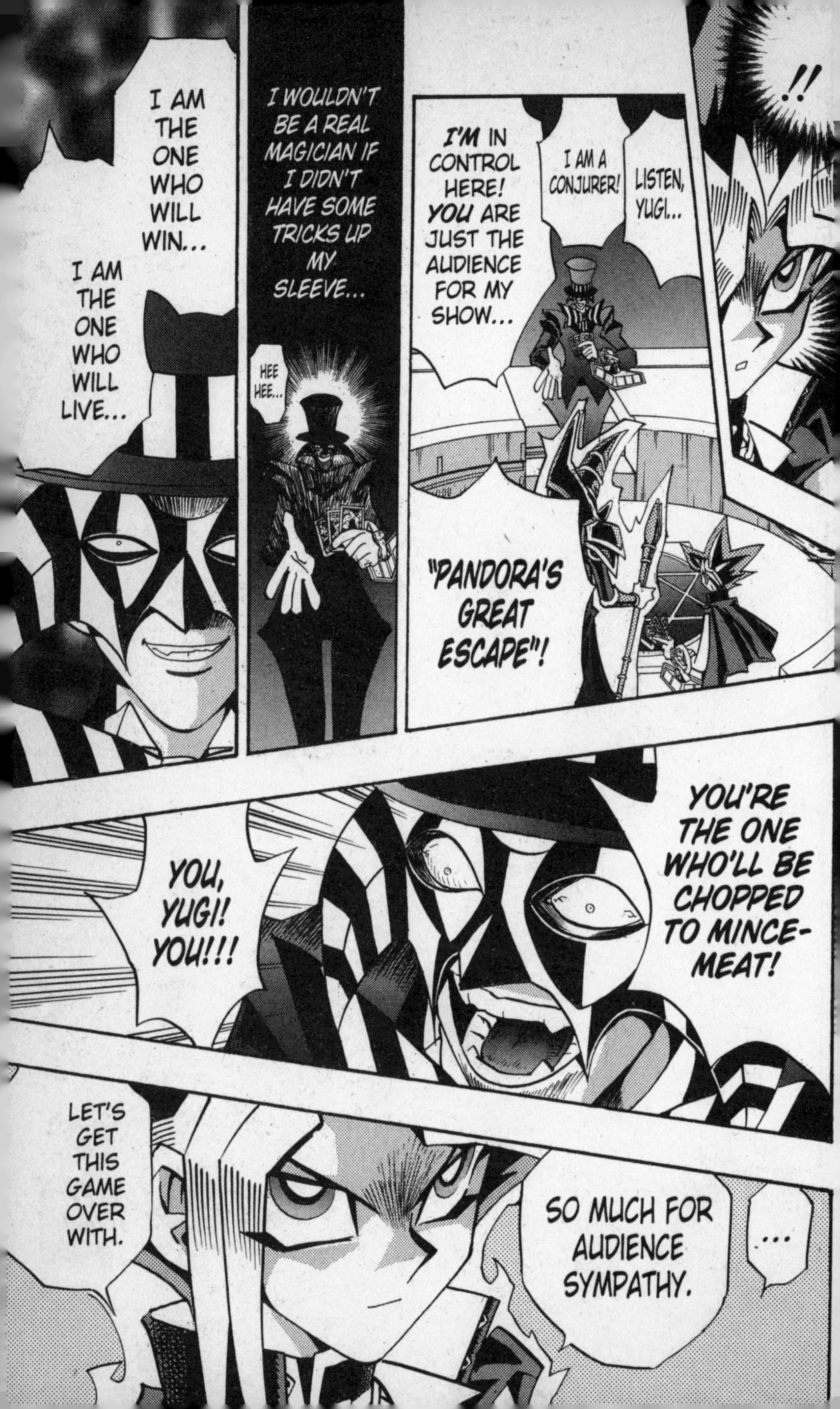
!!
LISTEN, YUGI...
I AM A CONJURER!
I'M IN CONTROL HERE! YOU ARE JUST THE AUDIENCE FOR MY SHOW...
"PANDORA'S GREAT ESCAPE"!
I WOULDN'T BE A REAL MAGICIAN IF I DIDN'T HAVE SOME TRICKS UP MY SLEEVE...
HEE HEE...
I AM THE ONE WHO WILL WIN...
I AM THE ONE WHO WILL LIVE...
YOU'RE THE ONE WHO'LL BE CHOPPED TO MINCE-MEAT!
YOU, YUGI! YOU!!!
...
SO MUCH FOR AUDIENCE SYMPATHY.
LET'S GET THIS GAME OVER WITH.

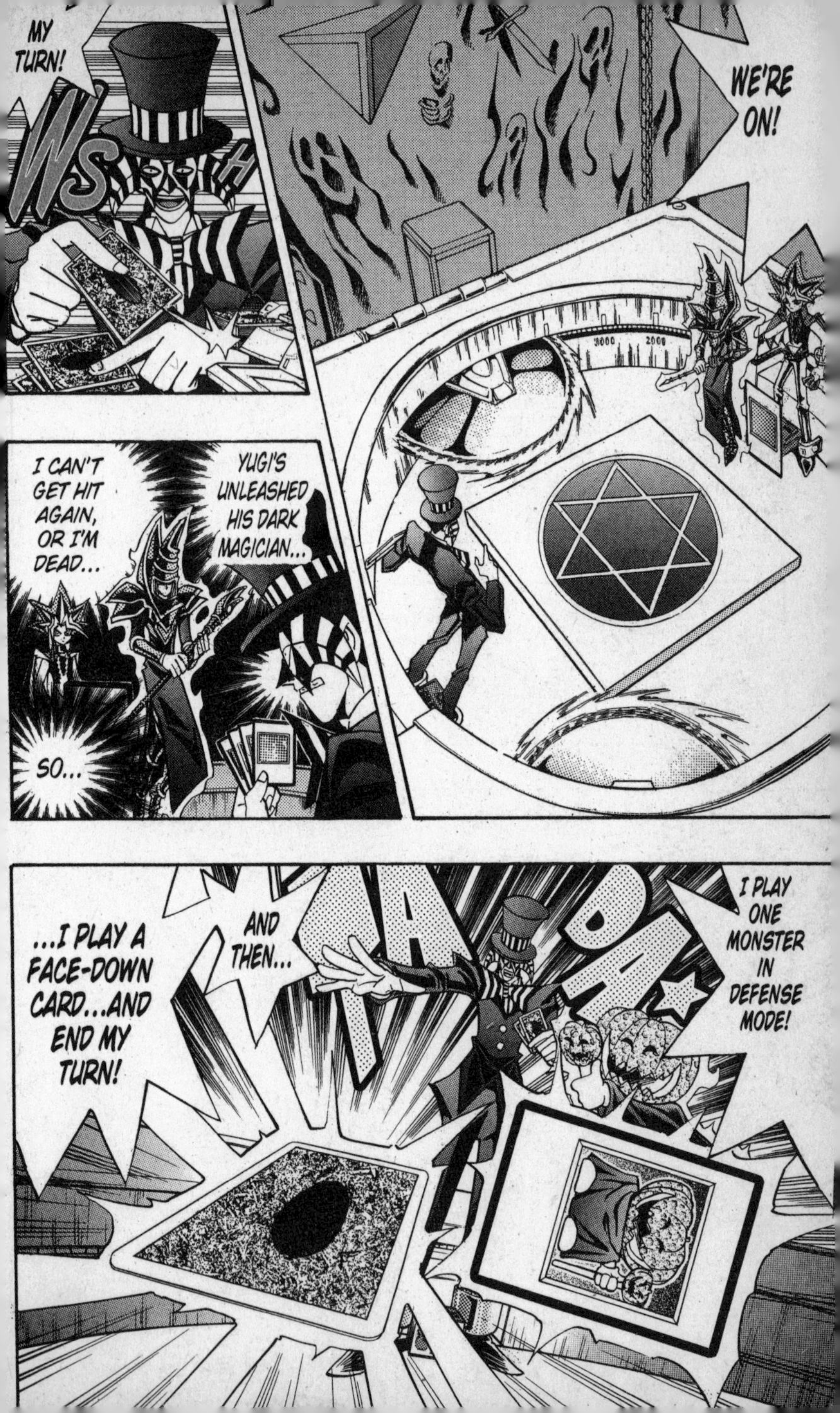
WE'RE ON!
MY TURN!
YUGI'S UNLEASHED HIS DARK MAGICIAN...
I CAN'T GET HIT AGAIN, OR I'M DEAD...
SO...
I PLAY ONE MONSTER IN DEFENSE MODE!
AND THEN...
...I PLAY A FACE-DOWN CARD...AND END MY TURN!

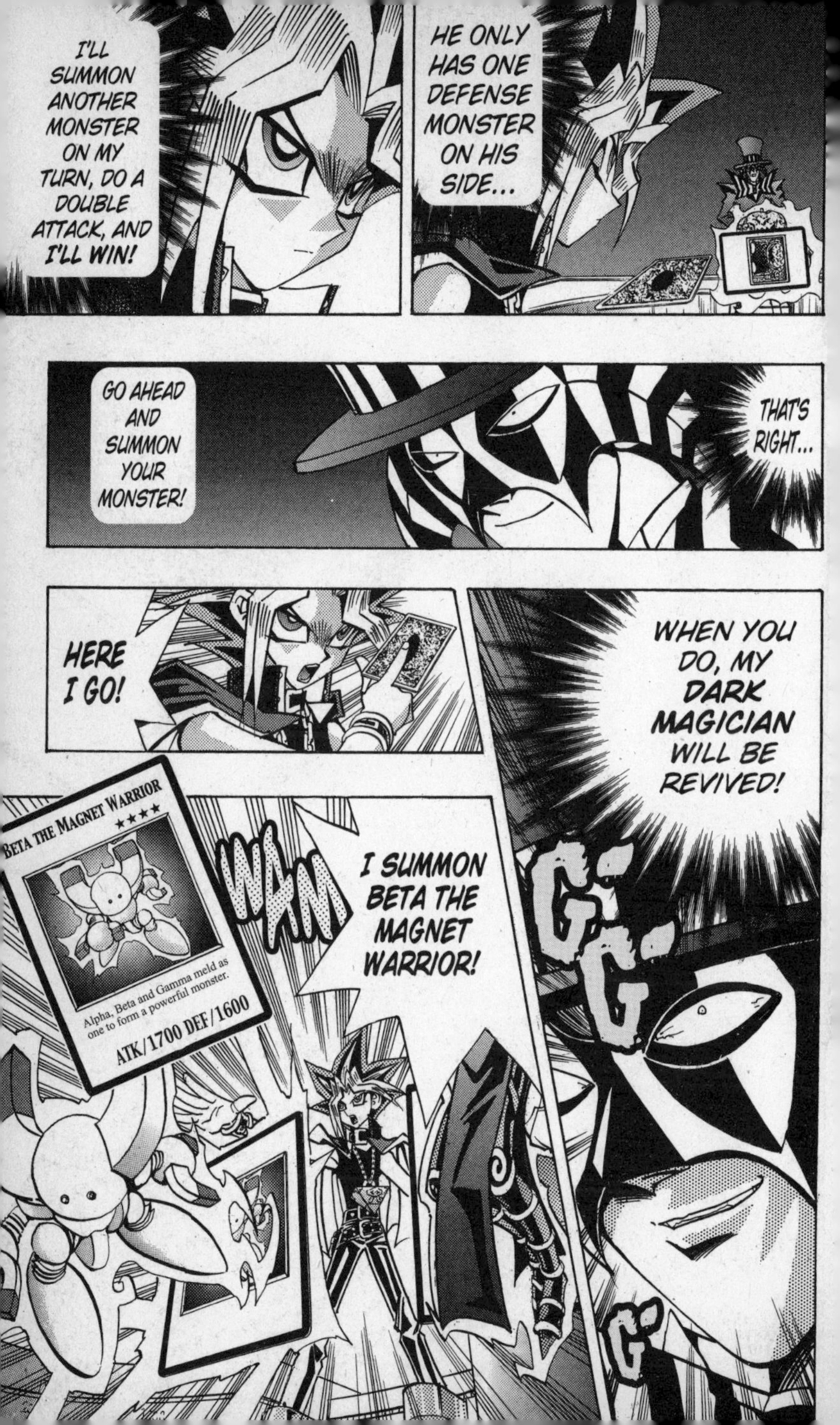
HE ONLY HAS ONE DEFENSE MONSTER ON HIS SIDE...
I'LL SUMMON ANOTHER MONSTER ON MY TURN, DO A DOUBLE ATTACK, AND I'LL WIN!
THAT'S RIGHT...
GO AHEAD AND SUMMON YOUR MONSTER!
WHEN YOU DO, MY DARK MAGICIAN WILL BE REVIVED!
GGG
HERE I GO!
I SUMMON BETA THE MAGNET WARRIOR!
WAM
BETA THE MAGNET WARRIOR
★★★★
Alpha, Beta and Gamma meld as one to form a powerful monster.
ATK/1700 DEF/1600

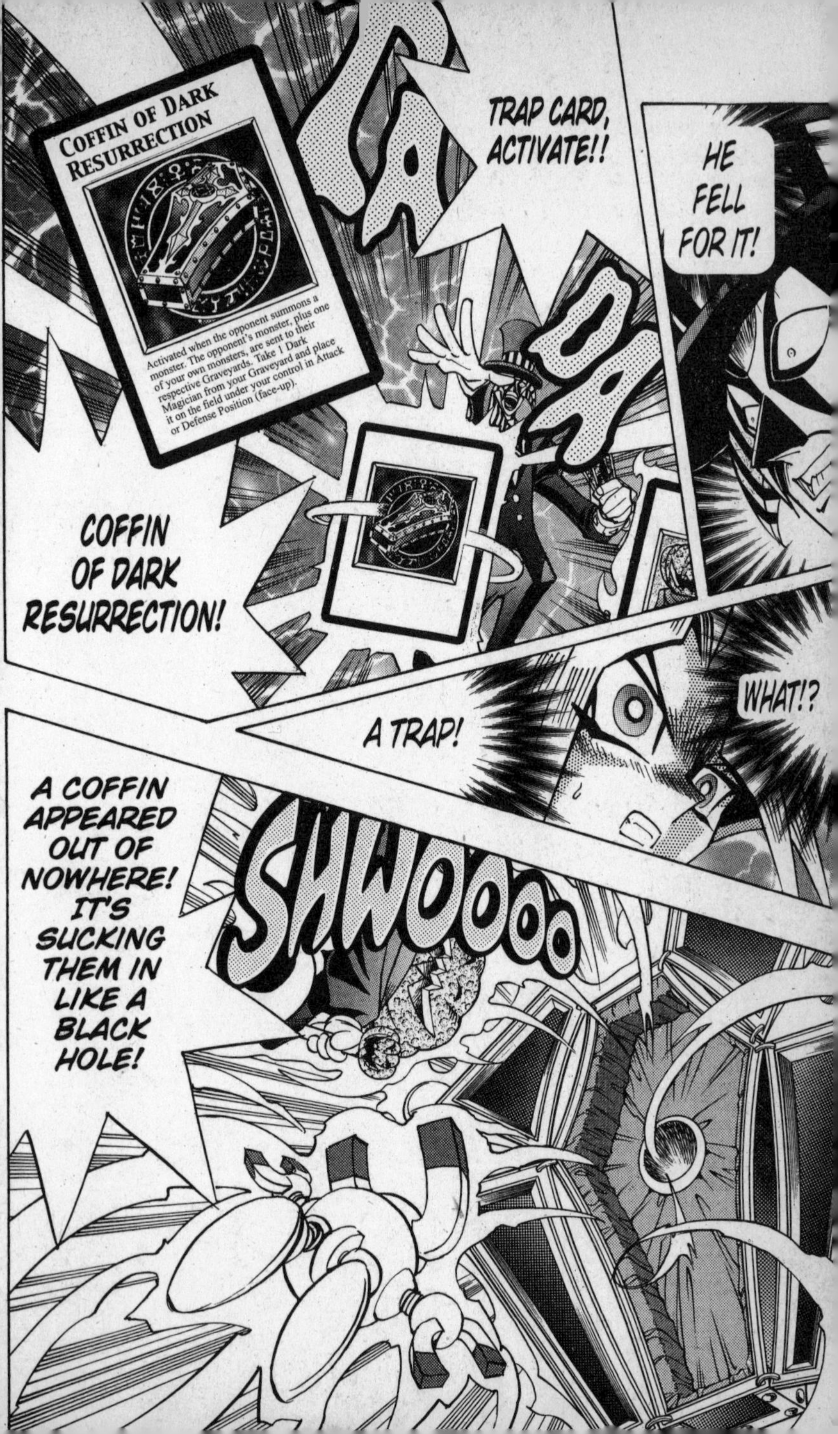
HE FELL FOR IT!
TRAP CARD, ACTIVATE!!
COFFIN OF DARK RESURRECTION
Activated when the opponent summons a monster. The opponent's monster, plus one of your own monsters, are sent to their respective Graveyards. Take 1 Dark Magician from your Graveyard and place it on the field under your control in Attack or Defense Position (face-up).
COFFIN OF DARK RESURRECTION!
WHAT!?
A TRAP!
SHWOOOO
A COFFIN APPEARED OUT OF NOWHERE! IT'S SUCKING THEM IN LIKE A BLACK HOLE!

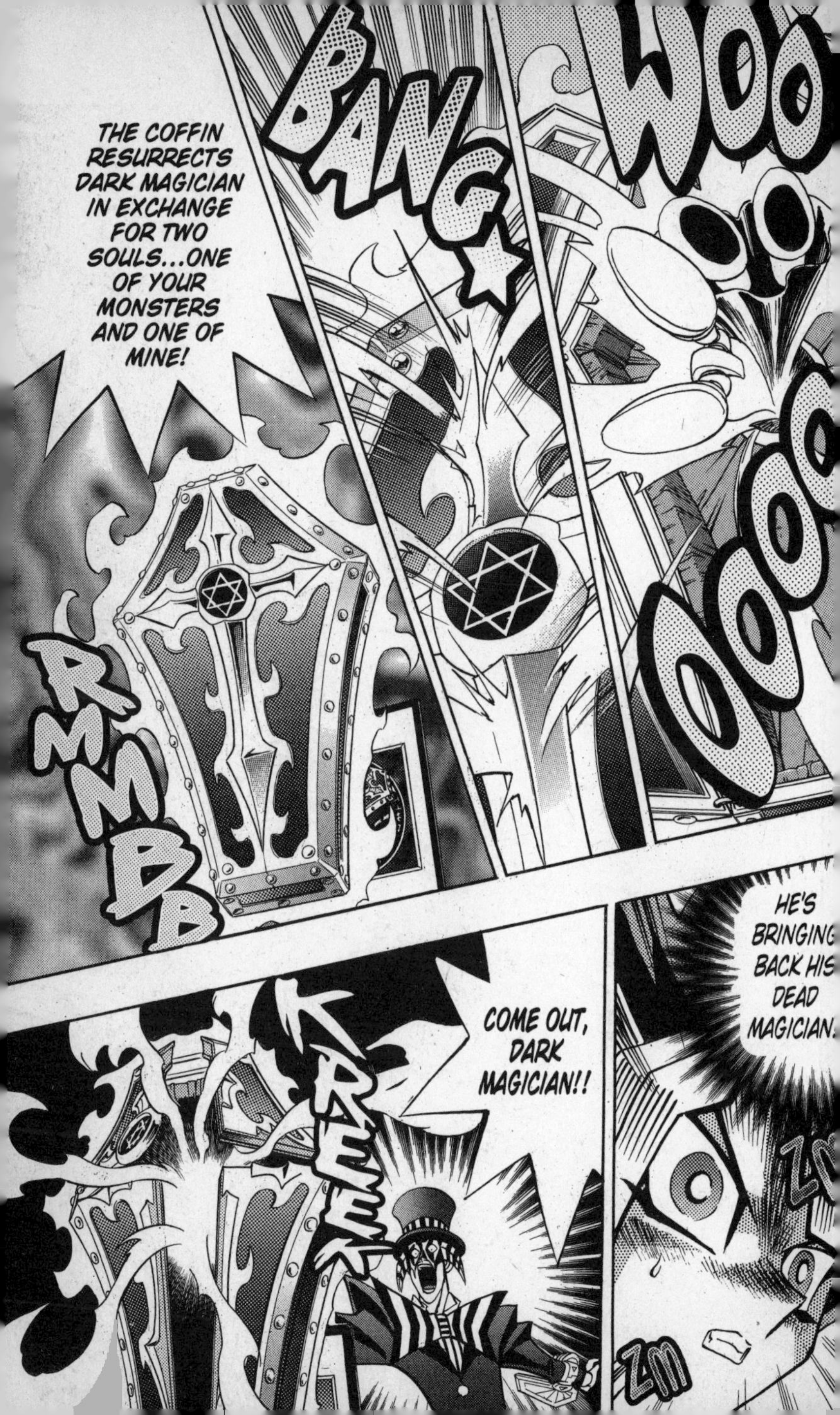
BANG
THE COFFIN RESURRECTS DARK MAGICIAN IN EXCHANGE FOR TWO SOULS...ONE OF YOUR MONSTERS AND ONE OF MINE!
RMMBB
HE'S BRINGING BACK HIS DEAD MAGICIAN!
COME OUT, DARK MAGICIAN!!

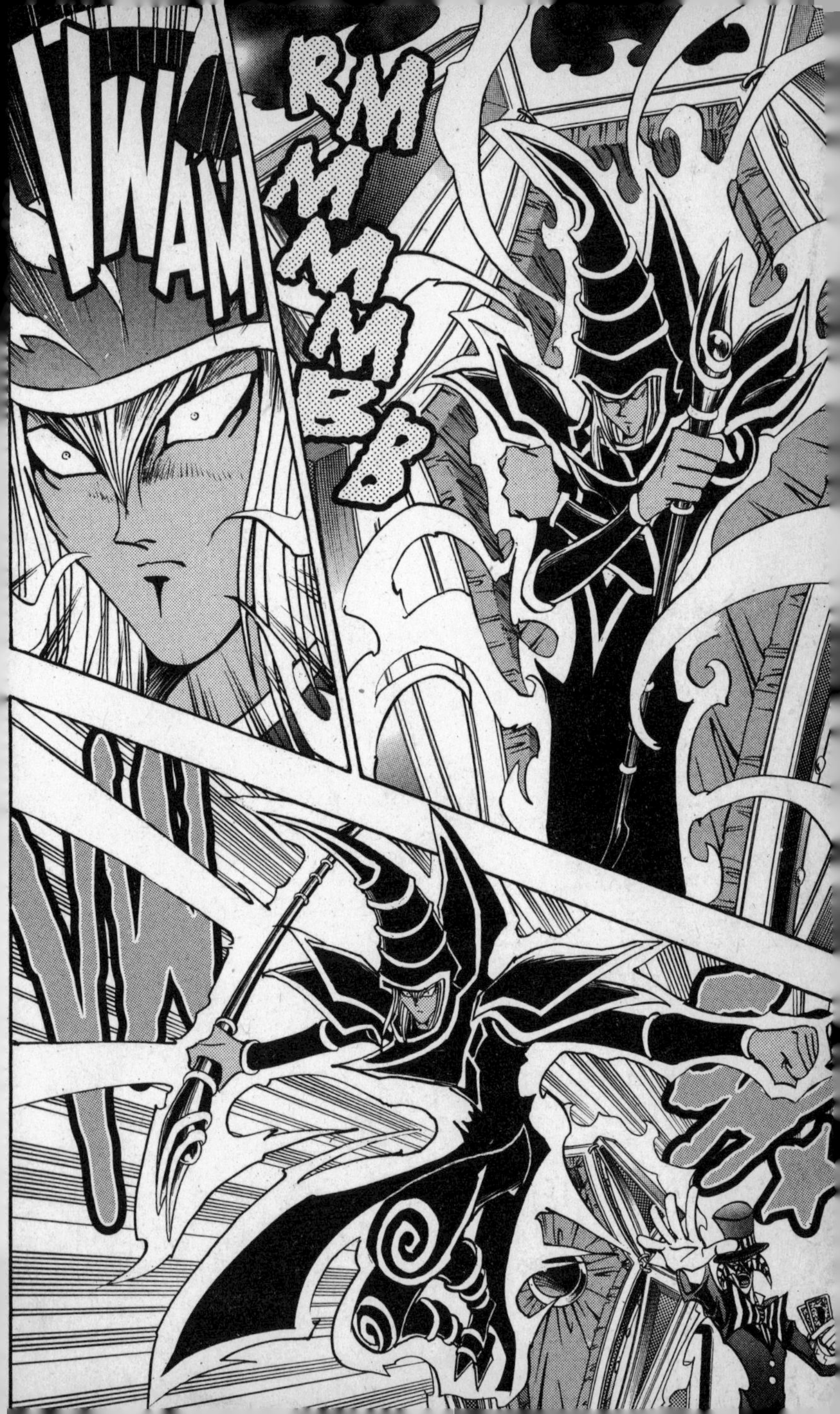
RMMMMBB
VWAM

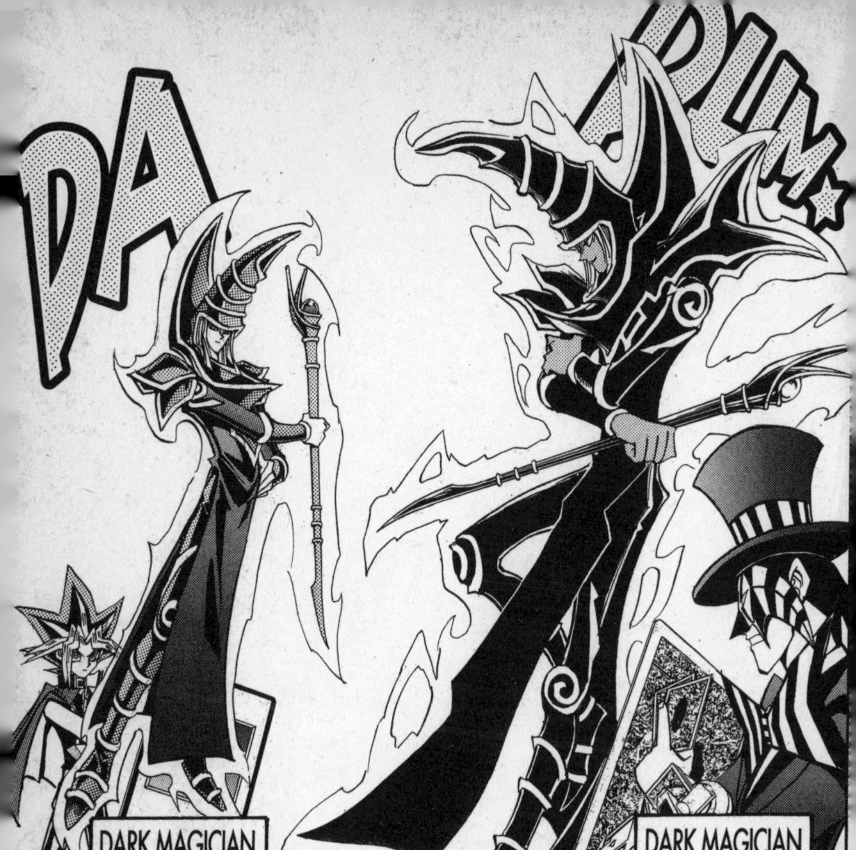
DA DUM.
DARK MAGICIAN Attack 2500
DARK MAGICIAN Attack 2500

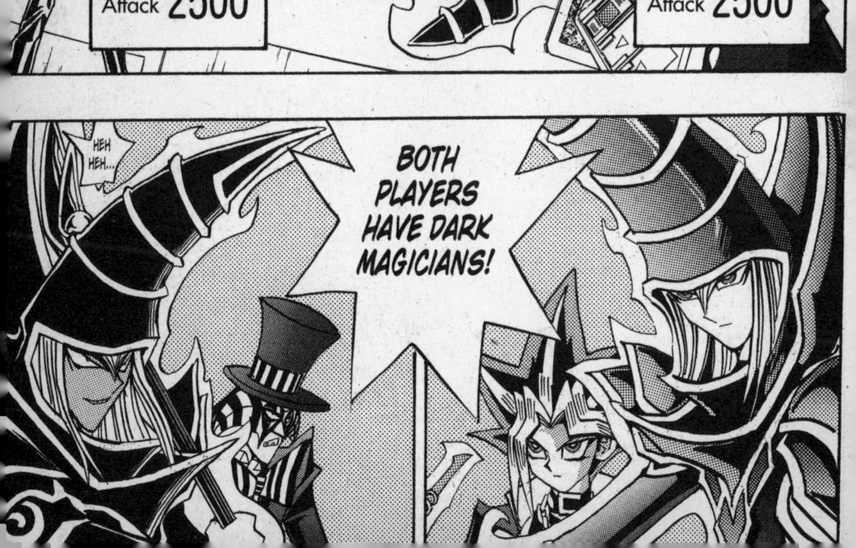
BOTH PLAYERS HAVE DARK MAGICIANS!
HEH HEH...

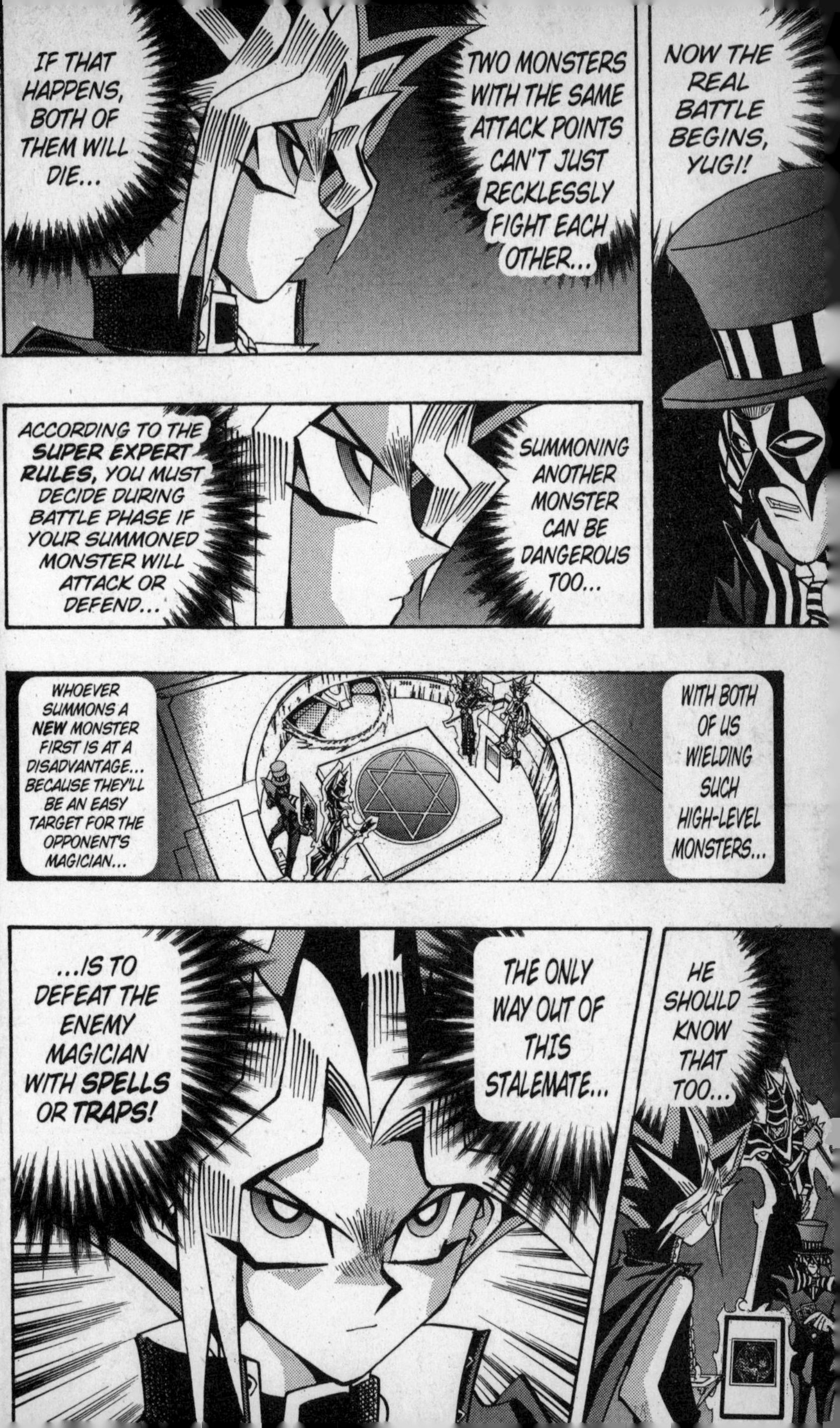
NOW THE REAL BATTLE BEGINS, YUGI!
TWO MONSTERS WITH THE SAME ATTACK POINTS CAN'T JUST RECKLESSLY FIGHT EACH OTHER...
IF THAT HAPPENS, BOTH OF THEM WILL DIE...
SUMMONING ANOTHER MONSTER CAN BE DANGEROUS TOO...
ACCORDING TO THE SUPER EXPERT RULES, YOU MUST DECIDE DURING BATTLE PHASE IF YOUR SUMMONED MONSTER WILL ATTACK OR DEFEND...
WITH BOTH OF US WIELDING SUCH HIGH-LEVEL MONSTERS...
WHOEVER SUMMONS A NEW MONSTER FIRST IS AT A DISADVANTAGE... BECAUSE THEY'LL BE AN EASY TARGET FOR THE OPPONENT'S MAGICIAN...
HE SHOULD KNOW THAT TOO...
THE ONLY WAY OUT OF THIS STALEMATE...
...IS TO DEFEAT THE ENEMY MAGICIAN WITH SPELLS OR TRAPS!

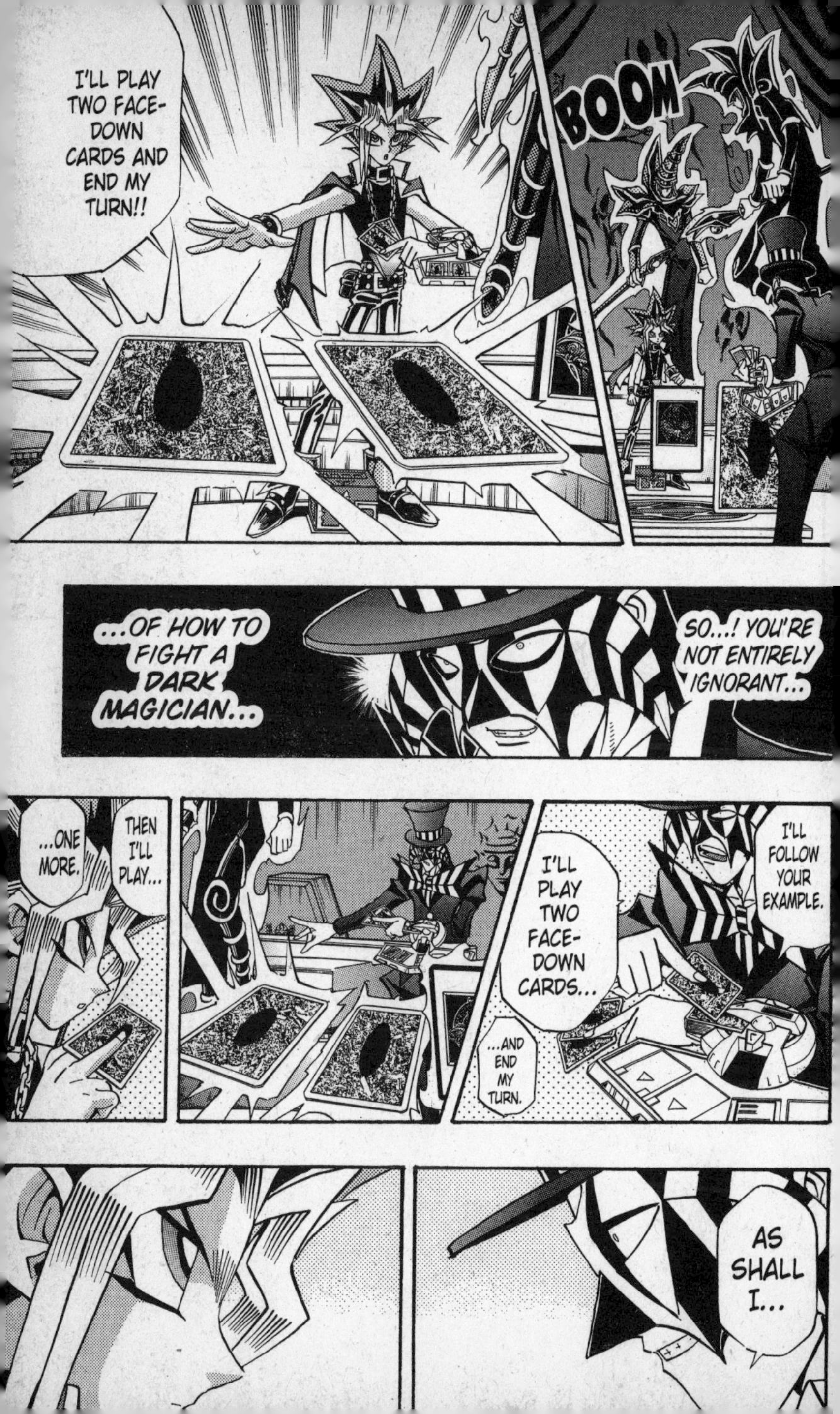
BOOM
I'LL PLAY TWO FACE-DOWN CARDS AND END MY TURN!!
SO...! YOU'RE NOT ENTIRELY IGNORANT...
...OF HOW TO FIGHT A DARK MAGICIAN...
I'LL FOLLOW YOUR EXAMPLE.
I'LL PLAY TWO FACE-DOWN CARDS...
...AND END MY TURN.
THEN I'LL PLAY...
...ONE MORE.
AS SHALL I...

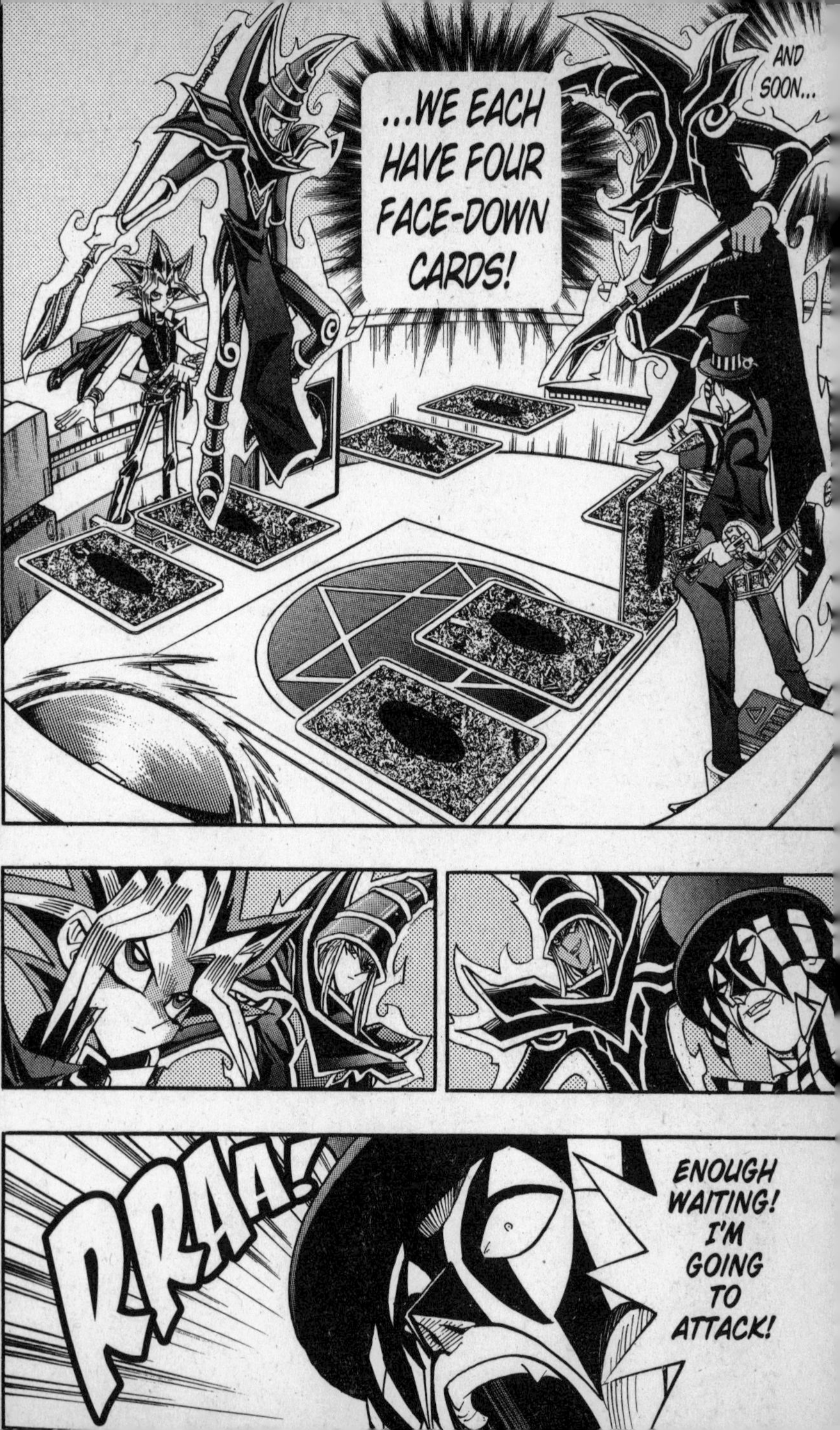
AND SOON...
...WE EACH HAVE FOUR FACE-DOWN CARDS!
ENOUGH WAITING! I'M GOING TO ATTACK!
RRAA!

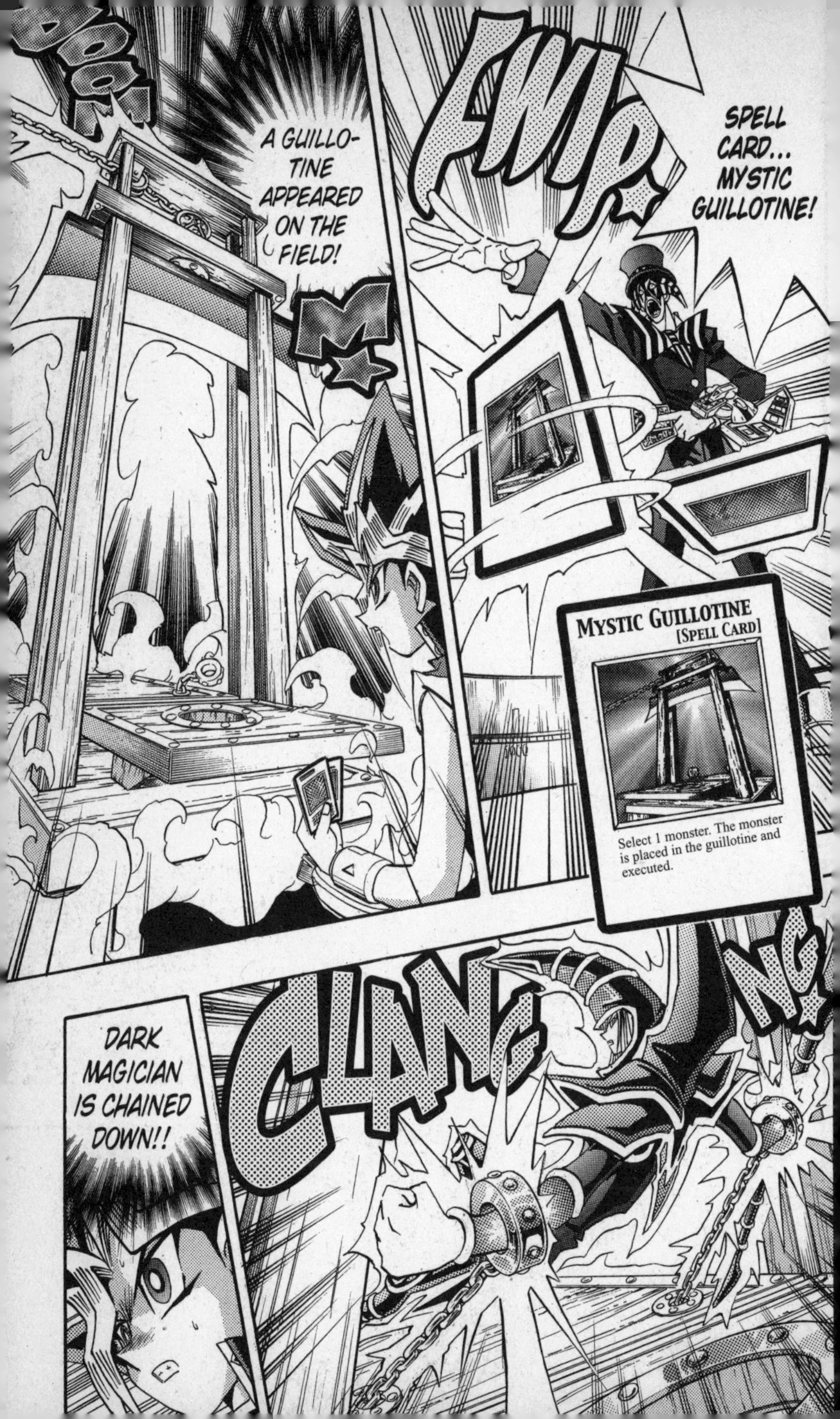
FWIP
SPELL CARD... MYSTIC GUILLOTINE!
MYSTIC GUILLOTINE
[SPELL CARD]
Select 1 monster. The monster is placed in the guillotine and executed.
DOOM
A GUILLO-TINE APPEARED ON THE FIELD!
CLANG
NG
DARK MAGICIAN IS CHAINED DOWN!!

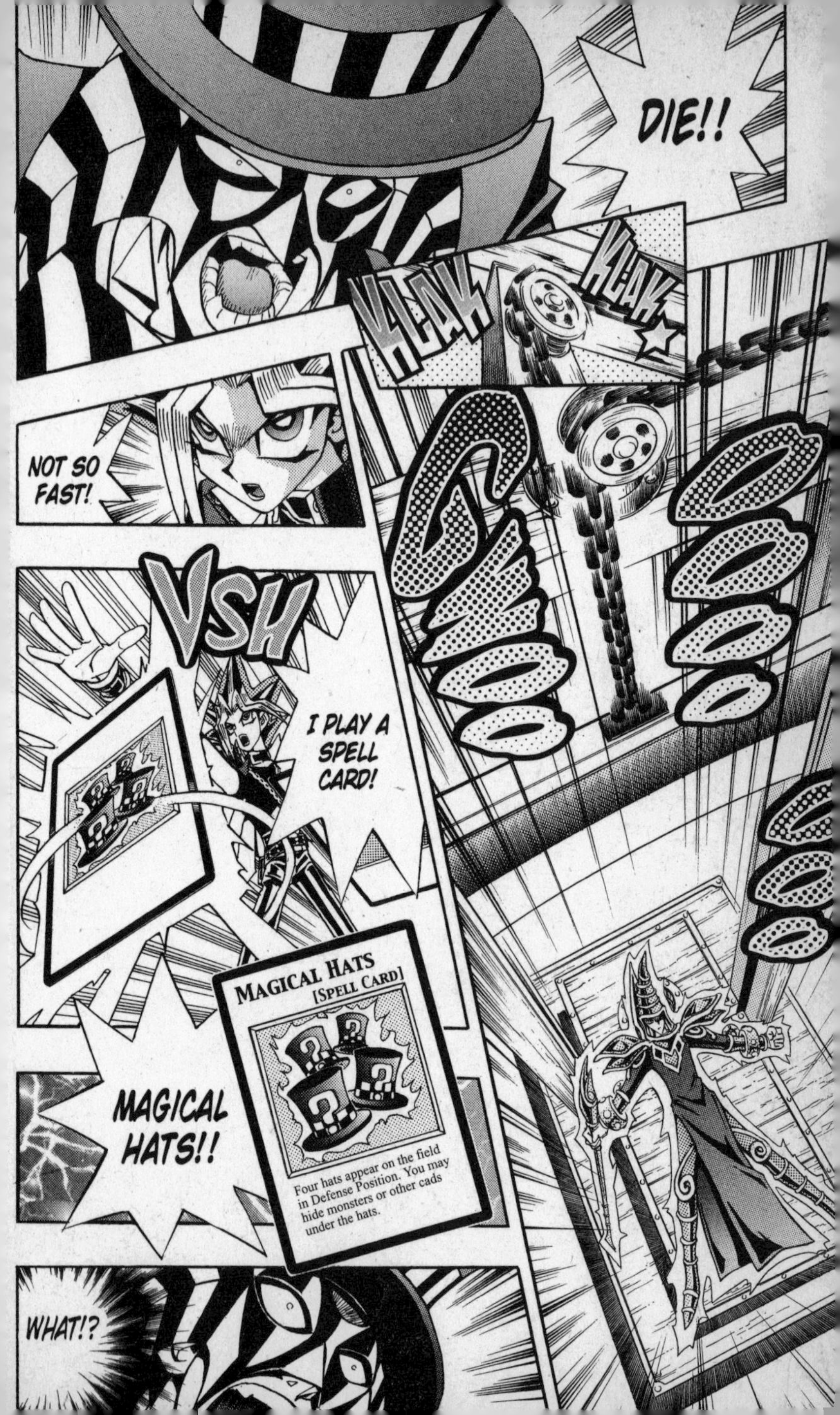
DIE!!
KLAK
KLAK
GWOOOOOOOOO
NOT SO FAST!
VSH
I PLAY A SPELL CARD!
MAGICAL HATS!!
MAGICAL HATS
[SPELL CARD]
Four hats appear on the field in Defense Position. You may hide monsters or other cads under the hats.
WHAT!?

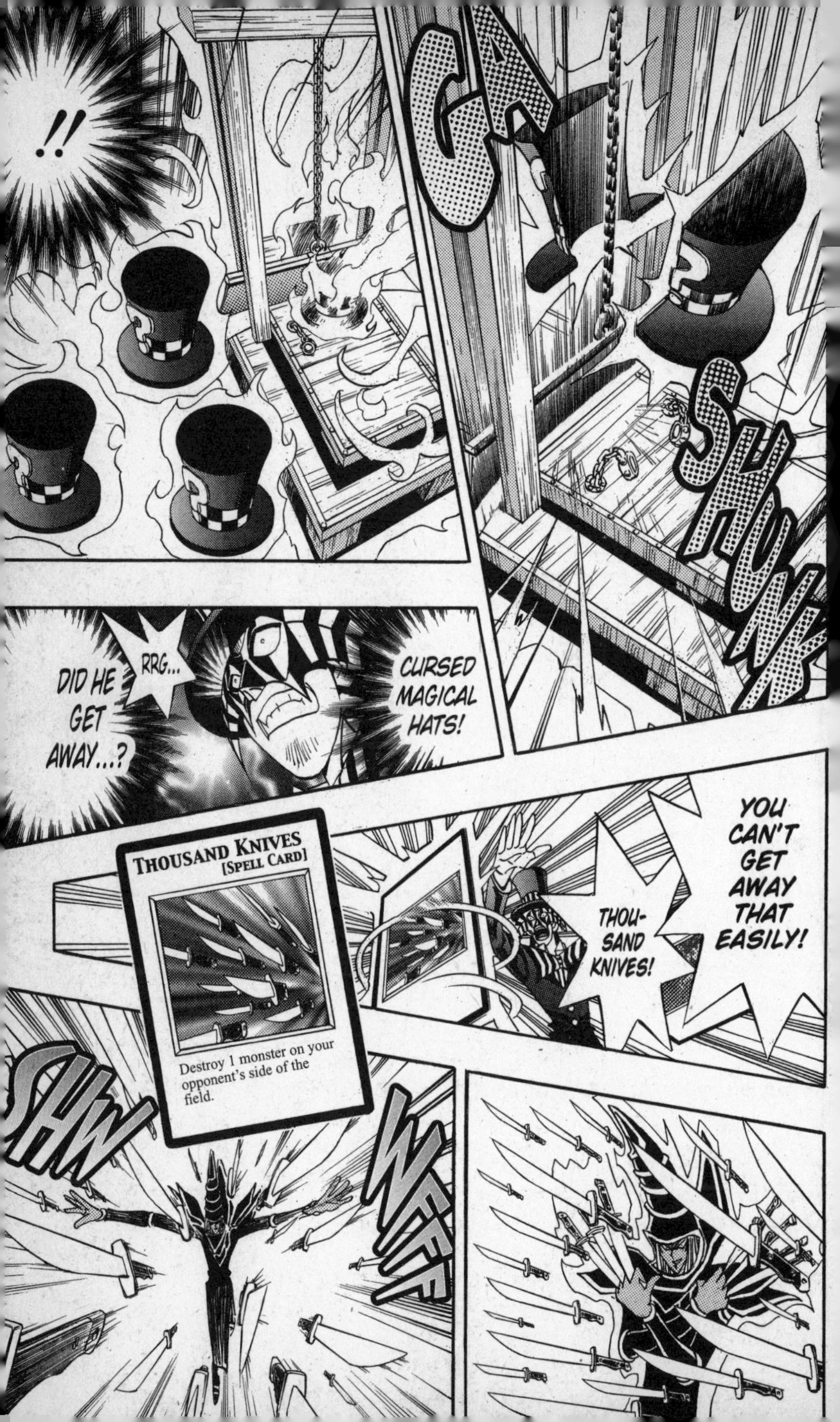

CA
SHUNK
!!
CURSED MAGICAL HATS!
RRG...
DID HE GET AWAY...?
YOU CAN'T GET AWAY THAT EASILY!
THOU-SAND KNIVES!
THOUSAND KNIVES [SPELL CARD]
Destroy 1 monster on your opponent's side of the field.
WFF
SHW

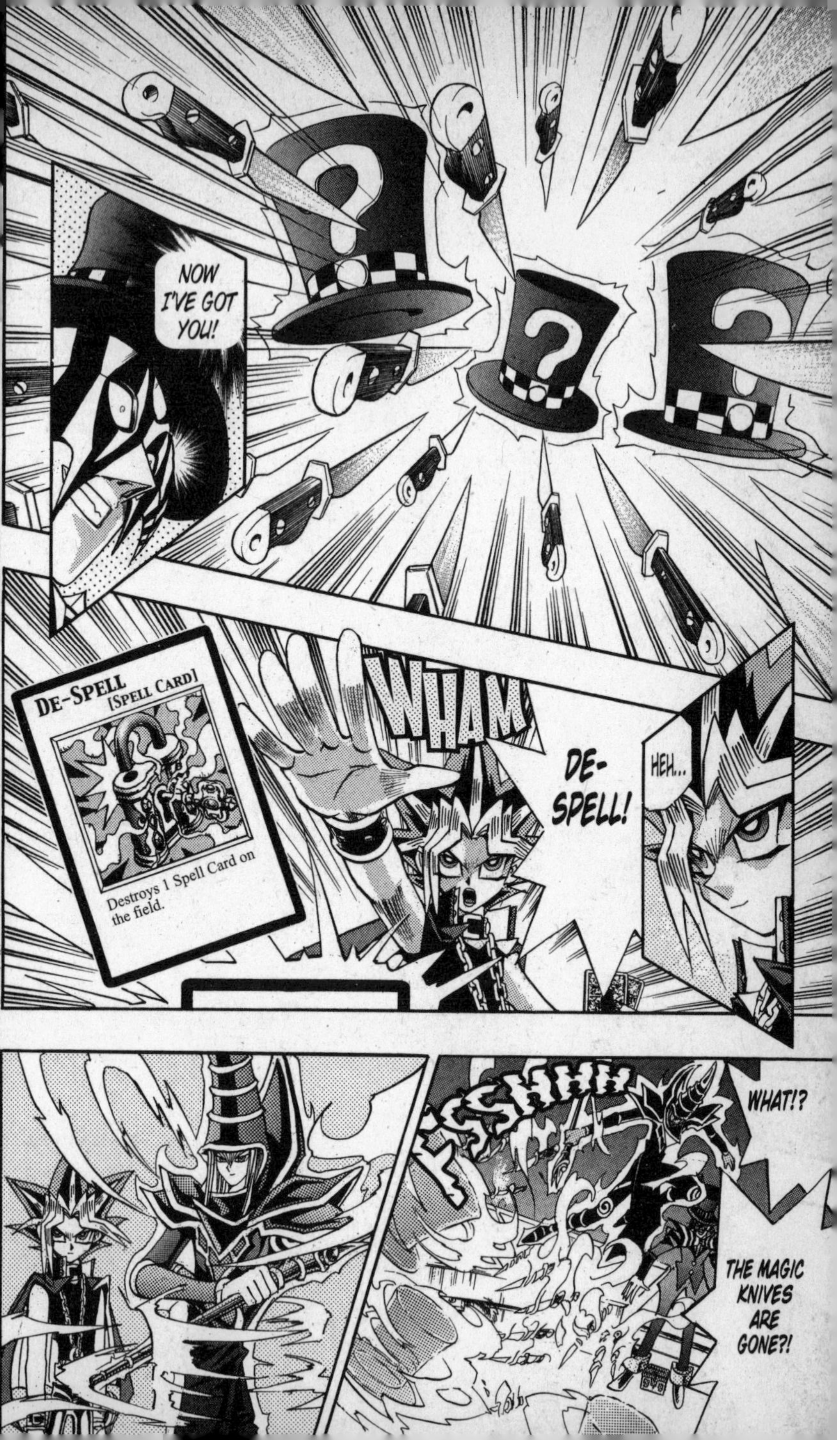
NOW I'VE GOT YOU!
HEH...
WHAM
DE-SPELL!
DE-SPELL
[SPELL CARD]
Destroys 1 Spell Card on the field.
WHAT!?
THE MAGIC KNIVES ARE GONE?!

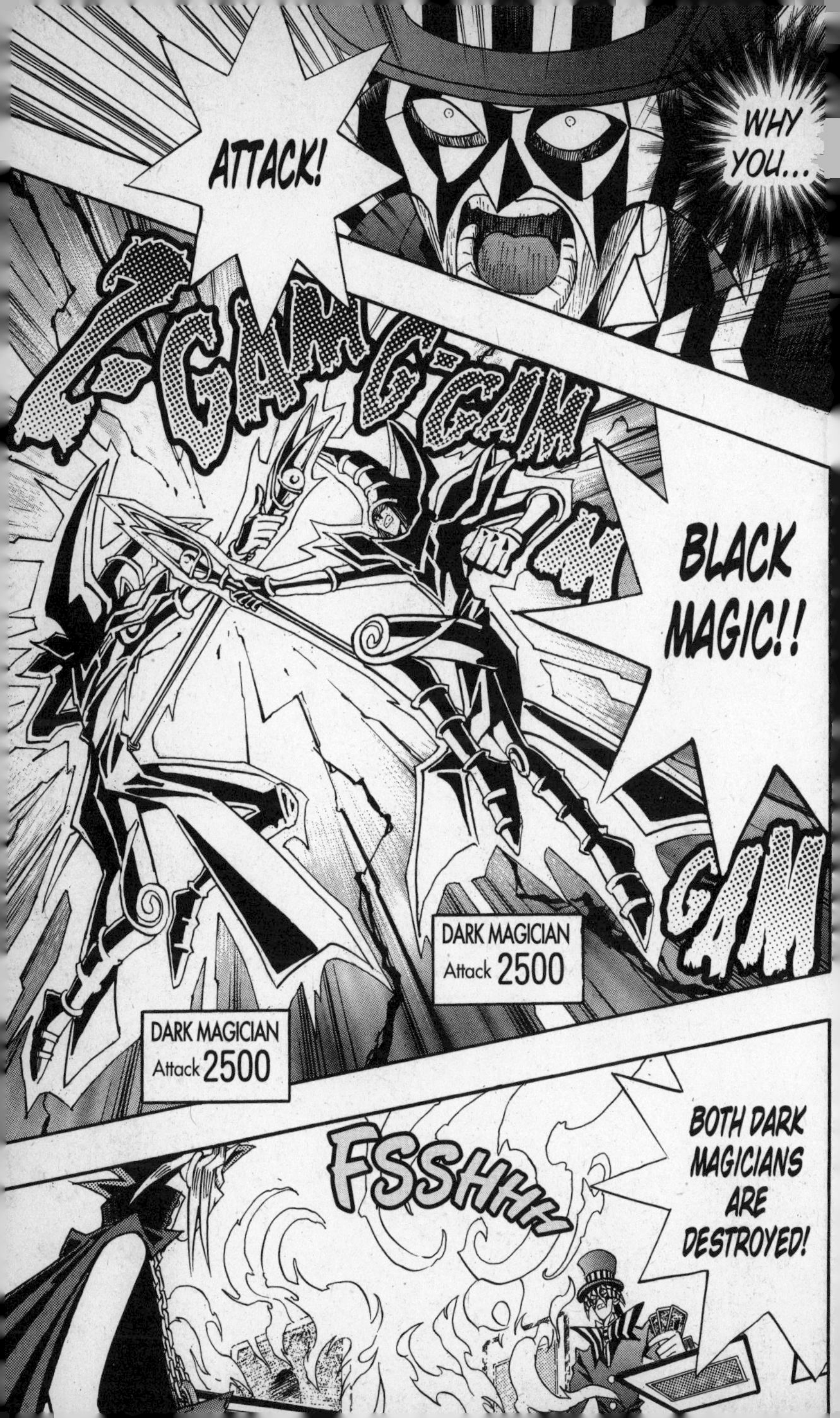
WHY YOU...
ATTACK!
GAM GAM
BLACK MAGIC!!
GAM
DARK MAGICIAN Attack 2500
DARK MAGICIAN Attack 2500
BOTH DARK MAGICIANS ARE DESTROYED!
FSSHHH

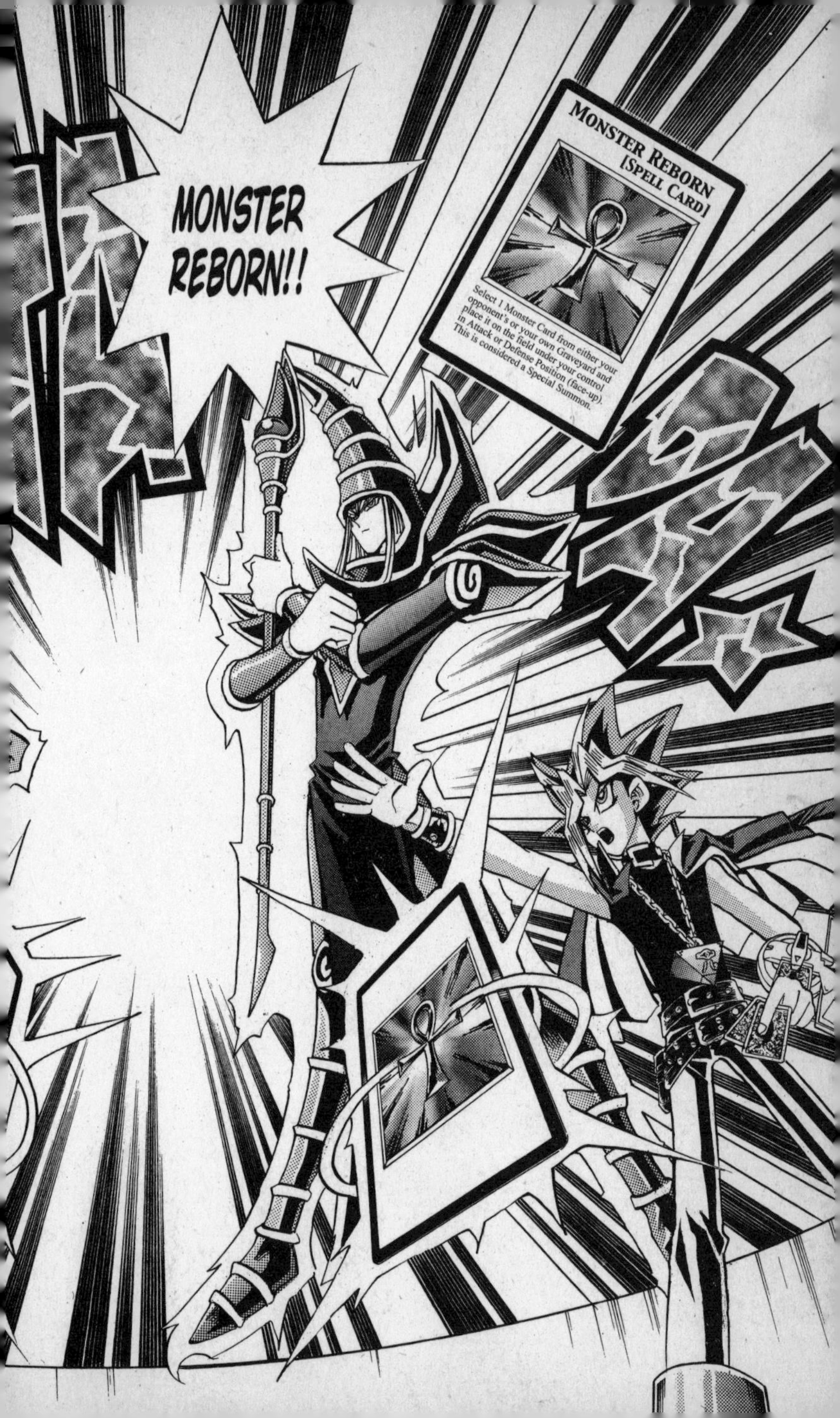
MONSTER REBORN!!
MONSTER REBORN
[SPELL CARD]
Select 1 Monster Card from either your opponent's or your own Graveyard and place it on the field under your control in Attack or Defense Position (face-up). This is considered a Special Summon.

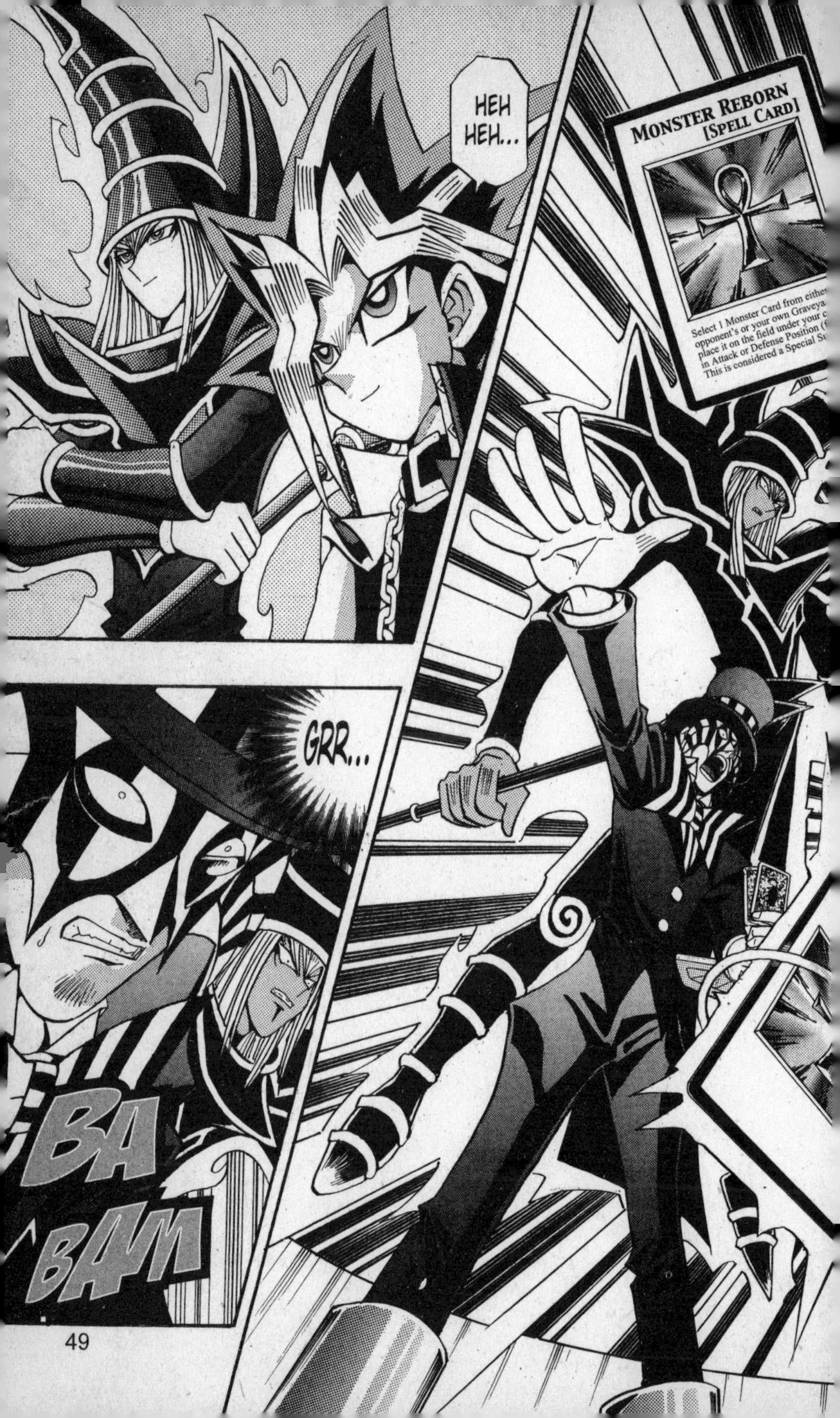
MONSTER REBORN
[SPELL CARD]
Select 1 Monster Card from either
opponent's or your own Graveya
place it on the field under your c
in Attack or Defense Position (
This is considered a Special S
HEH HEH...
GRR...
BA BAM

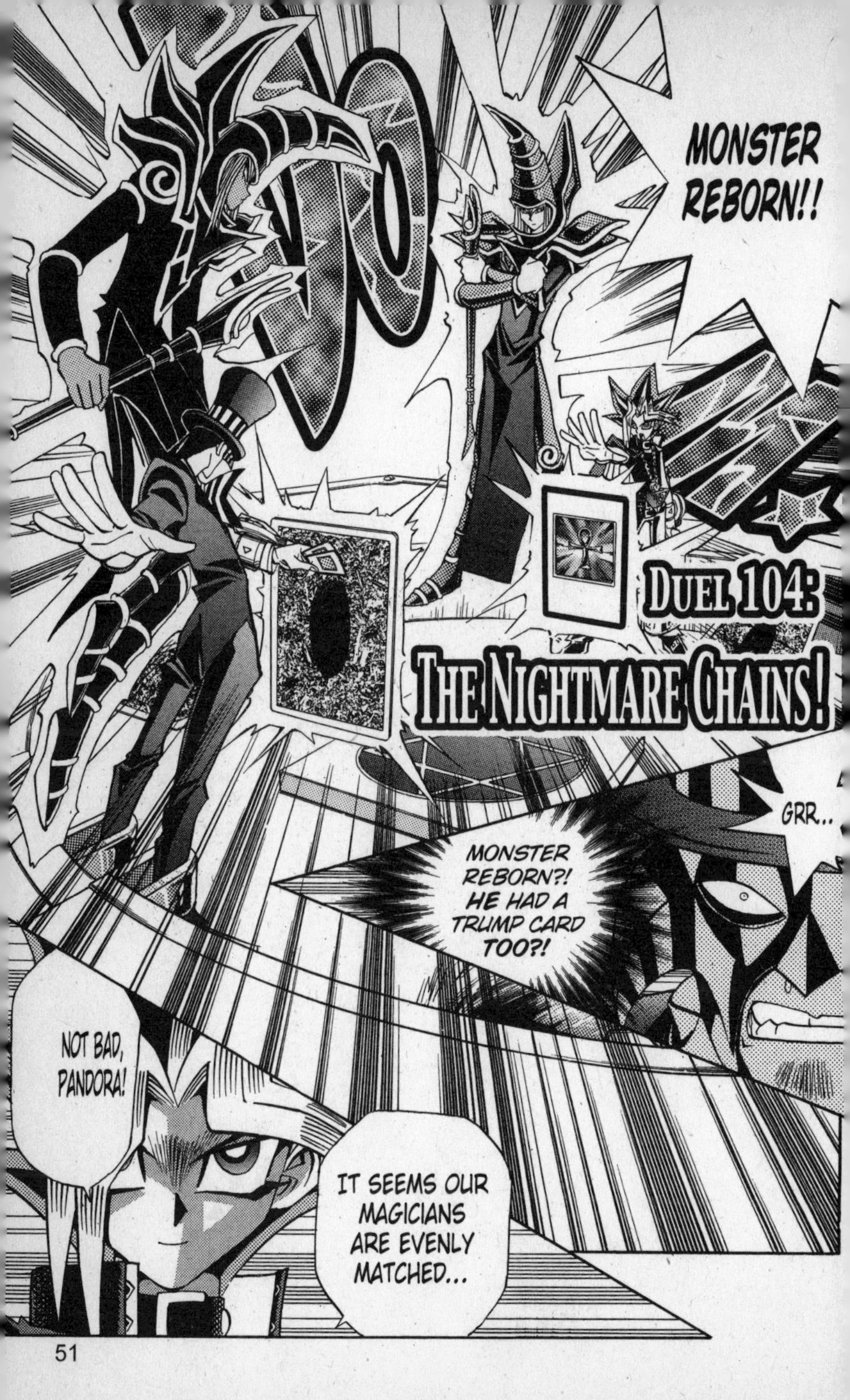
MONSTER REBORN!!
DUEL 104:
THE NIGHTMARE CHAINS!
GRR...
MONSTER REBORN?! HE HAD A TRUMP CARD TOO?!
NOT BAD, PANDORA!
IT SEEMS OUR MAGICIANS ARE EVENLY MATCHED...

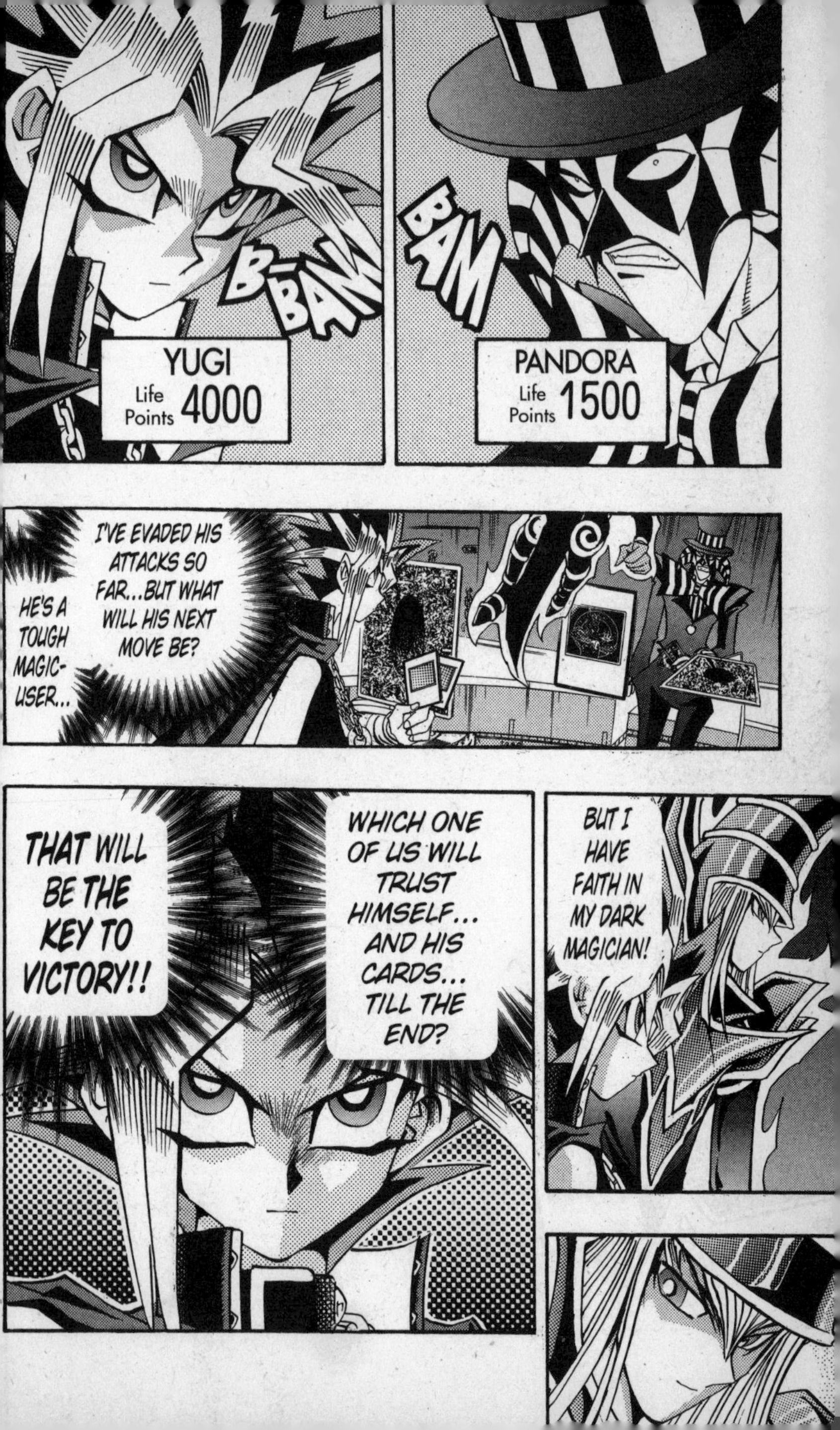
BAM
PANDORA Life Points 1500
B-BAM
YUGI Life Points 4000
I'VE EVADED HIS ATTACKS SO FAR...BUT WHAT WILL HIS NEXT MOVE BE?
HE'S A TOUGH MAGIC-USER...
BUT I HAVE FAITH IN MY DARK MAGICIAN!
WHICH ONE OF US WILL TRUST HIMSELF... AND HIS CARDS... TILL THE END?
THAT WILL BE THE KEY TO VICTORY!!

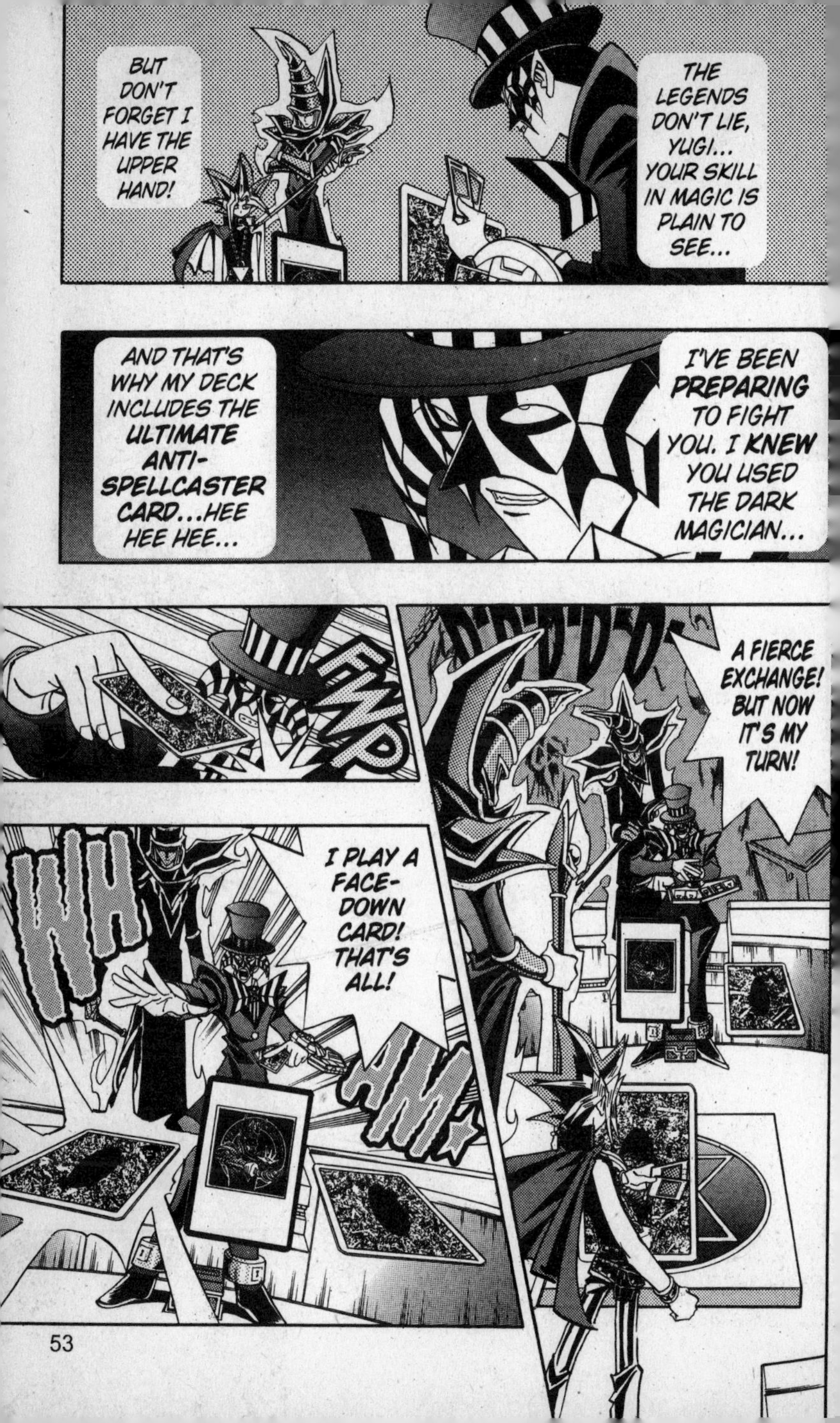

THE LEGENDS DON'T LIE, YUGI... YOUR SKILL IN MAGIC IS PLAIN TO SEE...
BUT DON'T FORGET I HAVE THE UPPER HAND!
I'VE BEEN PREPARING TO FIGHT YOU. I KNEW YOU USED THE DARK MAGICIAN...
AND THAT'S WHY MY DECK INCLUDES THE ULTIMATE ANTI-SPELLCASTER CARD...HEE HEE HEE...
A FIERCE EXCHANGE! BUT NOW IT'S MY TURN!
FWIP
WHAM!
I PLAY A FACE-DOWN CARD! THAT'S ALL!

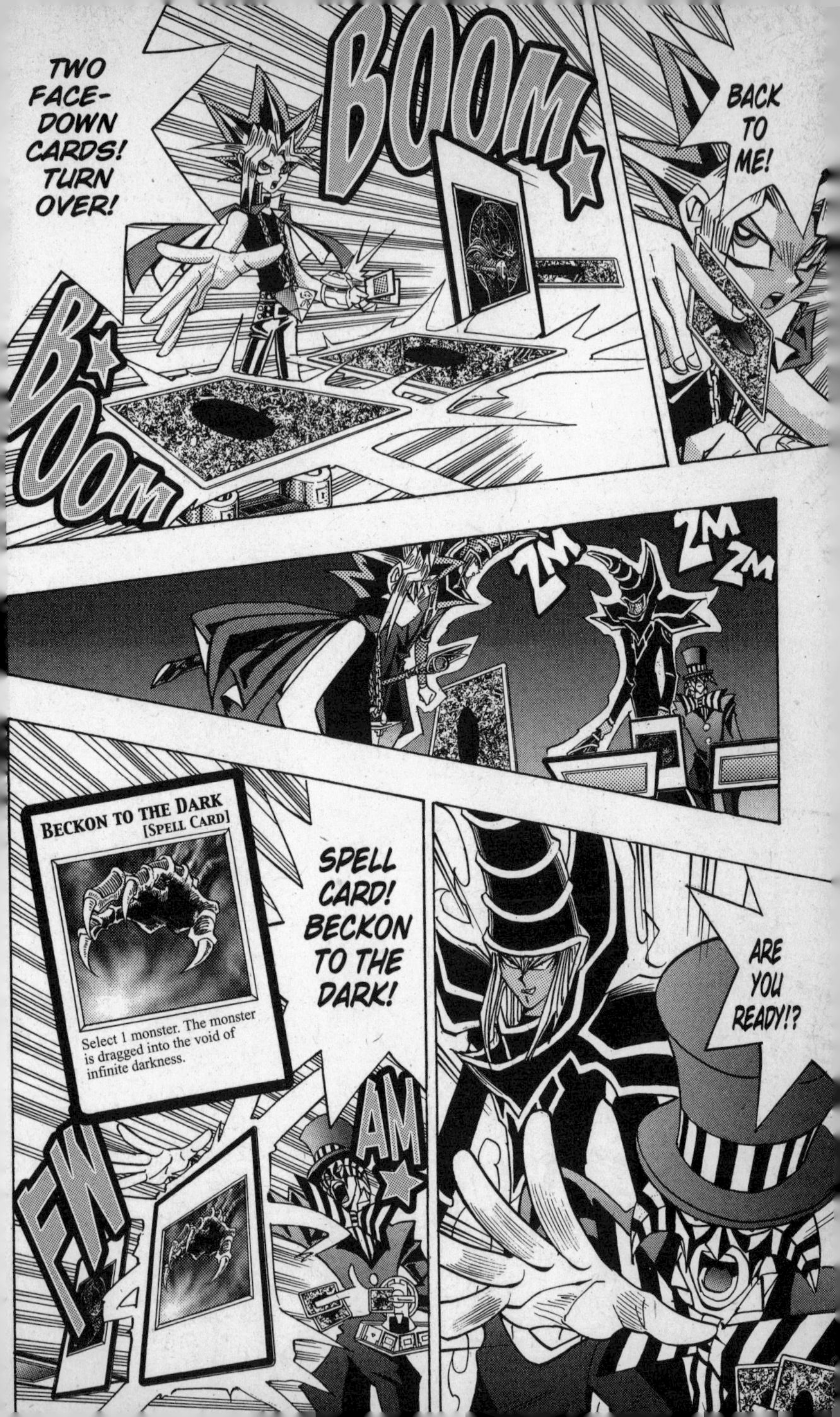
BACK TO ME!
BOOM
TWO FACE-DOWN CARDS! TURN OVER!
B☆DOOM
ZM
ZM
ZM
ARE YOU READY!?
BECKON TO THE DARK
[SPELL CARD]
Select 1 monster. The monster is dragged into the void of infinite darkness.
SPELL CARD! BECKON TO THE DARK!
AM
FW

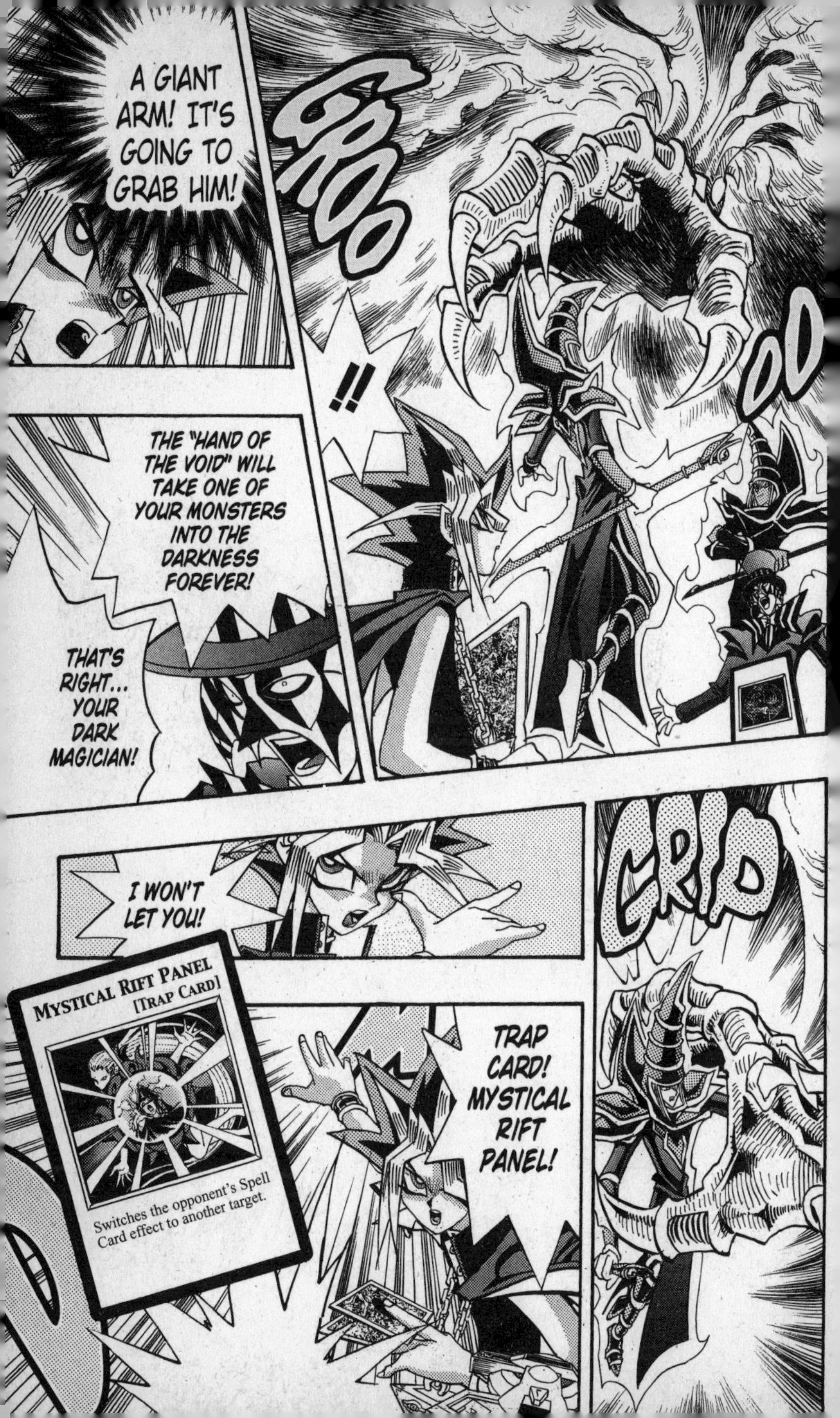
GROO
OO
!!
A GIANT ARM! IT'S GOING TO GRAB HIM!
THE "HAND OF THE VOID" WILL TAKE ONE OF YOUR MONSTERS INTO THE DARKNESS FOREVER!
THAT'S RIGHT... YOUR DARK MAGICIAN!
GRIP
I WON'T LET YOU!
TRAP CARD! MYSTICAL RIFT PANEL!
MYSTICAL RIFT PANEL
[TRAP CARD]
Switches the opponent's Spell Card effect to another target.

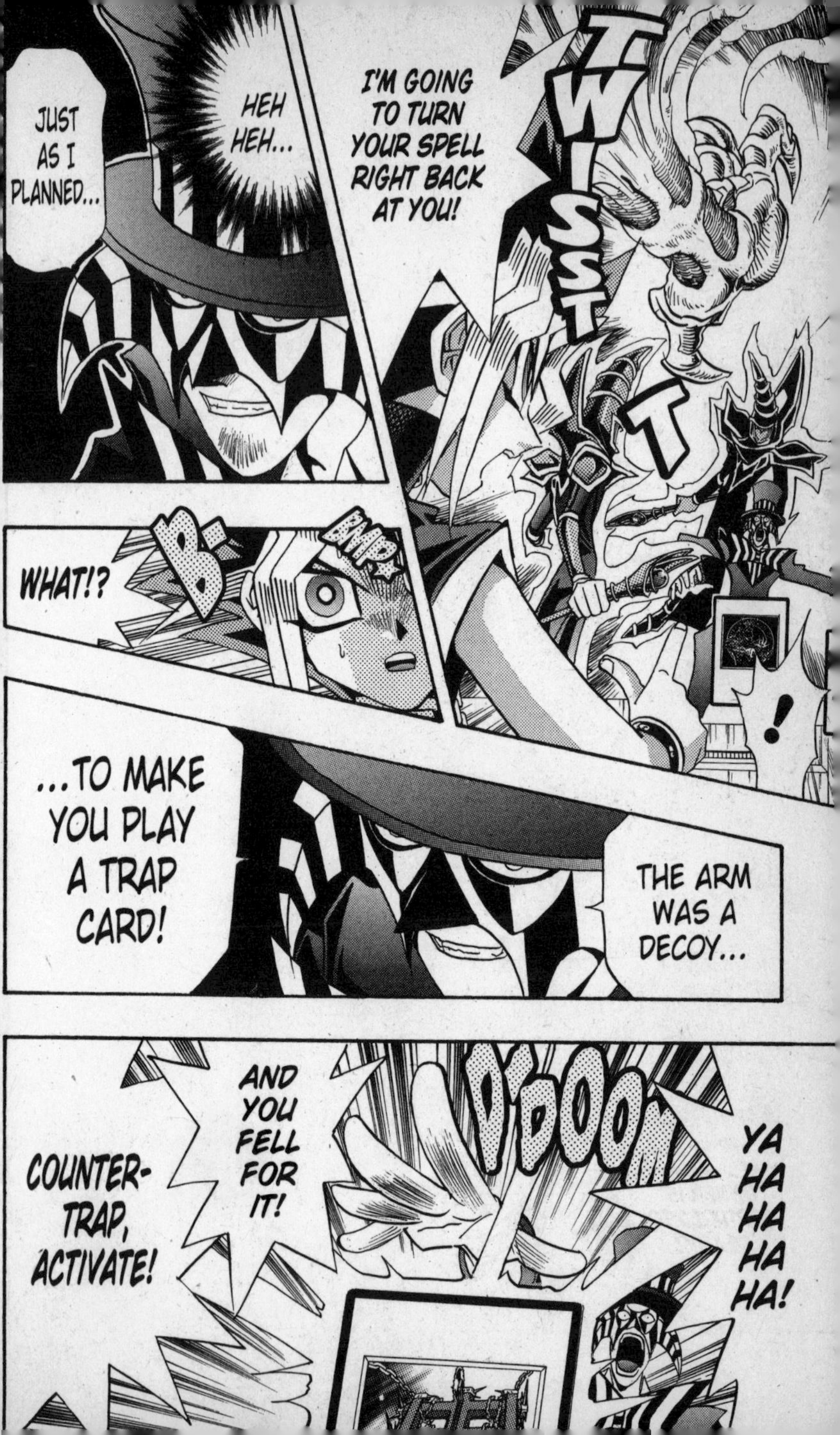
I'M GOING TO TURN YOUR SPELL RIGHT BACK AT YOU!
TWISST
T
!
HEH HEH...
JUST AS I PLANNED...
BMP
B
WHAT!?
THE ARM WAS A DECOY...
...TO MAKE YOU PLAY A TRAP CARD!
YA HA HA HA HA!
D'DOOM
AND YOU FELL FOR IT!
COUNTER-TRAP, ACTIVATE!

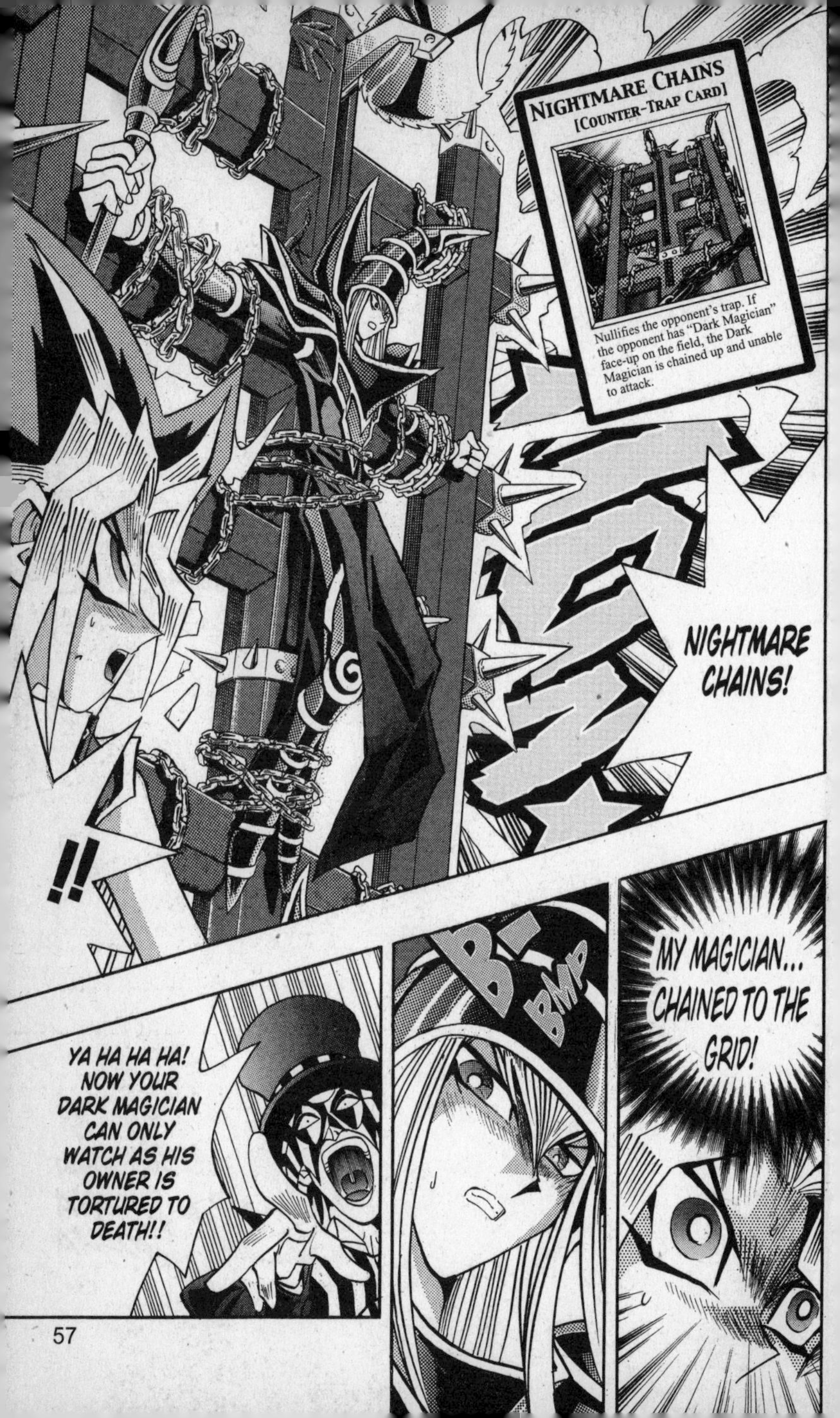
NIGHTMARE CHAINS
[COUNTER-TRAP CARD]
Nullifies the opponent's trap. If the opponent has "Dark Magician" face-up on the field, the Dark Magician is chained up and unable to attack.
NIGHTMARE CHAINS!
!!
MY MAGICIAN... CHAINED TO THE GRID!
B-BMP
YA HA HA HA! NOW YOUR DARK MAGICIAN CAN ONLY WATCH AS HIS OWNER IS TORTURED TO DEATH!!

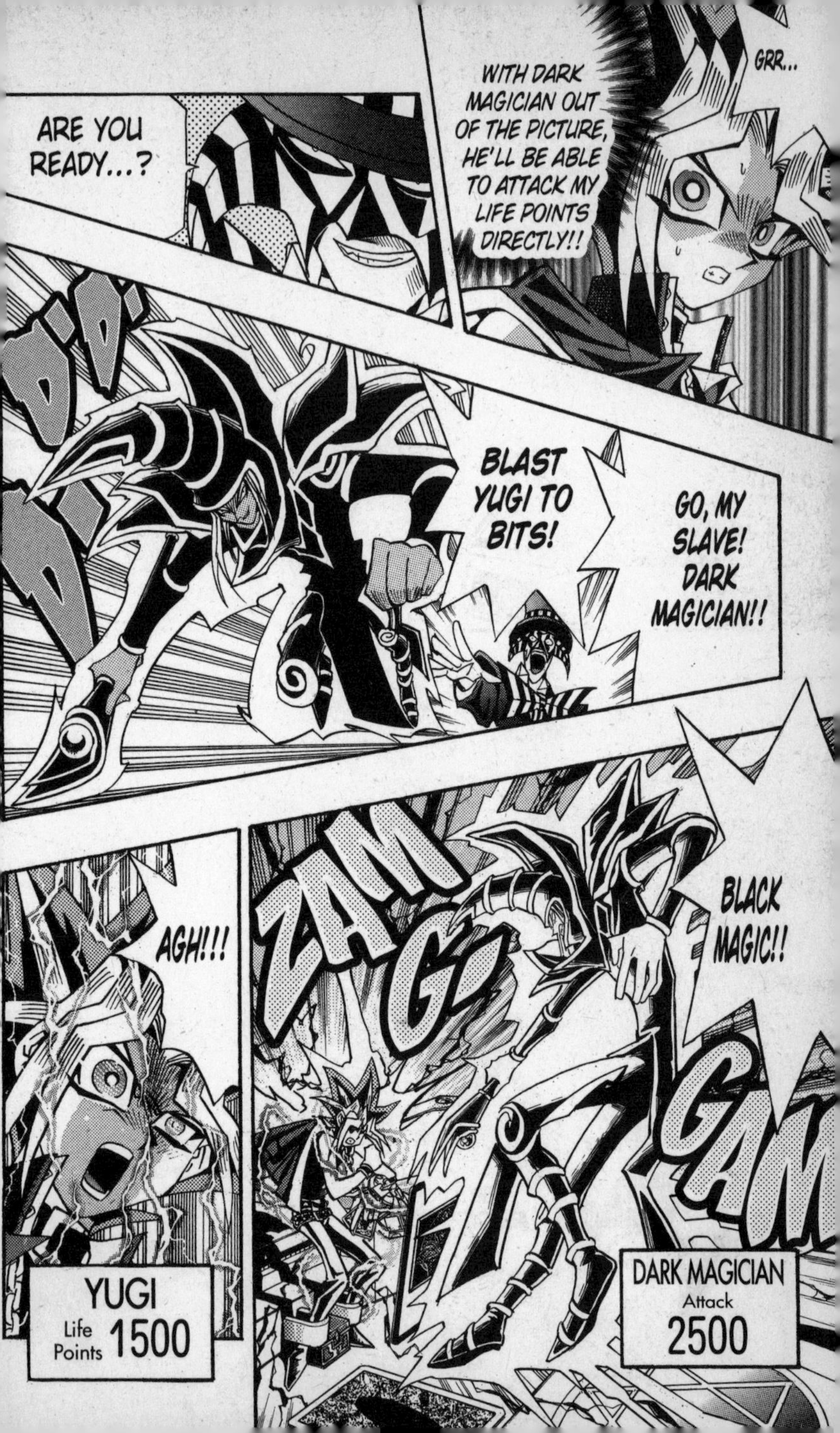
GRR...
WITH DARK MAGICIAN OUT OF THE PICTURE, HE'LL BE ABLE TO ATTACK MY LIFE POINTS DIRECTLY!!
ARE YOU READY...?
GO, MY SLAVE! DARK MAGICIAN!!
BLAST YUGI TO BITS!
BLACK MAGIC!!
ZAM
DARK MAGICIAN Attack 2500
AGH!!!
YUGI Life Points 1500

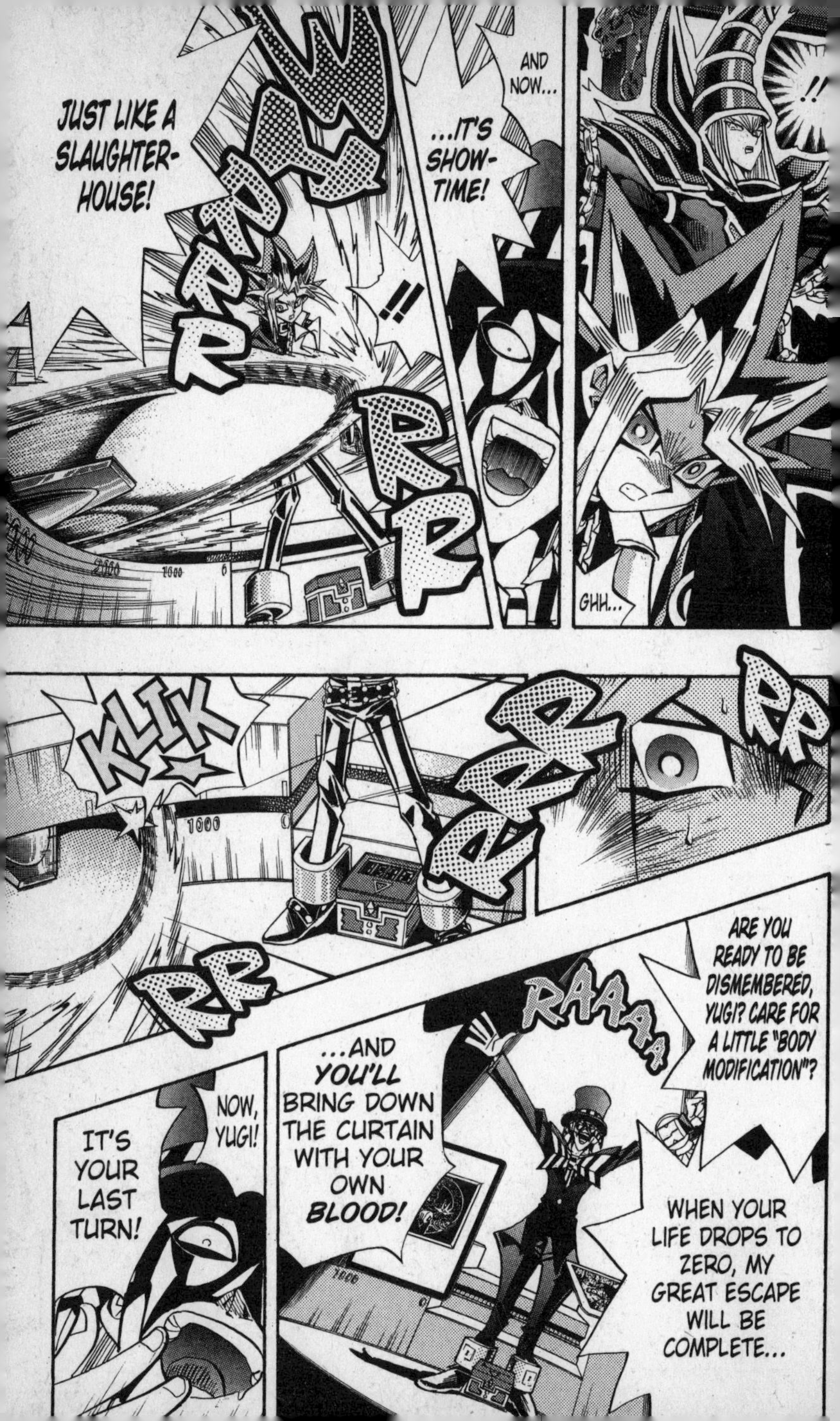

!!
GHH...
AND NOW...
...IT'S SHOW-TIME!
!!
WHIRR
RRR
JUST LIKE A SLAUGHTER-HOUSE!
RR
KLIK
RRRR
RR
ARE YOU READY TO BE DISMEMBERED, YUGI? CARE FOR A LITTLE "BODY MODIFICATION"?
RAAAA
WHEN YOUR LIFE DROPS TO ZERO, MY GREAT ESCAPE WILL BE COMPLETE...
...AND *YOU'LL* BRING DOWN THE CURTAIN WITH YOUR OWN *BLOOD!*
NOW, YUGI!
IT'S YOUR LAST TURN!

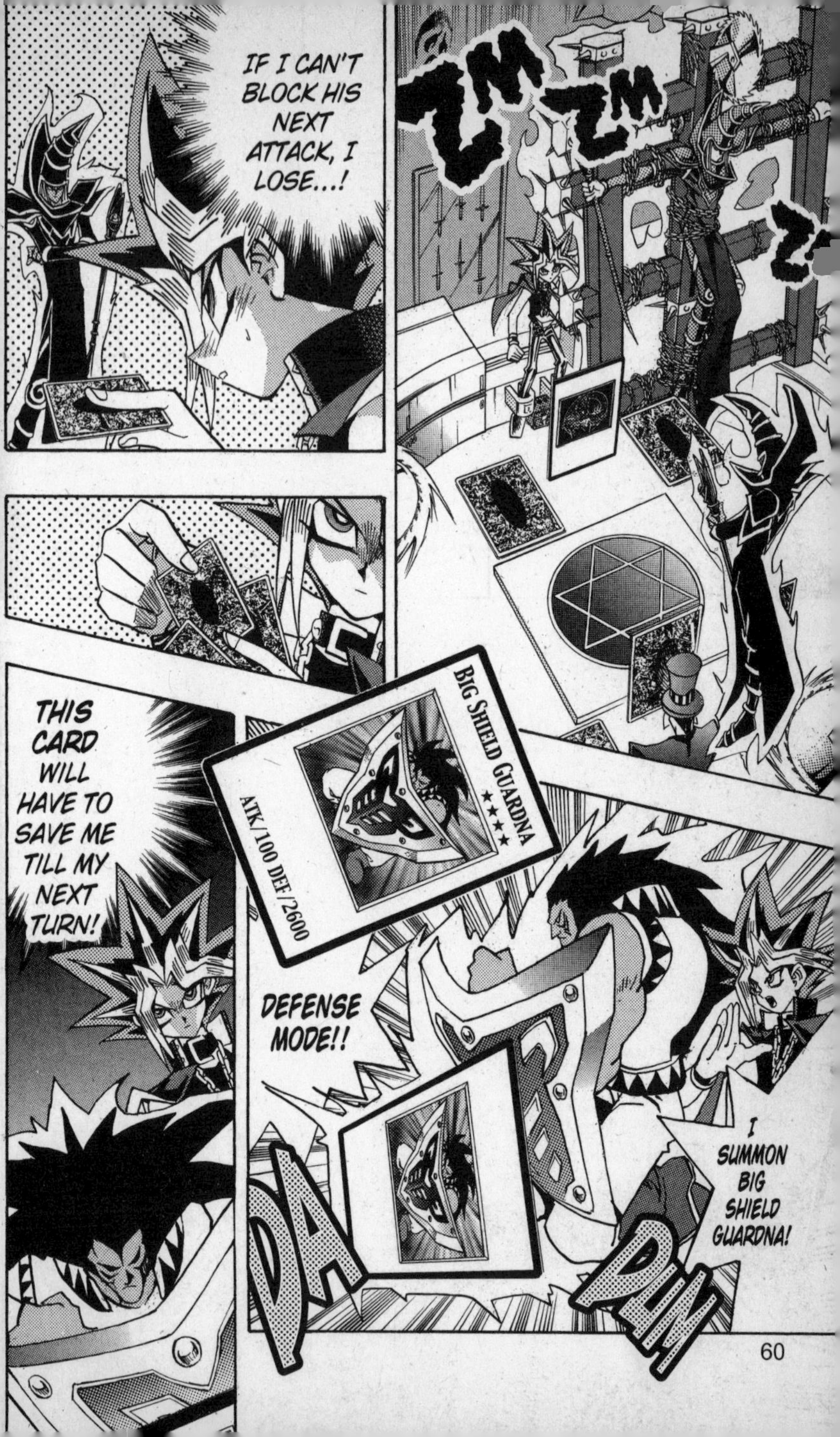
ZM ZM
IF I CAN'T BLOCK HIS NEXT ATTACK, I LOSE...!
I SUMMON BIG SHIELD GUARDNA!
BIG SHIELD GUARDNA
ATK/100 DEF/2600
DEFENSE MODE!!
DA DAN
THIS CARD WILL HAVE TO SAVE ME TILL MY NEXT TURN!

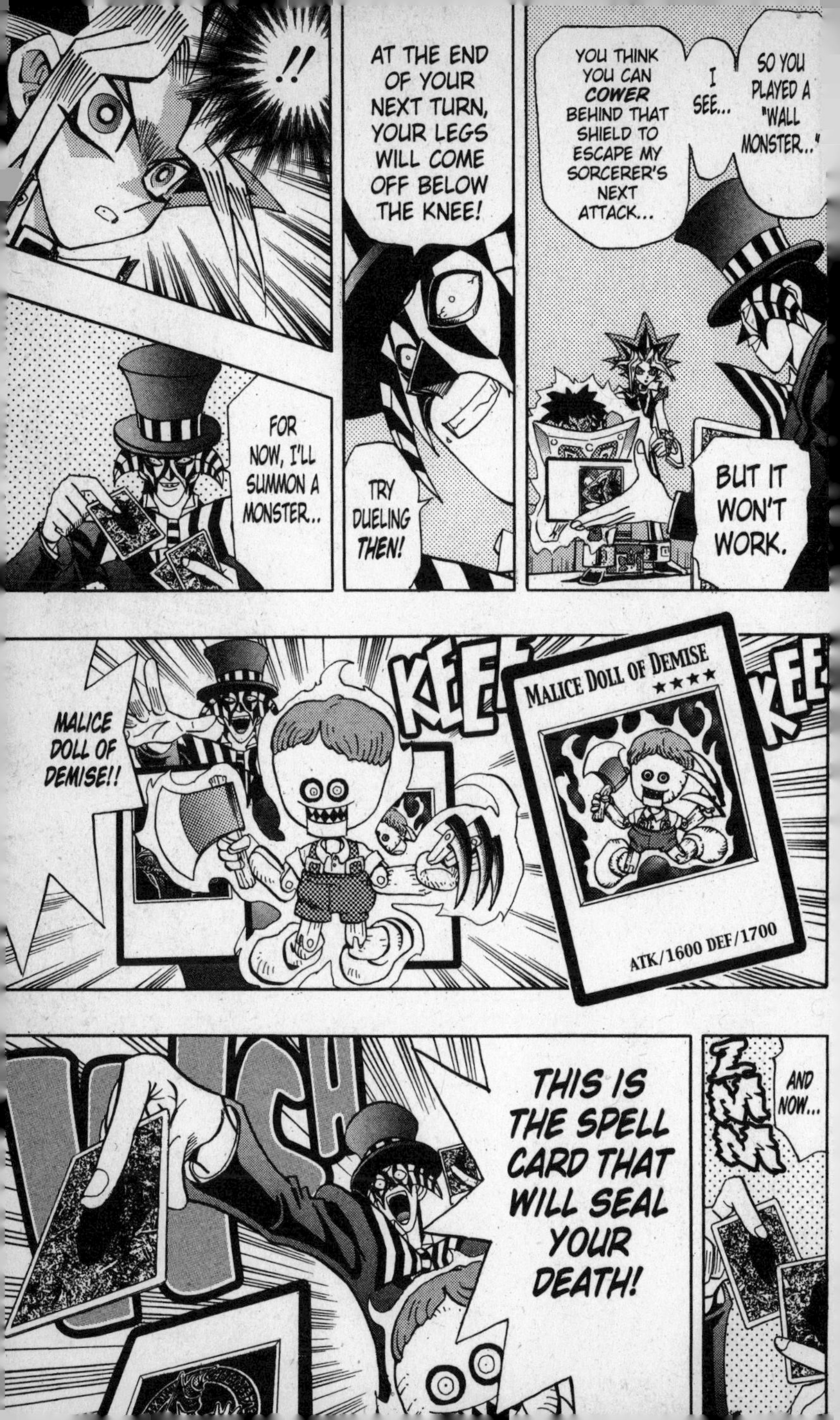
SO YOU PLAYED A "WALL MONSTER..."
I SEE...
YOU THINK YOU CAN COWER BEHIND THAT SHIELD TO ESCAPE MY SORCERER'S NEXT ATTACK...
BUT IT WON'T WORK.
AT THE END OF YOUR NEXT TURN, YOUR LEGS WILL COME OFF BELOW THE KNEE!
TRY DUELING THEN!
!!
FOR NOW, I'LL SUMMON A MONSTER...
KEE
MALICE DOLL OF DEMISE
★★★★
ATK/1600 DEF/1700
KEE
MALICE DOLL OF DEMISE!!
AND NOW...
THIS IS THE SPELL CARD THAT WILL SEAL YOUR DEATH!

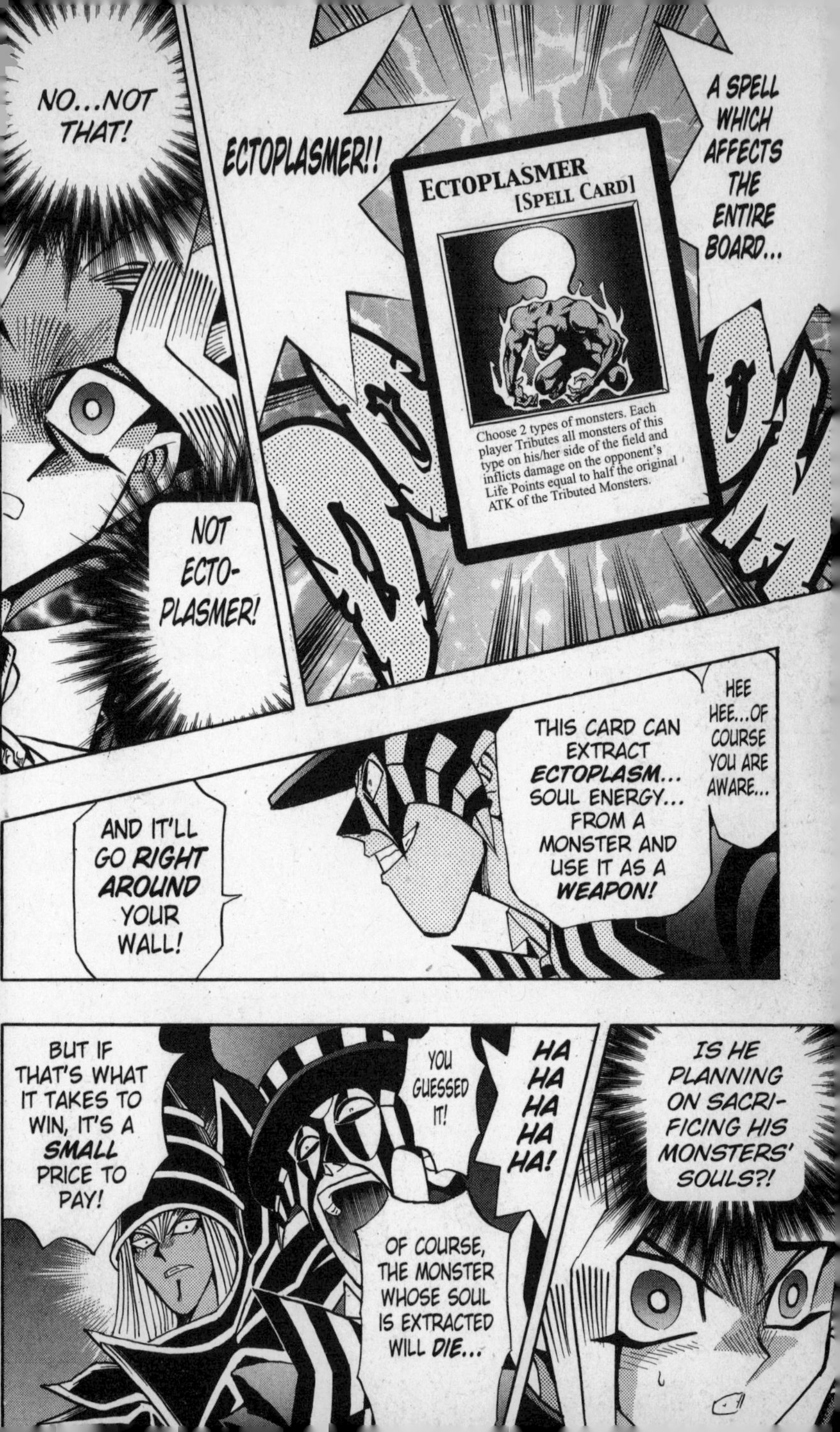

A SPELL WHICH AFFECTS THE ENTIRE BOARD...
ECTOPLASMER!!
ECTOPLASMER [SPELL CARD]
Choose 2 types of monsters. Each player Tributes all monsters of this type on his/her side of the field and inflicts damage on the opponent's Life Points equal to half the original ATK of the Tributed Monsters.
NO...NOT THAT!
NOT ECTO-PLASMER!
HEE HEE...OF COURSE YOU ARE AWARE...
THIS CARD CAN EXTRACT ECTOPLASM... SOUL ENERGY... FROM A MONSTER AND USE IT AS A WEAPON!
AND IT'LL GO RIGHT AROUND YOUR WALL!
IS HE PLANNING ON SACRI-FICING HIS MONSTERS' SOULS?!
HA HA HA HA HA!
YOU GUESSED IT!
OF COURSE, THE MONSTER WHOSE SOUL IS EXTRACTED WILL DIE...
BUT IF THAT'S WHAT IT TAKES TO WIN, IT'S A SMALL PRICE TO PAY!

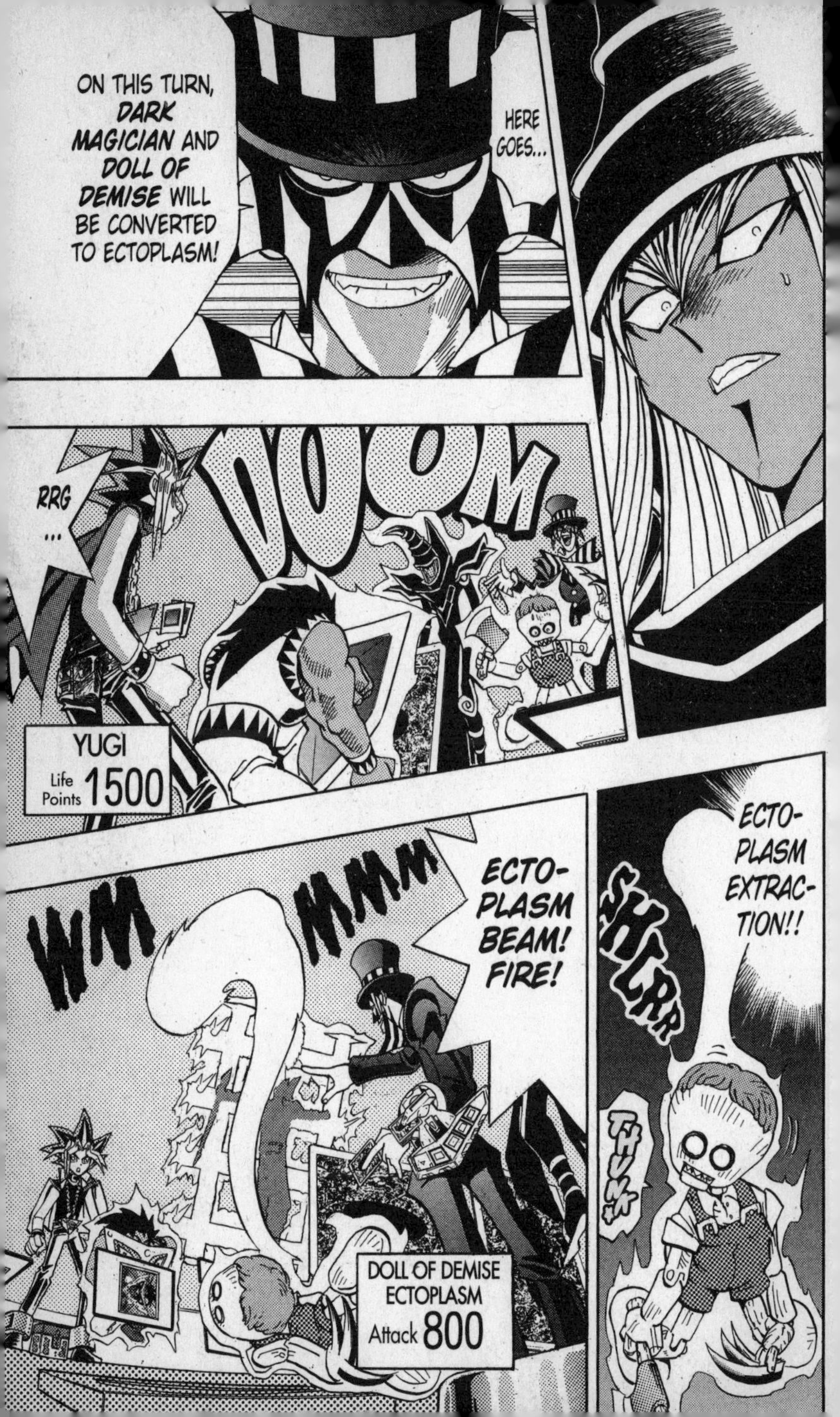
HERE GOES...
ON THIS TURN, DARK MAGICIAN AND DOLL OF DEMISE WILL BE CONVERTED TO ECTOPLASM!
DOOM
RRG ...
YUGI Life Points 1500
ECTO-PLASM EXTRAC-TION!!
SHLRR
THUNK
ECTO-PLASM BEAM! FIRE!
MMMM
WM
DOLL OF DEMISE ECTOPLASM Attack 800

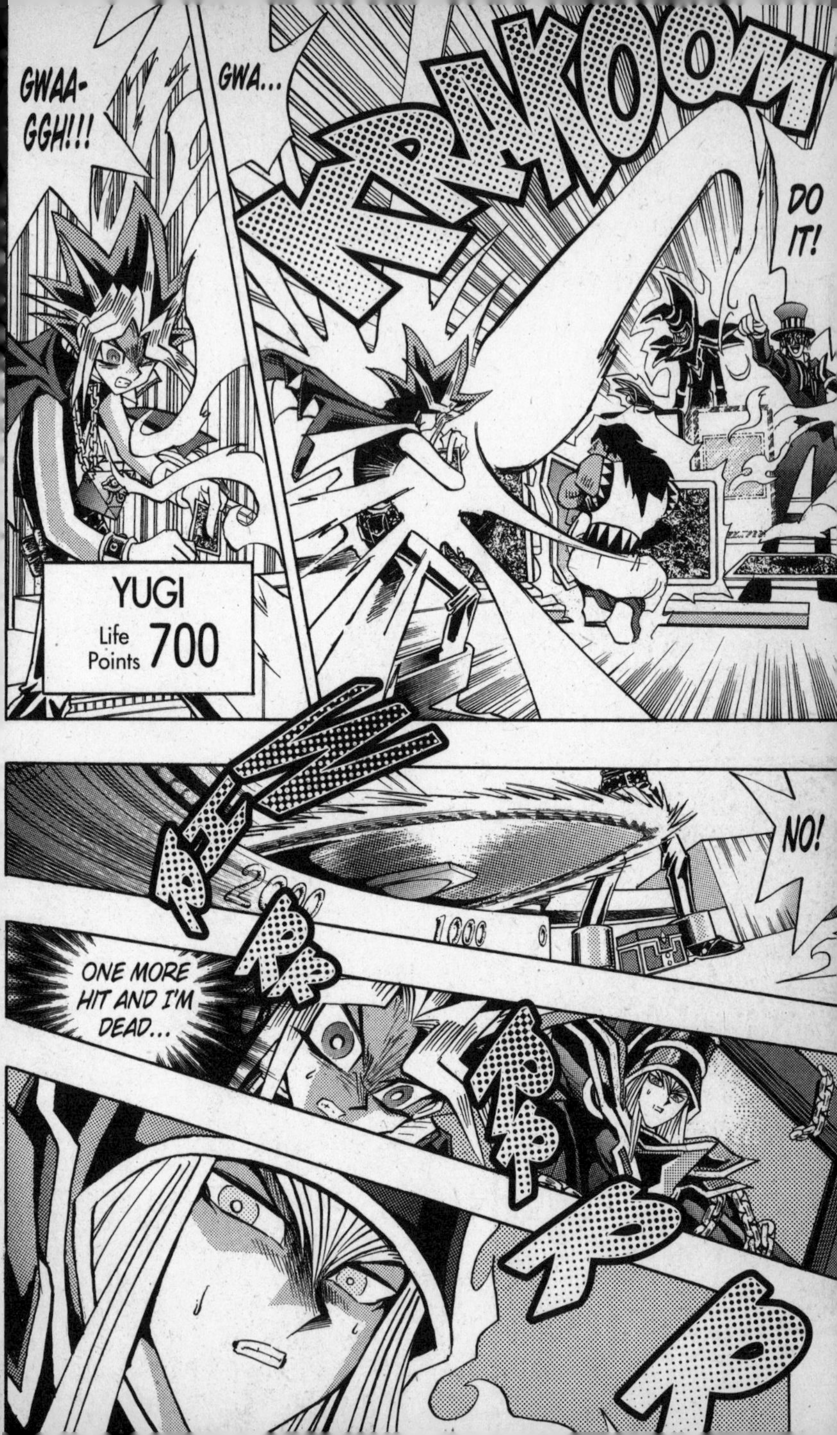
KRAKOOM
DO IT!
GWA...
GWAA-GGH!!!
YUGI Life Points 700
NO!
2000
1000
ONE MORE HIT AND I'M DEAD...

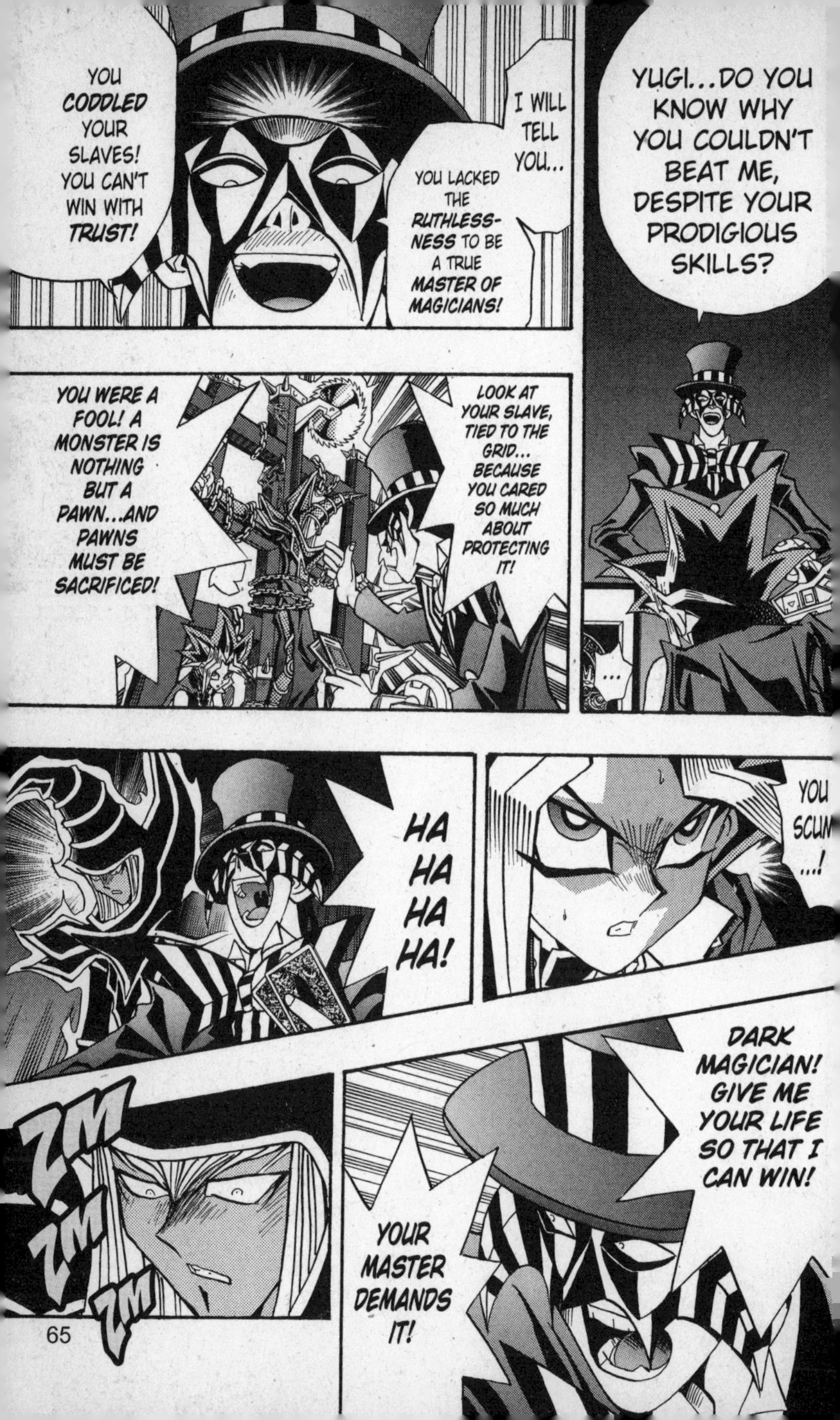
YUGI...DO YOU KNOW WHY YOU COULDN'T BEAT ME, DESPITE YOUR PRODIGIOUS SKILLS?
...
I WILL TELL YOU...
YOU LACKED THE RUTHLESSNESS TO BE A TRUE MASTER OF MAGICIANS!
YOU CODDLED YOUR SLAVES! YOU CAN'T WIN WITH TRUST!
LOOK AT YOUR SLAVE, TIED TO THE GRID... BECAUSE YOU CARED SO MUCH ABOUT PROTECTING IT!
YOU WERE A FOOL! A MONSTER IS NOTHING BUT A PAWN...AND PAWNS MUST BE SACRIFICED!
YOU SCUM...!
HA HA HA HA!
DARK MAGICIAN! GIVE ME YOUR LIFE SO THAT I CAN WIN!
YOUR MASTER DEMANDS IT!
ZM ZM ZM

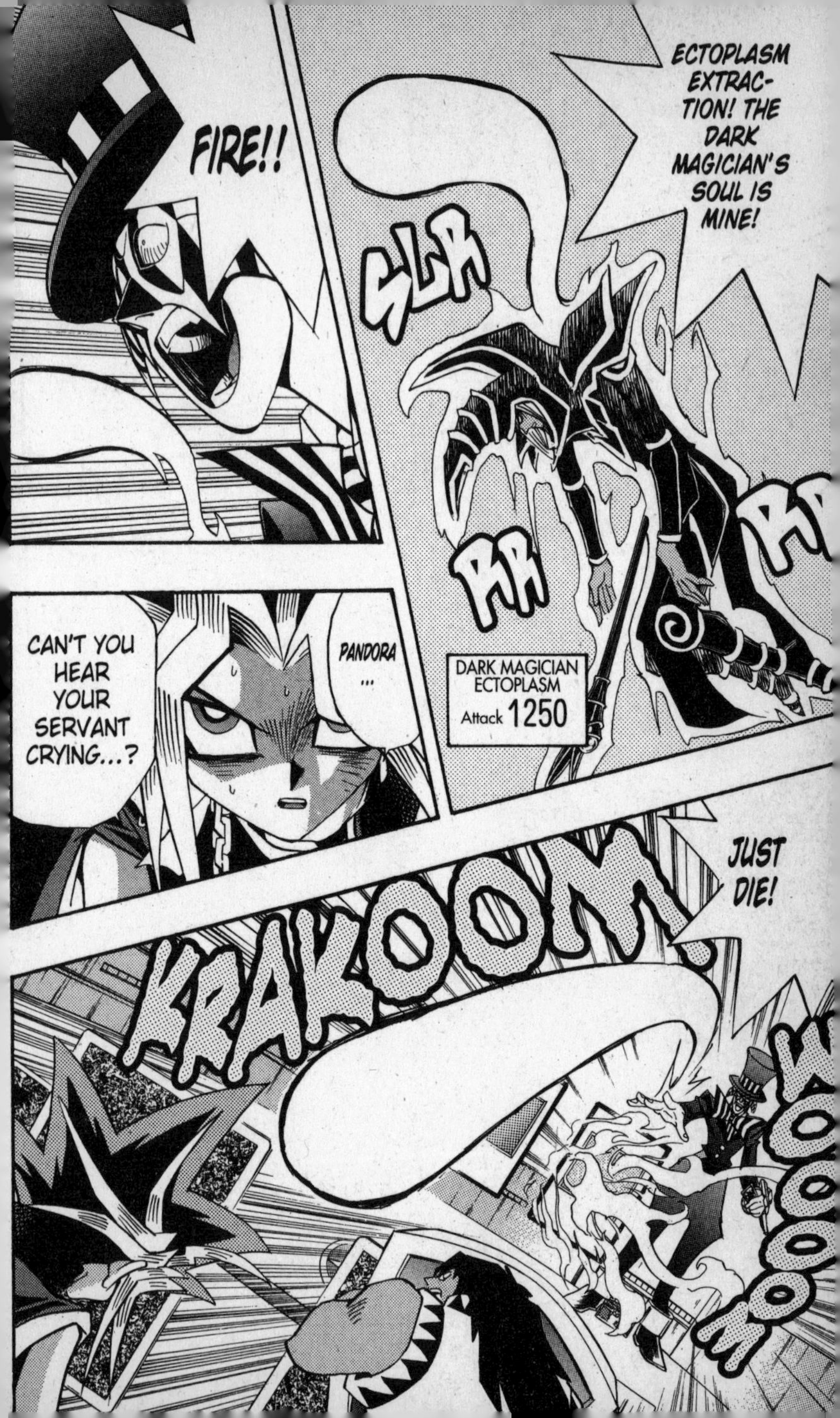
ECTOPLASM EXTRACTION! THE DARK MAGICIAN'S SOUL IS MINE!
SLR
RR
RR
DARK MAGICIAN ECTOPLASM Attack 1250
FIRE!!
PANDORA ...
CAN'T YOU HEAR YOUR SERVANT CRYING...?
JUST DIE!
KRAKOOM

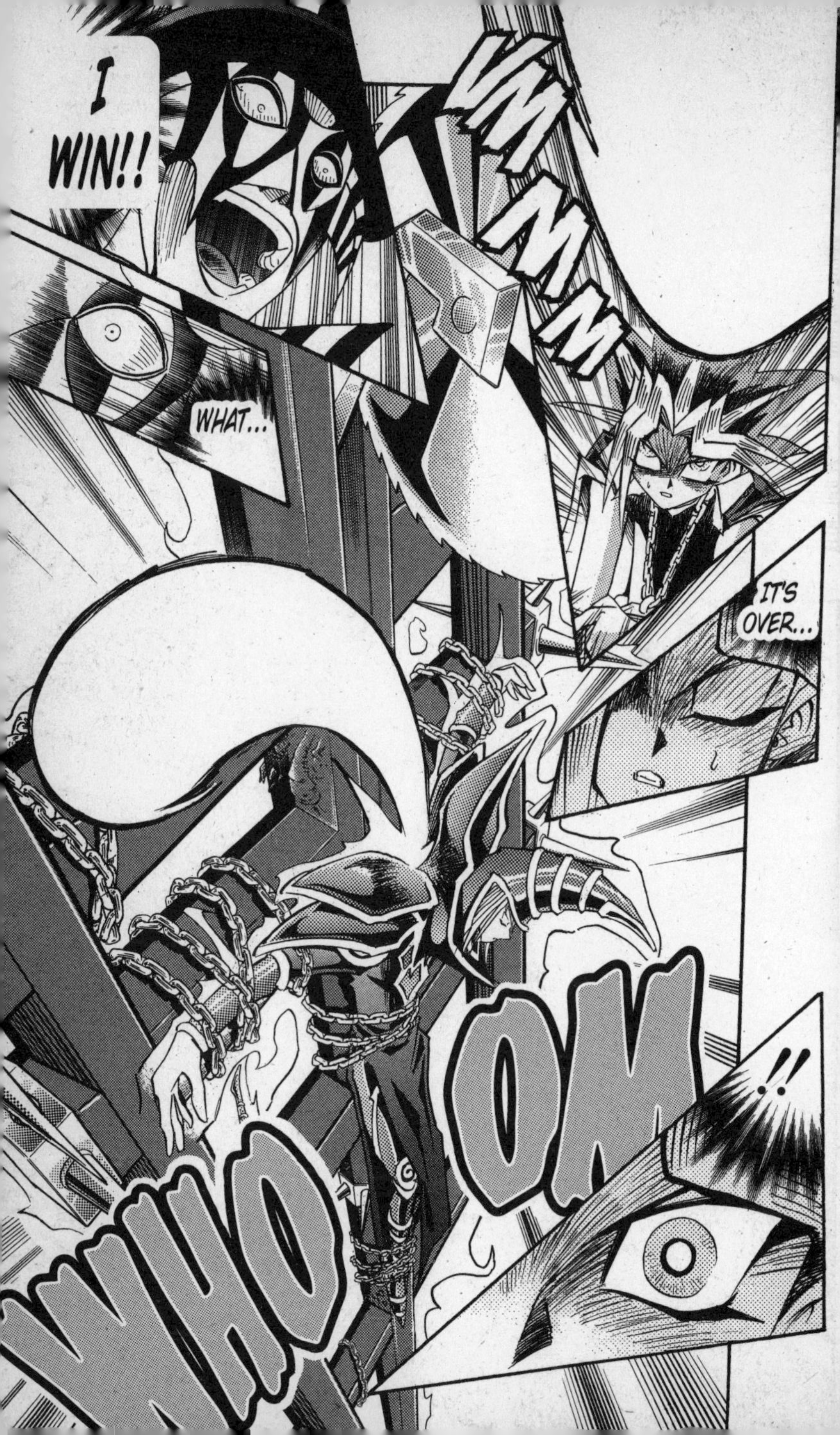
VMMMM
I WIN!!
IT'S OVER...
WHAT...
WHOOM!!

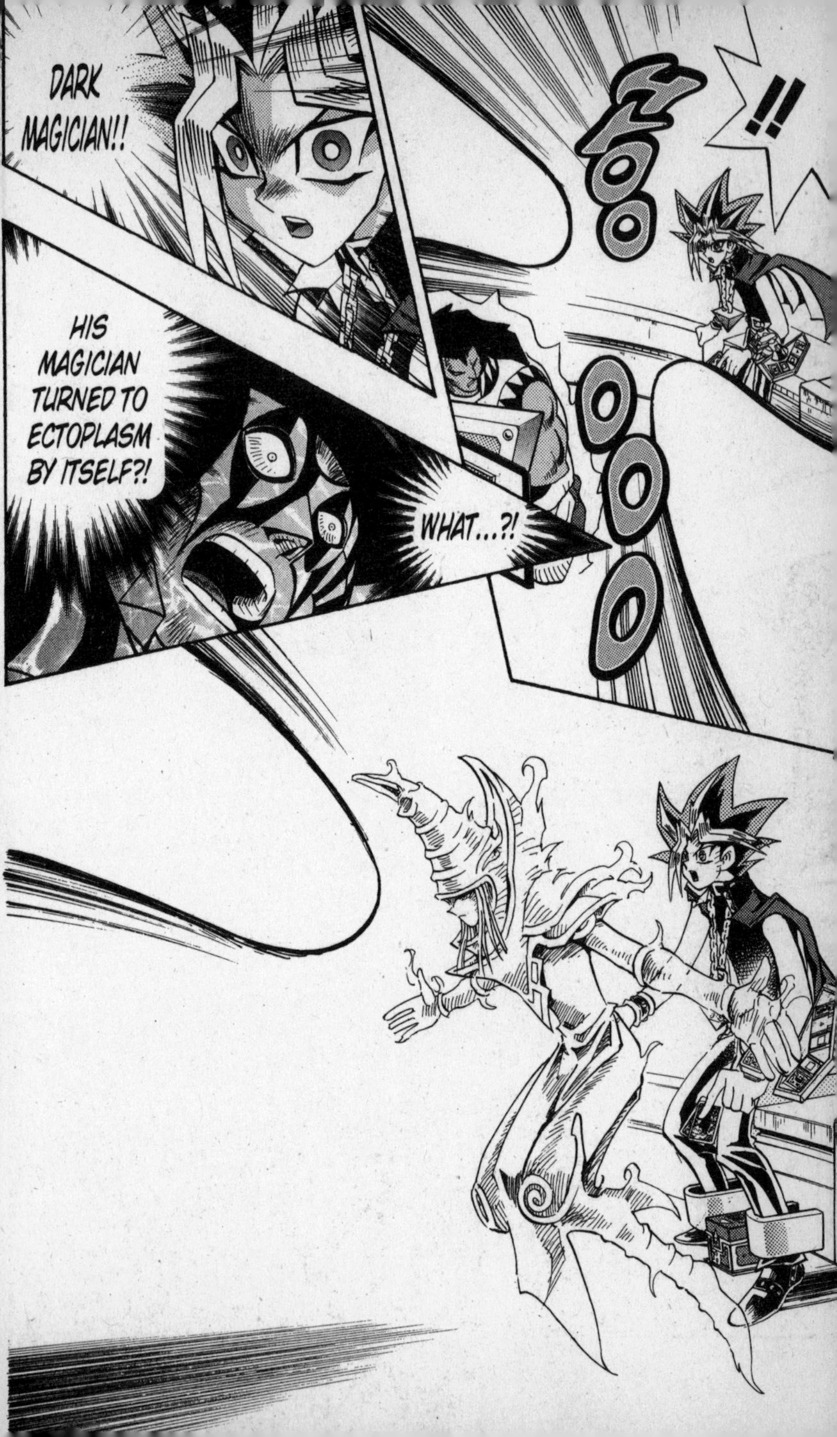
!!
DARK MAGICIAN!!
HIS MAGICIAN TURNED TO ECTOPLASM BY ITSELF?!
WHAT...?!

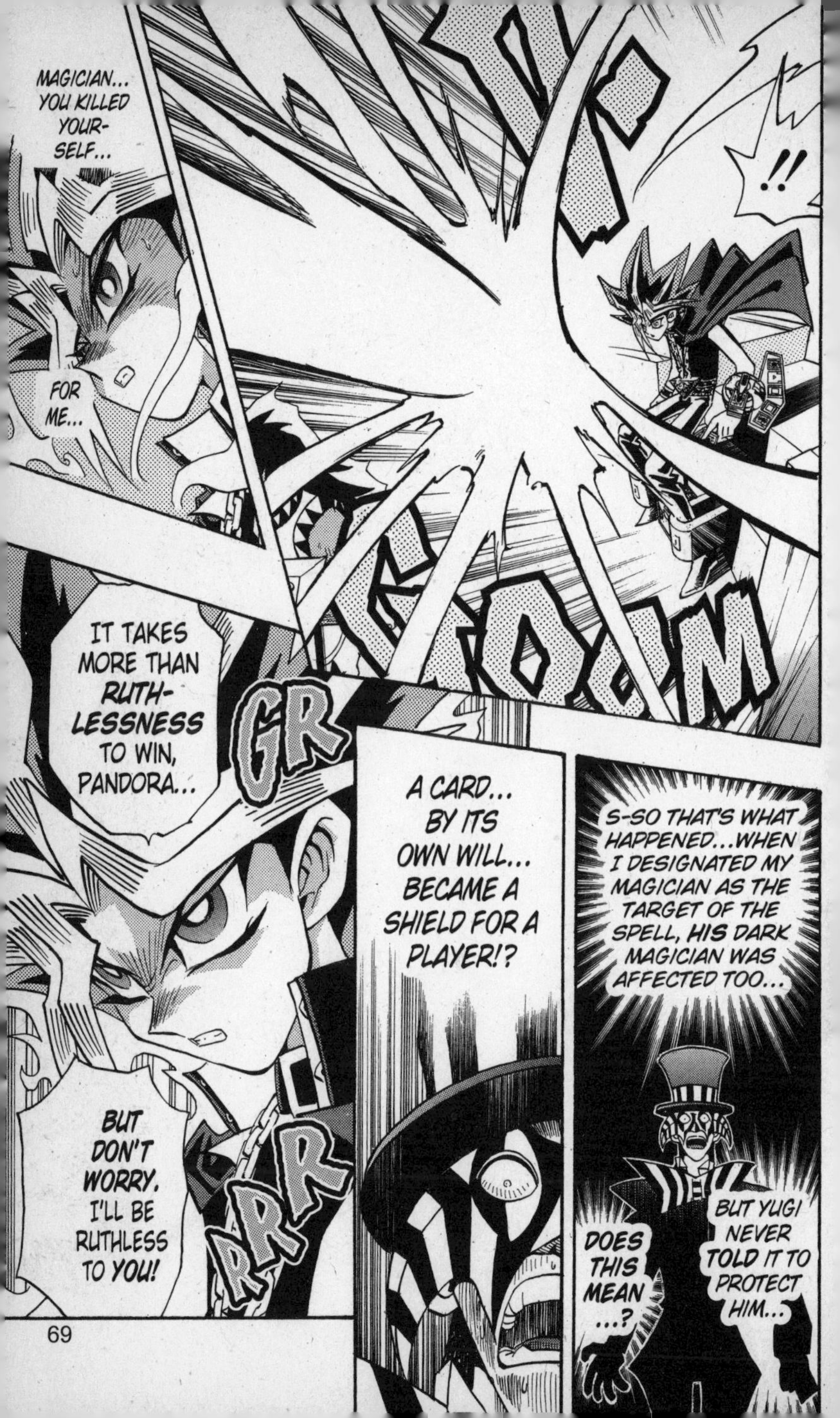

!!
MAGICIAN... YOU KILLED YOURSELF...
FOR ME...
S-SO THAT'S WHAT HAPPENED...WHEN I DESIGNATED MY MAGICIAN AS THE TARGET OF THE SPELL, HIS DARK MAGICIAN WAS AFFECTED TOO...
BUT YUGI NEVER TOLD IT TO PROTECT HIM...
DOES THIS MEAN ...?
A CARD... BY ITS OWN WILL... BECAME A SHIELD FOR A PLAYER!?
IT TAKES MORE THAN RUTHLESSNESS TO WIN, PANDORA...
GRRRR
BUT DON'T WORRY. I'LL BE RUTHLESS TO YOU!

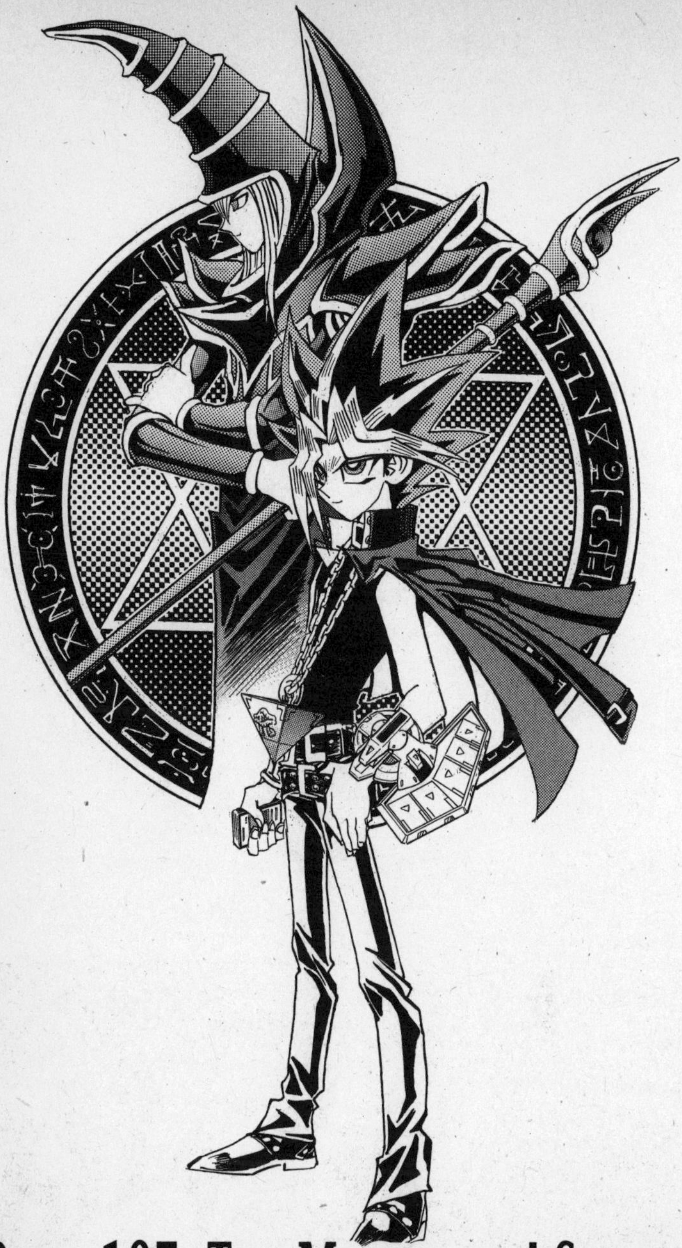

Duel 105: The Magicians' Souls

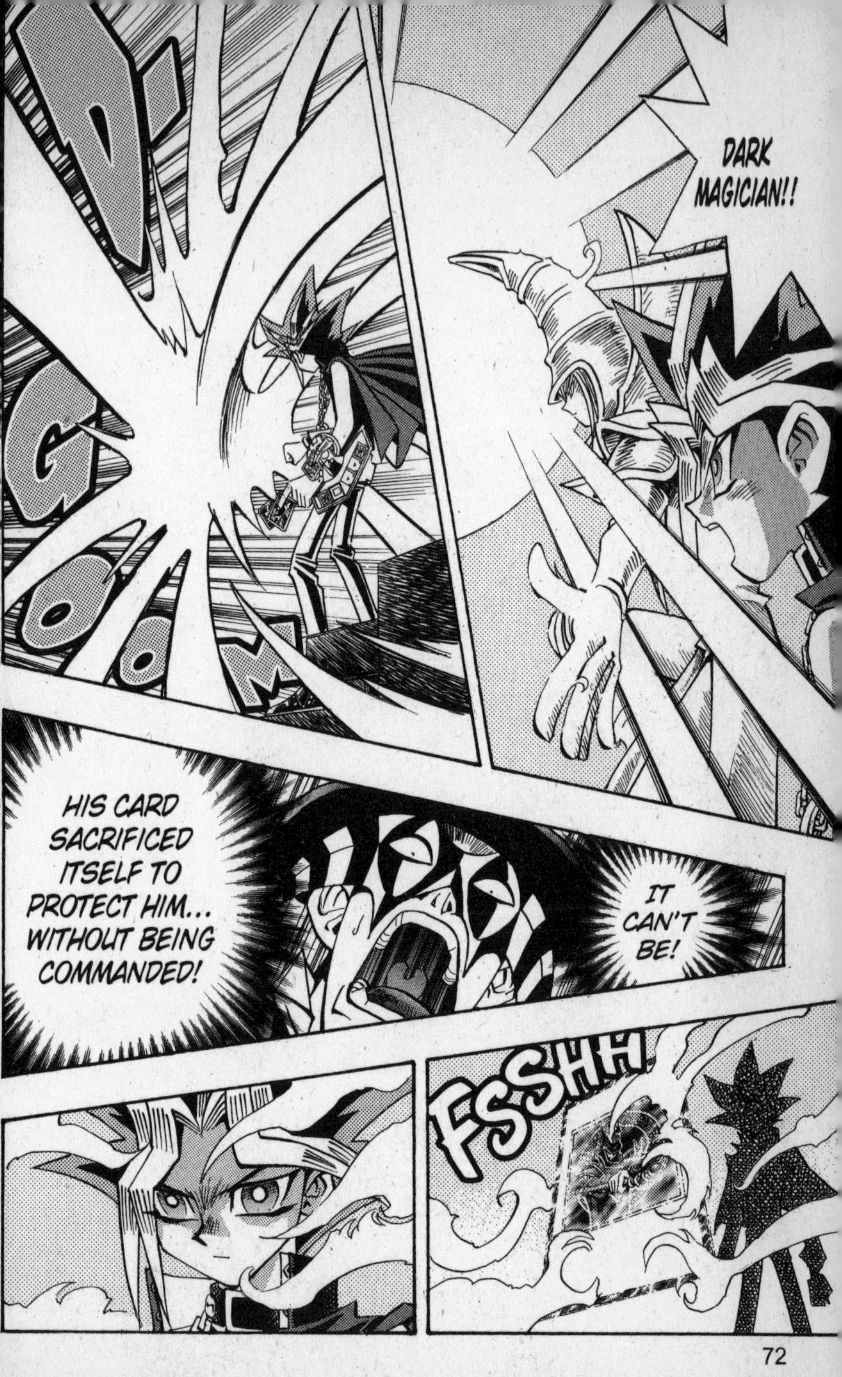
DARK MAGICIAN!!
D! GOOM
IT CAN'T BE!
HIS CARD SACRIFICED ITSELF TO PROTECT HIM... WITHOUT BEING COMMANDED!
FSSHH

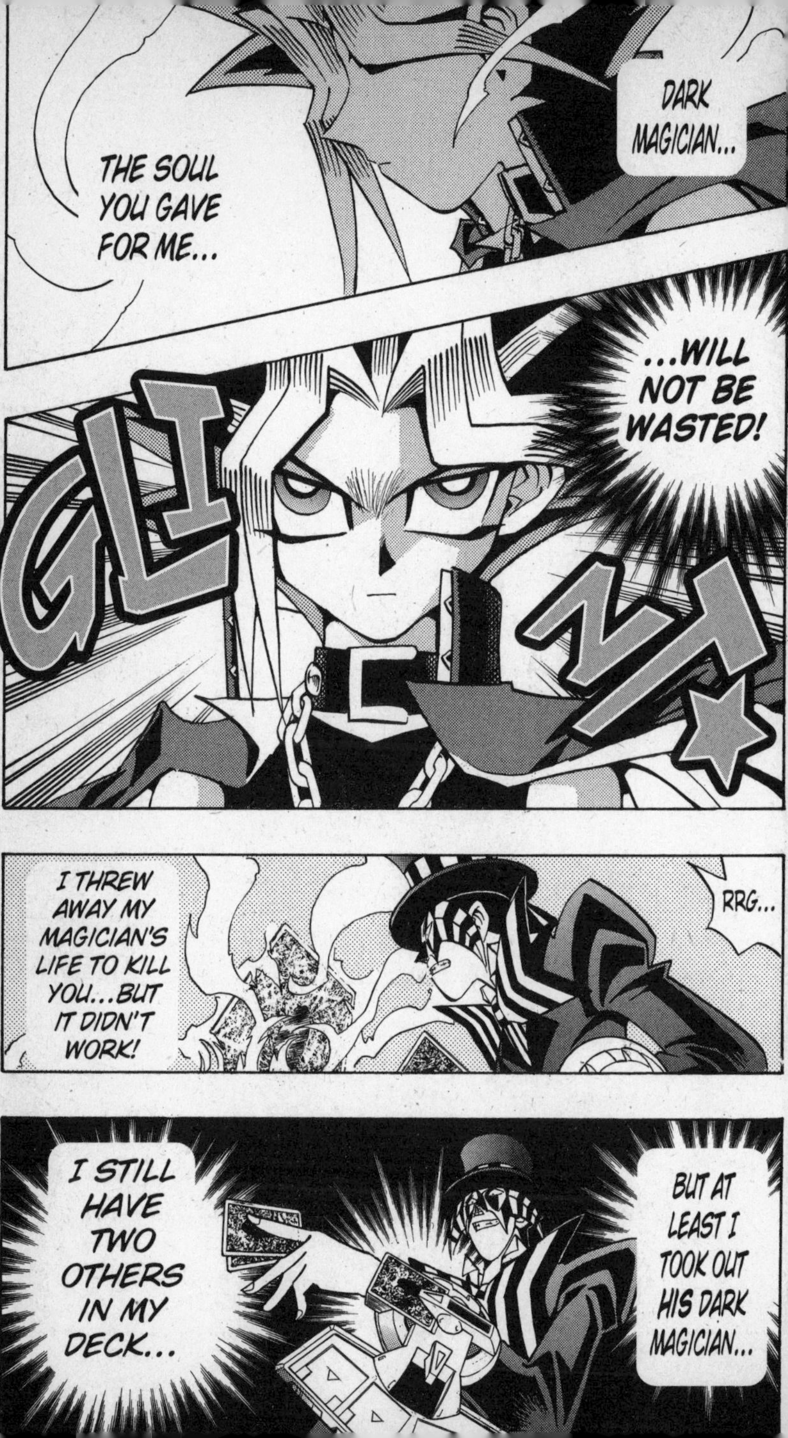
DARK MAGICIAN...
THE SOUL YOU GAVE FOR ME...
...WILL NOT BE WASTED!
GLINT
RRG...
I THREW AWAY MY MAGICIAN'S LIFE TO KILL YOU...BUT IT DIDN'T WORK!
BUT AT LEAST I TOOK OUT HIS DARK MAGICIAN...
I STILL HAVE TWO OTHERS IN MY DECK...

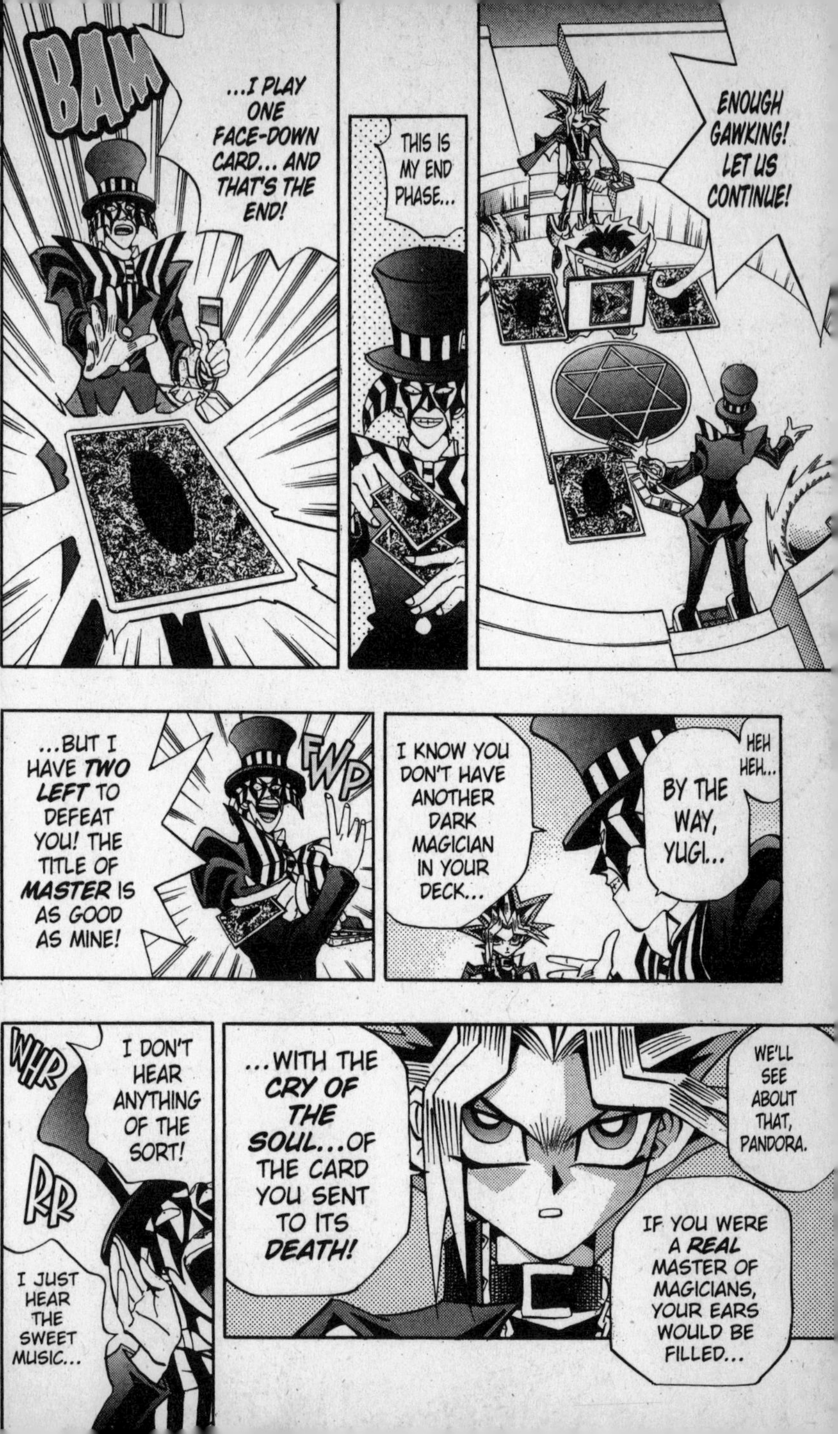
ENOUGH GAWKING! LET US CONTINUE!
THIS IS MY END PHASE...
BAM
...I PLAY ONE FACE-DOWN CARD... AND THAT'S THE END!
HEH HEH...
BY THE WAY, YUGI...
I KNOW YOU DON'T HAVE ANOTHER DARK MAGICIAN IN YOUR DECK...
FWP
...BUT I HAVE TWO LEFT TO DEFEAT YOU! THE TITLE OF MASTER IS AS GOOD AS MINE!
WE'LL SEE ABOUT THAT, PANDORA.
IF YOU WERE A REAL MASTER OF MAGICIANS, YOUR EARS WOULD BE FILLED...
...WITH THE CRY OF THE SOUL...OF THE CARD YOU SENT TO ITS DEATH!
WHR
I DON'T HEAR ANYTHING OF THE SORT!
RR
I JUST HEAR THE SWEET MUSIC...

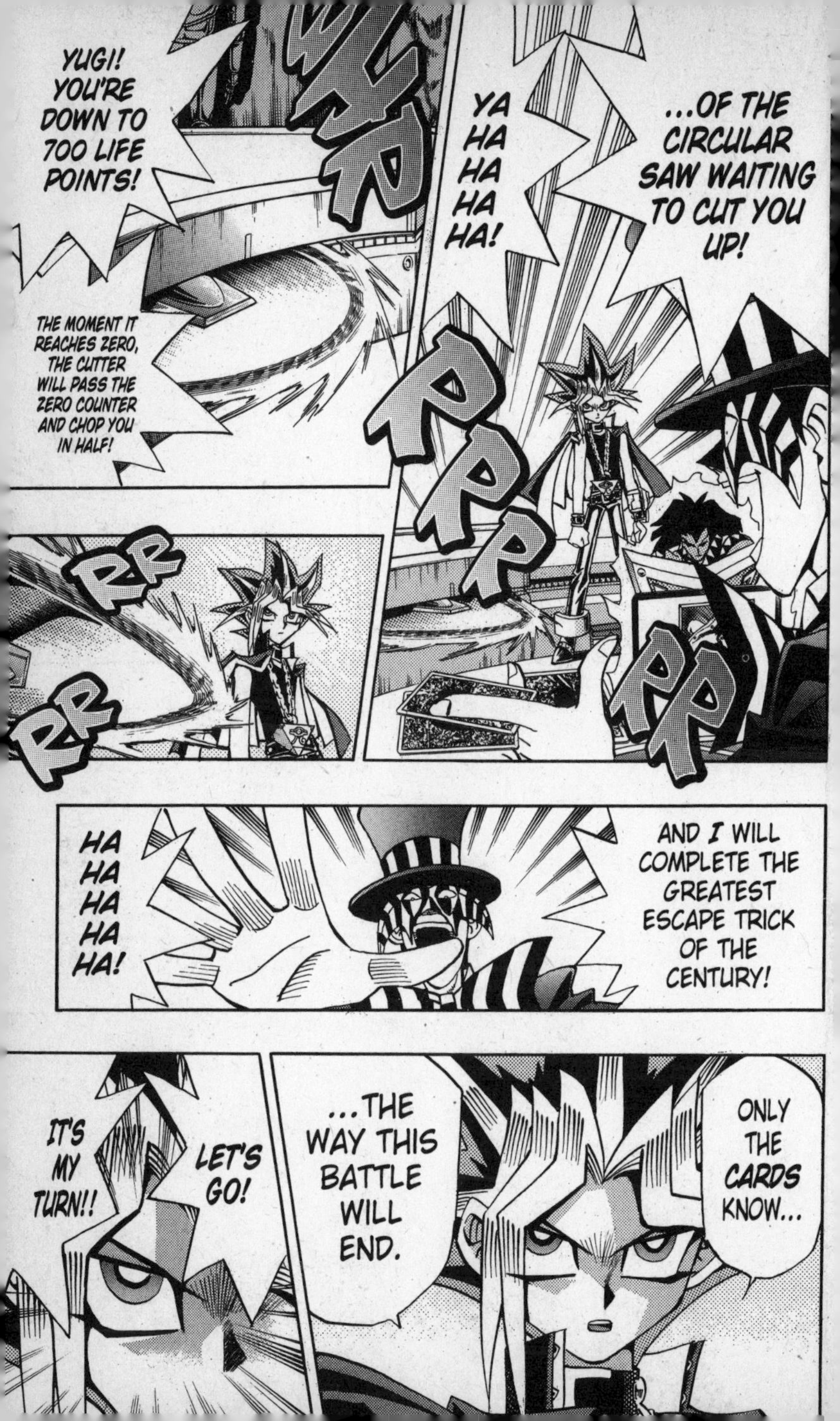
...OF THE CIRCULAR SAW WAITING TO CUT YOU UP!
YA HA HA HA HA!
RRR
RR
YUGI! YOU'RE DOWN TO 700 LIFE POINTS!
THE MOMENT IT REACHES ZERO, THE CUTTER WILL PASS THE ZERO COUNTER AND CHOP YOU IN HALF!
RR
RR
AND I WILL COMPLETE THE GREATEST ESCAPE TRICK OF THE CENTURY!
HA HA HA HA HA HA!
ONLY THE CARDS KNOW...
...THE WAY THIS BATTLE WILL END.
LET'S GO!
IT'S MY TURN!!

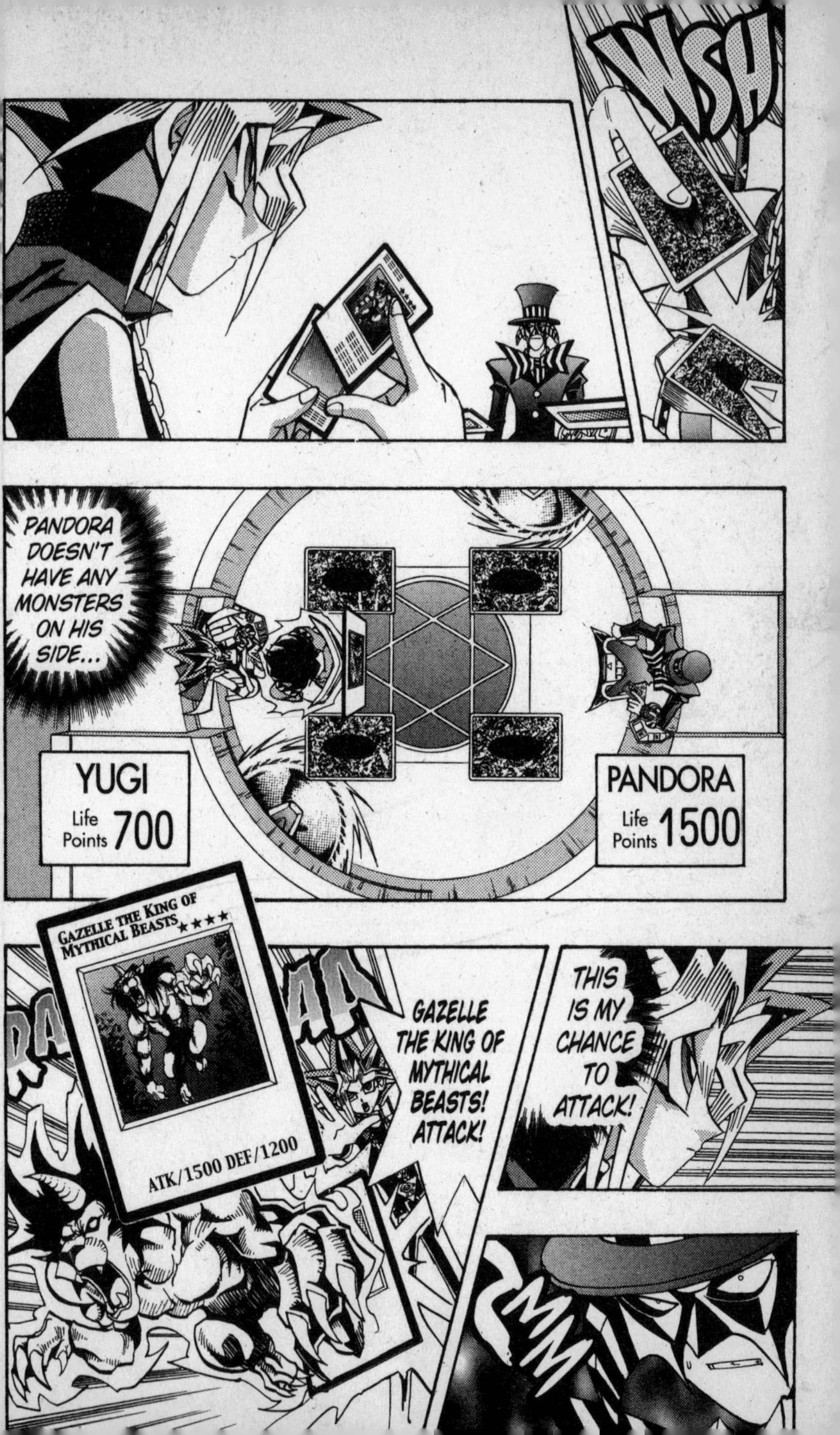
WSH
PANDORA DOESN'T HAVE ANY MONSTERS ON HIS SIDE...
YUGI
Life Points 700
PANDORA
Life Points 1500
THIS IS MY CHANCE TO ATTACK!
GAZELLE THE KING OF MYTHICAL BEASTS! ATTACK!
GAZELLE THE KING OF MYTHICAL BEASTS ★★★★
ATK/1500 DEF/1200

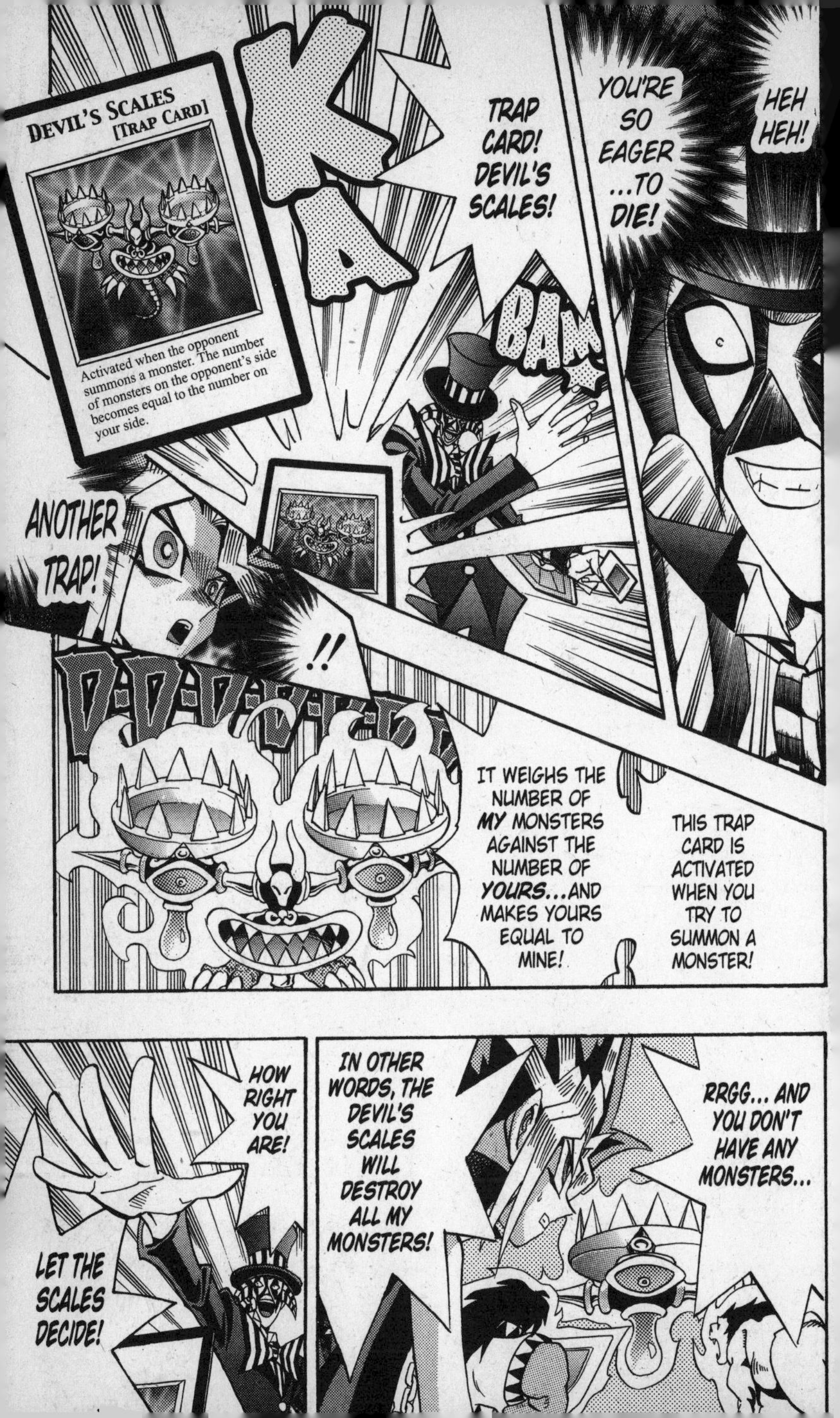

HEH HEH!
YOU'RE SO EAGER ...TO DIE!
TRAP CARD! DEVIL'S SCALES!
BAM
KA
DEVIL'S SCALES
[TRAP CARD]
Activated when the opponent summons a monster. The number of monsters on the opponent's side becomes equal to the number on your side.
ANOTHER TRAP!
!!
THIS TRAP CARD IS ACTIVATED WHEN YOU TRY TO SUMMON A MONSTER!
IT WEIGHS THE NUMBER OF MY MONSTERS AGAINST THE NUMBER OF YOURS...AND MAKES YOURS EQUAL TO MINE!
RRGG... AND YOU DON'T HAVE ANY MONSTERS...
IN OTHER WORDS, THE DEVIL'S SCALES WILL DESTROY ALL MY MONSTERS!
HOW RIGHT YOU ARE!
LET THE SCALES DECIDE!

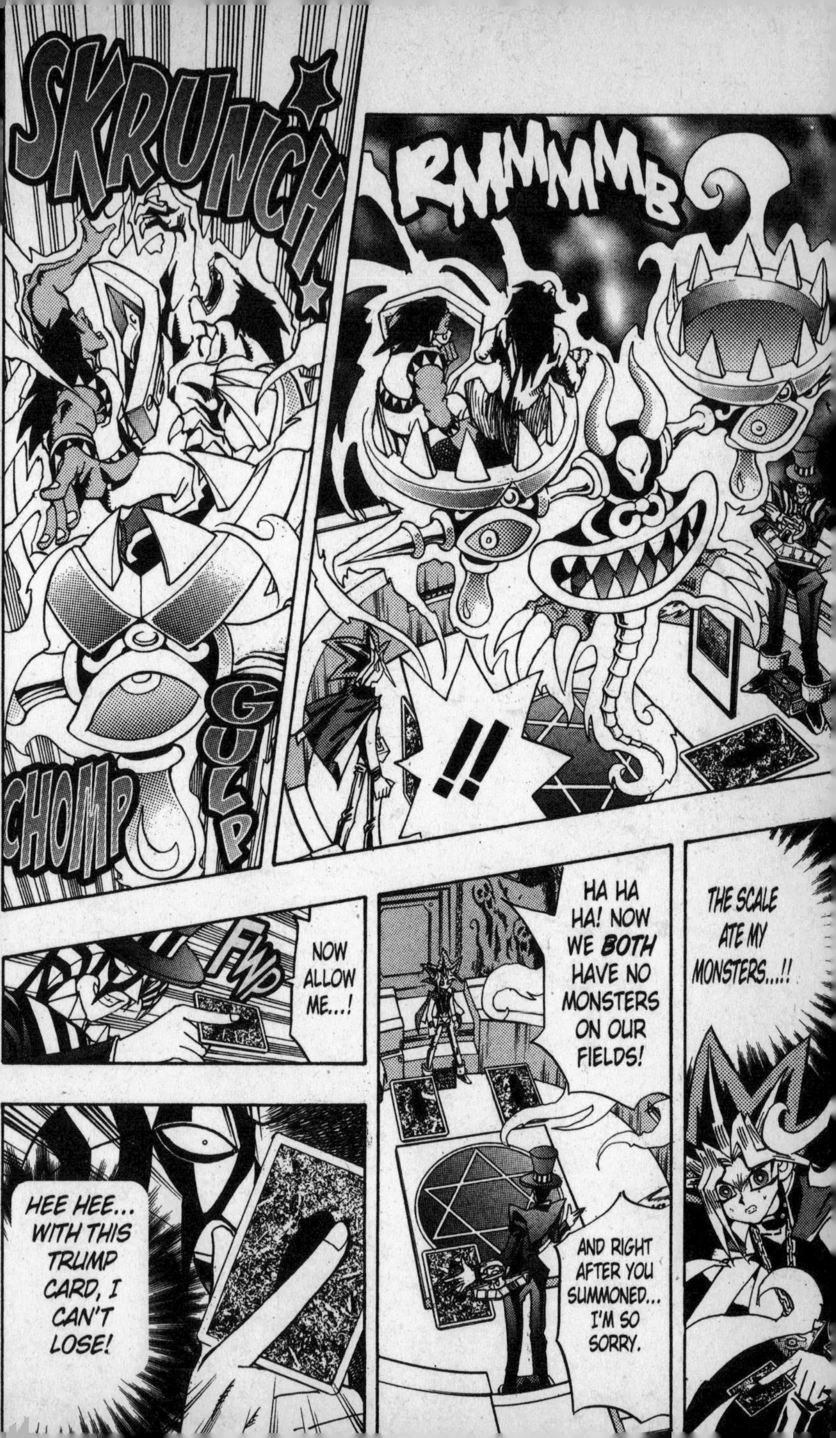
RMMMMB
!!
SKRUNCH
GULP
CHOMP
THE SCALE ATE MY MONSTERS...!!
HA HA HA! NOW WE *BOTH* HAVE NO MONSTERS ON OUR FIELDS!
AND RIGHT AFTER YOU SUMMONED... I'M SO SORRY.
NOW ALLOW ME...!
FWP
HEE HEE... WITH THIS TRUMP CARD, I CAN'T LOSE!

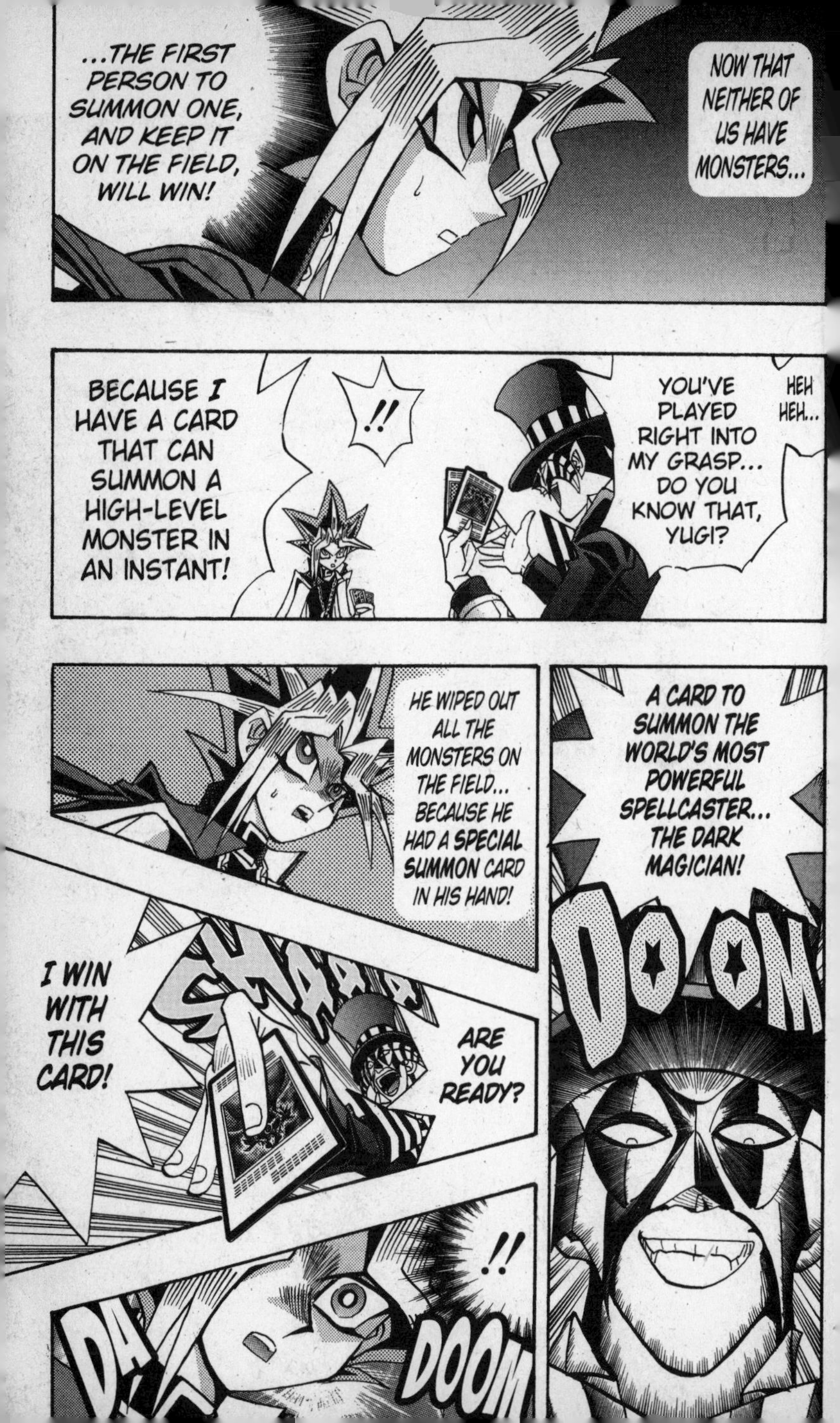
NOW THAT NEITHER OF US HAVE MONSTERS...
...THE FIRST PERSON TO SUMMON ONE, AND KEEP IT ON THE FIELD, WILL WIN!
HEH HEH...
YOU'VE PLAYED RIGHT INTO MY GRASP... DO YOU KNOW THAT, YUGI?
!!
BECAUSE I HAVE A CARD THAT CAN SUMMON A HIGH-LEVEL MONSTER IN AN INSTANT!
A CARD TO SUMMON THE WORLD'S MOST POWERFUL SPELLCASTER... THE DARK MAGICIAN!
DOOM
HE WIPED OUT ALL THE MONSTERS ON THE FIELD... BECAUSE HE HAD A SPECIAL SUMMON CARD IN HIS HAND!
ARE YOU READY?
I WIN WITH THIS CARD!
!!
DOOM

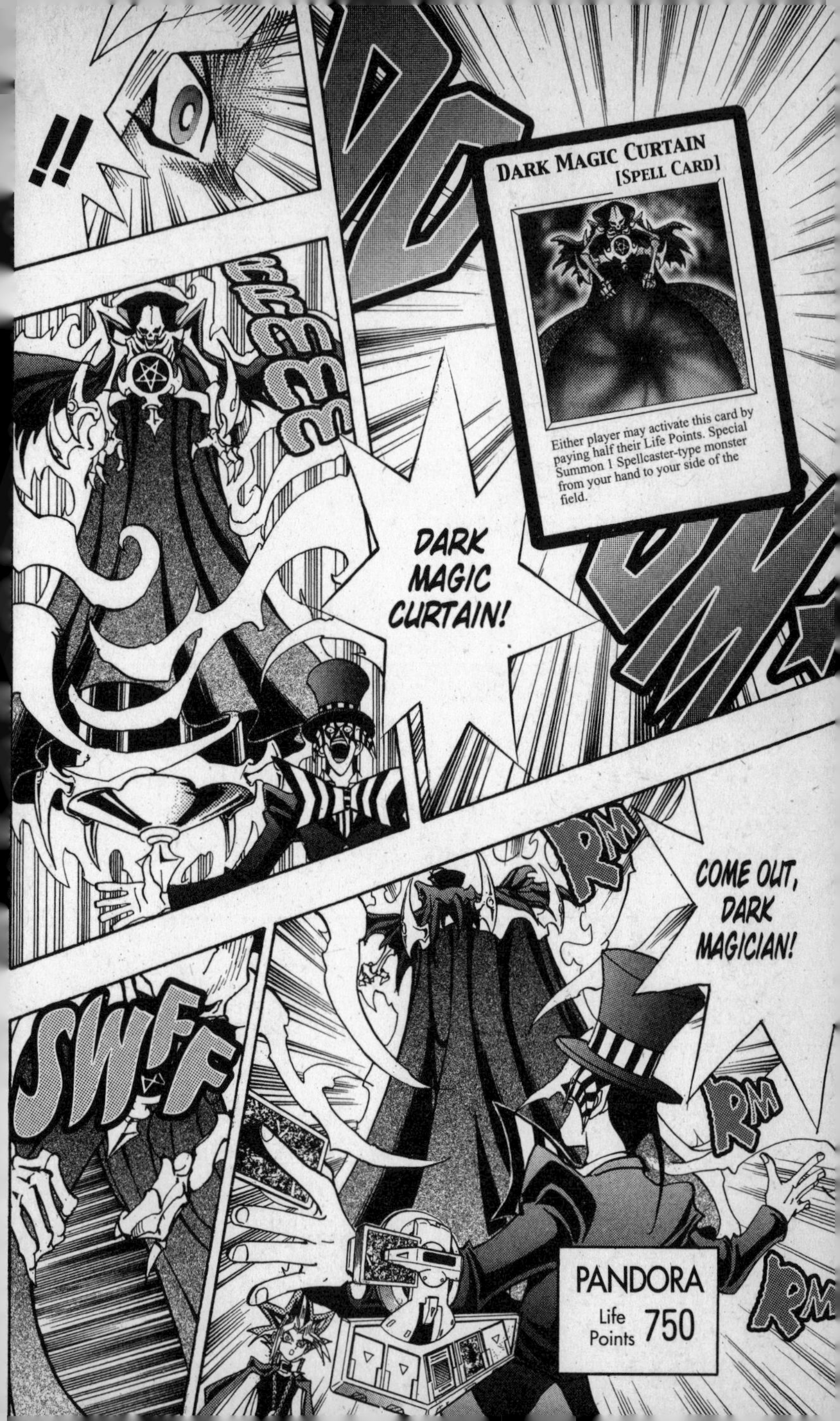

DARK MAGIC CURTAIN
[SPELL CARD]
Either player may activate this card by paying half their Life Points. Special Summon 1 Spellcaster-type monster from your hand to your side of the field.
!!
DARK MAGIC CURTAIN!
RM
COME OUT, DARK MAGICIAN!
RM
RM
PANDORA
Life Points 750
SWFF

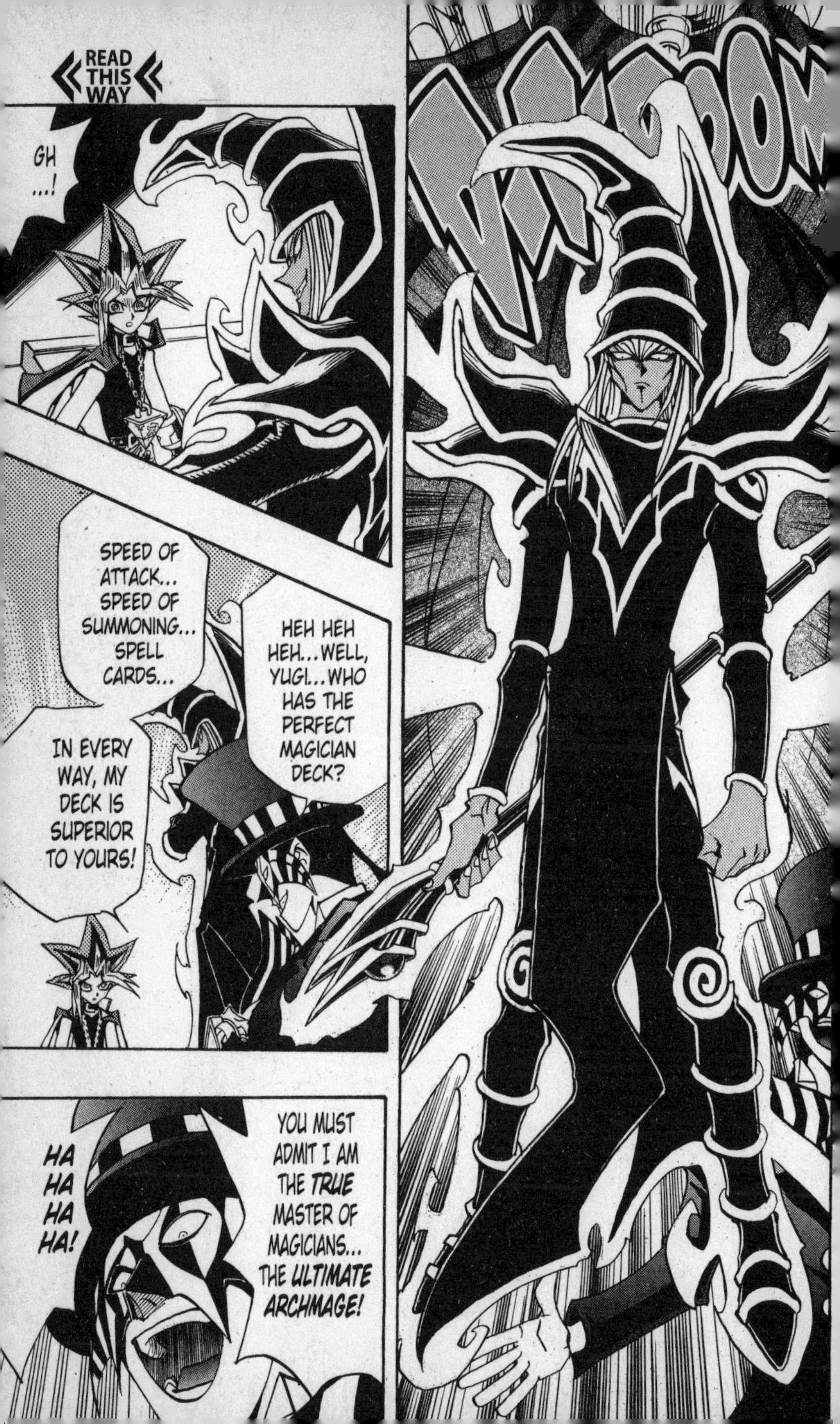
READ THIS WAY
GH ...!
HEH HEH HEH...WELL, YUGI...WHO HAS THE PERFECT MAGICIAN DECK?
SPEED OF ATTACK... SPEED OF SUMMONING... SPELL CARDS...
IN EVERY WAY, MY DECK IS SUPERIOR TO YOURS!
YOU MUST ADMIT I AM THE *TRUE* MASTER OF MAGICIANS... THE *ULTIMATE ARCHMAGE!*
HA HA HA HA!

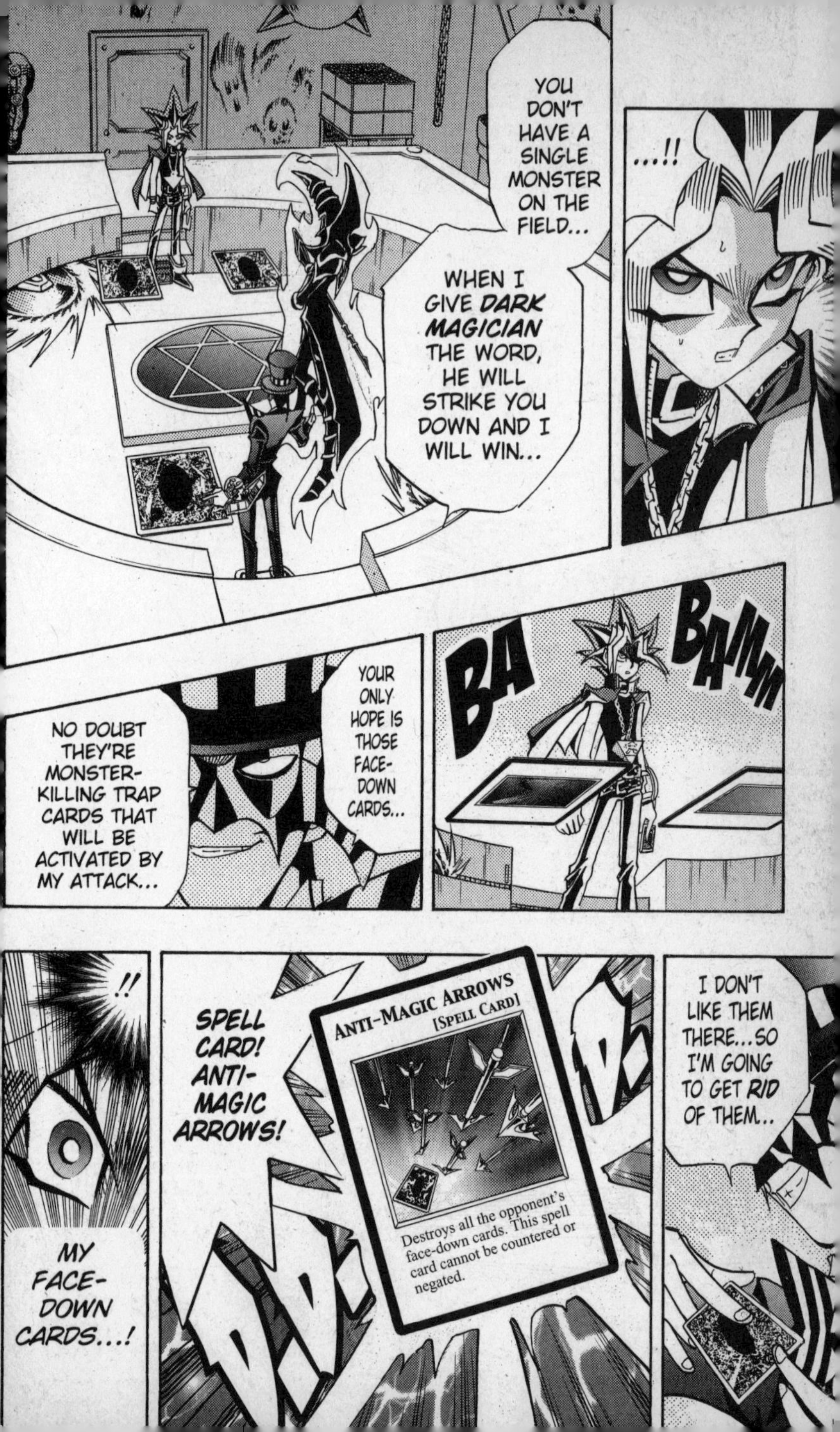
...!!
YOU DON'T HAVE A SINGLE MONSTER ON THE FIELD...
WHEN I GIVE DARK MAGICIAN THE WORD, HE WILL STRIKE YOU DOWN AND I WILL WIN...
BAMM
BA
YOUR ONLY HOPE IS THOSE FACE-DOWN CARDS...
NO DOUBT THEY'RE MONSTER-KILLING TRAP CARDS THAT WILL BE ACTIVATED BY MY ATTACK...
I DON'T LIKE THEM THERE...SO I'M GOING TO GET RID OF THEM...
ANTI-MAGIC ARROWS
[SPELL CARD]
Destroys all the opponent's face-down cards. This spell card cannot be countered or negated.
SPELL CARD! ANTI-MAGIC ARROWS!
!!
MY FACE-DOWN CARDS...!

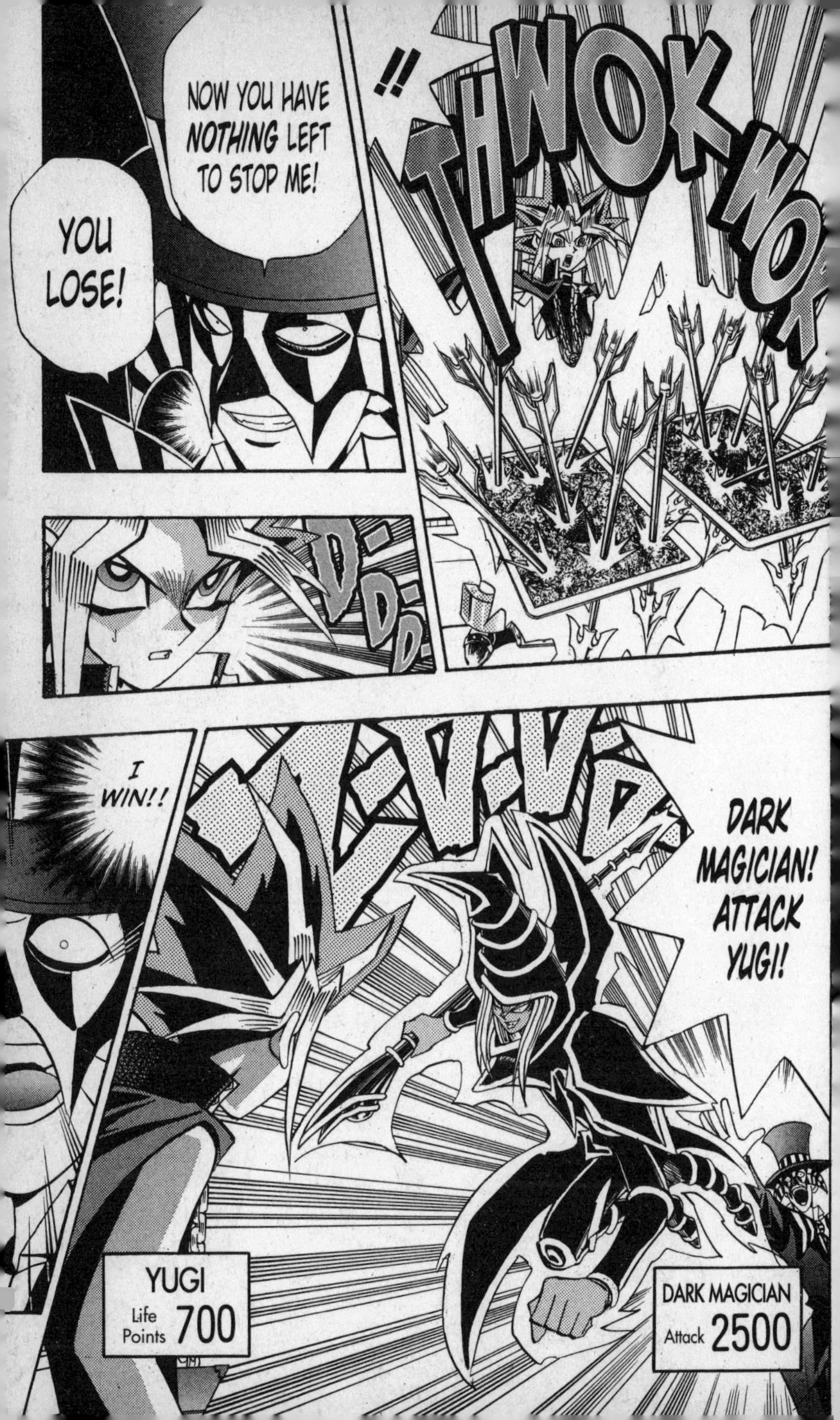
!!
THWOK WOK
NOW YOU HAVE NOTHING LEFT TO STOP ME!
YOU LOSE!
D-D-D-
DARK MAGICIAN! ATTACK YUGI!
DARK MAGICIAN Attack 2500
I WIN!!
YUGI Life Points 700

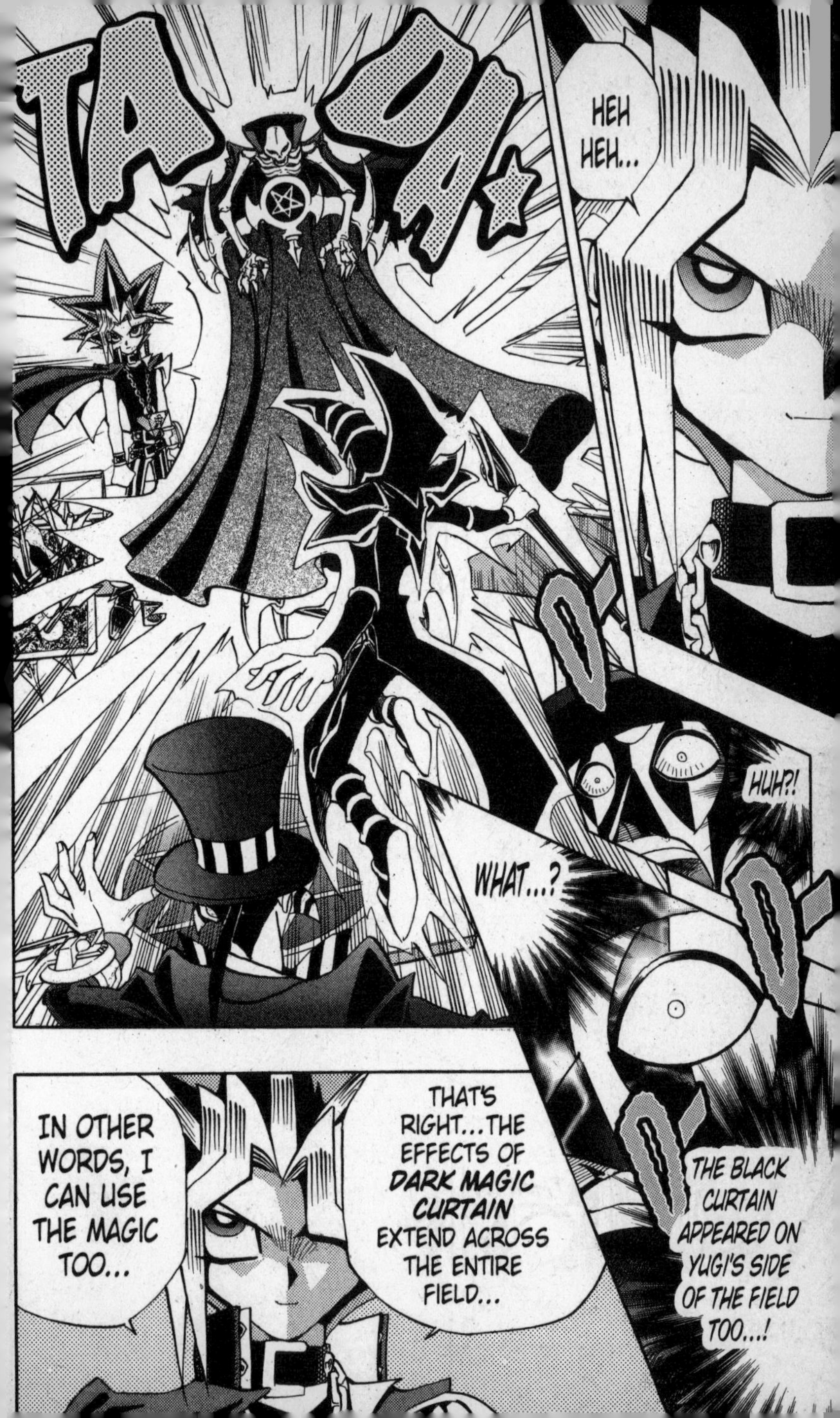

HEH HEH...
TA DA
HUH?!
WHAT...?
THE BLACK CURTAIN APPEARED ON YUGI'S SIDE OF THE FIELD TOO...!
THAT'S RIGHT... THE EFFECTS OF ***DARK MAGIC CURTAIN*** EXTEND ACROSS THE ENTIRE FIELD...
IN OTHER WORDS, I CAN USE THE MAGIC TOO...

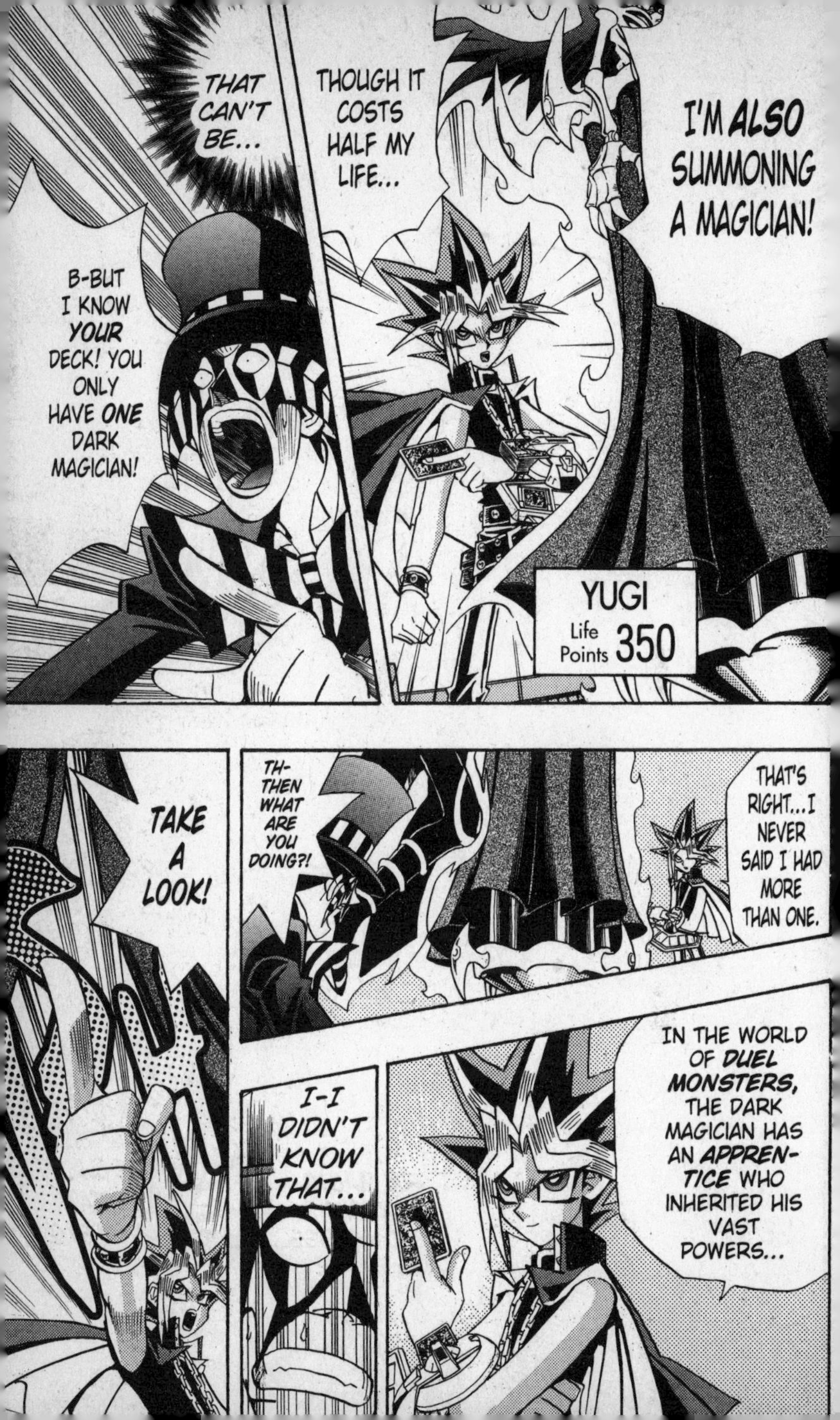
I'M ALSO SUMMONING A MAGICIAN!
THOUGH IT COSTS HALF MY LIFE...
YUGI Life Points 350
THAT CAN'T BE...
B-BUT I KNOW YOUR DECK! YOU ONLY HAVE ONE DARK MAGICIAN!
THAT'S RIGHT...I NEVER SAID I HAD MORE THAN ONE.
TH-THEN WHAT ARE YOU DOING?!
IN THE WORLD OF DUEL MONSTERS, THE DARK MAGICIAN HAS AN APPREN-TICE WHO INHERITED HIS VAST POWERS...
I-I DIDN'T KNOW THAT...
TAKE A LOOK!

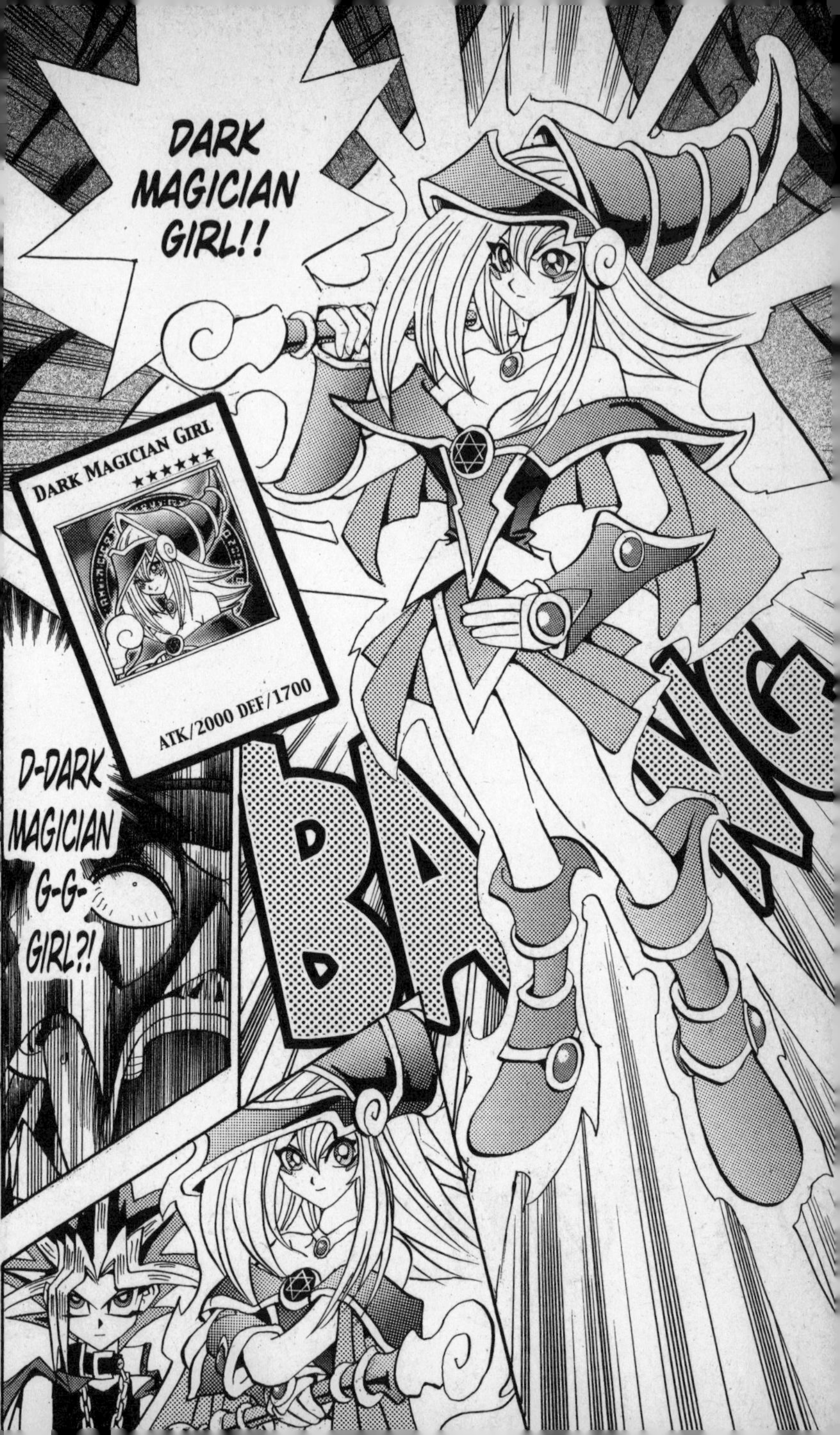
DARK MAGICIAN GIRL!!
DARK MAGICIAN GIRL
★★★★★★
ATK/2000 DEF/1700
BANG
D-DARK MAGICIAN G-G-GIRL?!

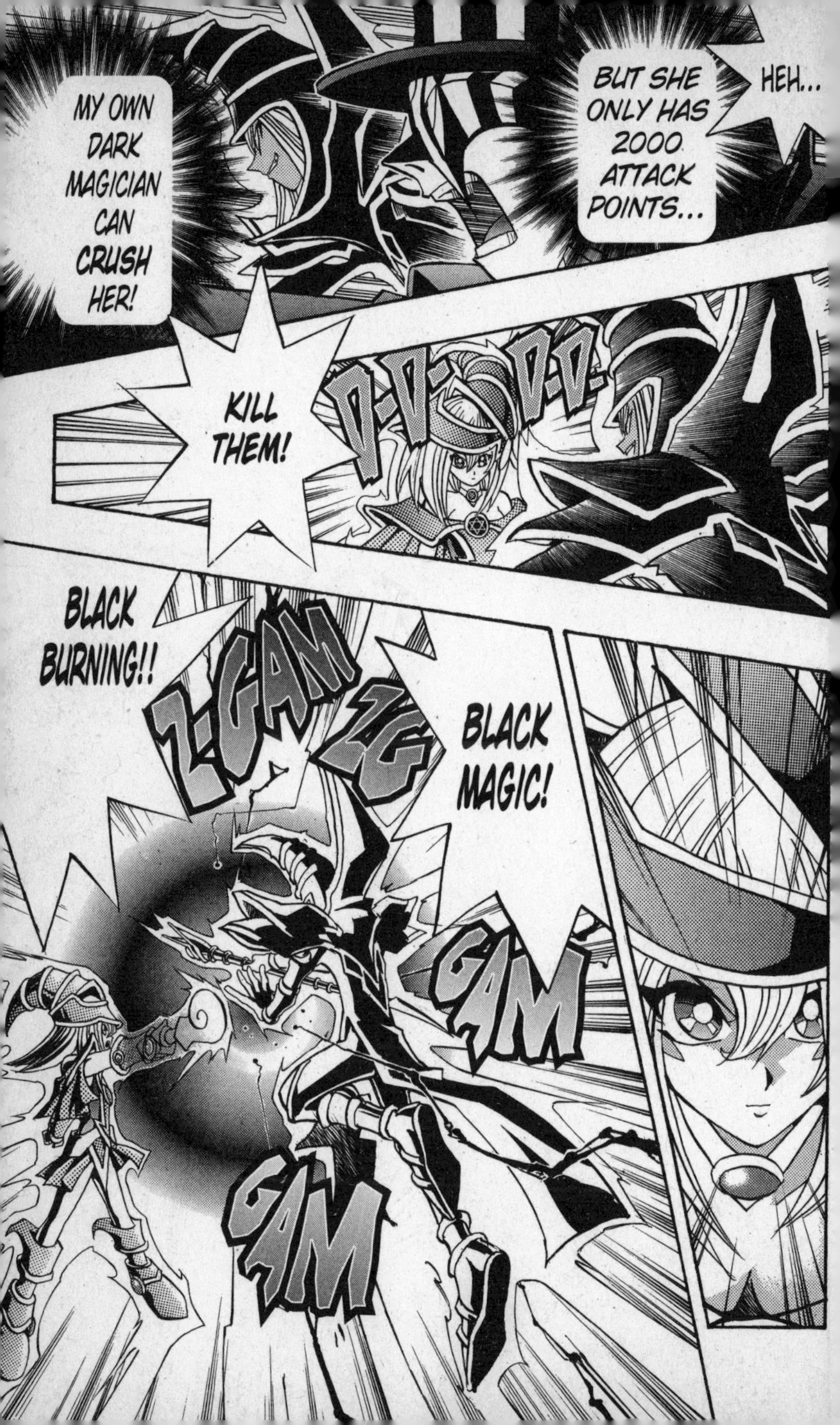
HEH...
BUT SHE ONLY HAS 2000 ATTACK POINTS...
MY OWN DARK MAGICIAN CAN CRUSH HER!
D-D-D-D
KILL THEM!
BLACK MAGIC!
ZG
Z-GAM
BLACK BURNING!!
GAM
GAM

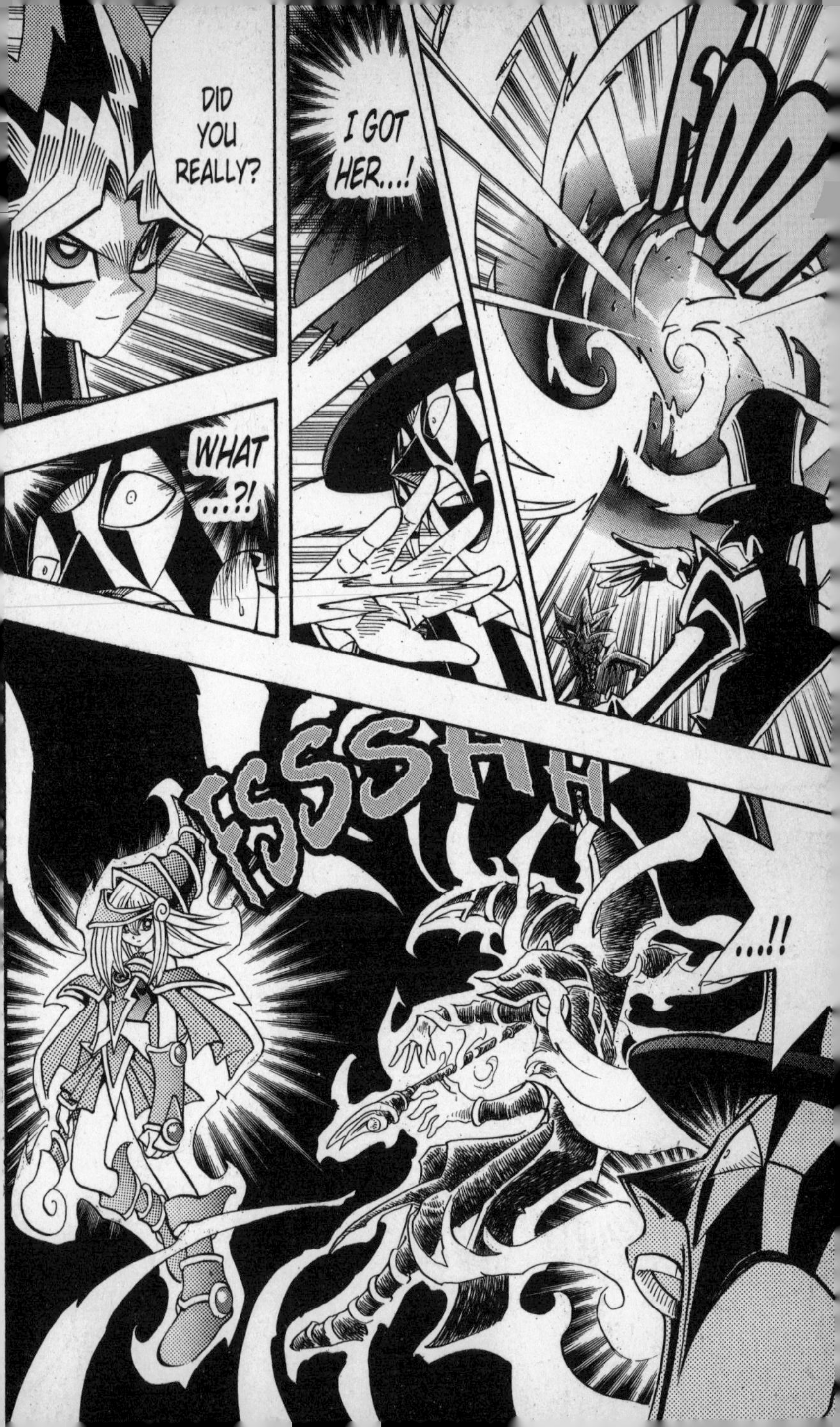
FOO
I GOT HER...!
DID YOU REALLY?
WHAT ...?!
FSSSHH
...!!

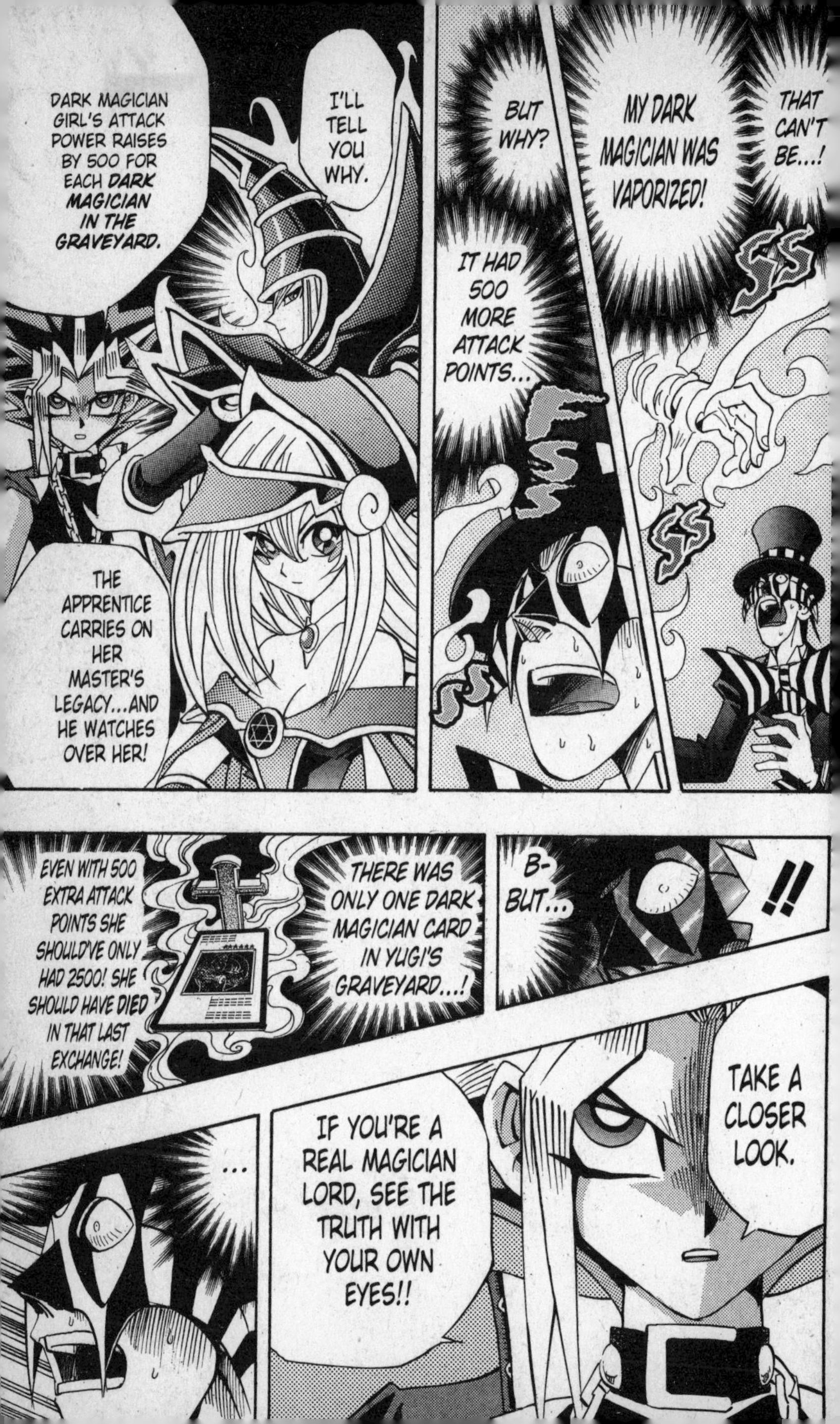
THAT CAN'T BE...!
MY DARK MAGICIAN WAS VAPORIZED!
BUT WHY?
IT HAD 500 MORE ATTACK POINTS...
I'LL TELL YOU WHY.
DARK MAGICIAN GIRL'S ATTACK POWER RAISES BY 500 FOR EACH DARK MAGICIAN IN THE GRAVEYARD.
THE APPRENTICE CARRIES ON HER MASTER'S LEGACY...AND HE WATCHES OVER HER!
B-BUT...
!!
THERE WAS ONLY ONE DARK MAGICIAN CARD IN YUGI'S GRAVEYARD...!
EVEN WITH 500 EXTRA ATTACK POINTS SHE SHOULD'VE ONLY HAD 2500! SHE SHOULD HAVE DIED IN THAT LAST EXCHANGE!
TAKE A CLOSER LOOK.
IF YOU'RE A REAL MAGICIAN LORD, SEE THE TRUTH WITH YOUR OWN EYES!!
...

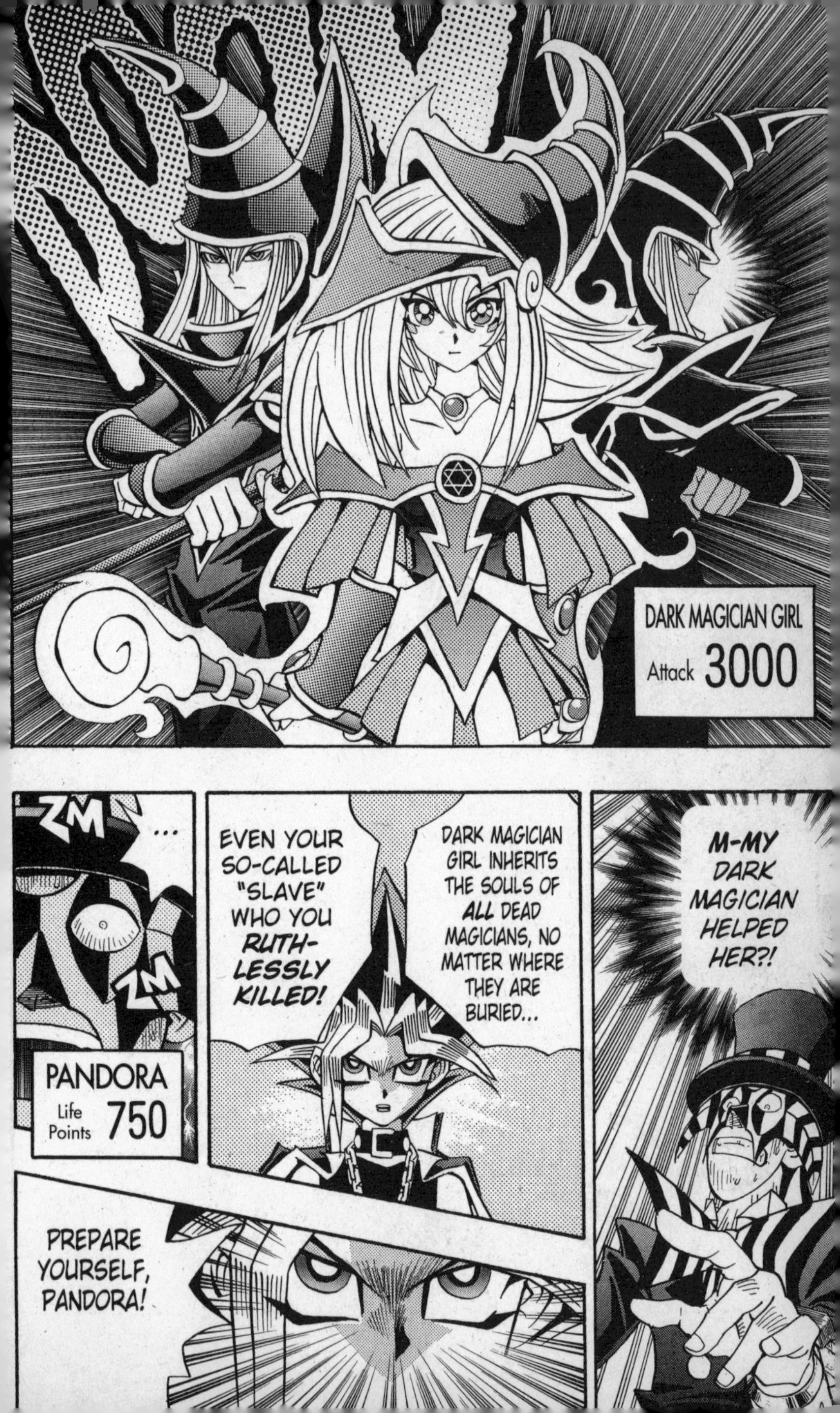
DARK MAGICIAN GIRL
Attack 3000
M-MY DARK MAGICIAN HELPED HER?!
DARK MAGICIAN GIRL INHERITS THE SOULS OF ALL DEAD MAGICIANS, NO MATTER WHERE THEY ARE BURIED...
EVEN YOUR SO-CALLED "SLAVE" WHO YOU RUTHLESSLY KILLED!
ZM
...
ZM
PANDORA
Life Points 750
PREPARE YOURSELF, PANDORA!

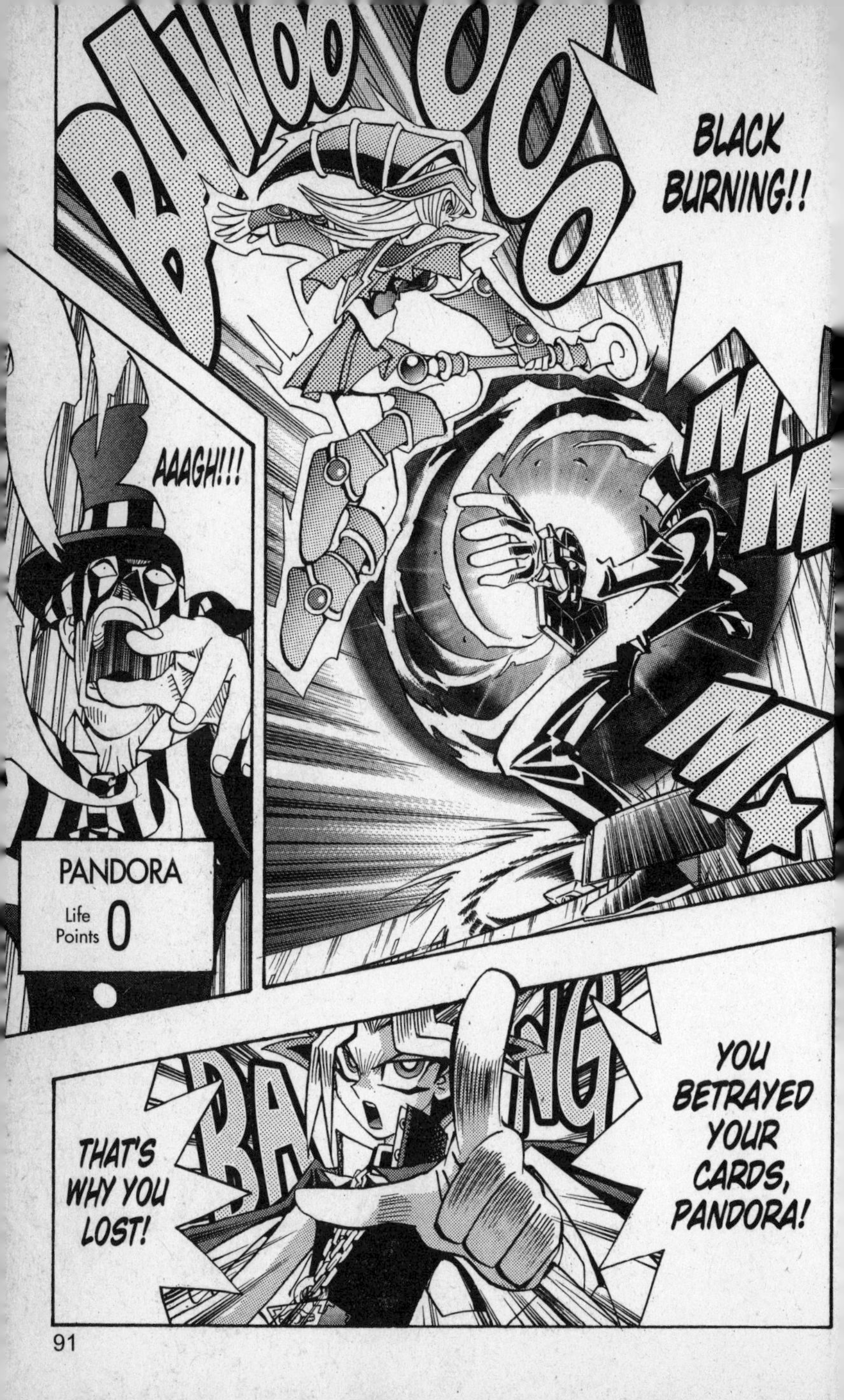
BLACK BURNING!!
AAAGH!!!
PANDORA
Life Points 0
YOU BETRAYED YOUR CARDS, PANDORA!
THAT'S WHY YOU LOST!

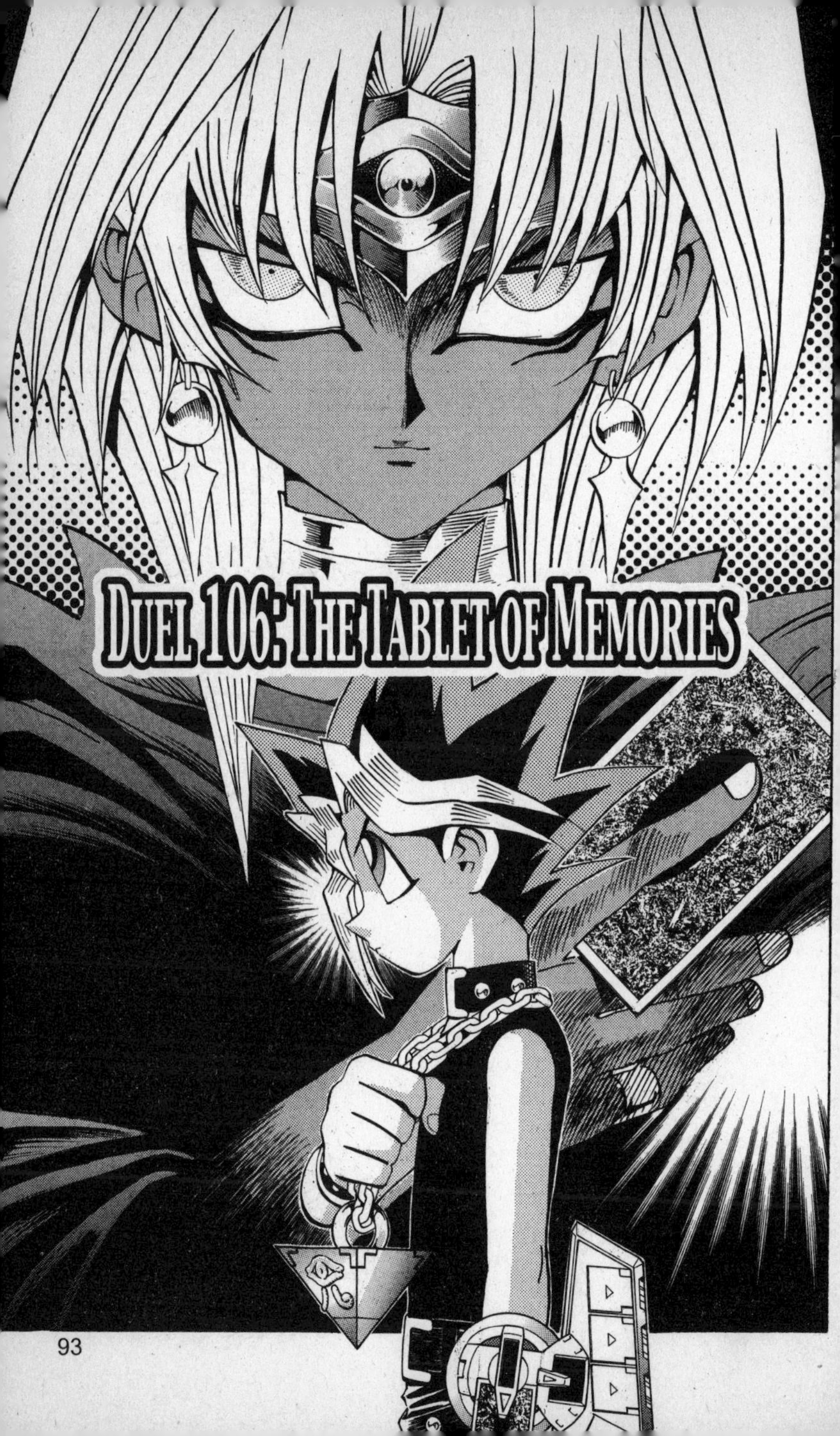
DUEL 106: THE TABLET OF MEMORIES

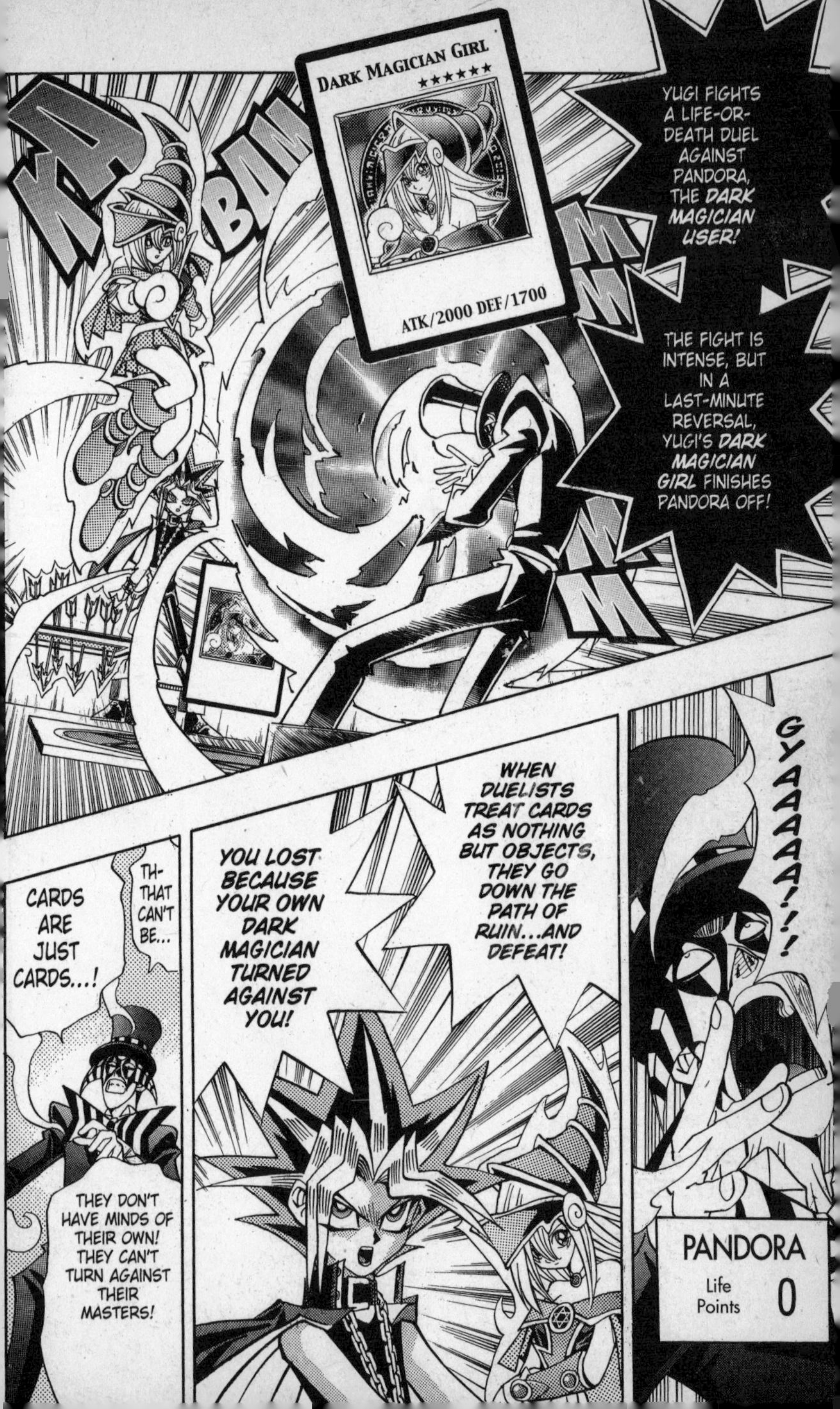
YUGI FIGHTS A LIFE-OR-DEATH DUEL AGAINST PANDORA, THE DARK MAGICIAN USER!
THE FIGHT IS INTENSE, BUT IN A LAST-MINUTE REVERSAL, YUGI'S DARK MAGICIAN GIRL FINISHES PANDORA OFF!
DARK MAGICIAN GIRL
ATK/2000 DEF/1700
GYAAAAAA!!!
PANDORA
Life Points 0
WHEN DUELISTS TREAT CARDS AS NOTHING BUT OBJECTS, THEY GO DOWN THE PATH OF RUIN...AND DEFEAT!
YOU LOST BECAUSE YOUR OWN DARK MAGICIAN TURNED AGAINST YOU!
TH-THAT CAN'T BE...
CARDS ARE JUST CARDS...!
THEY DON'T HAVE MINDS OF THEIR OWN! THEY CAN'T TURN AGAINST THEIR MASTERS!

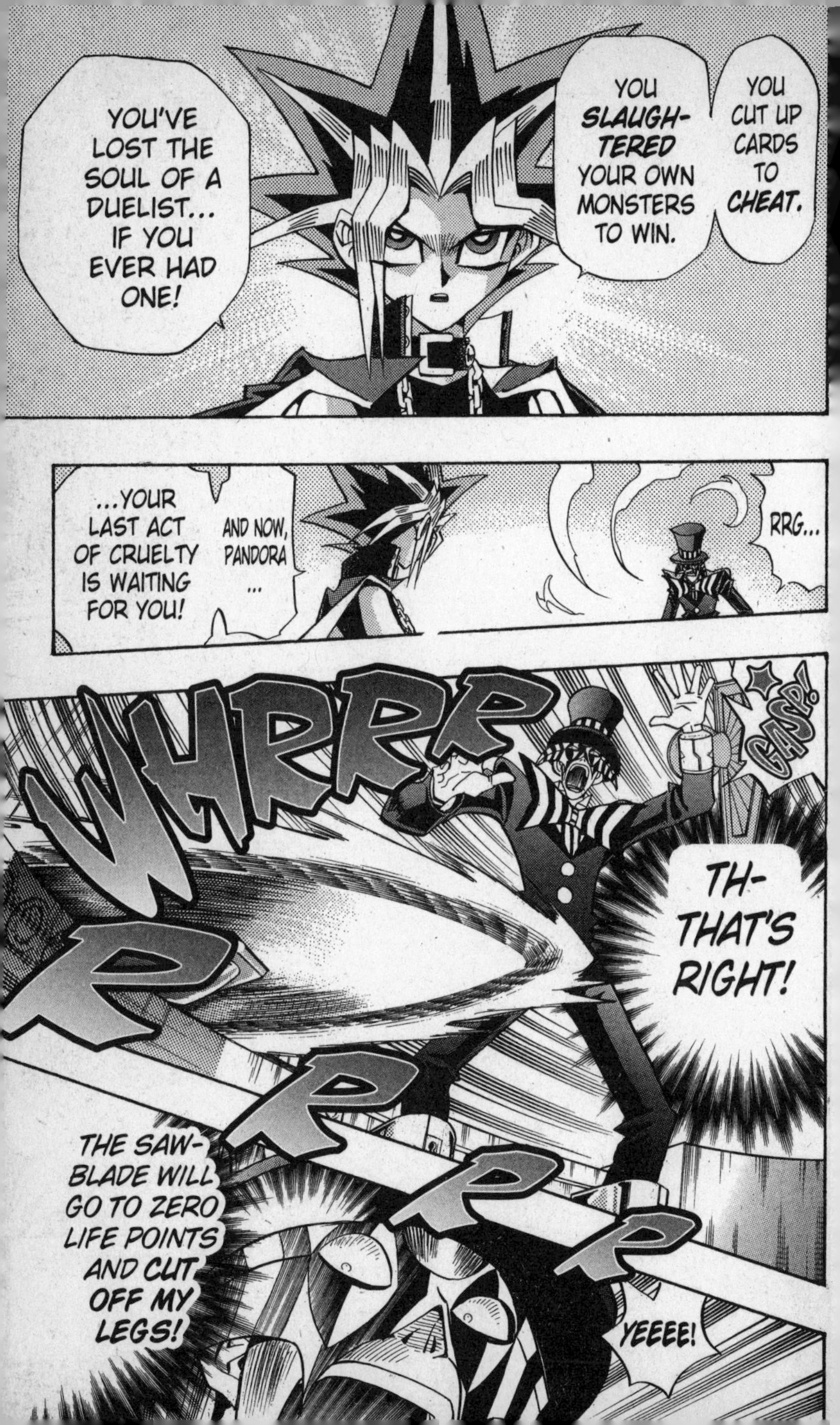
YOU CUT UP CARDS TO CHEAT.
YOU SLAUGHTERED YOUR OWN MONSTERS TO WIN.
YOU'VE LOST THE SOUL OF A DUELIST... IF YOU EVER HAD ONE!
RRG...
AND NOW, PANDORA...
...YOUR LAST ACT OF CRUELTY IS WAITING FOR YOU!
GASP!
WHRRRRRRR
TH-THAT'S RIGHT!
YEEEE!
THE SAW-BLADE WILL GO TO ZERO LIFE POINTS AND CUT OFF MY LEGS!

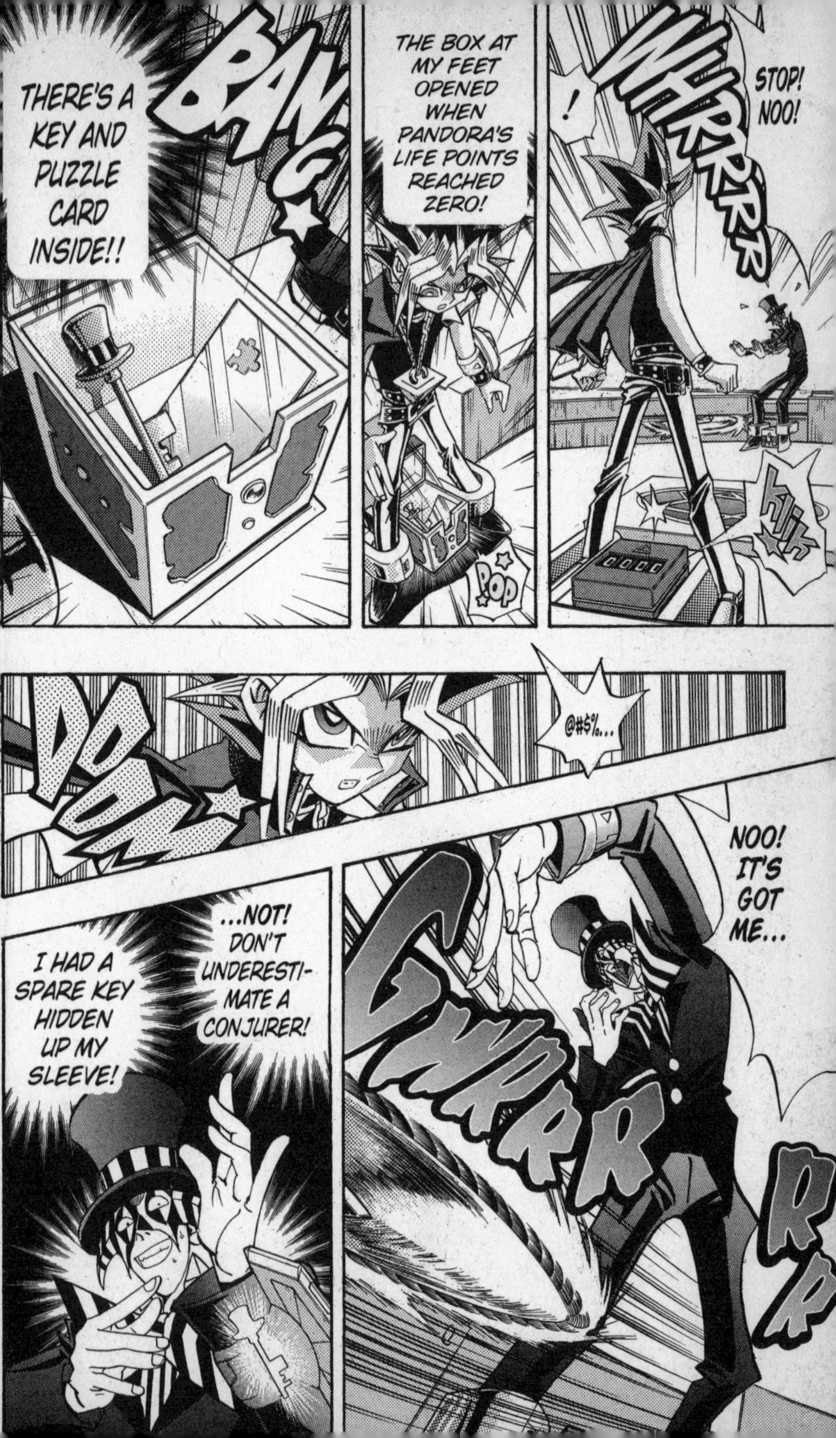
!
STOP! NOO!
klik
THE BOX AT MY FEET OPENED WHEN PANDORA'S LIFE POINTS REACHED ZERO!
POP
BANG
THERE'S A KEY AND PUZZLE CARD INSIDE!!
@#$%...
NOO! IT'S GOT ME...
...NOT! DON'T UNDERESTI-MATE A CONJURER!
I HAD A SPARE KEY HIDDEN UP MY SLEEVE!

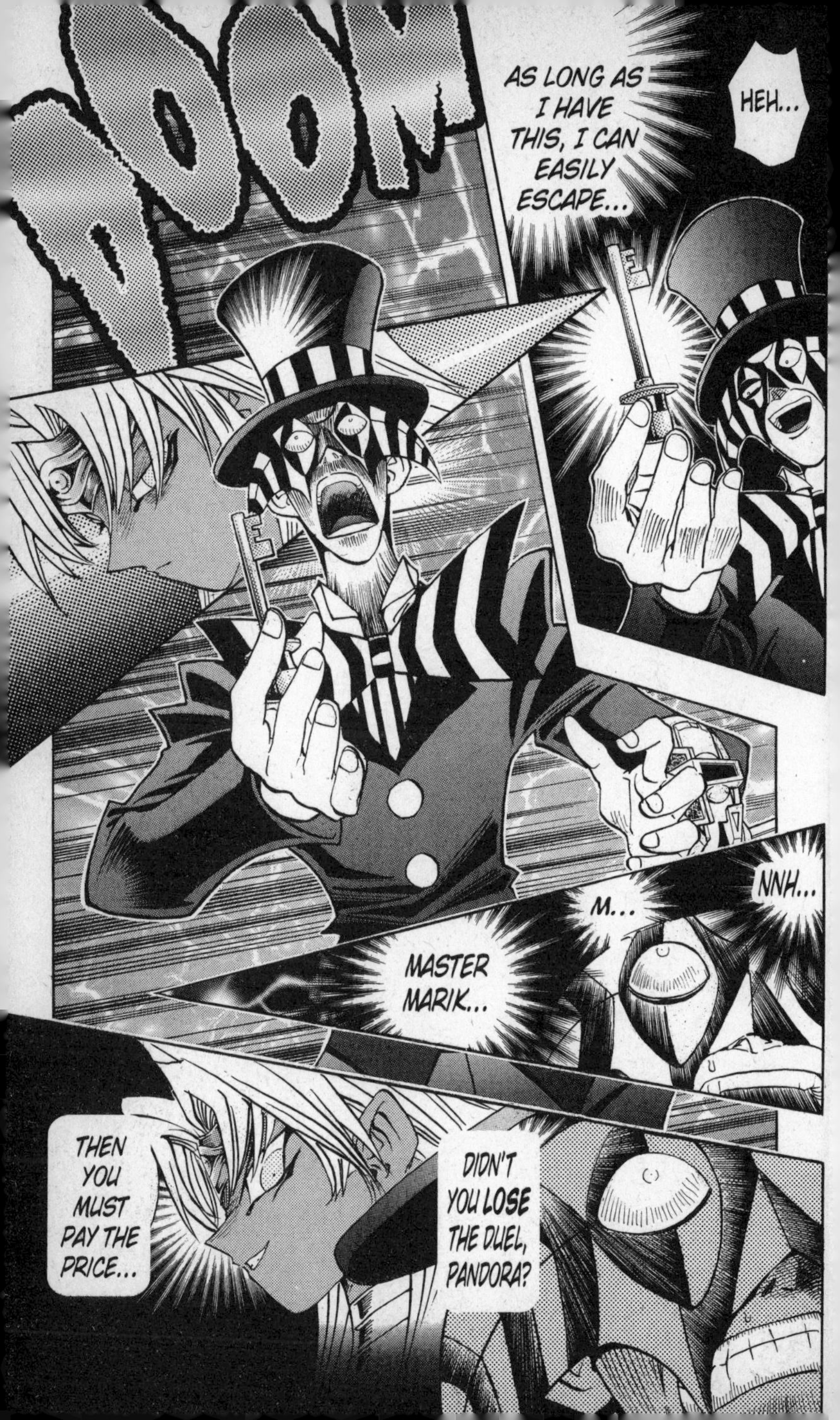
DOOM
HEH...
AS LONG AS I HAVE THIS, I CAN EASILY ESCAPE...
NNH...
M...
MASTER MARIK...
DIDN'T YOU LOSE THE DUEL, PANDORA?
THEN YOU MUST PAY THE PRICE...

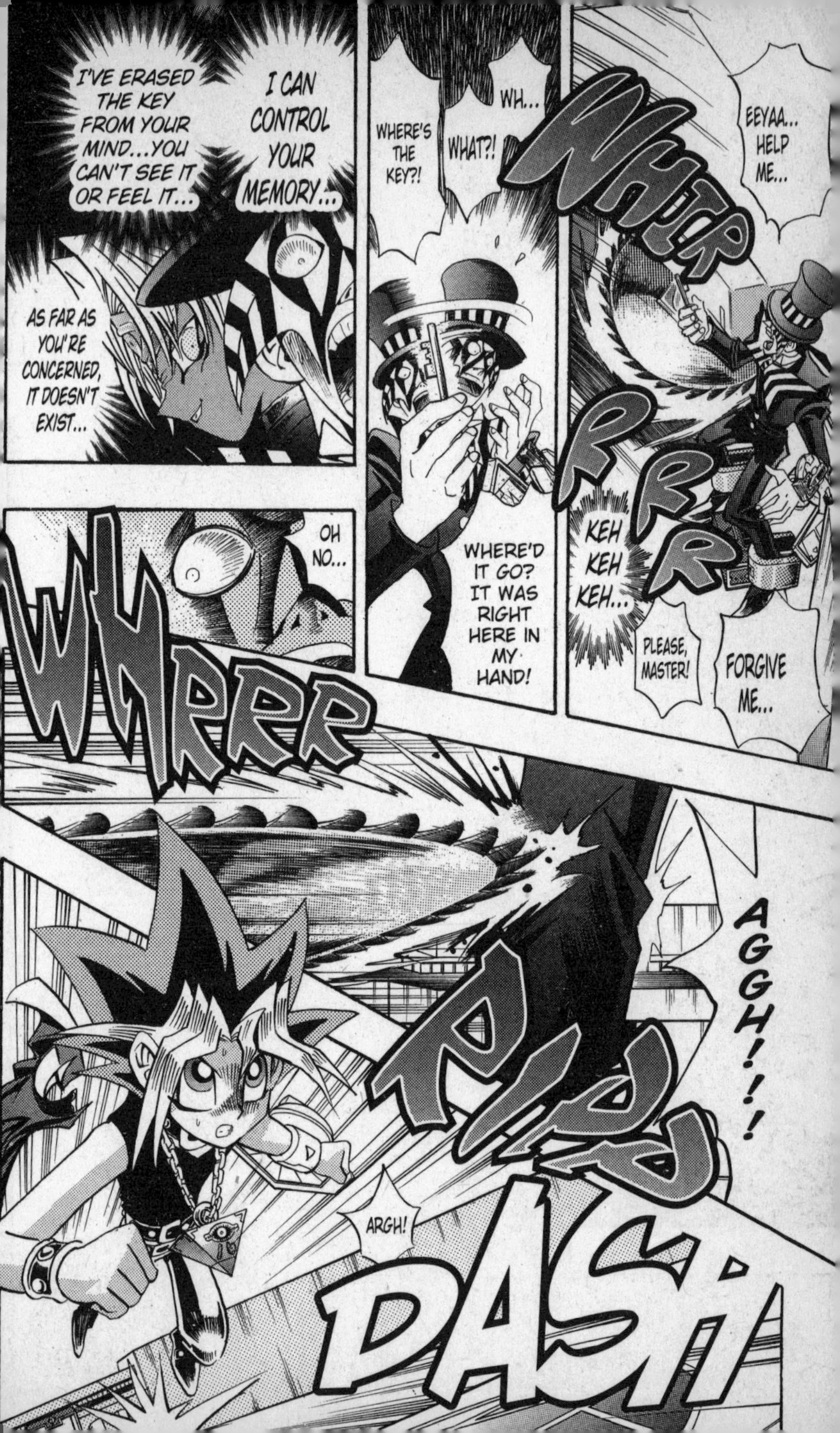
EEYAA... HELP ME...
WHIRR
RRRR
KEH KEH KEH...
PLEASE, MASTER!
FORGIVE ME...
WH...
WHAT?!
WHERE'S THE KEY?!
WHERE'D IT GO? IT WAS RIGHT HERE IN MY HAND!
I CAN CONTROL YOUR MEMORY...
I'VE ERASED THE KEY FROM YOUR MIND...YOU CAN'T SEE IT OR FEEL IT...
AS FAR AS YOU'RE CONCERNED, IT DOESN'T EXIST...
OH NO...
WHRRR
AGGH!!!
RIP
ARGH!
DASH!

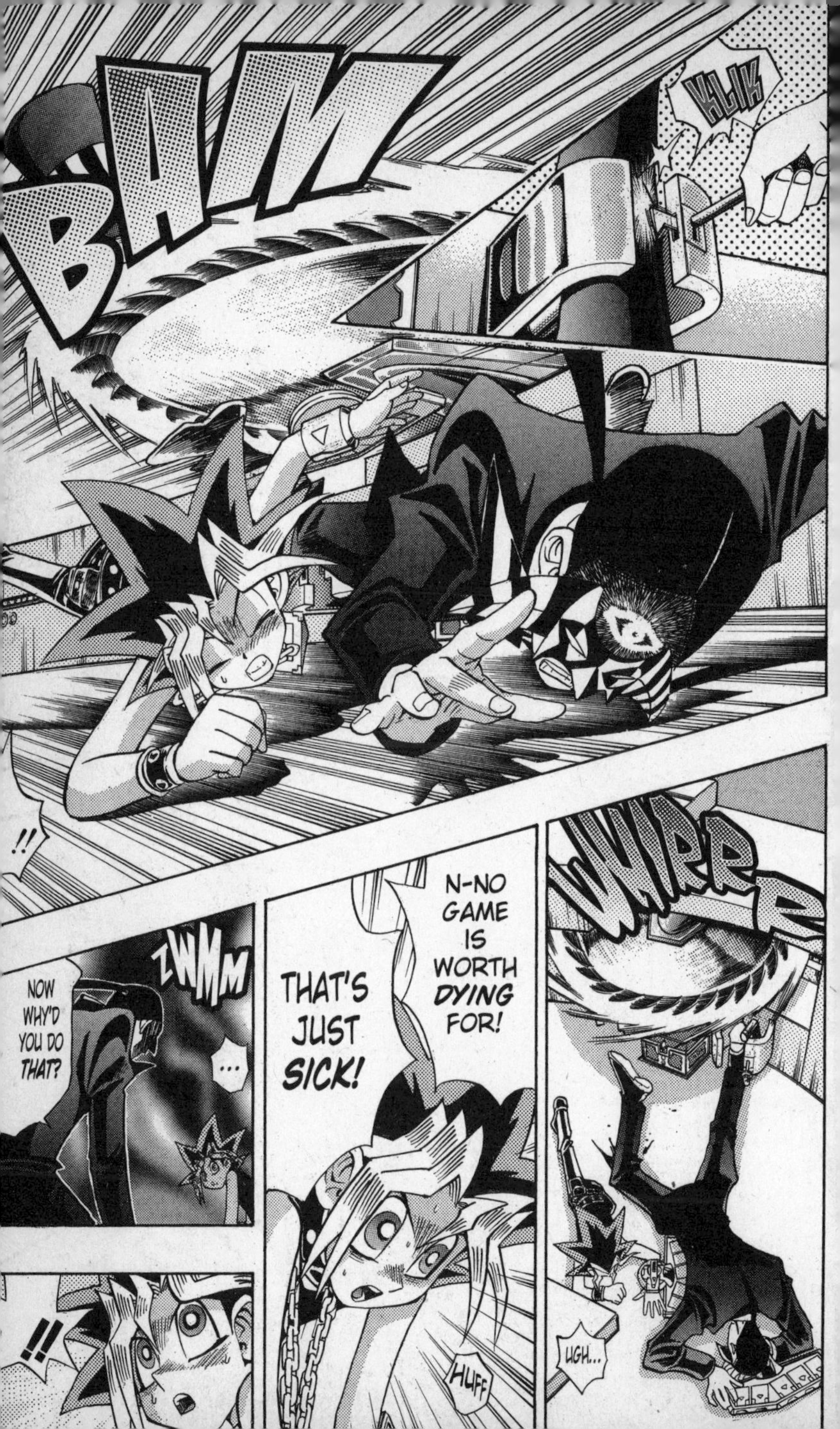
KLIK
BAM
!!
WHIRR
UGH...
N-NO GAME IS WORTH DYING FOR!
THAT'S JUST SICK!
HUFF
ZWMM
NOW WHY'D YOU DO THAT?
...
!!

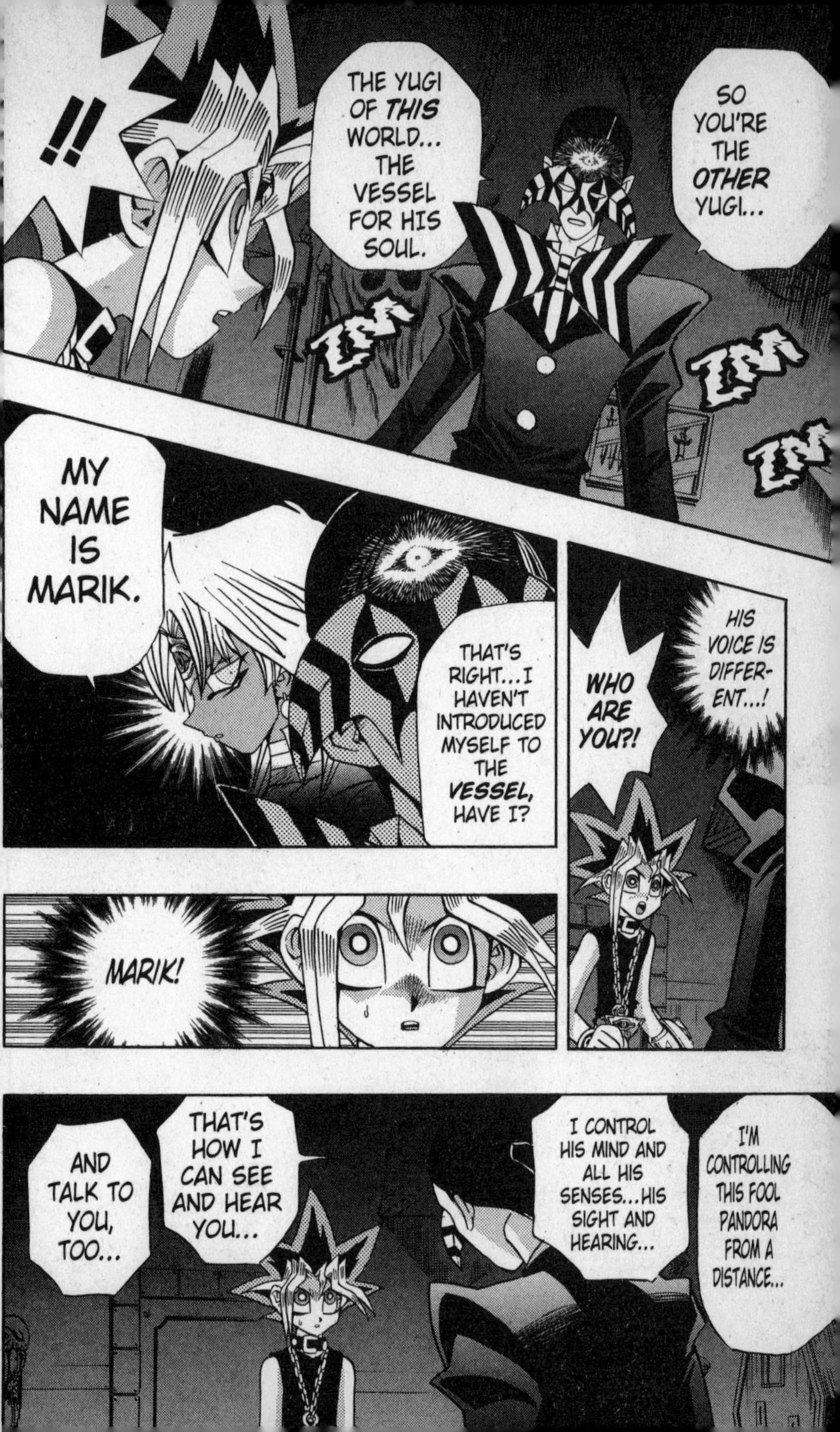
SO YOU'RE THE OTHER YUGI...
THE YUGI OF THIS WORLD... THE VESSEL FOR HIS SOUL.
!!
HIS VOICE IS DIFFERENT...!
WHO ARE YOU?!
THAT'S RIGHT...I HAVEN'T INTRODUCED MYSELF TO THE VESSEL, HAVE I?
MY NAME IS MARIK.
MARIK!
I'M CONTROLLING THIS FOOL PANDORA FROM A DISTANCE...
I CONTROL HIS MIND AND ALL HIS SENSES...HIS SIGHT AND HEARING...
THAT'S HOW I CAN SEE AND HEAR YOU...
AND TALK TO YOU, TOO...

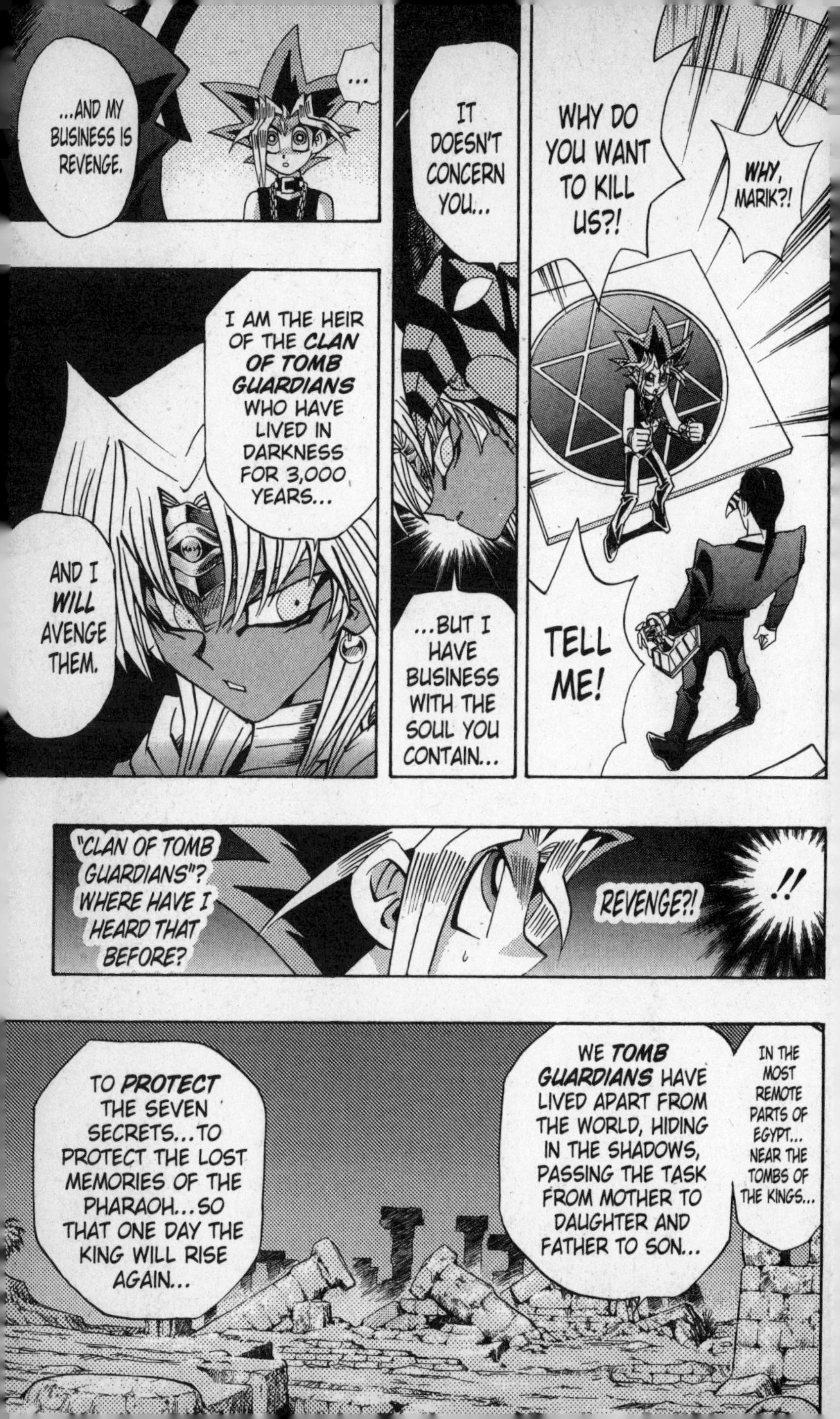
WHY, MARIK?!
WHY DO YOU WANT TO KILL US?!
TELL ME!
IT DOESN'T CONCERN YOU...
...BUT I HAVE BUSINESS WITH THE SOUL YOU CONTAIN...
...AND MY BUSINESS IS REVENGE.
...
I AM THE HEIR OF THE CLAN OF TOMB GUARDIANS WHO HAVE LIVED IN DARKNESS FOR 3,000 YEARS...
AND I WILL AVENGE THEM.
!!
REVENGE?!
"CLAN OF TOMB GUARDIANS"? WHERE HAVE I HEARD THAT BEFORE?
IN THE MOST REMOTE PARTS OF EGYPT... NEAR THE TOMBS OF THE KINGS...
WE TOMB GUARDIANS HAVE LIVED APART FROM THE WORLD, HIDING IN THE SHADOWS, PASSING THE TASK FROM MOTHER TO DAUGHTER AND FATHER TO SON...
TO PROTECT THE SEVEN SECRETS...TO PROTECT THE LOST MEMORIES OF THE PHARAOH...SO THAT ONE DAY THE KING WILL RISE AGAIN...

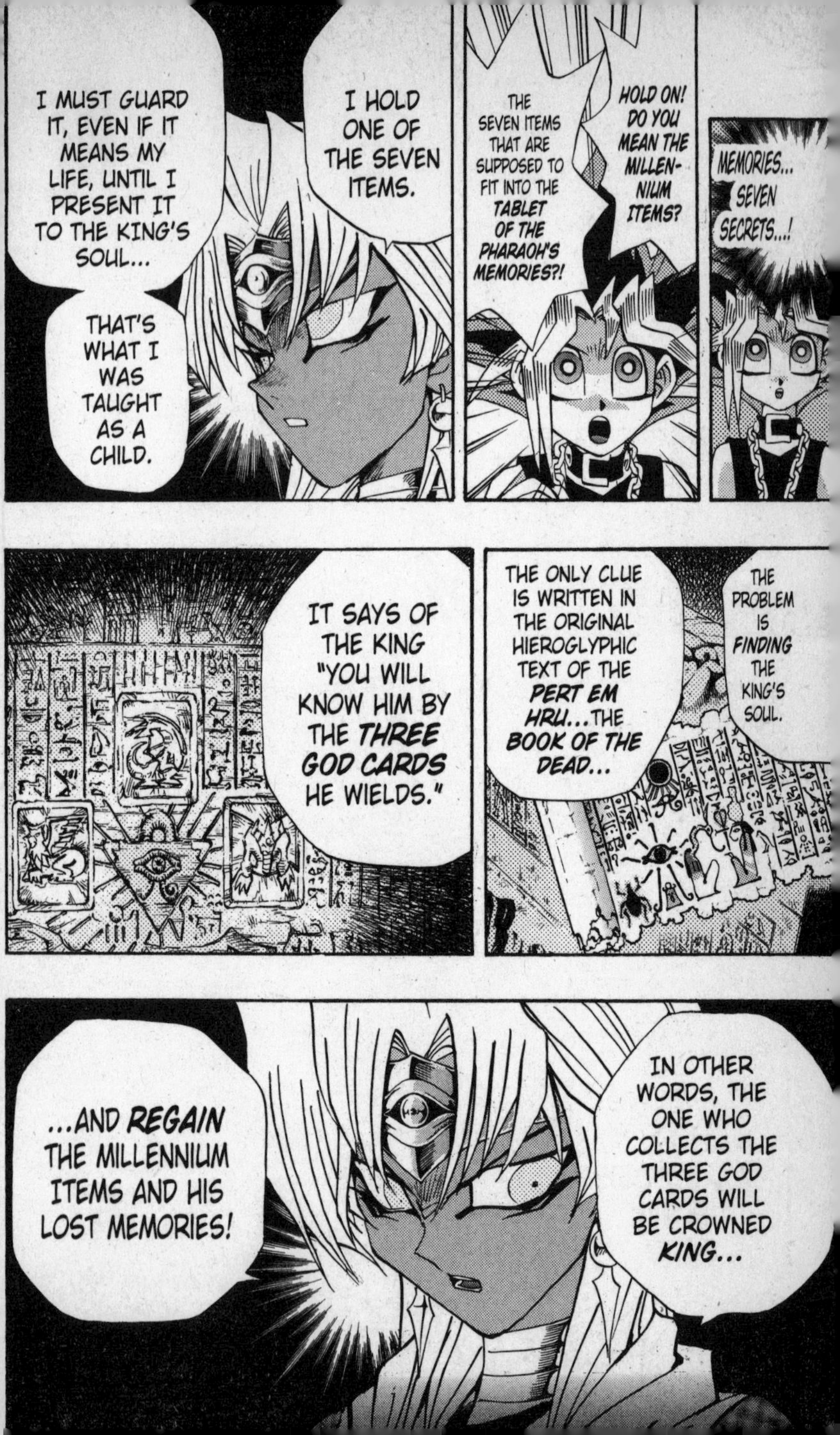
MEMORIES... SEVEN SECRETS...!
HOLD ON! DO YOU MEAN THE MILLENNIUM ITEMS?
THE SEVEN ITEMS THAT ARE SUPPOSED TO FIT INTO THE TABLET OF THE PHARAOH'S MEMORIES?!
I HOLD ONE OF THE SEVEN ITEMS.
I MUST GUARD IT, EVEN IF IT MEANS MY LIFE, UNTIL I PRESENT IT TO THE KING'S SOUL...
THAT'S WHAT I WAS TAUGHT AS A CHILD.
THE PROBLEM IS FINDING THE KING'S SOUL.
THE ONLY CLUE IS WRITTEN IN THE ORIGINAL HIEROGLYPHIC TEXT OF THE PERT EM HRU...THE BOOK OF THE DEAD...
IT SAYS OF THE KING "YOU WILL KNOW HIM BY THE THREE GOD CARDS HE WIELDS."
IN OTHER WORDS, THE ONE WHO COLLECTS THE THREE GOD CARDS WILL BE CROWNED KING...
...AND REGAIN THE MILLENNIUM ITEMS AND HIS LOST MEMORIES!

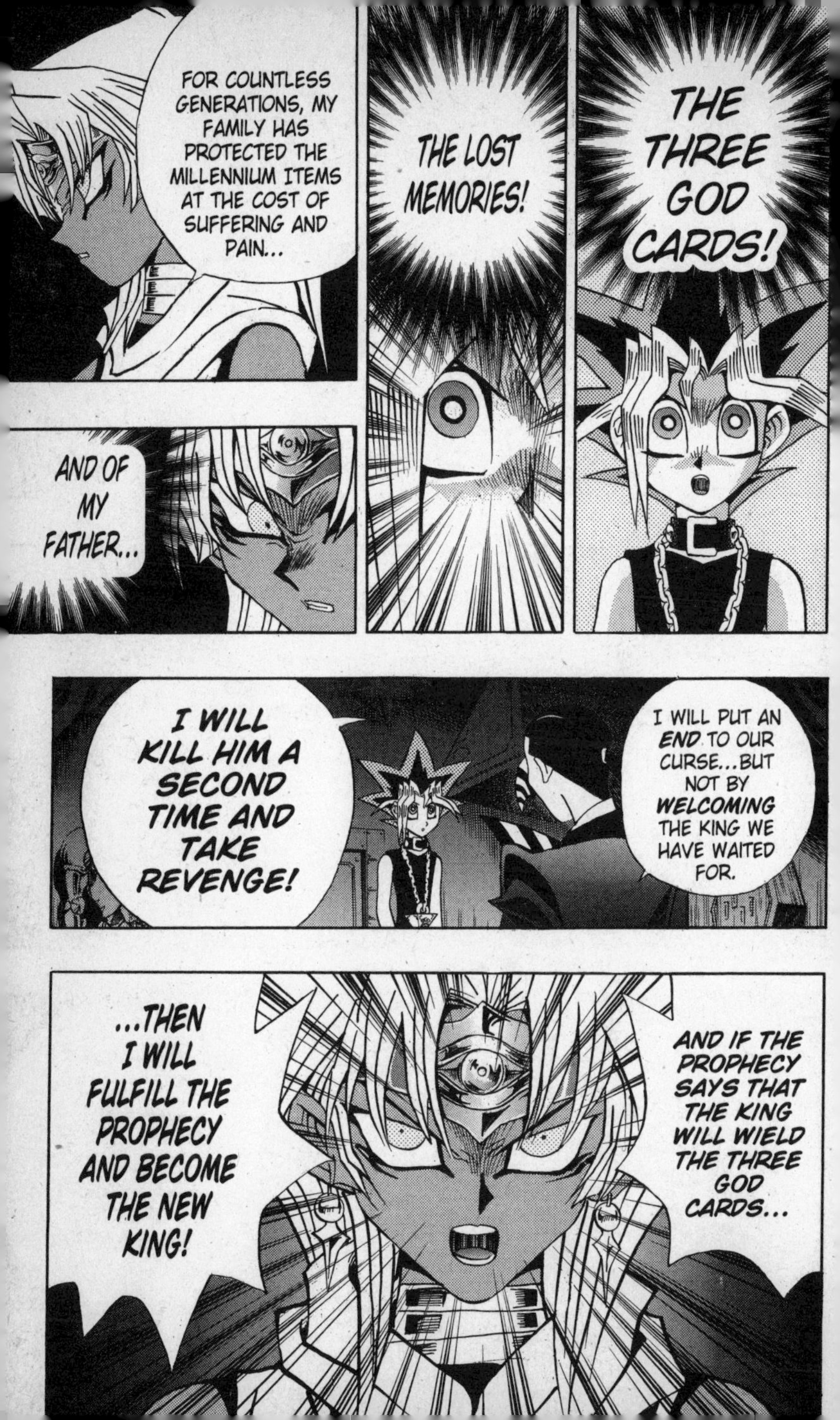
THE THREE GOD CARDS!
THE LOST MEMORIES!
FOR COUNTLESS GENERATIONS, MY FAMILY HAS PROTECTED THE MILLENNIUM ITEMS AT THE COST OF SUFFERING AND PAIN...
AND OF MY FATHER...
I WILL PUT AN END TO OUR CURSE...BUT NOT BY WELCOMING THE KING WE HAVE WAITED FOR.
I WILL KILL HIM A SECOND TIME AND TAKE REVENGE!
AND IF THE PROPHECY SAYS THAT THE KING WILL WIELD THE THREE GOD CARDS...
...THEN I WILL FULFILL THE PROPHECY AND BECOME THE NEW KING!

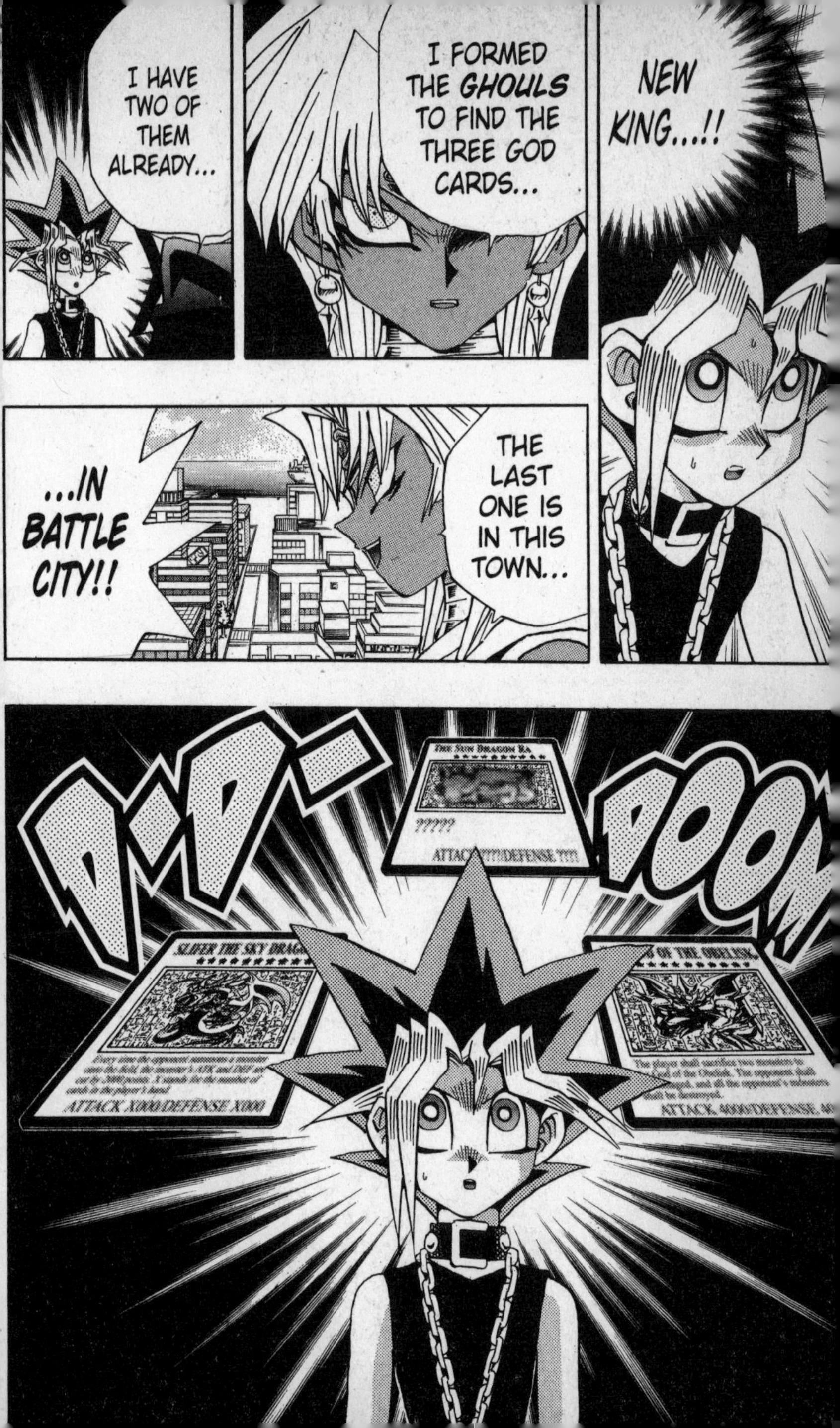

NEW KING...!!
I FORMED THE GHOULS TO FIND THE THREE GOD CARDS...
I HAVE TWO OF THEM ALREADY...
THE LAST ONE IS IN THIS TOWN...
...IN BATTLE CITY!!
D-D-DOOM
THE SUN DRAGON RA
ATTACK X000/DEFENSE X000

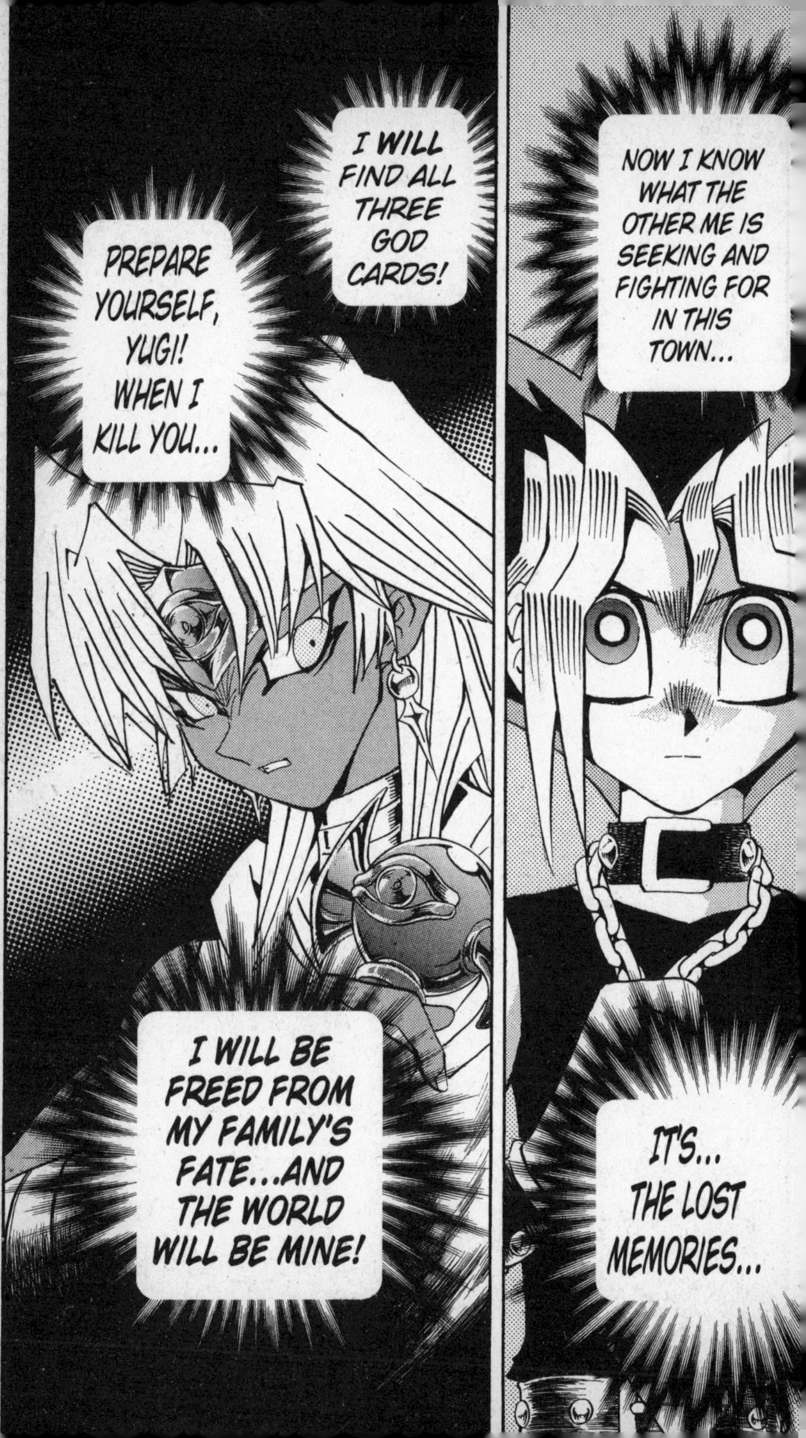
NOW I KNOW WHAT THE OTHER ME IS SEEKING AND FIGHTING FOR IN THIS TOWN...
IT'S... THE LOST MEMORIES...
I WILL FIND ALL THREE GOD CARDS!
PREPARE YOURSELF, YUGI! WHEN I KILL YOU...
I WILL BE FREED FROM MY FAMILY'S FATE...AND THE WORLD WILL BE MINE!

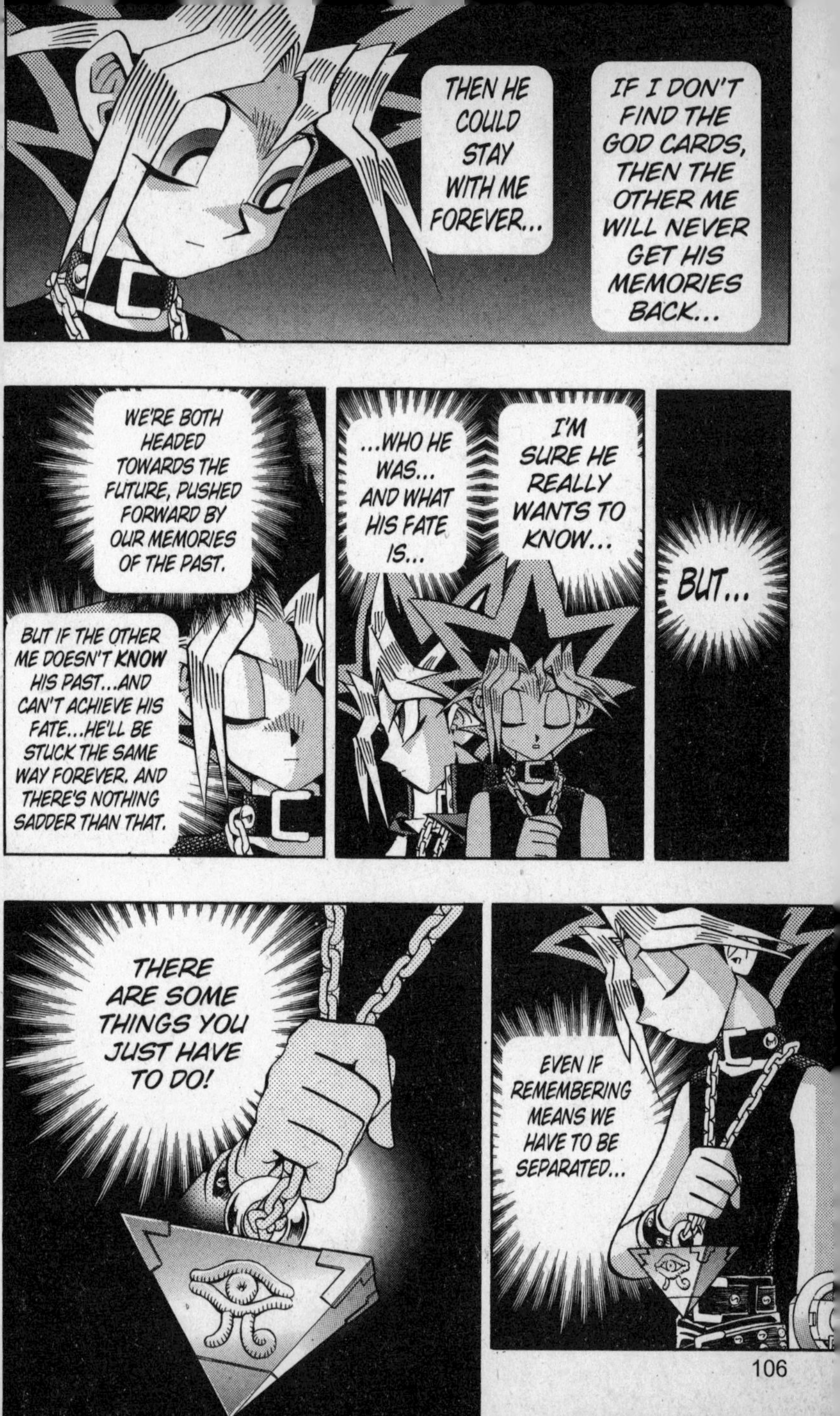
IF I DON'T FIND THE GOD CARDS, THEN THE OTHER ME WILL NEVER GET HIS MEMORIES BACK...
THEN HE COULD STAY WITH ME FOREVER...
BUT...
I'M SURE HE REALLY WANTS TO KNOW...
...WHO HE WAS... AND WHAT HIS FATE IS...
WE'RE BOTH HEADED TOWARDS THE FUTURE, PUSHED FORWARD BY OUR MEMORIES OF THE PAST.
BUT IF THE OTHER ME DOESN'T **KNOW** HIS PAST...AND CAN'T ACHIEVE HIS FATE...HE'LL BE STUCK THE SAME WAY FOREVER. AND THERE'S NOTHING SADDER THAN THAT.
EVEN IF REMEMBERING MEANS WE HAVE TO BE SEPARATED...
THERE ARE SOME THINGS YOU JUST HAVE TO DO!

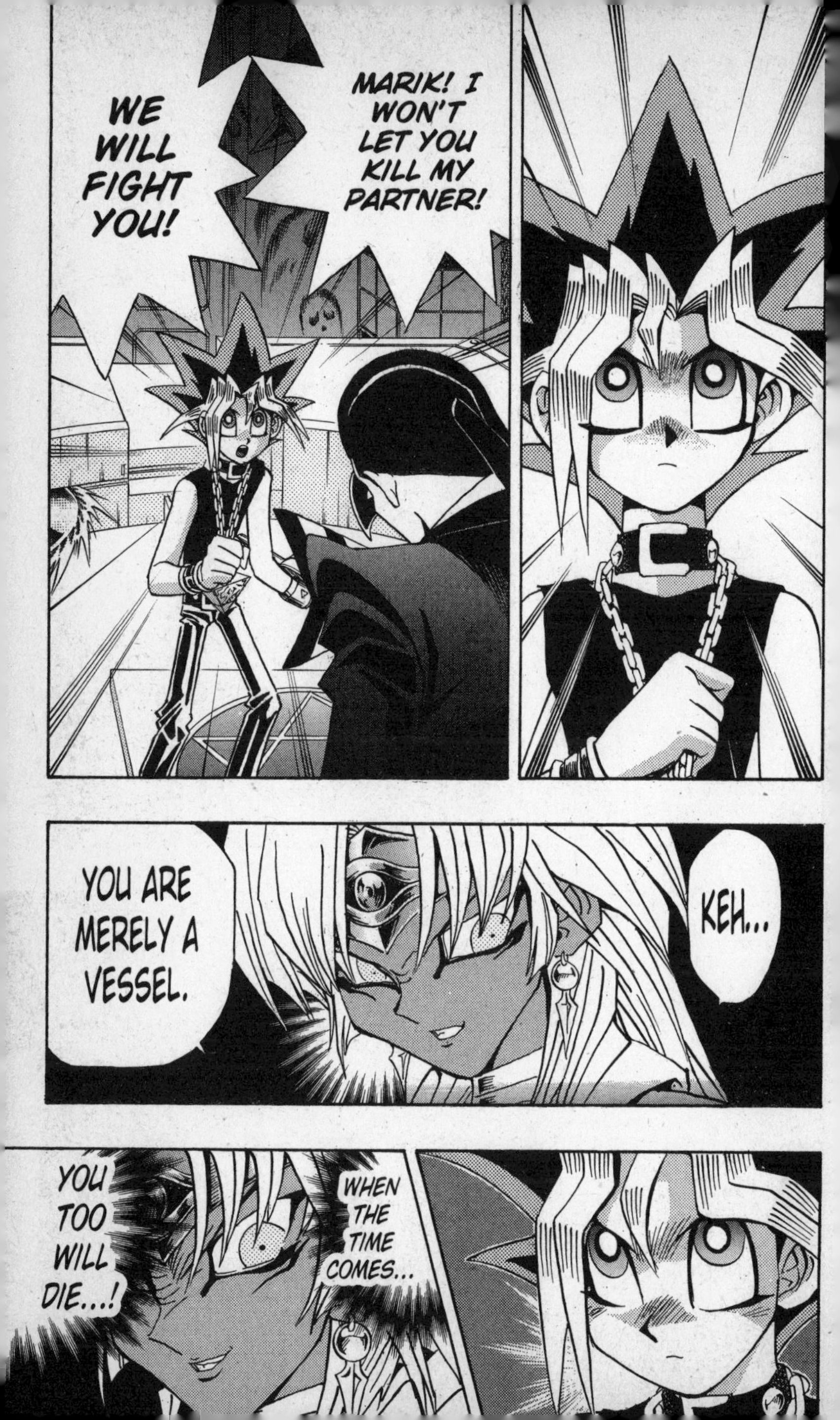
MARIK! I WON'T LET YOU KILL MY PARTNER!
WE WILL FIGHT YOU!
KEH...
YOU ARE MERELY A VESSEL.
WHEN THE TIME COMES...
YOU TOO WILL DIE...!

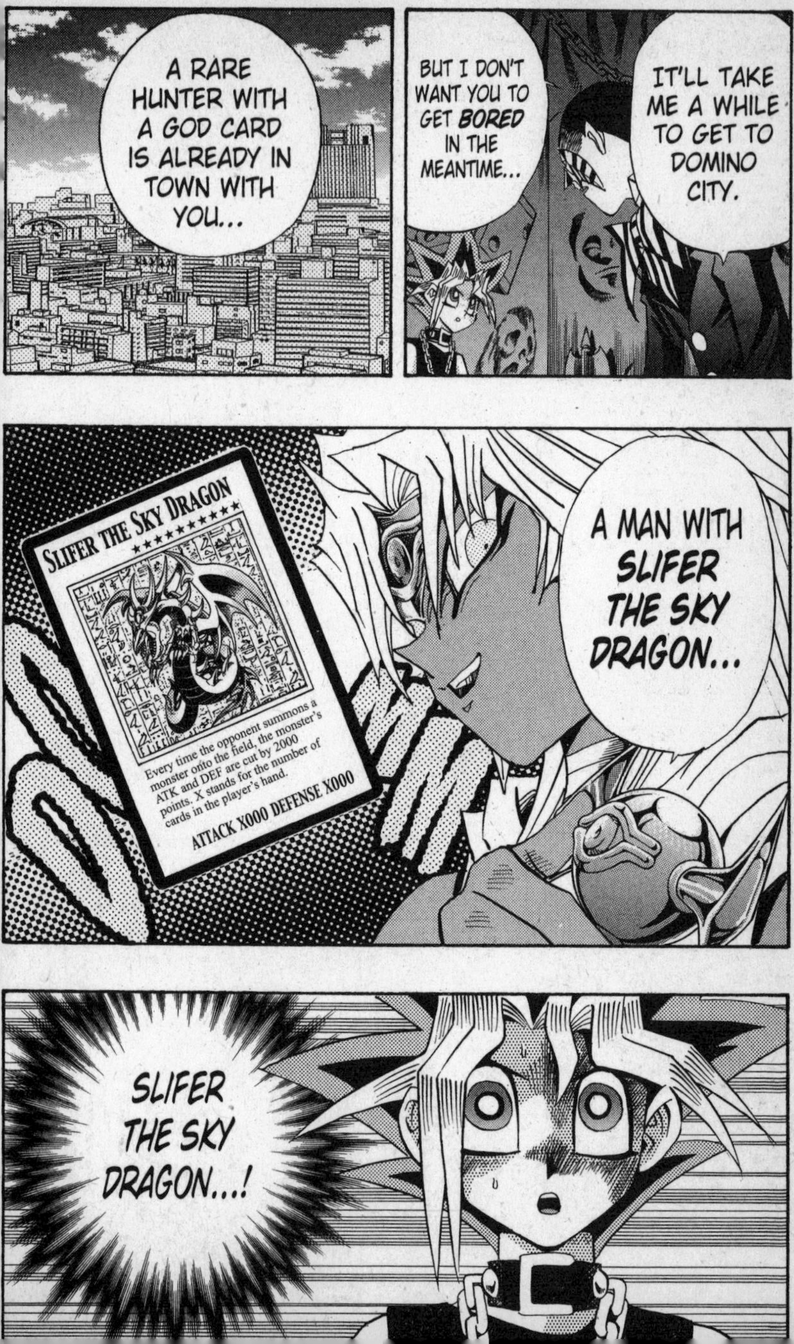
IT'LL TAKE ME A WHILE TO GET TO DOMINO CITY.
BUT I DON'T WANT YOU TO GET *BORED* IN THE MEANTIME...
A RARE HUNTER WITH A GOD CARD IS ALREADY IN TOWN WITH YOU...
A MAN WITH *SLIFER THE SKY DRAGON...*
SLIFER THE SKY DRAGON
Every time the opponent summons a monster onto the field, the monster's ATK and DEF are cut by 2000 points. X stands for the number of cards in the player's hand.
ATTACK X000 DEFENSE X000
SLIFER THE SKY DRAGON...!

READ THIS WAY

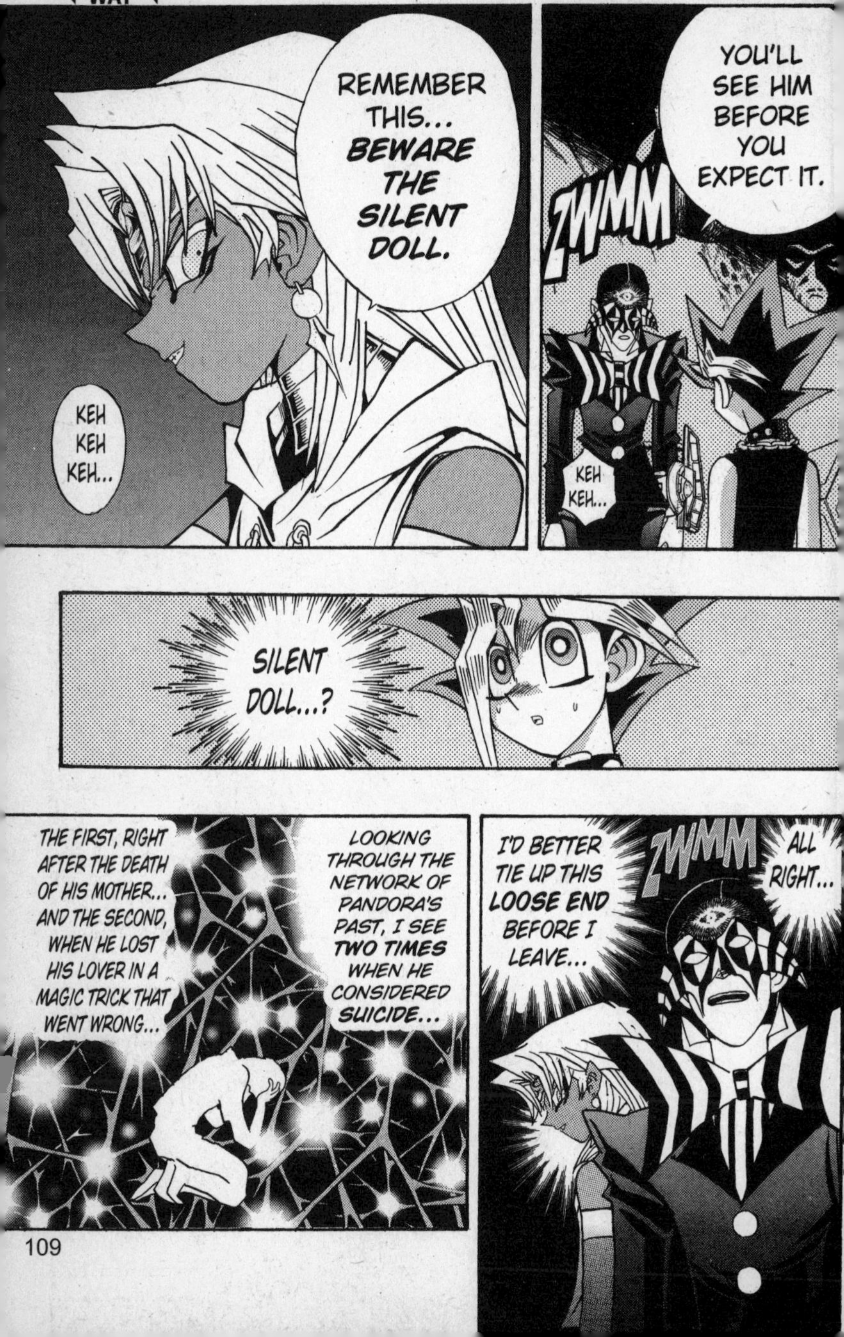

YOU'LL SEE HIM BEFORE YOU EXPECT IT.
ZWMM
KEH KEH...
REMEMBER THIS... **BEWARE THE SILENT DOLL.**
KEH KEH KEH...
SILENT DOLL...?
ALL RIGHT...
ZWMM
I'D BETTER TIE UP THIS **LOOSE END** BEFORE I LEAVE...
LOOKING THROUGH THE NETWORK OF PANDORA'S PAST, I SEE **TWO TIMES** WHEN HE CONSIDERED **SUICIDE...**
THE FIRST, RIGHT AFTER THE DEATH OF HIS MOTHER... AND THE SECOND, WHEN HE LOST HIS LOVER IN A MAGIC TRICK THAT WENT WRONG...

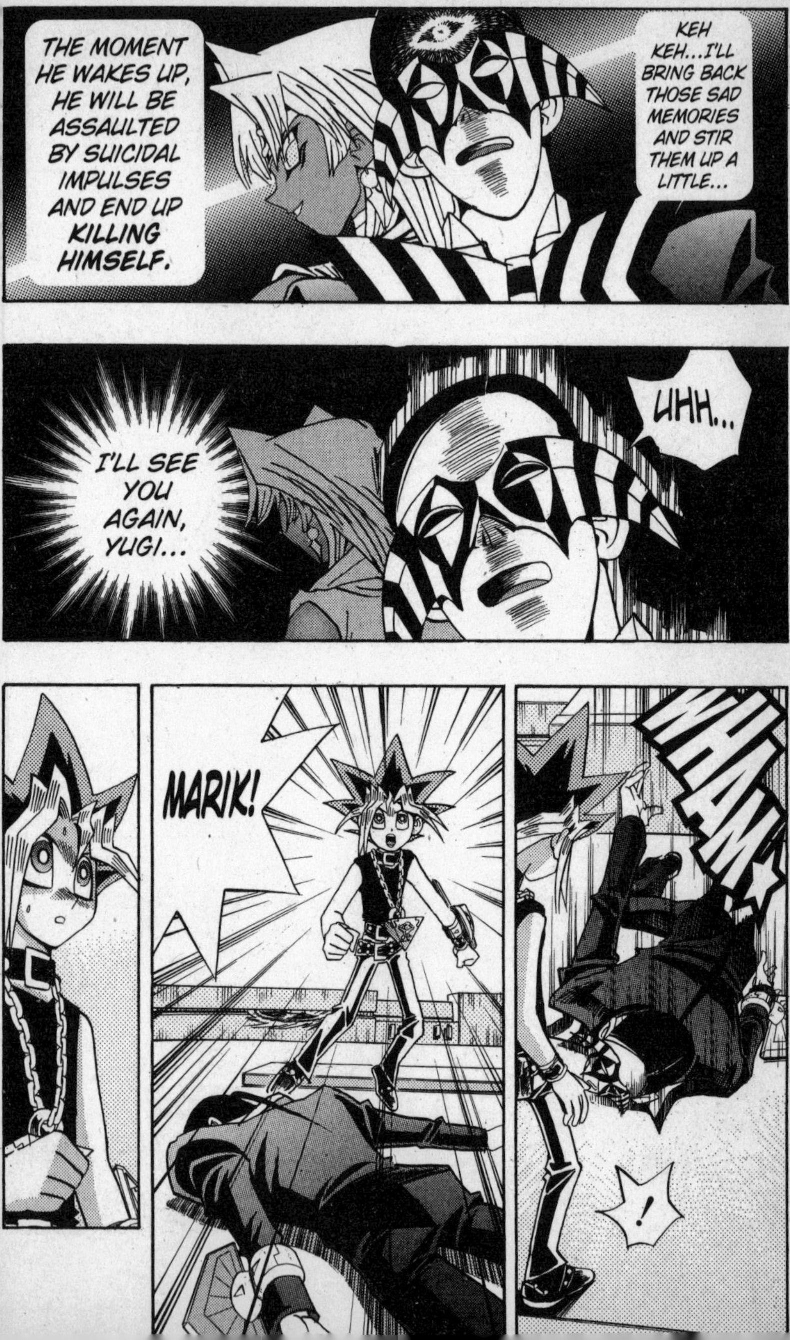
KEH KEH...I'LL BRING BACK THOSE SAD MEMORIES AND STIR THEM UP A LITTLE...
THE MOMENT HE WAKES UP, HE WILL BE ASSAULTED BY SUICIDAL IMPULSES AND END UP KILLING HIMSELF.
UHH...
I'LL SEE YOU AGAIN, YUGI...
WHAM
!
MARIK!

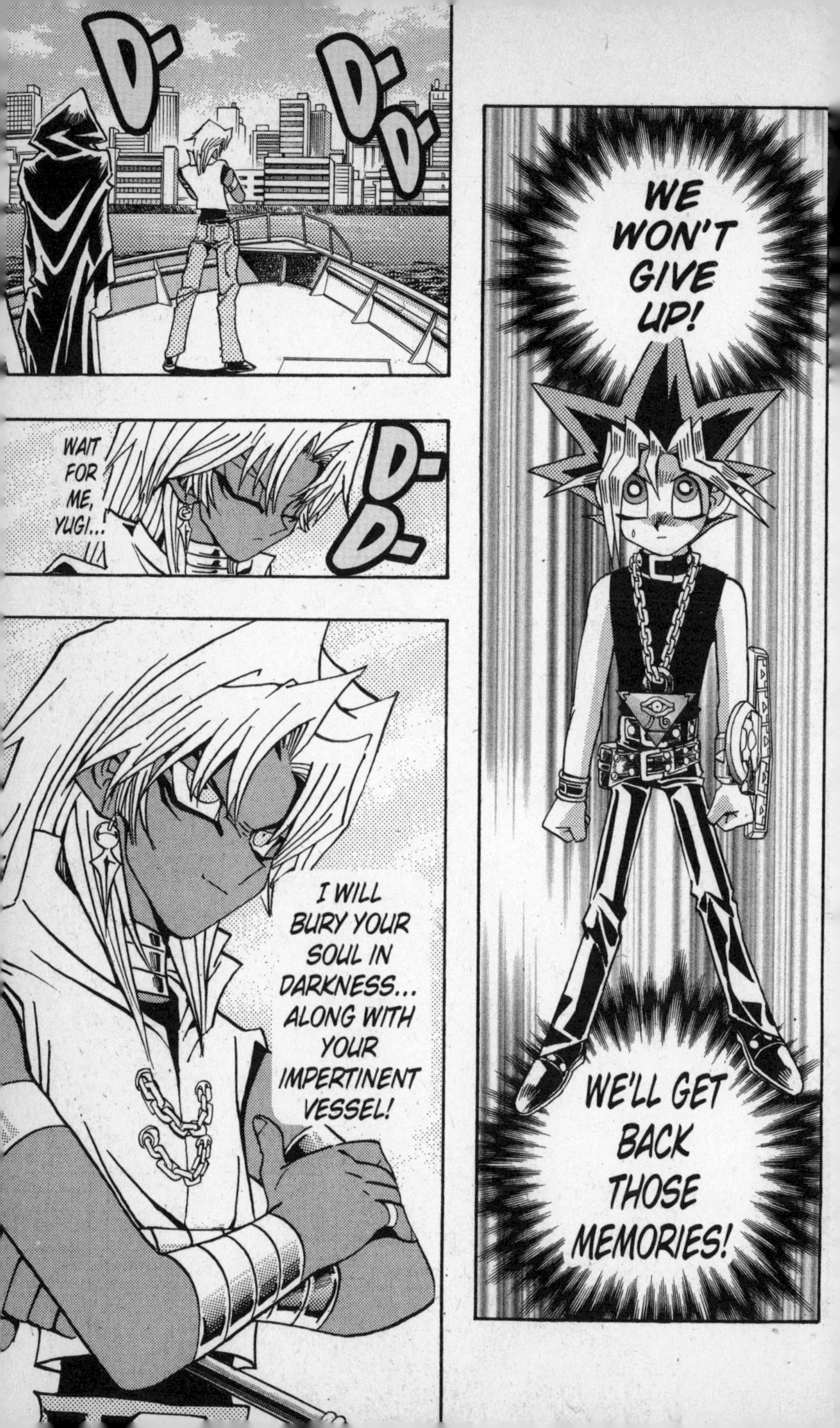
WE WON'T GIVE UP!
WE'LL GET BACK THOSE MEMORIES!
D- D- D-
D-
D- D-
WAIT FOR ME, YUGI...
I WILL BURY YOUR SOUL IN DARKNESS... ALONG WITH YOUR IMPERTINENT VESSEL!

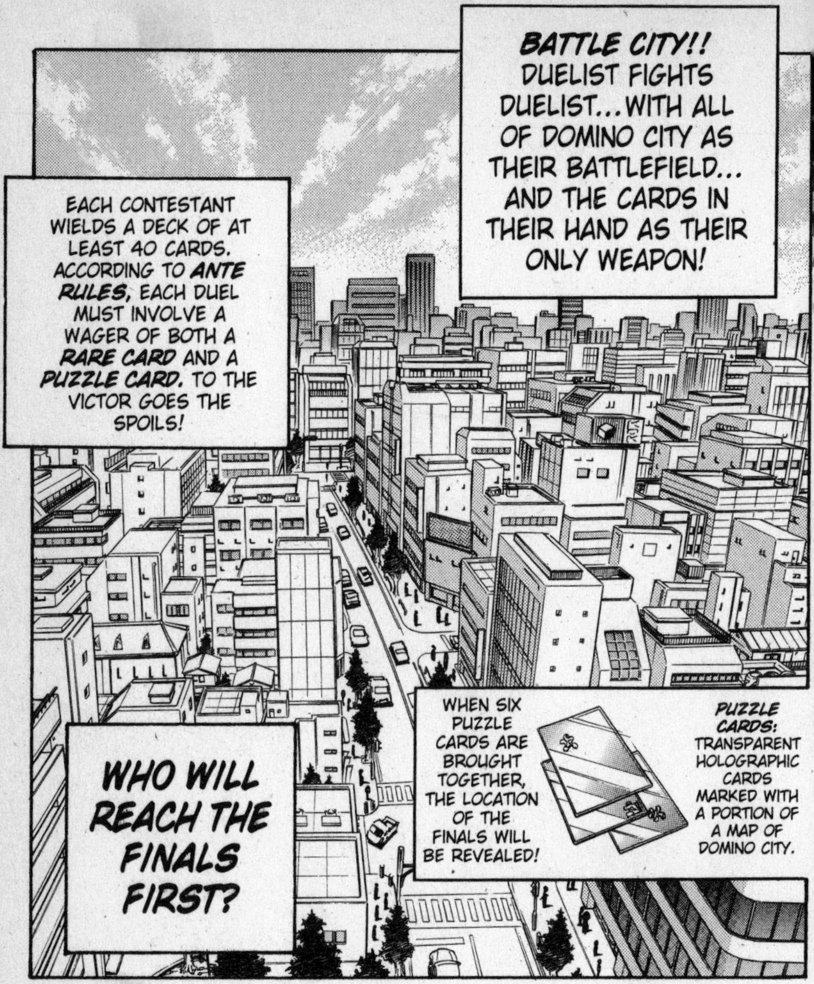
BATTLE CITY!! DUELIST FIGHTS DUELIST...WITH ALL OF DOMINO CITY AS THEIR BATTLEFIELD... AND THE CARDS IN THEIR HAND AS THEIR ONLY WEAPON!
EACH CONTESTANT WIELDS A DECK OF AT LEAST 40 CARDS. ACCORDING TO ANTE RULES, EACH DUEL MUST INVOLVE A WAGER OF BOTH A RARE CARD AND A PUZZLE CARD. TO THE VICTOR GOES THE SPOILS!
PUZZLE CARDS: TRANSPARENT HOLOGRAPHIC CARDS MARKED WITH A PORTION OF A MAP OF DOMINO CITY.
WHEN SIX PUZZLE CARDS ARE BROUGHT TOGETHER, THE LOCATION OF THE FINALS WILL BE REVEALED!
WHO WILL REACH THE FINALS FIRST?

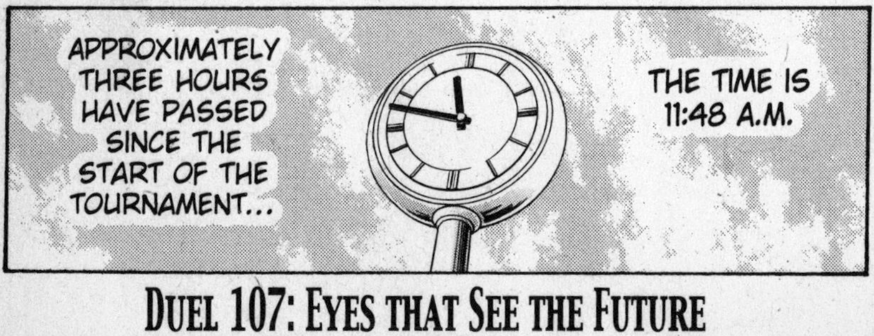
THE TIME IS 11:48 A.M.
APPROXIMATELY THREE HOURS HAVE PASSED SINCE THE START OF THE TOURNAMENT...

Duel 107: Eyes that See the Future

Duel 107: Eyes that See the Future

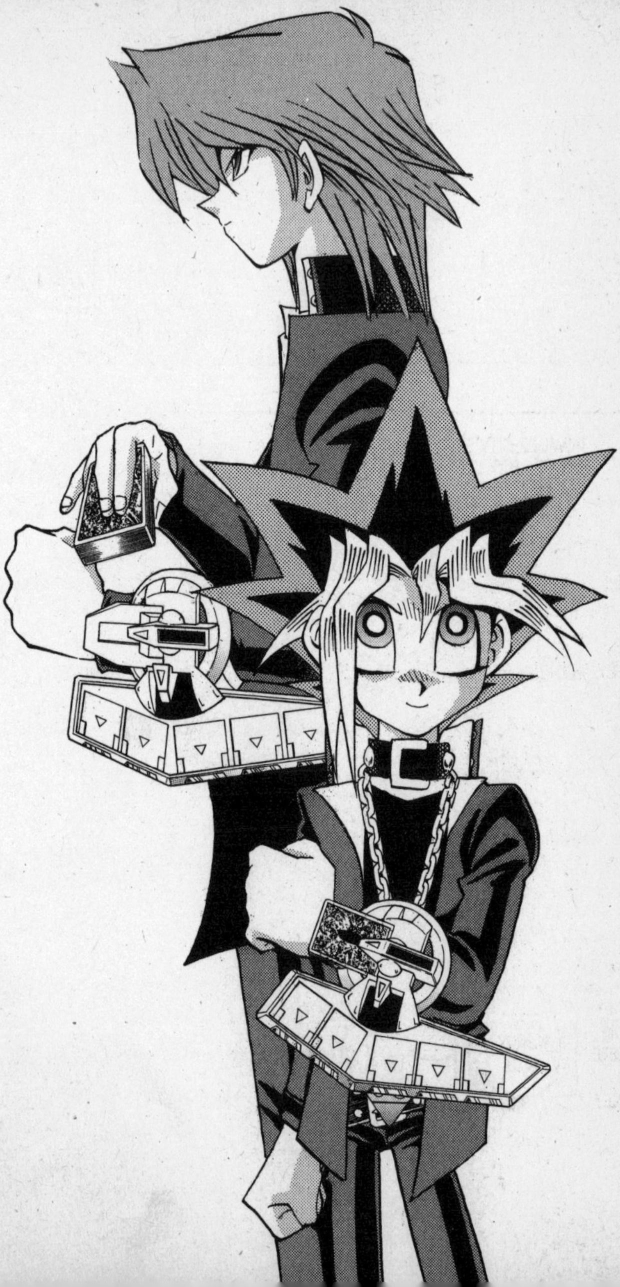

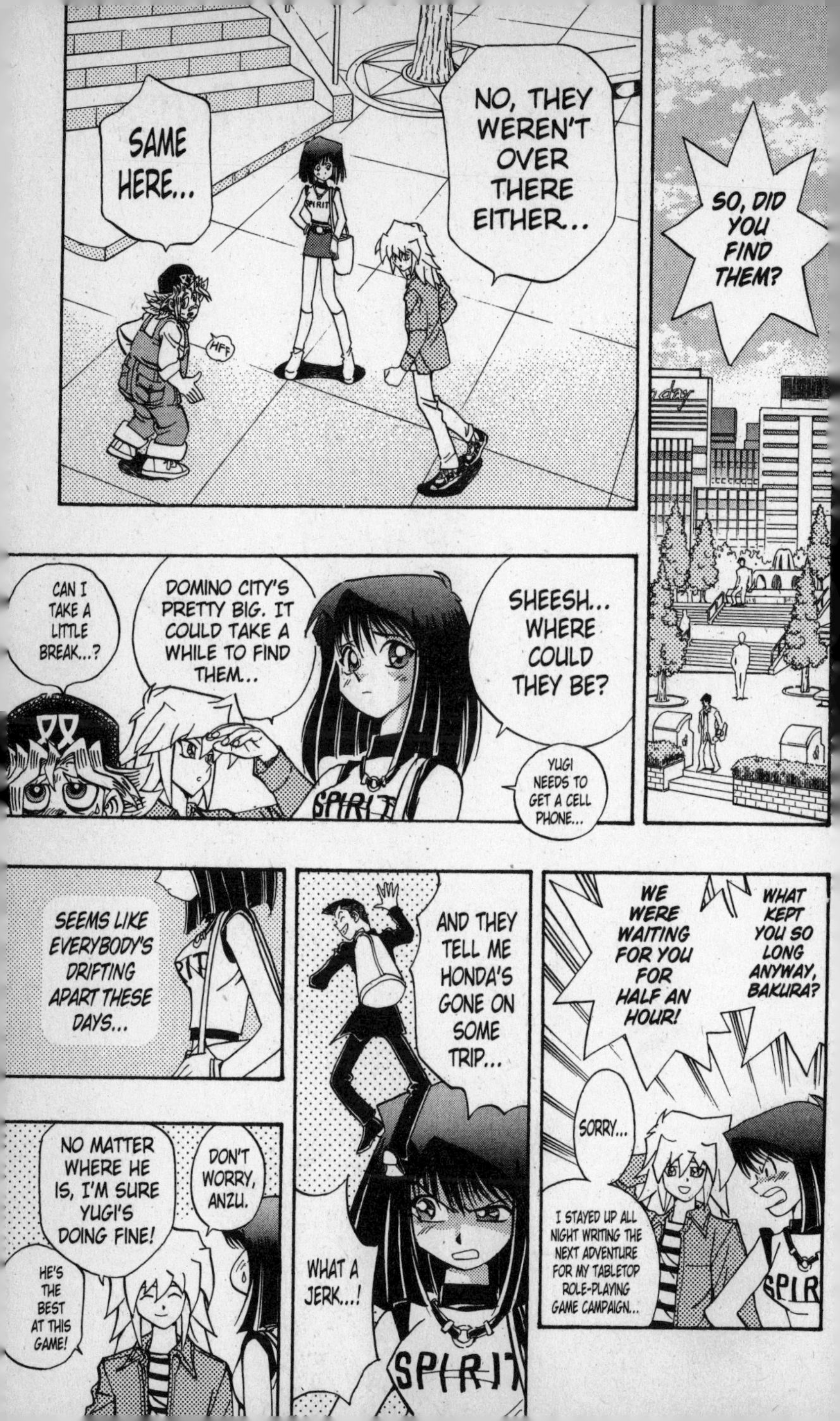
SO, DID YOU FIND THEM?
NO, THEY WEREN'T OVER THERE EITHER...
SAME HERE...
HFF
SHEESH... WHERE COULD THEY BE?
YUGI NEEDS TO GET A CELL PHONE...
DOMINO CITY'S PRETTY BIG. IT COULD TAKE A WHILE TO FIND THEM...
CAN I TAKE A LITTLE BREAK...?
WHAT KEPT YOU SO LONG ANYWAY, BAKURA?
WE WERE WAITING FOR YOU FOR HALF AN HOUR!
SORRY...
I STAYED UP ALL NIGHT WRITING THE NEXT ADVENTURE FOR MY TABLETOP ROLE-PLAYING GAME CAMPAIGN...
AND THEY TELL ME HONDA'S GONE ON SOME TRIP...
WHAT A JERK...!
SEEMS LIKE EVERYBODY'S DRIFTING APART THESE DAYS...
DON'T WORRY, ANZU.
NO MATTER WHERE HE IS, I'M SURE YUGI'S DOING FINE!
HE'S THE BEST AT THIS GAME!

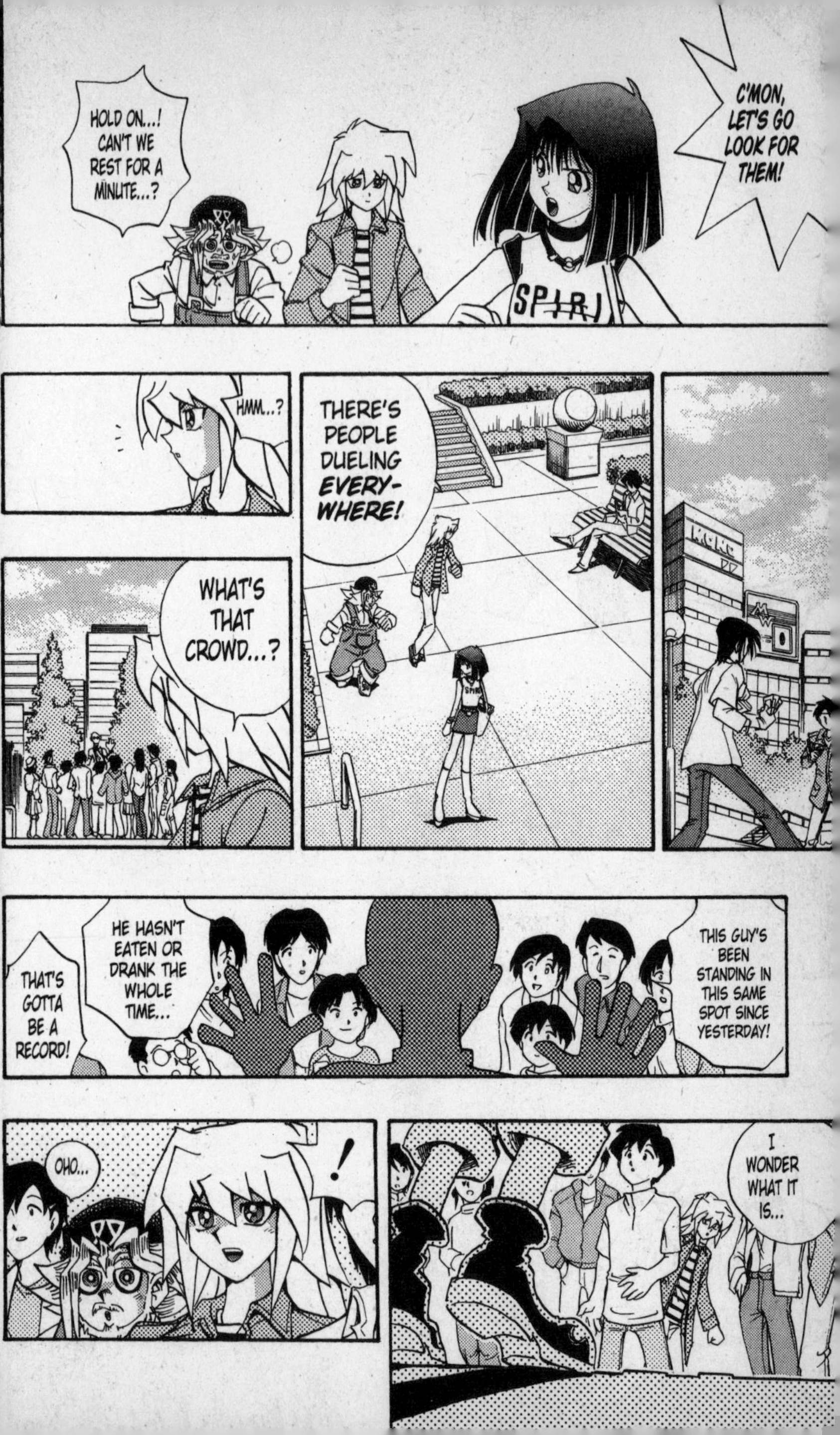
C'MON, LET'S GO LOOK FOR THEM!
HOLD ON...! CAN'T WE REST FOR A MINUTE...?
THERE'S PEOPLE DUELING EVERY-WHERE!
HMM...?
WHAT'S THAT CROWD...?
THIS GUY'S BEEN STANDING IN THIS SAME SPOT SINCE YESTERDAY!
HE HASN'T EATEN OR DRANK THE WHOLE TIME...
THAT'S GOTTA BE A RECORD!
I WONDER WHAT IT IS...
!
OHO...

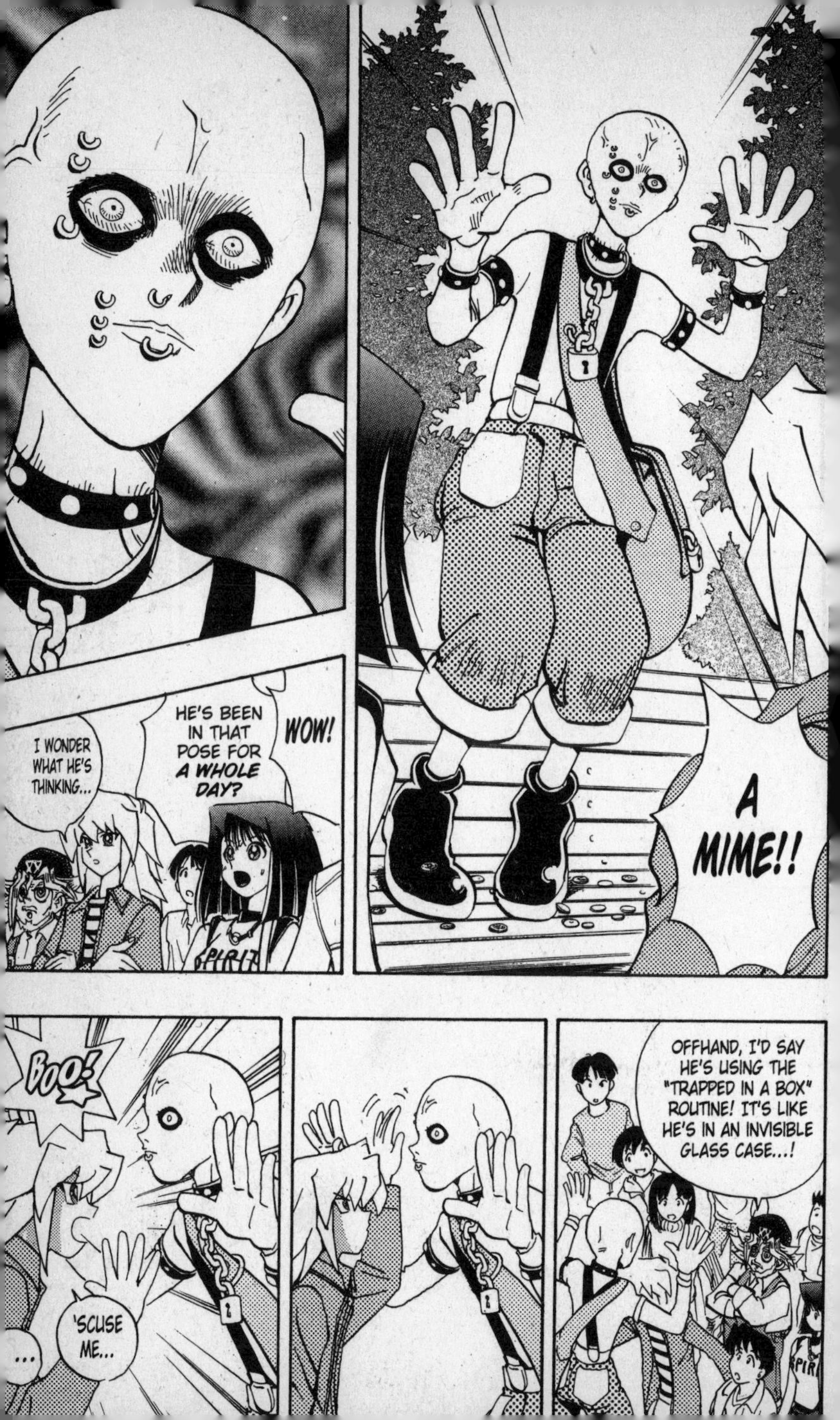
A MIME!!
WOW!
HE'S BEEN IN THAT POSE FOR A WHOLE DAY?
I WONDER WHAT HE'S THINKING...
OFFHAND, I'D SAY HE'S USING THE "TRAPPED IN A BOX" ROUTINE! IT'S LIKE HE'S IN AN INVISIBLE GLASS CASE...!
BOO!
'SCUSE ME...
...

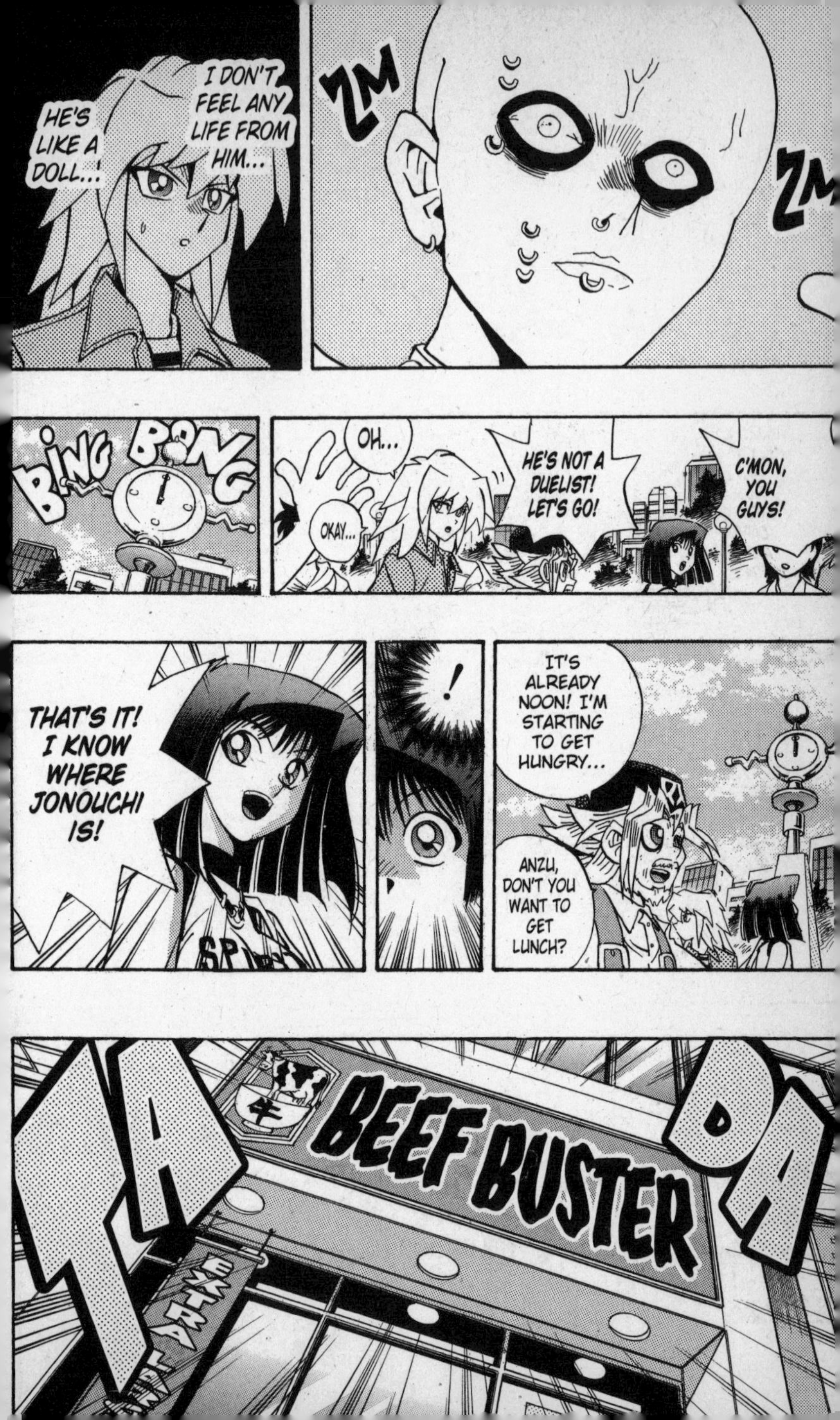
ZM
ZM
I DON'T FEEL ANY LIFE FROM HIM...
HE'S LIKE A DOLL...
C'MON, YOU GUYS!
HE'S NOT A DUELIST! LET'S GO!
OH...
OKAY...
BING BONG
IT'S ALREADY NOON! I'M STARTING TO GET HUNGRY...
ANZU, DON'T YOU WANT TO GET LUNCH?
!
THAT'S IT! I KNOW WHERE JONOUCHI IS!
TA
DA
BEEF BUSTER
EXTRA

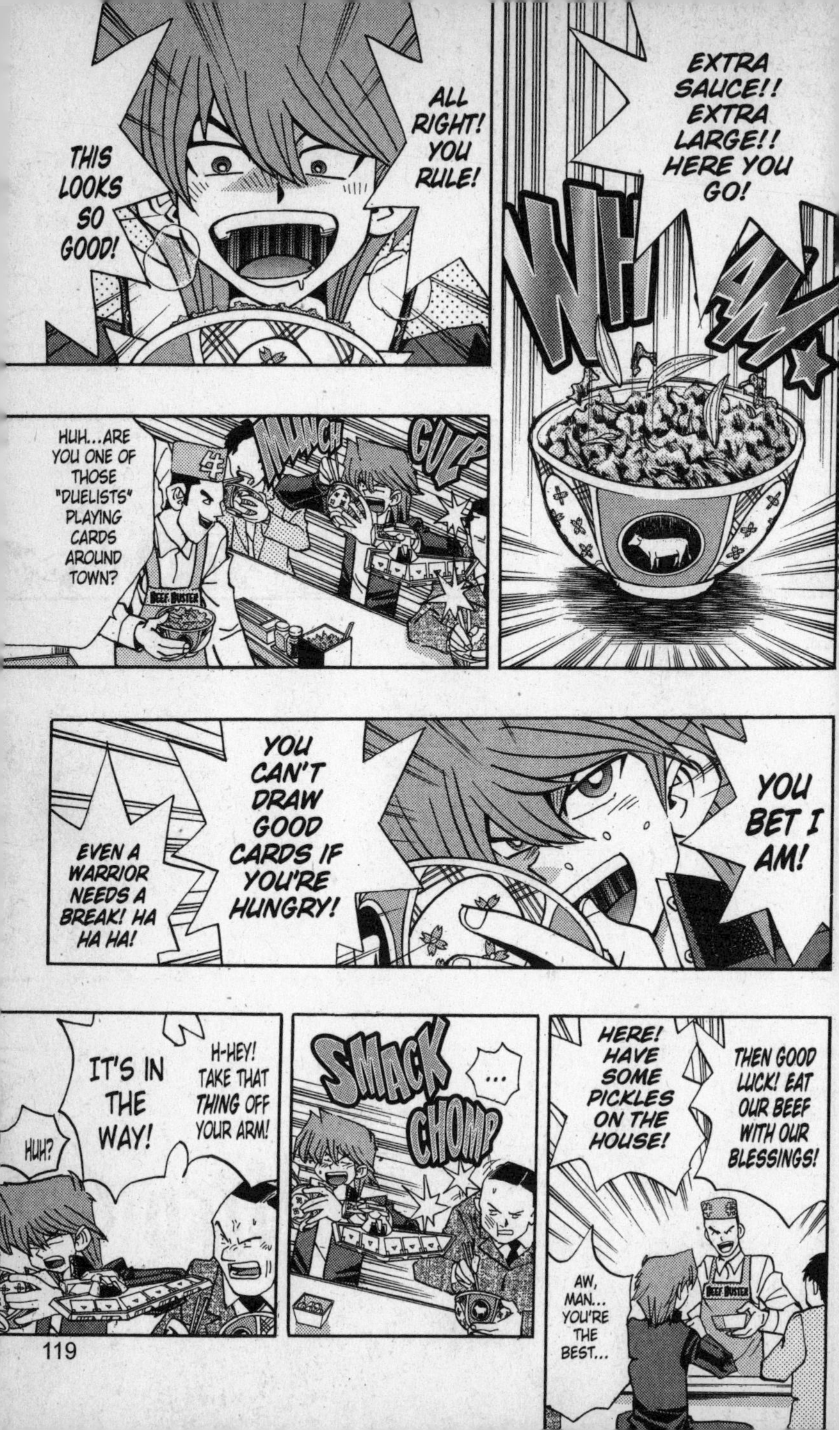
EXTRA SAUCE!! EXTRA LARGE!! HERE YOU GO!
WHAM
ALL RIGHT! YOU RULE!
THIS LOOKS SO GOOD!
MUNCH
GULP
HUH...ARE YOU ONE OF THOSE "DUELISTS" PLAYING CARDS AROUND TOWN?
BEEF BUSTER
YOU BET I AM!
YOU CAN'T DRAW GOOD CARDS IF YOU'RE HUNGRY!
EVEN A WARRIOR NEEDS A BREAK! HA HA HA!
THEN GOOD LUCK! EAT OUR BEEF WITH OUR BLESSINGS!
HERE! HAVE SOME PICKLES ON THE HOUSE!
BEEF BUSTER
AW, MAN... YOU'RE THE BEST...
...
SMACK
CHOMP
H-HEY! TAKE THAT THING OFF YOUR ARM!
IT'S IN THE WAY!
HUH?

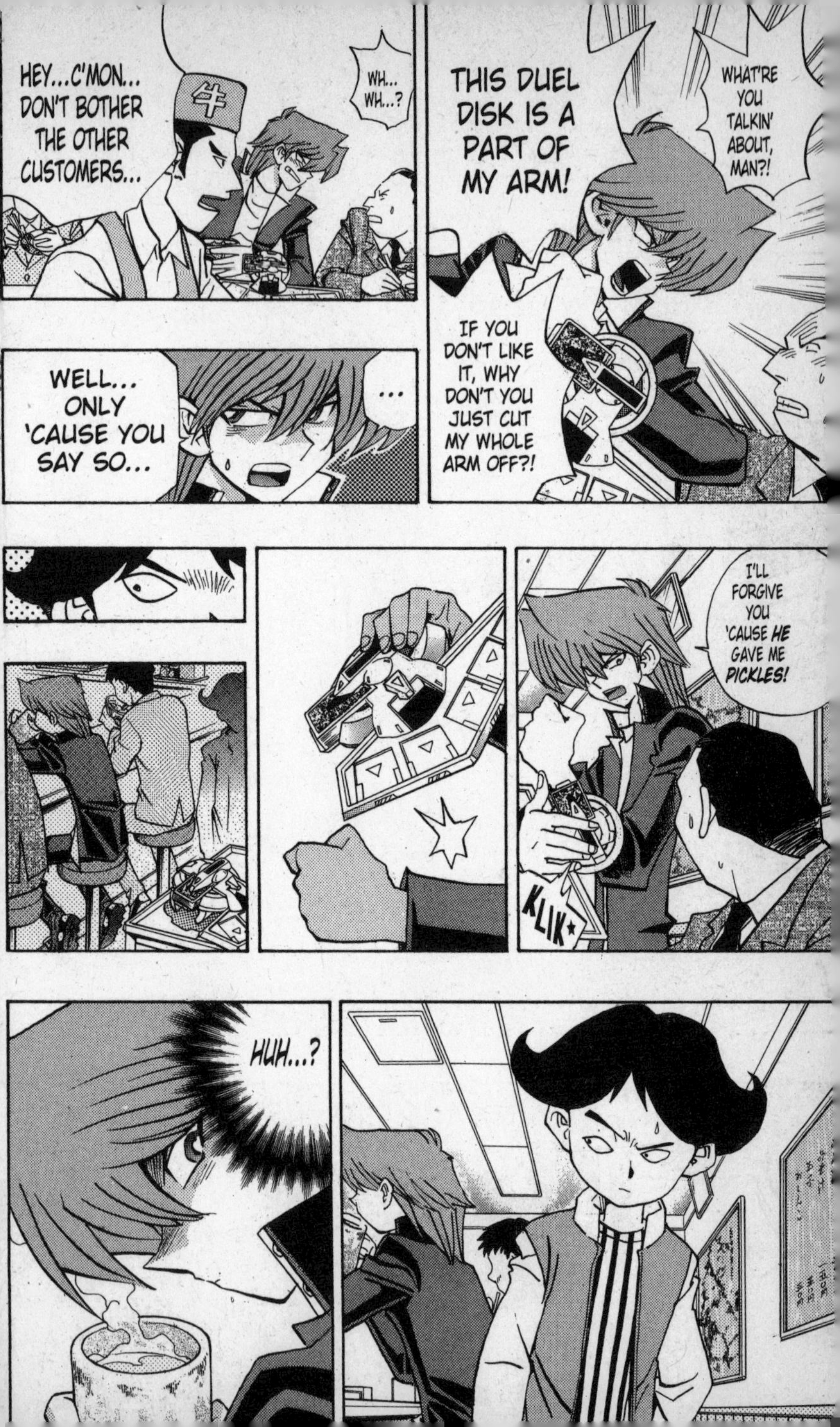
WHAT'RE YOU TALKIN' ABOUT, MAN?!
THIS DUEL DISK IS A PART OF MY ARM!
IF YOU DON'T LIKE IT, WHY DON'T YOU JUST CUT MY WHOLE ARM OFF?!
WH... WH...?
HEY...C'MON... DON'T BOTHER THE OTHER CUSTOMERS...
...
WELL... ONLY 'CAUSE YOU SAY SO...
I'LL FORGIVE YOU 'CAUSE HE GAVE ME PICKLES!
KLIK
HUH...?

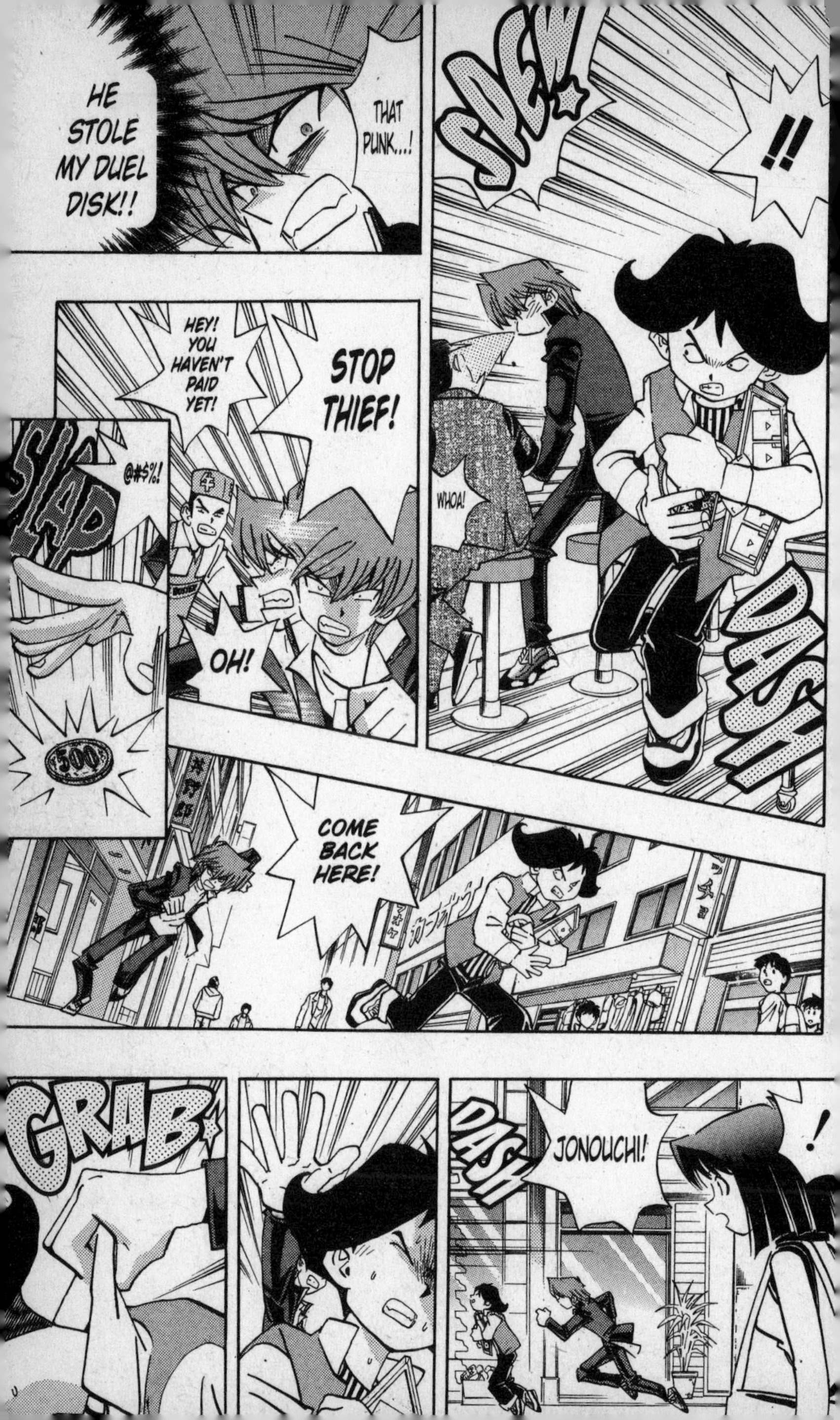
SPEW!
!!
WHOA!
DASH!!
THAT PUNK...!
HE STOLE MY DUEL DISK!!
STOP THIEF!
HEY! YOU HAVEN'T PAID YET!
OH!
@#$%!
SLAP
500
COME BACK HERE!
!
JONOUCHI!
DASH
GRAB

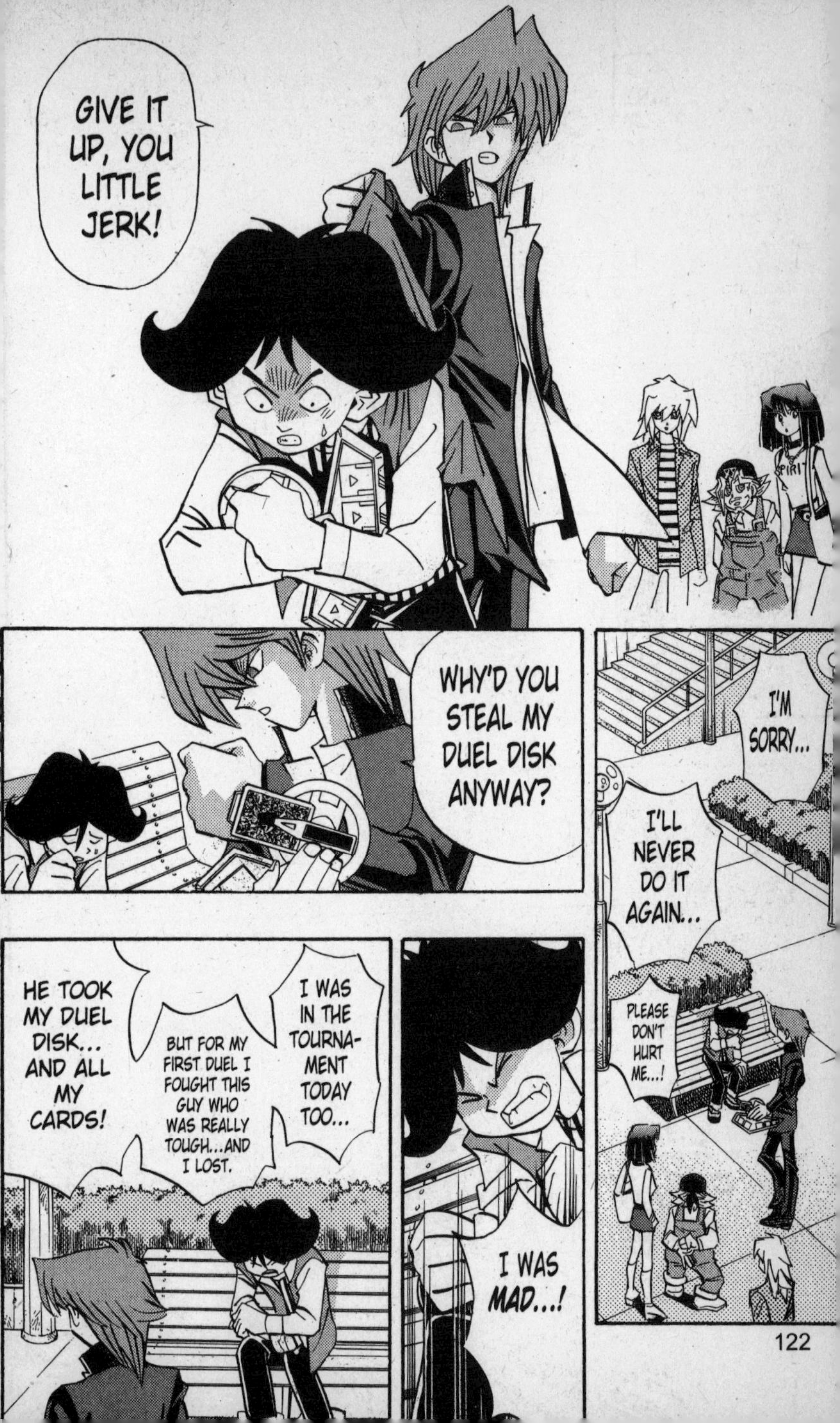
GIVE IT UP, YOU LITTLE JERK!
I'M SORRY...
I'LL NEVER DO IT AGAIN...
PLEASE DON'T HURT ME...!
WHY'D YOU STEAL MY DUEL DISK ANYWAY?
I WAS MAD...!
I WAS IN THE TOURNA-MENT TODAY TOO...
BUT FOR MY FIRST DUEL I FOUGHT THIS GUY WHO WAS REALLY TOUGH...AND I LOST.
HE TOOK MY DUEL DISK... AND ALL MY CARDS!

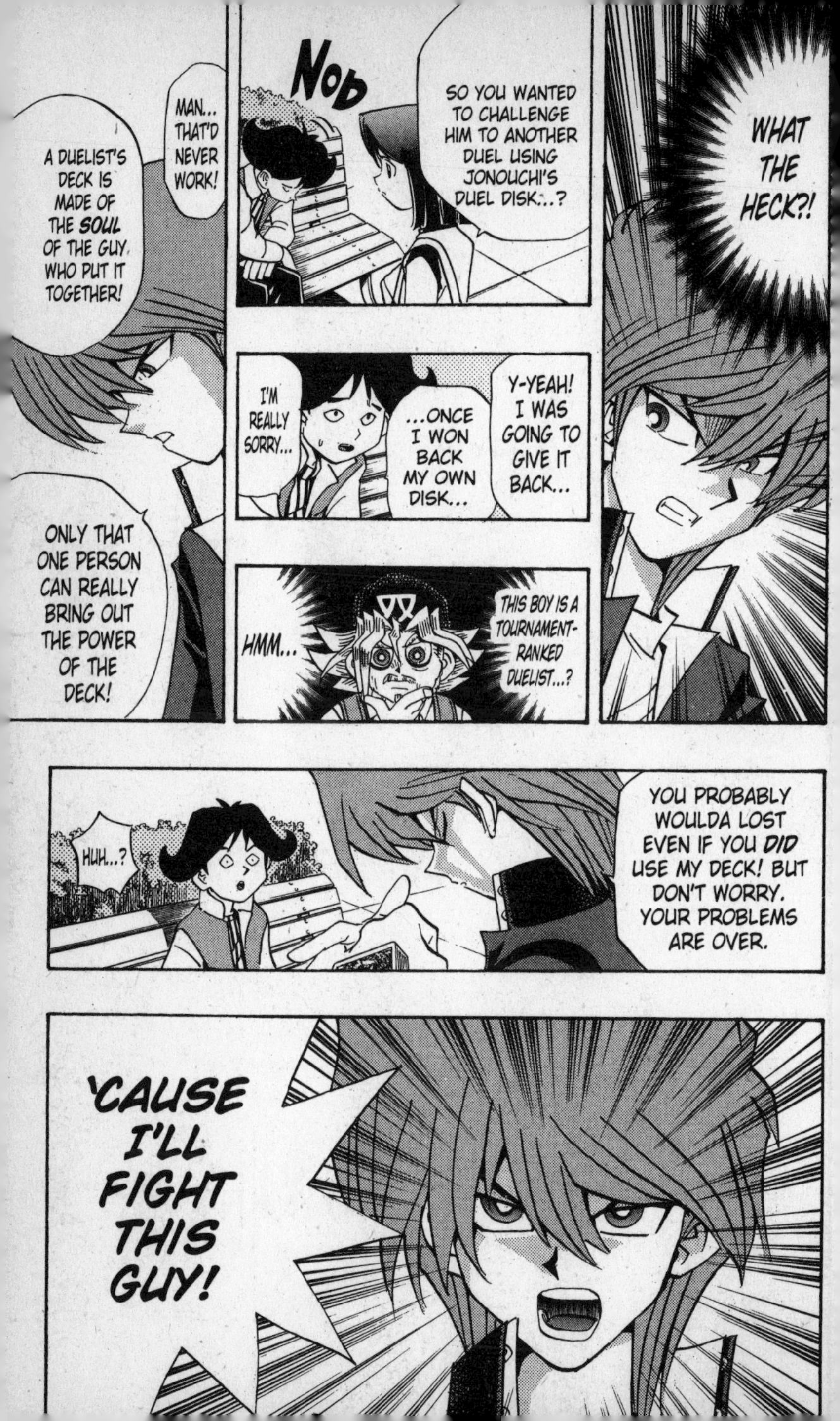
WHAT THE HECK?!
SO YOU WANTED TO CHALLENGE HIM TO ANOTHER DUEL USING JONOUCHI'S DUEL DISK...?
NOD
Y-YEAH! I WAS GOING TO GIVE IT BACK...
...ONCE I WON BACK MY OWN DISK...
I'M REALLY SORRY...
THIS BOY IS A TOURNAMENT-RANKED DUELIST...?
HMM...
MAN... THAT'D NEVER WORK!
A DUELIST'S DECK IS MADE OF THE **SOUL** OF THE GUY WHO PUT IT TOGETHER!
ONLY THAT ONE PERSON CAN REALLY BRING OUT THE POWER OF THE DECK!
YOU PROBABLY WOULDA LOST EVEN IF YOU *DID* USE MY DECK! BUT DON'T WORRY. YOUR PROBLEMS ARE OVER.
HUH...?
'CAUSE I'LL FIGHT THIS GUY!

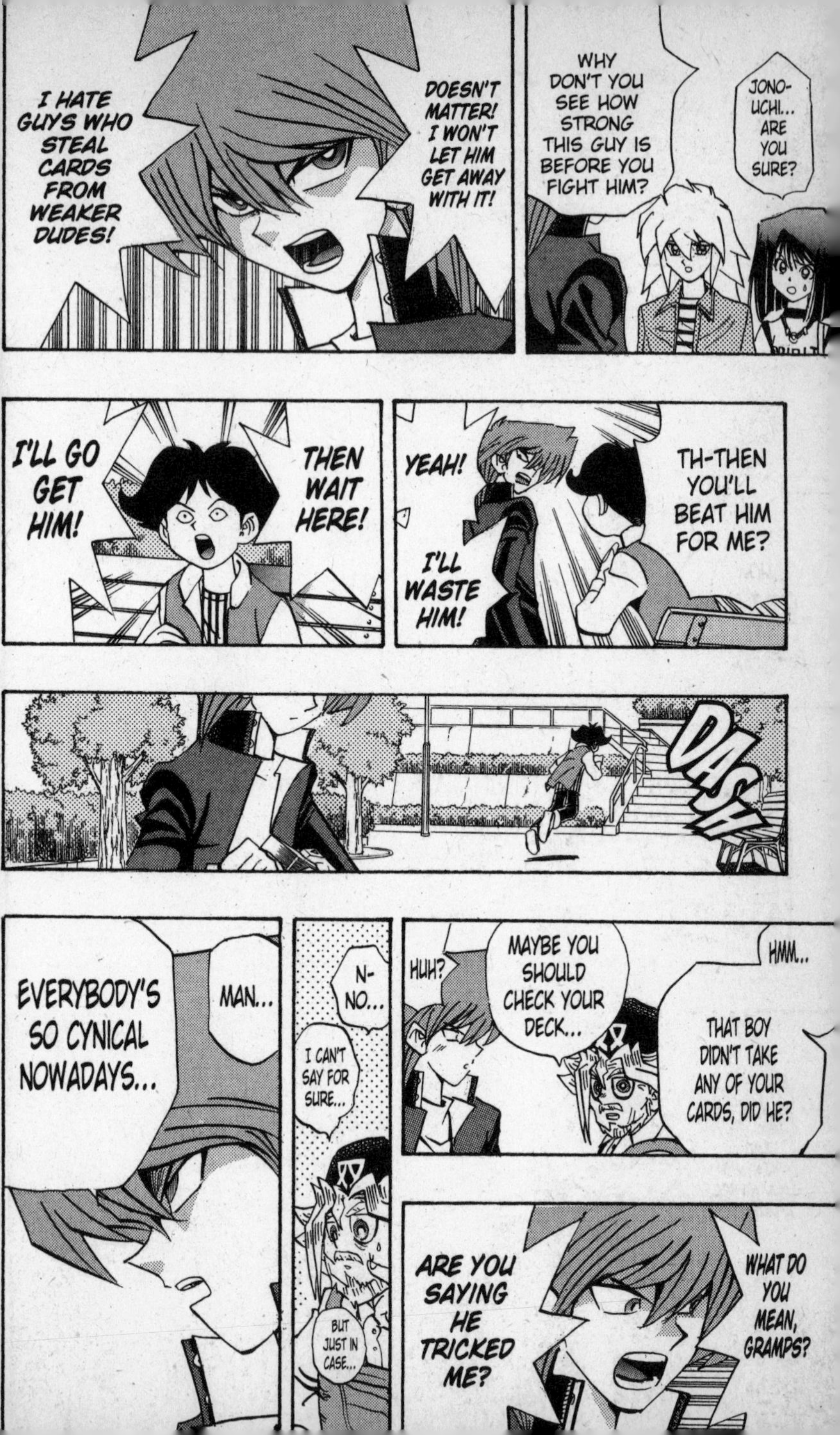
JONO-UCHI... ARE YOU SURE?
WHY DON'T YOU SEE HOW STRONG THIS GUY IS BEFORE YOU FIGHT HIM?
DOESN'T MATTER! I WON'T LET HIM GET AWAY WITH IT!
I HATE GUYS WHO STEAL CARDS FROM WEAKER DUDES!
TH-THEN YOU'LL BEAT HIM FOR ME?
YEAH!
I'LL WASTE HIM!
THEN WAIT HERE!
I'LL GO GET HIM!
DASH
HMM..
THAT BOY DIDN'T TAKE ANY OF YOUR CARDS, DID HE?
MAYBE YOU SHOULD CHECK YOUR DECK...
HUH?
WHAT DO YOU MEAN, GRAMPS?
ARE YOU SAYING HE TRICKED ME?
N-NO...
I CAN'T SAY FOR SURE...
BUT JUST IN CASE...
MAN...
EVERYBODY'S SO CYNICAL NOWADAYS...

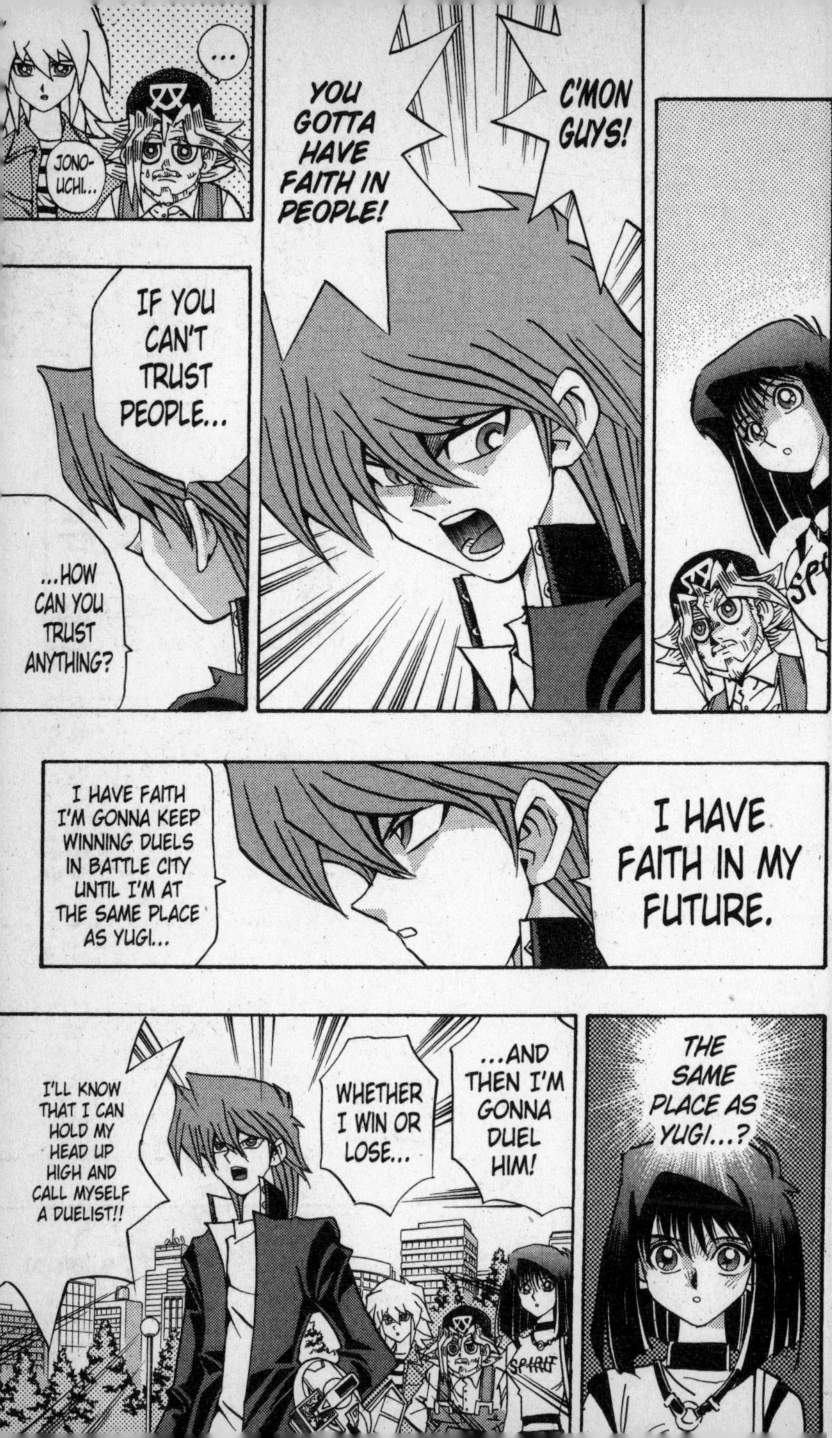
C'MON GUYS!
YOU GOTTA HAVE FAITH IN PEOPLE!
...
JONO-UCHI...
IF YOU CAN'T TRUST PEOPLE...
...HOW CAN YOU TRUST ANYTHING?
I HAVE FAITH IN MY FUTURE.
I HAVE FAITH I'M GONNA KEEP WINNING DUELS IN BATTLE CITY UNTIL I'M AT THE SAME PLACE AS YUGI...
THE SAME PLACE AS YUGI...?
...AND THEN I'M GONNA DUEL HIM!
WHETHER I WIN OR LOSE...
I'LL KNOW THAT I CAN HOLD MY HEAD UP HIGH AND CALL MYSELF A DUELIST!!
SPIRIT

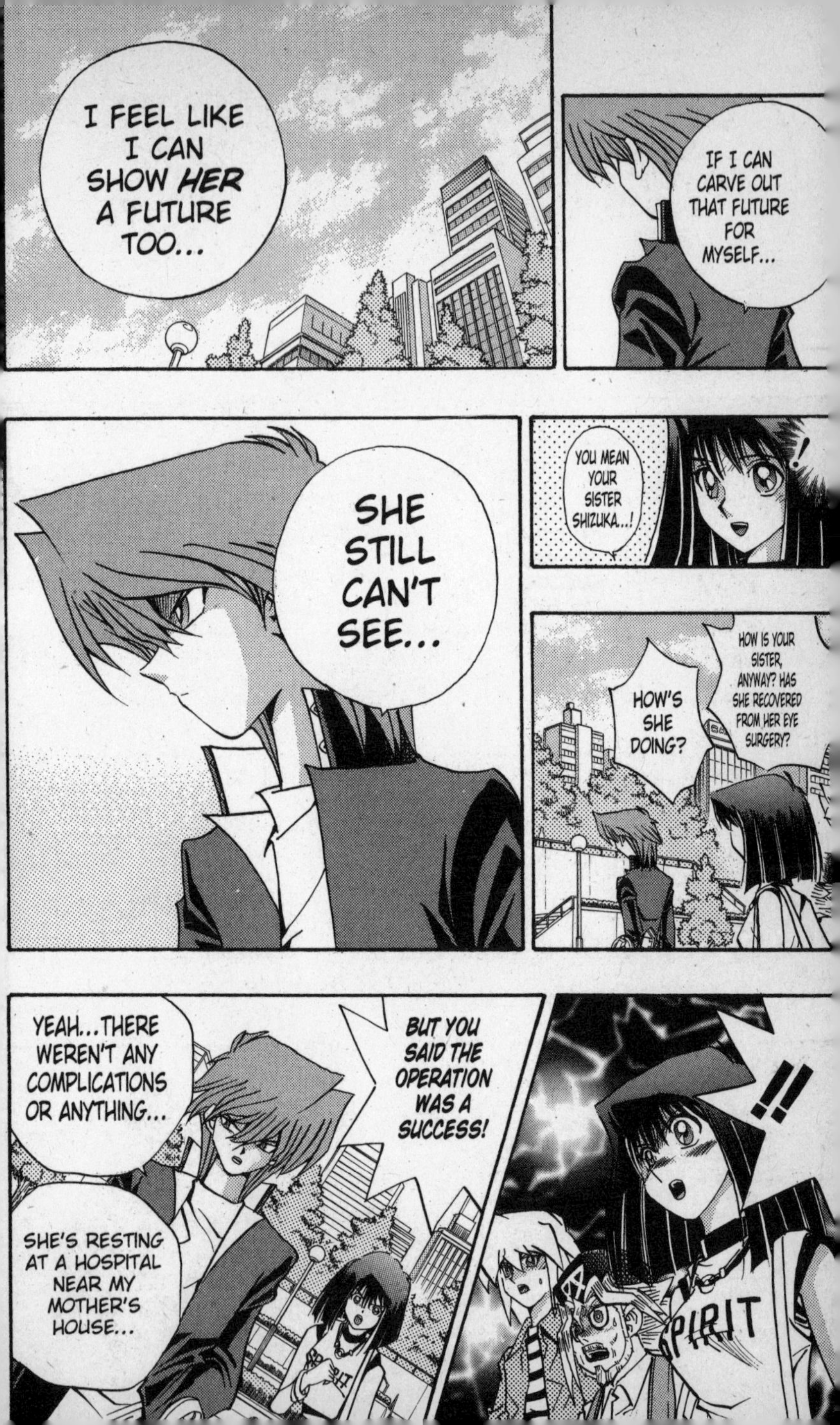
IF I CAN CARVE OUT THAT FUTURE FOR MYSELF...
I FEEL LIKE I CAN SHOW *HER* A FUTURE TOO...
!
YOU MEAN YOUR SISTER SHIZUKA...!
HOW IS YOUR SISTER, ANYWAY? HAS SHE RECOVERED FROM HER EYE SURGERY?
HOW'S SHE DOING?
SHE STILL CAN'T SEE...
!!
SPIRIT
BUT YOU SAID THE OPERATION WAS A SUCCESS!
YEAH...THERE WEREN'T ANY COMPLICATIONS OR ANYTHING...
SHE'S RESTING AT A HOSPITAL NEAR MY MOTHER'S HOUSE...

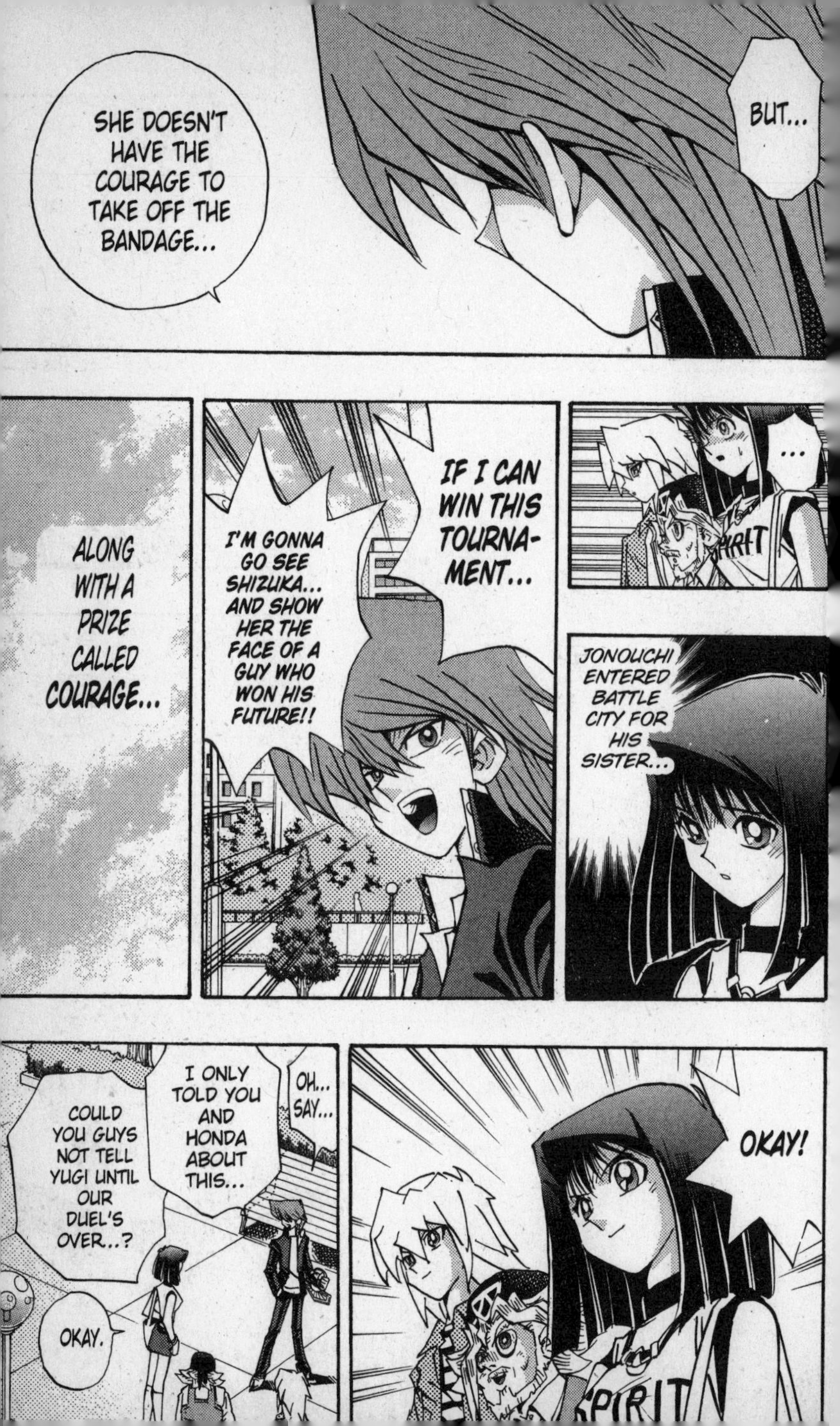
BUT...
SHE DOESN'T HAVE THE COURAGE TO TAKE OFF THE BANDAGE...
...
JONOUCHI ENTERED BATTLE CITY FOR HIS SISTER...
IF I CAN WIN THIS TOURNA-MENT...
I'M GONNA GO SEE SHIZUKA... AND SHOW HER THE FACE OF A GUY WHO WON HIS FUTURE!!
ALONG WITH A PRIZE CALLED COURAGE...
OKAY!
OH... SAY...
I ONLY TOLD YOU AND HONDA ABOUT THIS...
COULD YOU GUYS NOT TELL YUGI UNTIL OUR DUEL'S OVER...?
OKAY.

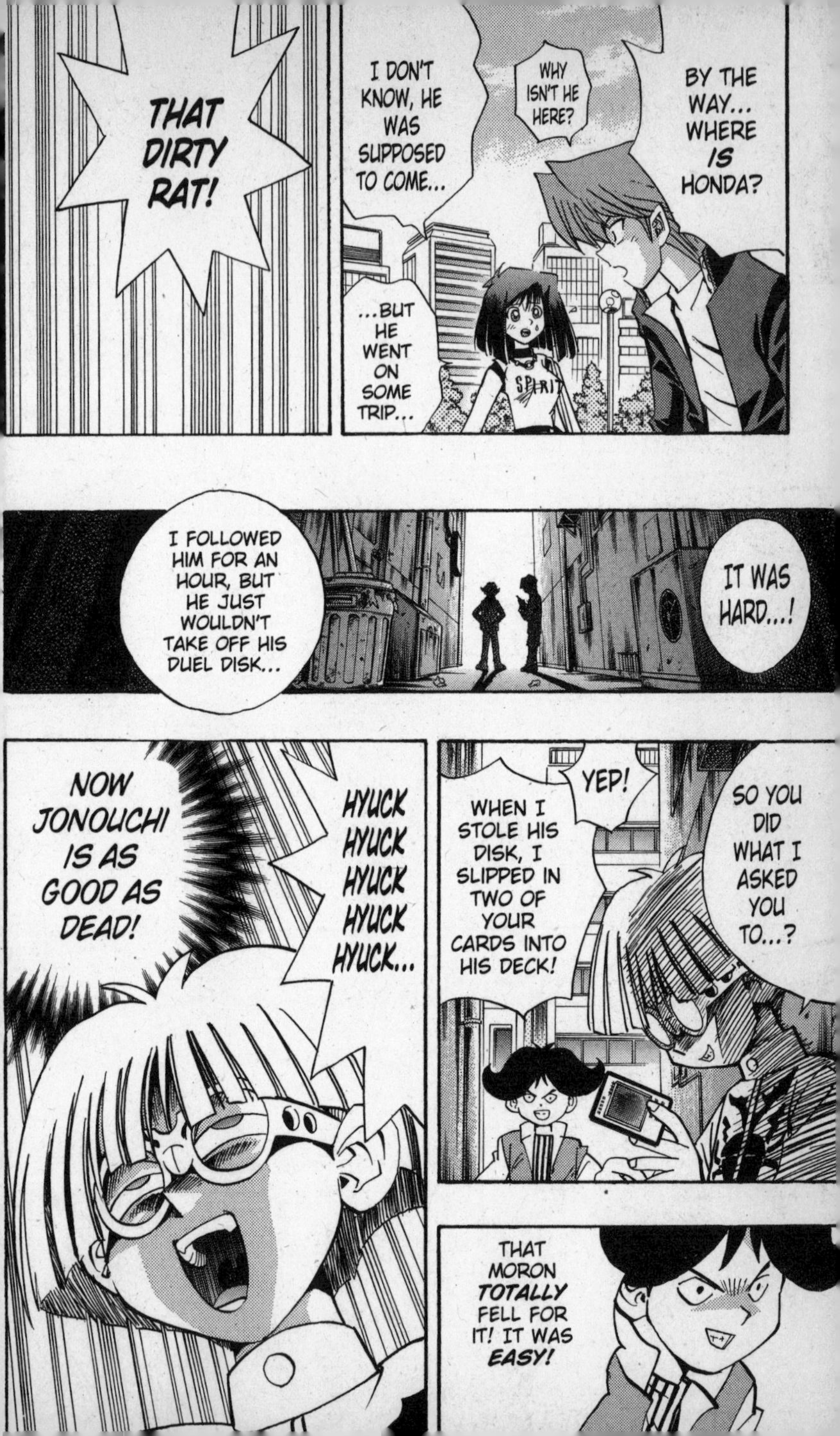
BY THE WAY... WHERE IS HONDA?
WHY ISN'T HE HERE?
I DON'T KNOW, HE WAS SUPPOSED TO COME...
...BUT HE WENT ON SOME TRIP...
SPIRIT
THAT DIRTY RAT!
IT WAS HARD...!
I FOLLOWED HIM FOR AN HOUR, BUT HE JUST WOULDN'T TAKE OFF HIS DUEL DISK...
SO YOU DID WHAT I ASKED YOU TO...?
YEP!
WHEN I STOLE HIS DISK, I SLIPPED IN TWO OF YOUR CARDS INTO HIS DECK!
THAT MORON TOTALLY FELL FOR IT! IT WAS EASY!
HYUCK HYUCK HYUCK HYUCK HYUCK...
NOW JONOUCHI IS AS GOOD AS DEAD!

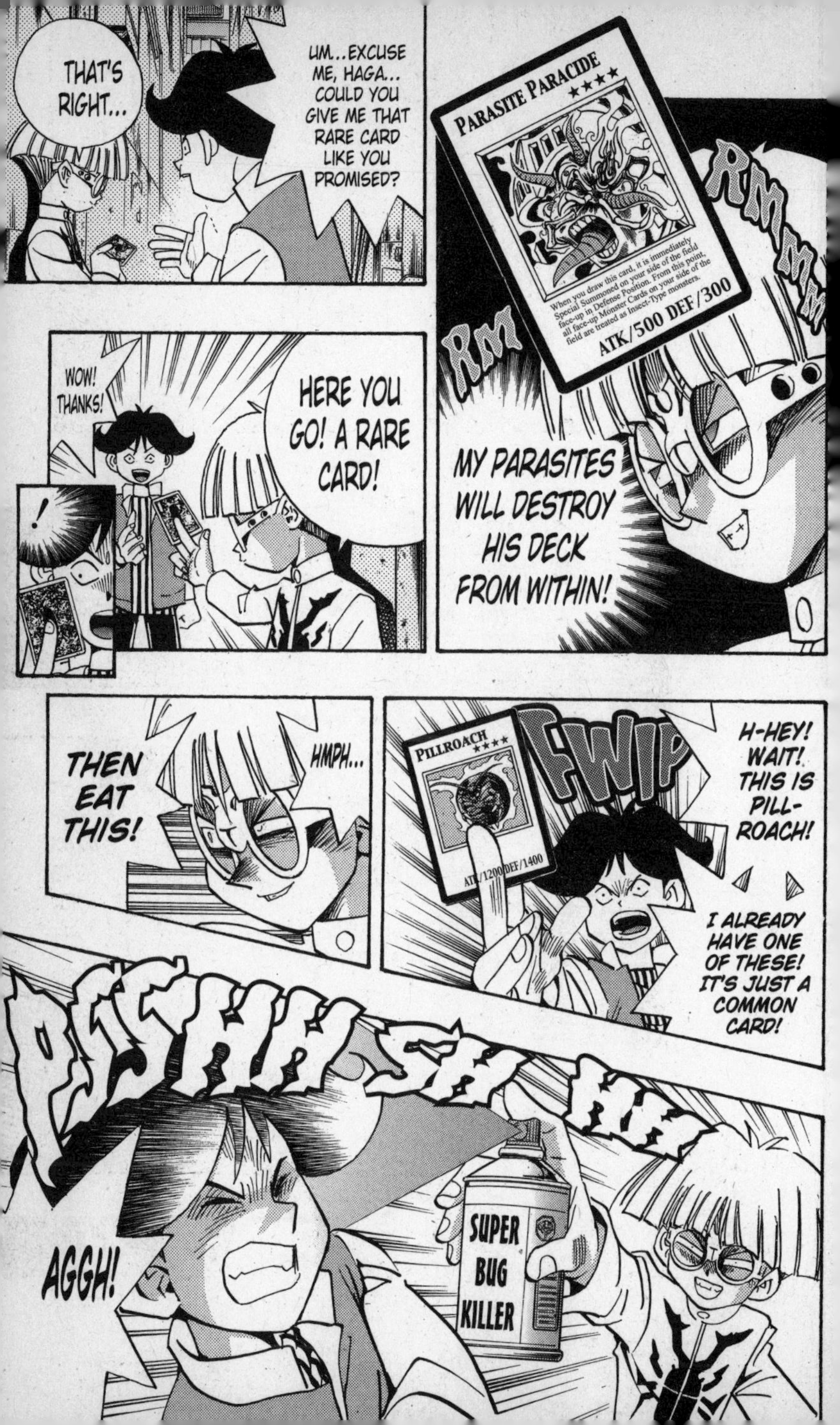
PARASITE PARACIDE ★★★★
When you draw this card, it is immediately Special Summoned on your side of the field face-up in Defense Position. From this point, all face-up Monster Cards on your side of the field are treated as Insect-Type monsters.
ATK/500 DEF/300
RMMMM
RM
MY PARASITES WILL DESTROY HIS DECK FROM WITHIN!
UM...EXCUSE ME, HAGA... COULD YOU GIVE ME THAT RARE CARD LIKE YOU PROMISED?
THAT'S RIGHT...
HERE YOU GO! A RARE CARD!
WOW! THANKS!
!
FWIP
H-HEY! WAIT! THIS IS PILL-ROACH!
PILLROACH ★★★★
ATK/1200 DEF/1400
I ALREADY HAVE ONE OF THESE! IT'S JUST A COMMON CARD!
HMPH...
THEN EAT THIS!
SUPER BUG KILLER
AGGH!

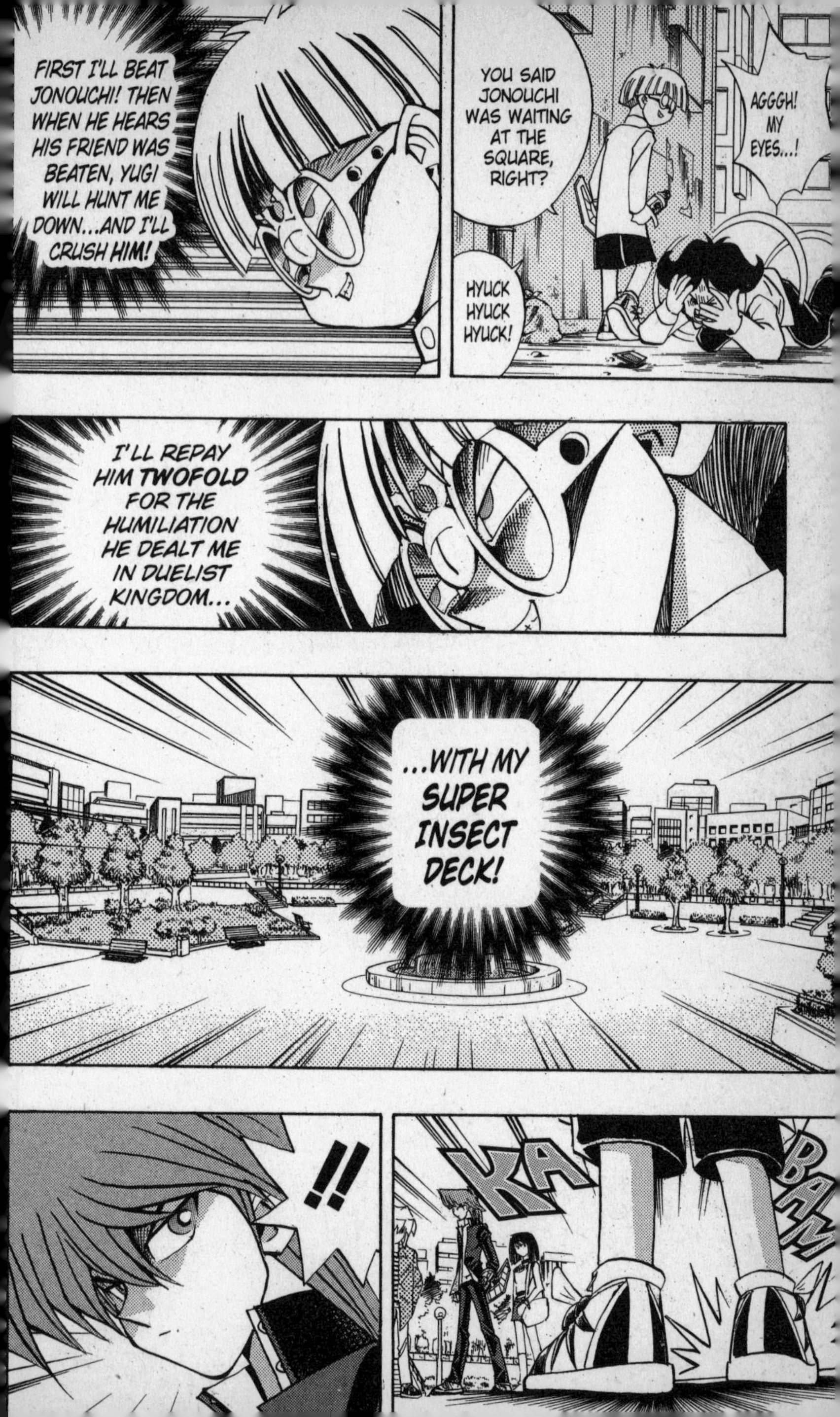
AGGGH! MY EYES...!
YOU SAID JONOUCHI WAS WAITING AT THE SQUARE, RIGHT?
HYUCK HYUCK HYUCK!
FIRST I'LL BEAT JONOUCHI! THEN WHEN HE HEARS HIS FRIEND WAS BEATEN, YUGI WILL HUNT ME DOWN...AND I'LL CRUSH HIM!
I'LL REPAY HIM TWOFOLD FOR THE HUMILIATION HE DEALT ME IN DUELIST KINGDOM...
...WITH MY SUPER INSECT DECK!
KA BAM
!!

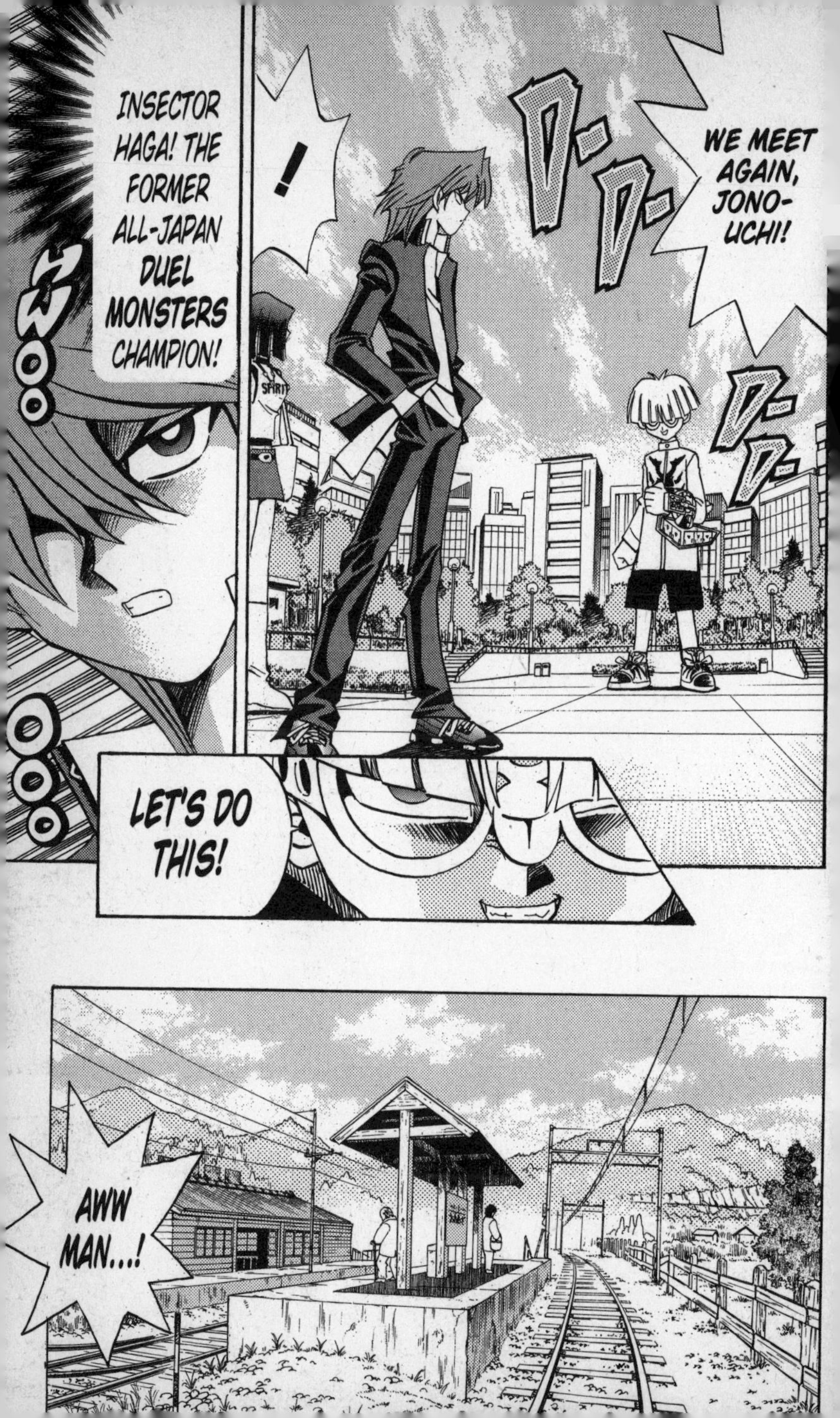

!
WE MEET AGAIN, JONO-UCHI!
LET'S DO THIS!
INSECTOR HAGA! THE FORMER ALL-JAPAN DUEL MONSTERS CHAMPION!
AWW MAN...!

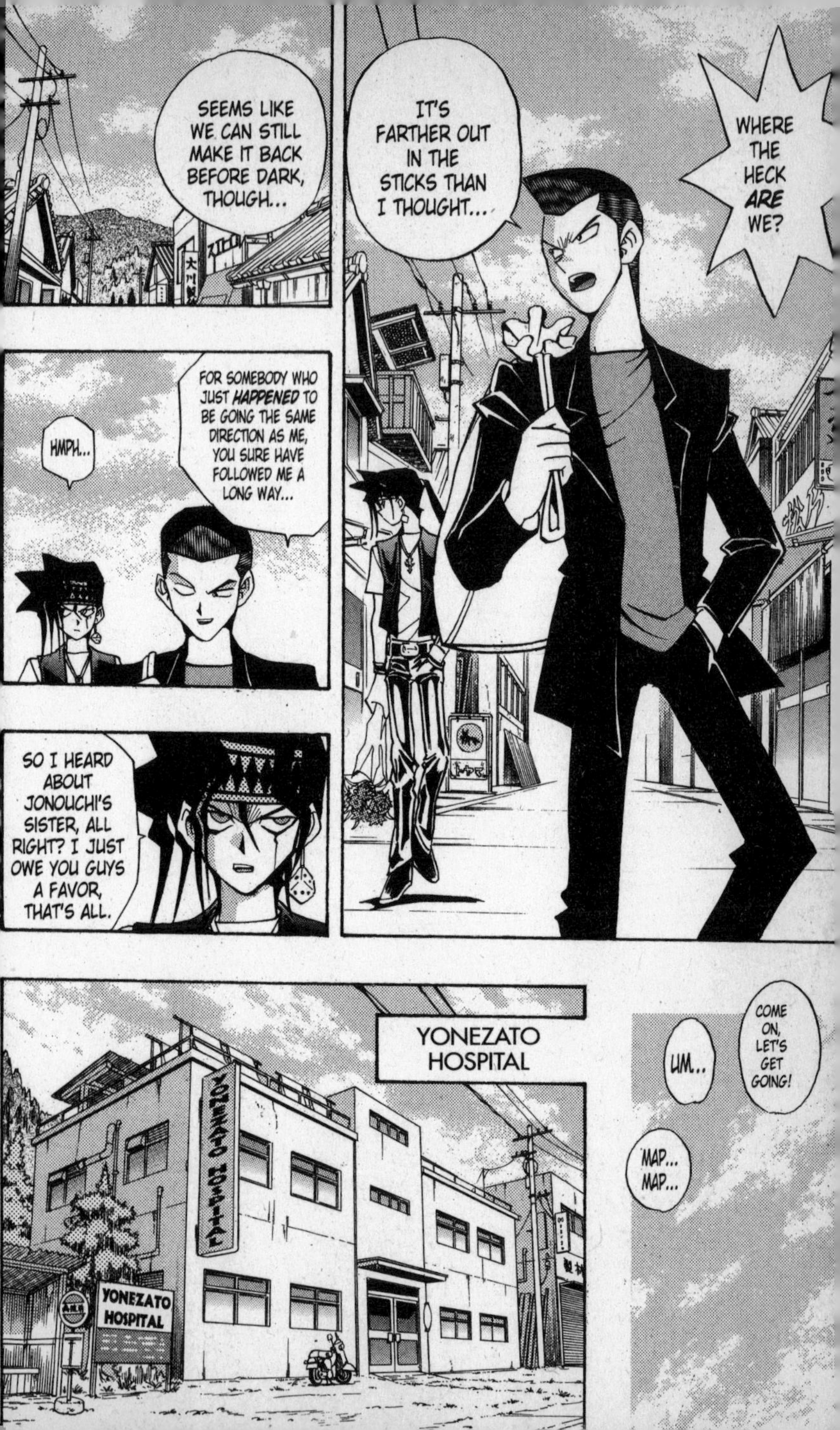
WHERE THE HECK *ARE* WE?
IT'S FARTHER OUT IN THE STICKS THAN I THOUGHT...
SEEMS LIKE WE CAN STILL MAKE IT BACK BEFORE DARK, THOUGH...
FOR SOMEBODY WHO JUST *HAPPENED* TO BE GOING THE SAME DIRECTION AS ME, YOU SURE HAVE FOLLOWED ME A LONG WAY...
HMPH...
SO I HEARD ABOUT JONOUCHI'S SISTER, ALL RIGHT? I JUST OWE YOU GUYS A FAVOR, THAT'S ALL.
COME ON, LET'S GET GOING!
UM...
MAP... MAP...
YONEZATO HOSPITAL
YONEZATO HOSPITAL
YONEZATO HOSPITAL

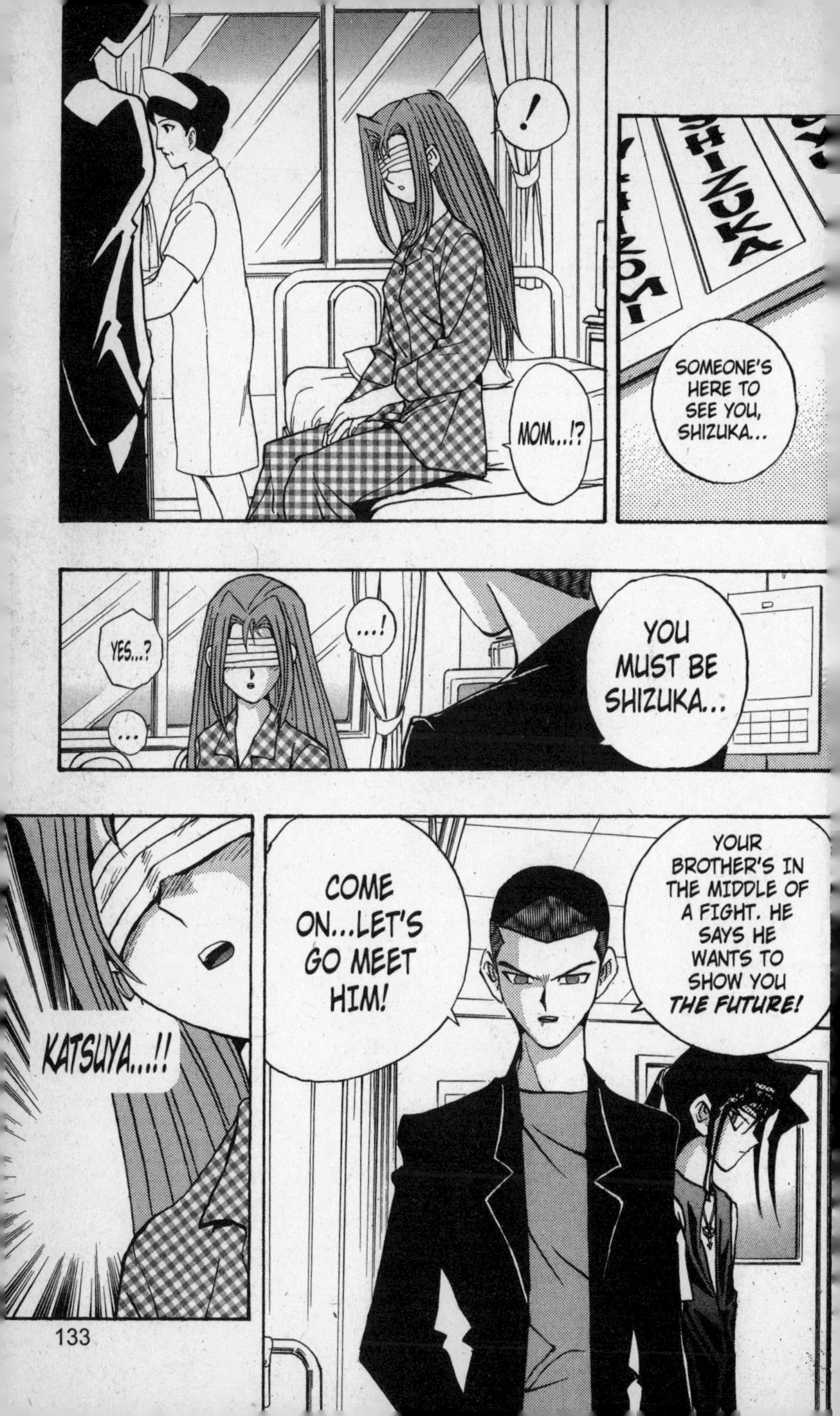
SHIZUKA
SOMEONE'S HERE TO SEE YOU, SHIZUKA...
!
MOM...!?
YOU MUST BE SHIZUKA...
...!
YES...?
...
YOUR BROTHER'S IN THE MIDDLE OF A FIGHT. HE SAYS HE WANTS TO SHOW YOU *THE FUTURE!*
COME ON...LET'S GO MEET HIM!
KATSUYA...!!

DUEL DISK DIAGRAM

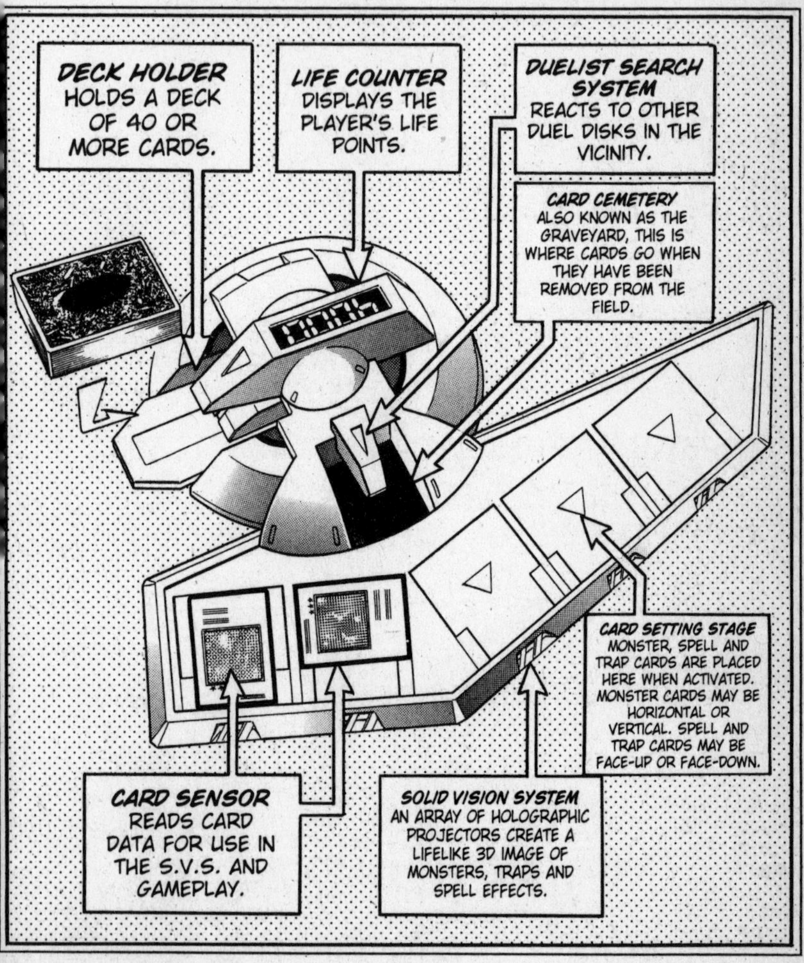
DECK HOLDER
HOLDS A DECK OF 40 OR MORE CARDS.
LIFE COUNTER
DISPLAYS THE PLAYER'S LIFE POINTS.
DUELIST SEARCH SYSTEM
REACTS TO OTHER DUEL DISKS IN THE VICINITY.
CARD CEMETERY
ALSO KNOWN AS THE GRAVEYARD, THIS IS WHERE CARDS GO WHEN THEY HAVE BEEN REMOVED FROM THE FIELD.
CARD SETTING STAGE
MONSTER, SPELL AND TRAP CARDS ARE PLACED HERE WHEN ACTIVATED. MONSTER CARDS MAY BE HORIZONTAL OR VERTICAL. SPELL AND TRAP CARDS MAY BE FACE-UP OR FACE-DOWN.
CARD SENSOR
READS CARD DATA FOR USE IN THE S.V.S. AND GAMEPLAY.
SOLID VISION SYSTEM
AN ARRAY OF HOLOGRAPHIC PROJECTORS CREATE A LIFELIKE 3D IMAGE OF MONSTERS, TRAPS AND SPELL EFFECTS.

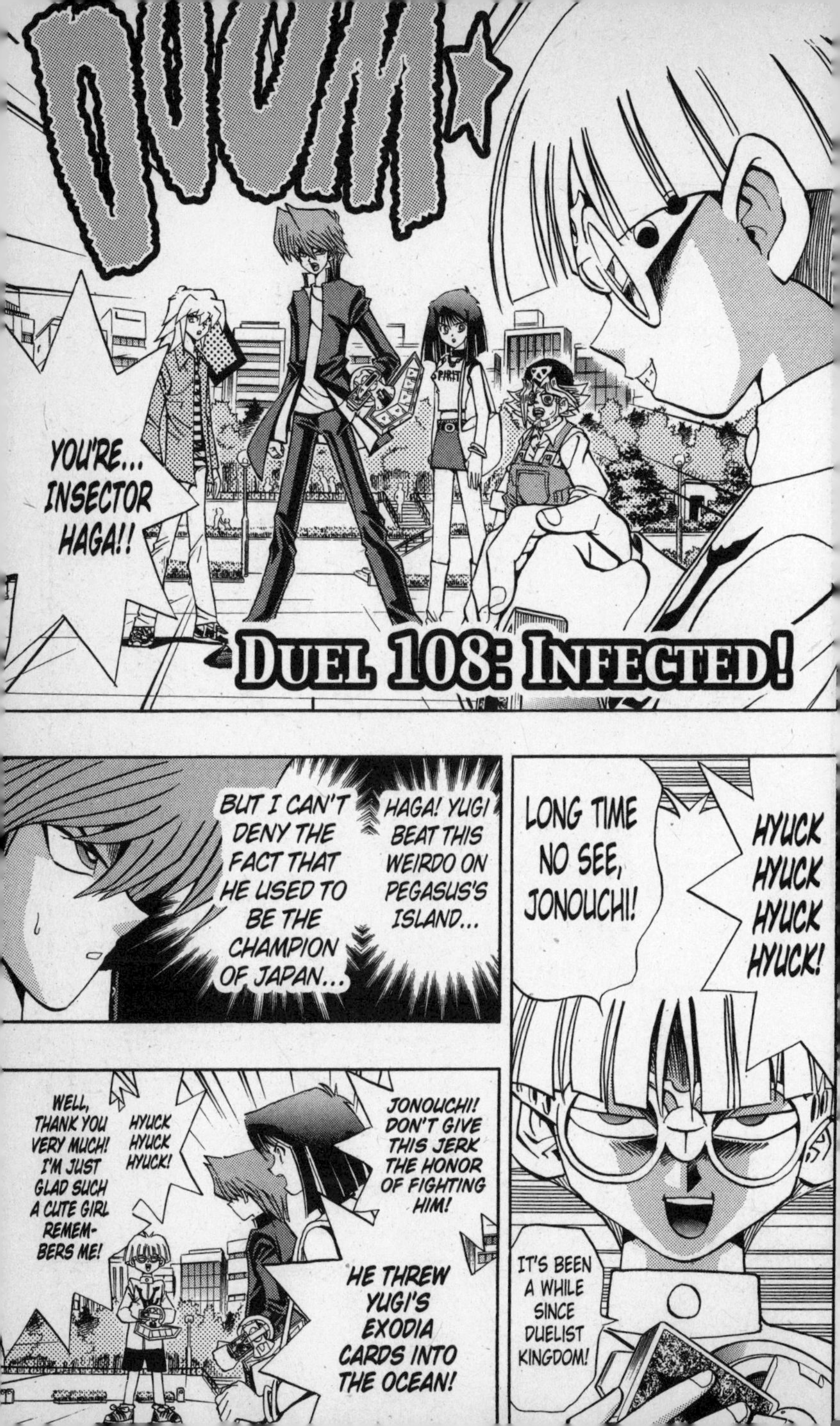
YOU'RE... INSECTOR HAGA!!
DUEL 108: INFECTED!
HYUCK HYUCK HYUCK HYUCK!
LONG TIME NO SEE, JONOUCHI!
IT'S BEEN A WHILE SINCE DUELIST KINGDOM!
HAGA! YUGI BEAT THIS WEIRDO ON PEGASUS'S ISLAND...
BUT I CAN'T DENY THE FACT THAT HE USED TO BE THE CHAMPION OF JAPAN...
JONOUCHI! DON'T GIVE THIS JERK THE HONOR OF FIGHTING HIM!
HE THREW YUGI'S EXODIA CARDS INTO THE OCEAN!
HYUCK HYUCK HYUCK!
WELL, THANK YOU VERY MUCH! I'M JUST GLAD SUCH A CUTE GIRL REMEMBERS ME!

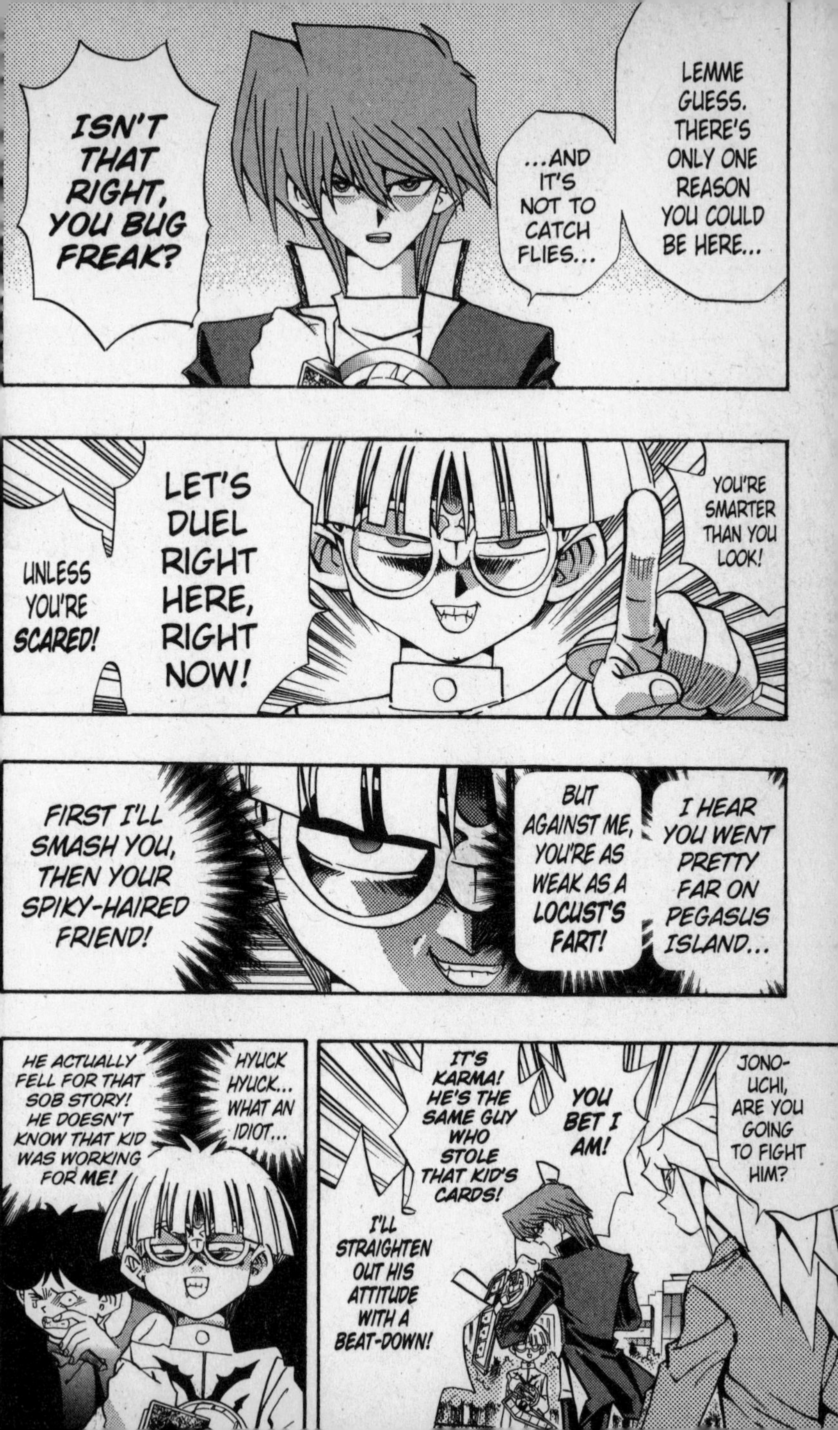

LEMME GUESS. THERE'S ONLY ONE REASON YOU COULD BE HERE...
...AND IT'S NOT TO CATCH FLIES...
ISN'T THAT RIGHT, YOU BUG FREAK?
YOU'RE SMARTER THAN YOU LOOK!
LET'S DUEL RIGHT HERE, RIGHT NOW!
UNLESS YOU'RE SCARED!
I HEAR YOU WENT PRETTY FAR ON PEGASUS ISLAND...
BUT AGAINST ME, YOU'RE AS WEAK AS A LOCUST'S FART!
FIRST I'LL SMASH YOU, THEN YOUR SPIKY-HAIRED FRIEND!
JONO-UCHI, ARE YOU GOING TO FIGHT HIM?
YOU BET I AM!
IT'S KARMA! HE'S THE SAME GUY WHO STOLE THAT KID'S CARDS!
I'LL STRAIGHTEN OUT HIS ATTITUDE WITH A BEAT-DOWN!
HYUCK HYUCK... WHAT AN IDIOT...
HE ACTUALLY FELL FOR THAT SOB STORY! HE DOESN'T KNOW THAT KID WAS WORKING FOR ME!

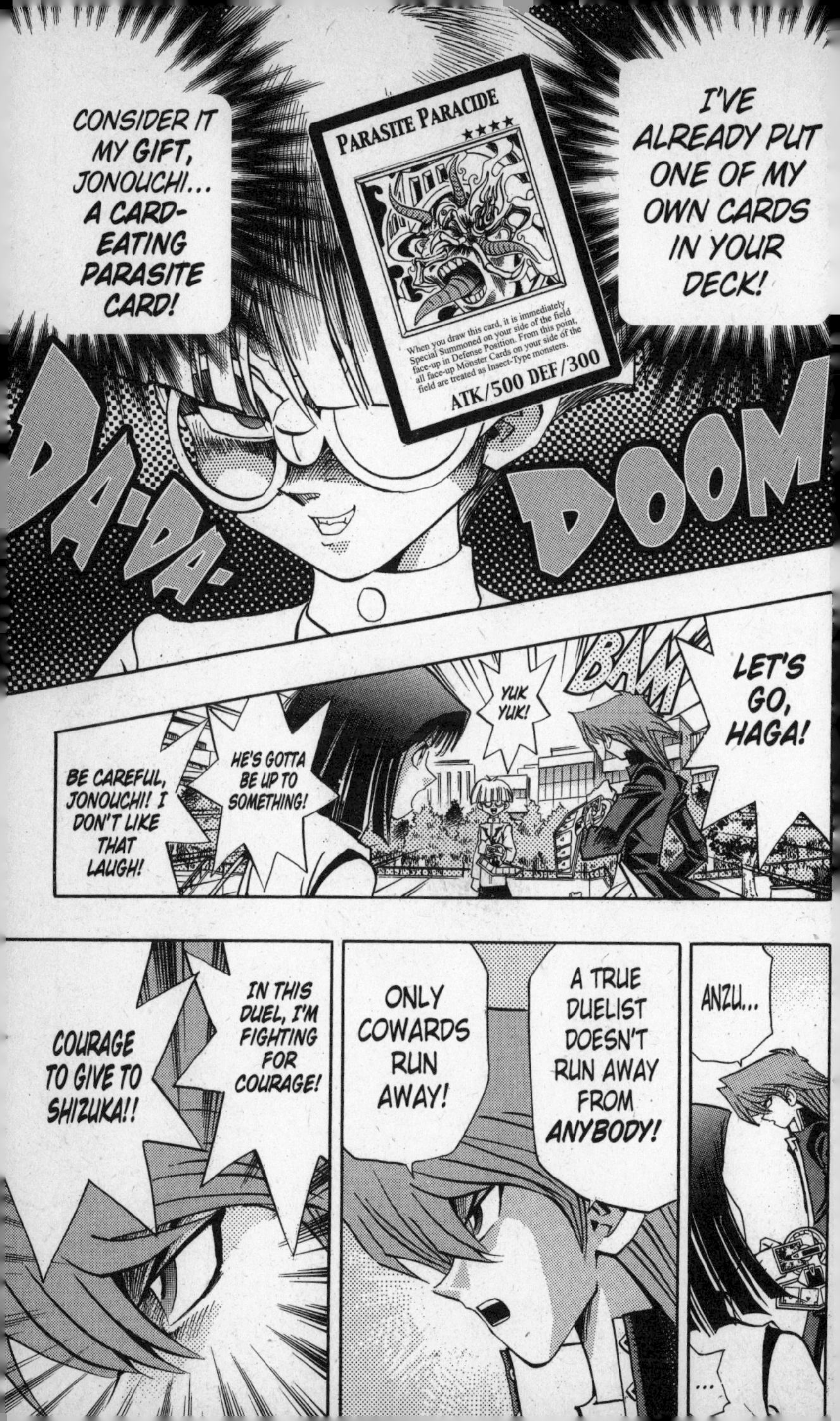
I'VE ALREADY PUT ONE OF MY OWN CARDS IN YOUR DECK!
CONSIDER IT MY GIFT, JONOUCHI... A CARD-EATING PARASITE CARD!
PARASITE PARACIDE
When you draw this card, it is immediately Special Summoned on your side of the field face-up in Defense Position. From this point, all face-up Monster Cards on your side of the field are treated as Insect-Type monsters.
ATK/500 DEF/300
DA-DA-DOOM
LET'S GO, HAGA!
BAM
YUK YUK!
HE'S GOTTA BE UP TO SOMETHING!
BE CAREFUL, JONOUCHI! I DON'T LIKE THAT LAUGH!
ANZU...
...
A TRUE DUELIST DOESN'T RUN AWAY FROM ANYBODY!
ONLY COWARDS RUN AWAY!
IN THIS DUEL, I'M FIGHTING FOR COURAGE!
COURAGE TO GIVE TO SHIZUKA!!

Duel 108: Infected!

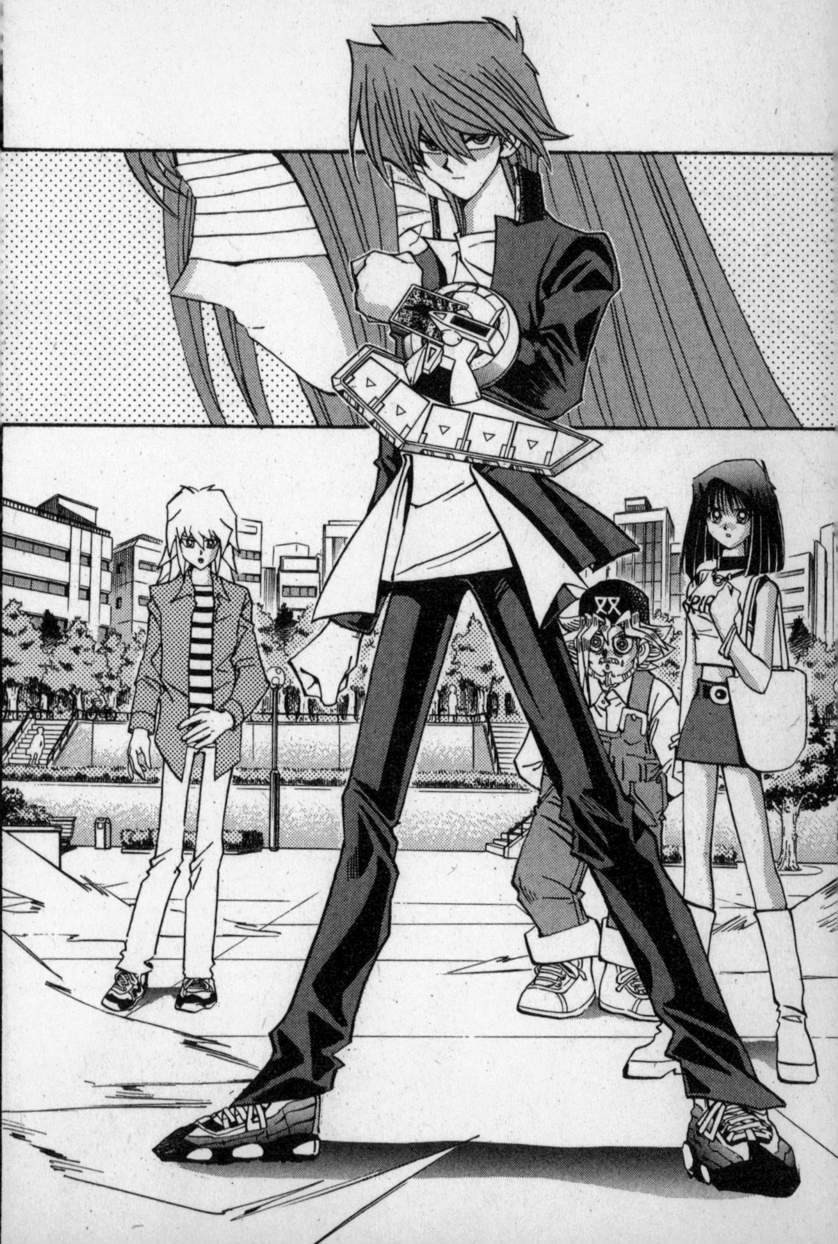

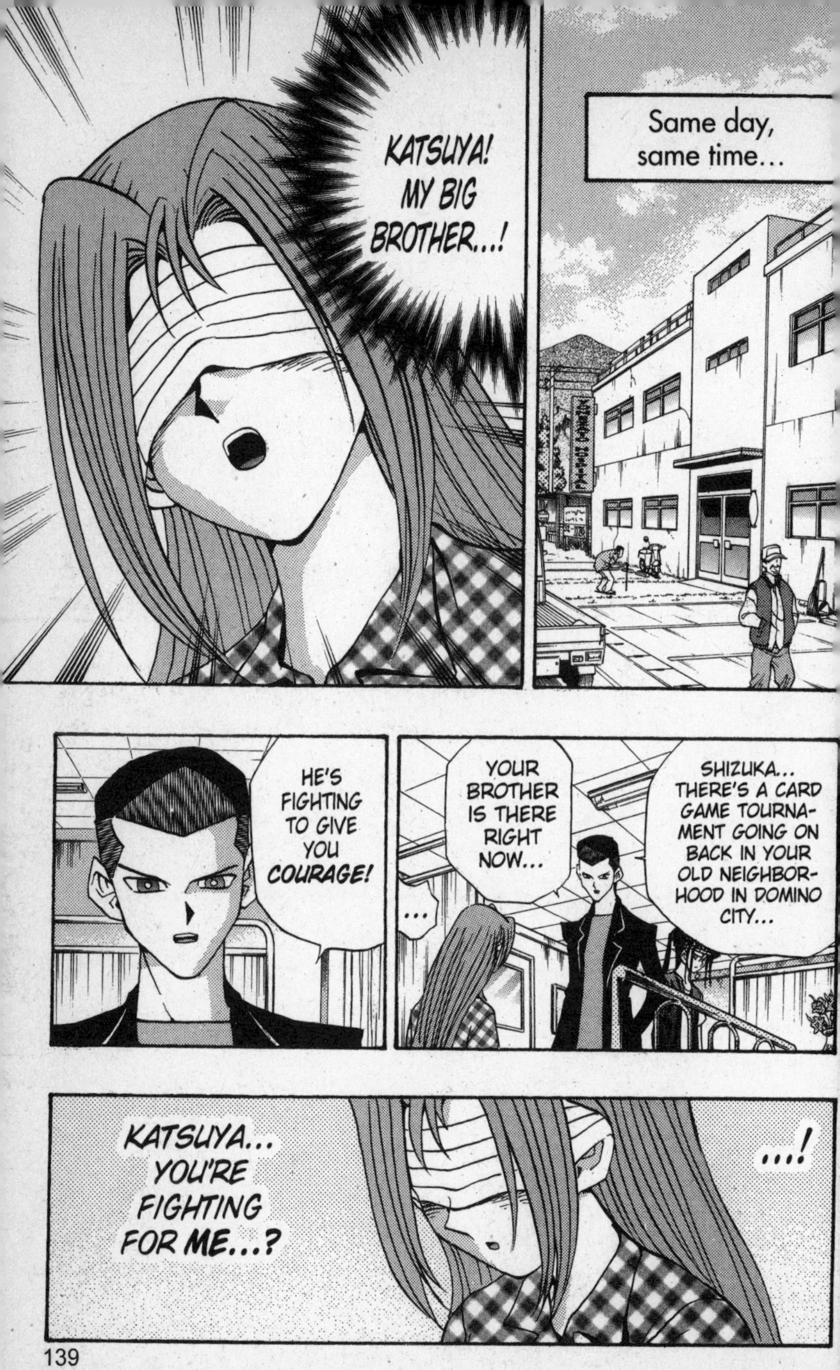
Same day, same time…
KATSUYA! MY BIG BROTHER…!
SHIZUKA… THERE'S A CARD GAME TOURNAMENT GOING ON BACK IN YOUR OLD NEIGHBORHOOD IN DOMINO CITY…
YOUR BROTHER IS THERE RIGHT NOW…
…
HE'S FIGHTING TO GIVE YOU COURAGE!
…!
KATSUYA… YOU'RE FIGHTING FOR ME…?

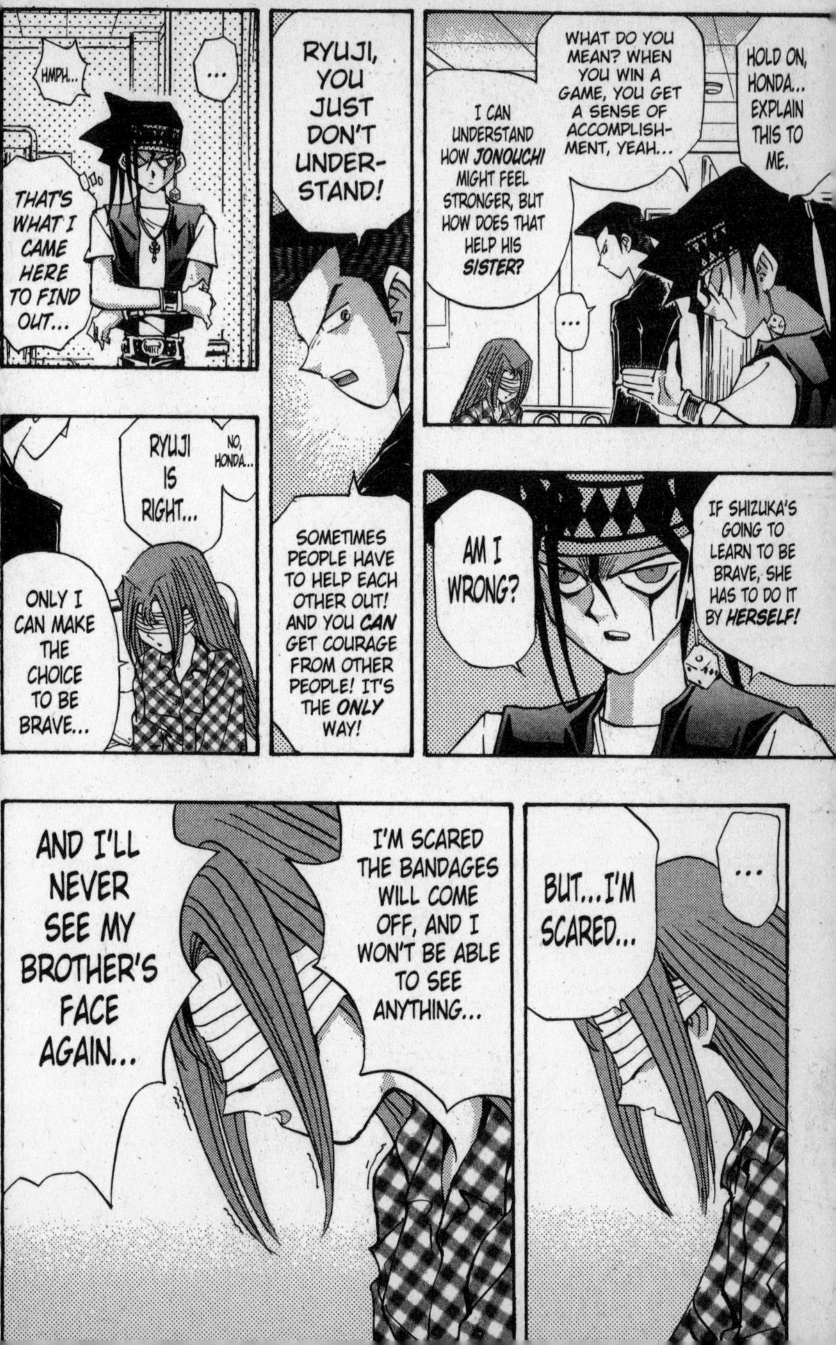
HOLD ON, HONDA... EXPLAIN THIS TO ME.
WHAT DO YOU MEAN? WHEN YOU WIN A GAME, YOU GET A SENSE OF ACCOMPLISHMENT, YEAH...
I CAN UNDERSTAND HOW *JONOUCHI* MIGHT FEEL STRONGER, BUT HOW DOES THAT HELP HIS *SISTER?*
...
IF SHIZUKA'S GOING TO LEARN TO BE BRAVE, SHE HAS TO DO IT BY *HERSELF!*
AM I WRONG?
RYUJI, YOU JUST DON'T UNDERSTAND!
SOMETIMES PEOPLE HAVE TO HELP EACH OTHER OUT! AND YOU *CAN* GET COURAGE FROM OTHER PEOPLE! IT'S THE *ONLY* WAY!
...
HMPH...
THAT'S WHAT I CAME HERE TO FIND OUT...
NO, HONDA...
RYUJI IS RIGHT...
ONLY I CAN MAKE THE CHOICE TO BE BRAVE...
...
BUT...I'M SCARED...
I'M SCARED THE BANDAGES WILL COME OFF, AND I WON'T BE ABLE TO SEE ANYTHING...
AND I'LL NEVER SEE MY BROTHER'S FACE AGAIN...

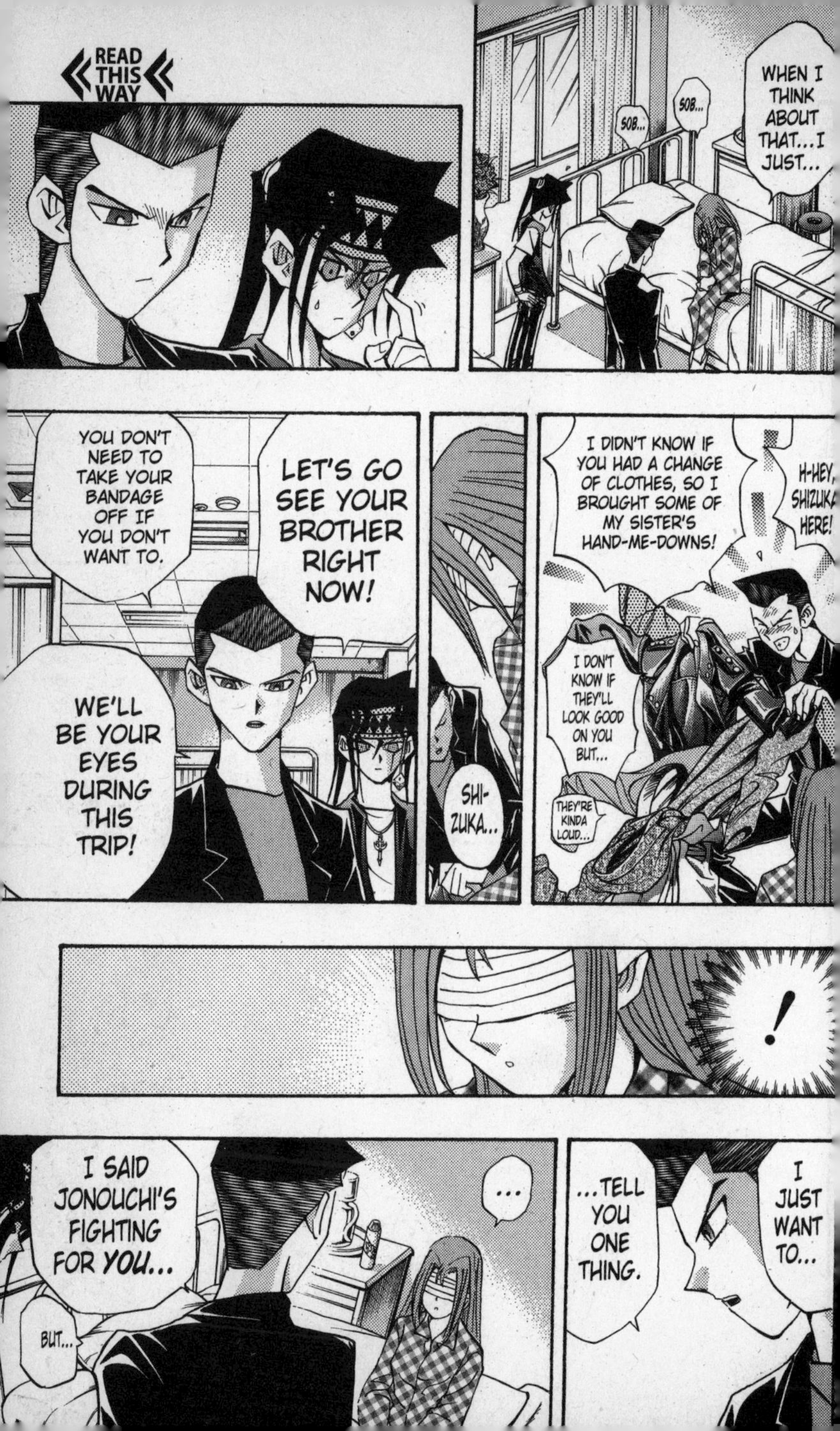
READ THIS WAY
WHEN I THINK ABOUT THAT...I JUST...
SOB...
SOB...
H-HEY, SHIZUKA HERE!
I DIDN'T KNOW IF YOU HAD A CHANGE OF CLOTHES, SO I BROUGHT SOME OF MY SISTER'S HAND-ME-DOWNS!
I DON'T KNOW IF THEY'LL LOOK GOOD ON YOU BUT...
THEY'RE KINDA LOUD...
SHI-ZUKA...
LET'S GO SEE YOUR BROTHER RIGHT NOW!
YOU DON'T NEED TO TAKE YOUR BANDAGE OFF IF YOU DON'T WANT TO.
WE'LL BE YOUR EYES DURING THIS TRIP!
!
I JUST WANT TO...
...TELL YOU ONE THING.
...
I SAID JONOUCHI'S FIGHTING FOR *YOU*...
BUT...

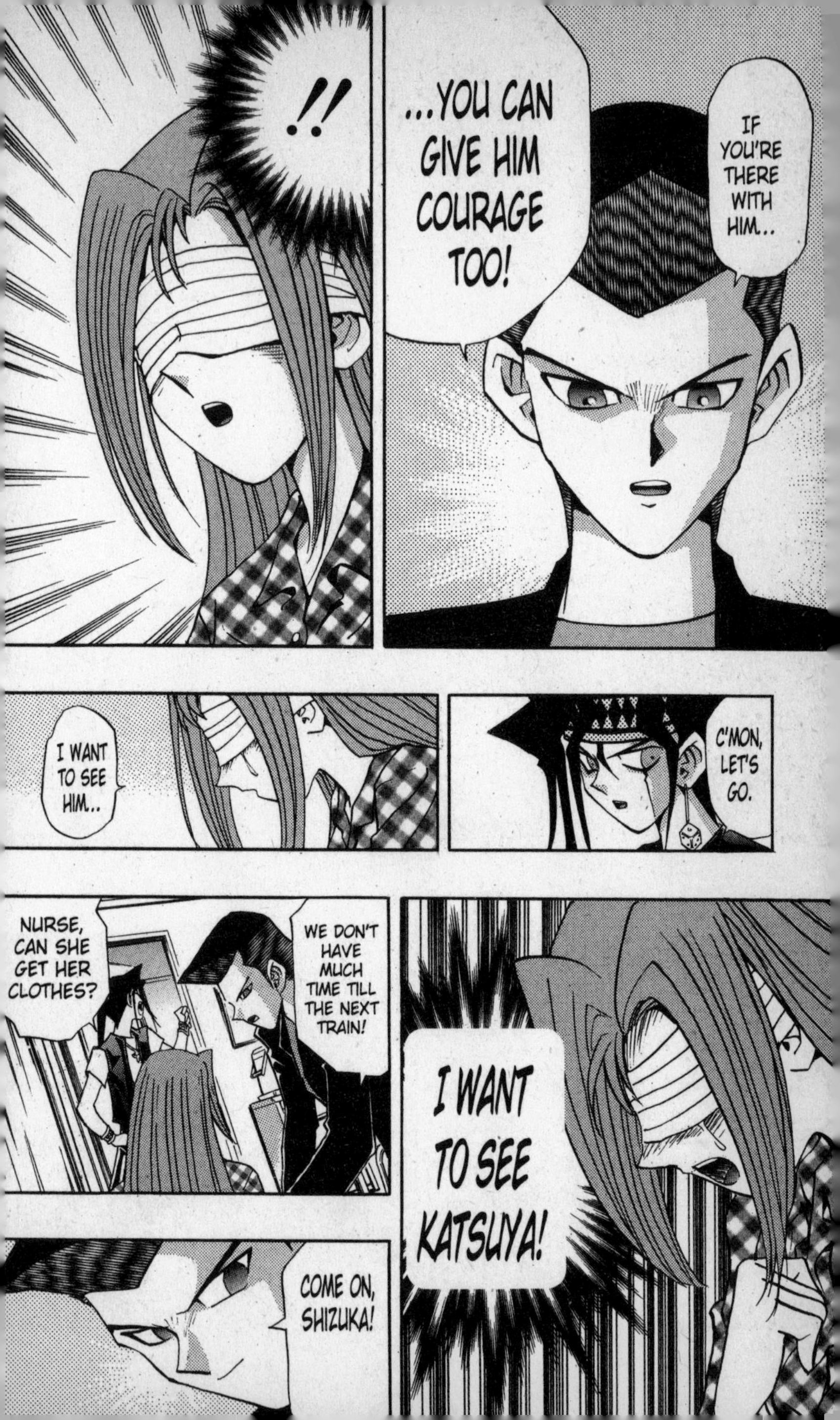
IF YOU'RE THERE WITH HIM...
...YOU CAN GIVE HIM COURAGE TOO!
!!
C'MON, LET'S GO.
I WANT TO SEE HIM...
I WANT TO SEE KATSUYA!
WE DON'T HAVE MUCH TIME TILL THE NEXT TRAIN!
NURSE, CAN SHE GET HER CLOTHES?
COME ON, SHIZUKA!

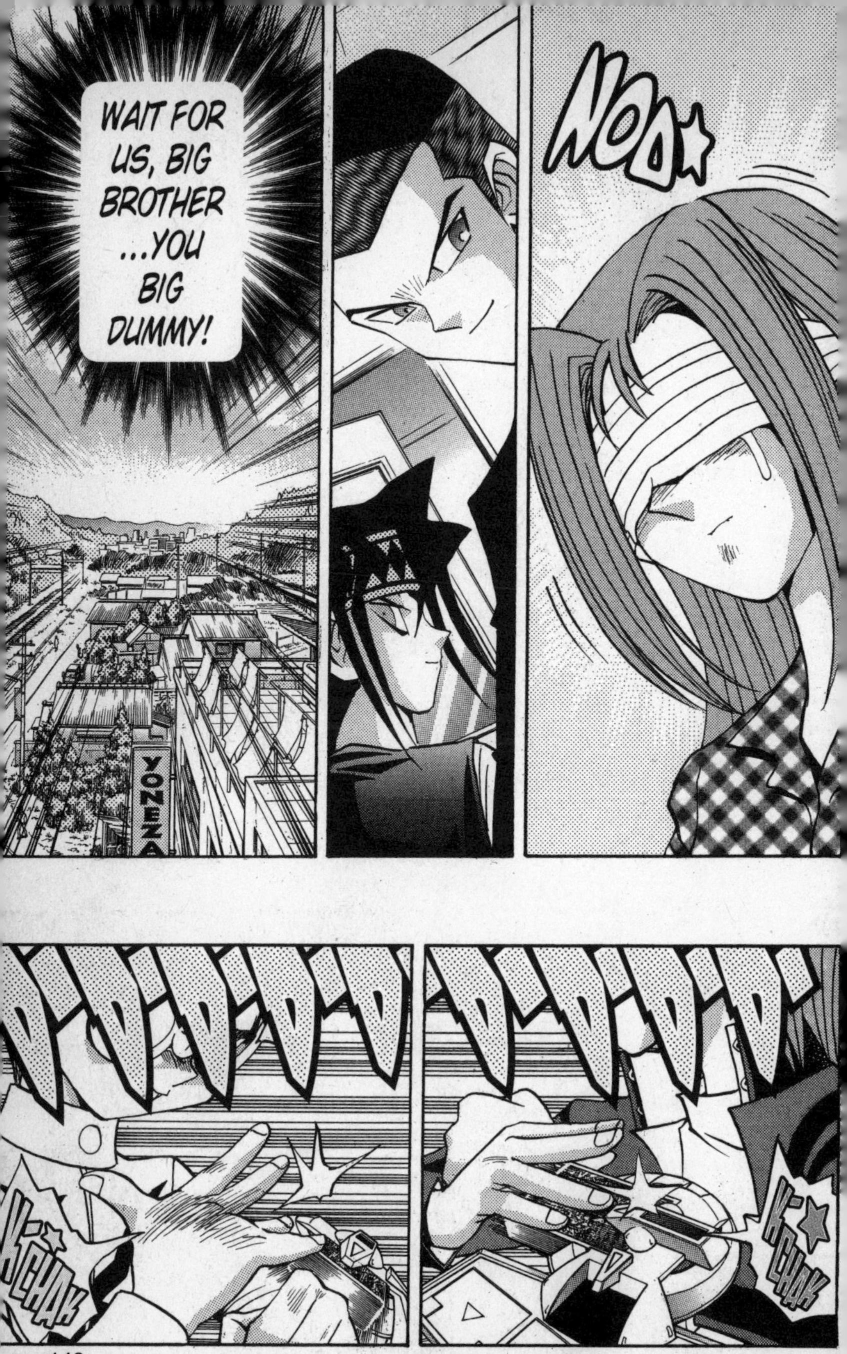
NOD☆
WAIT FOR US, BIG BROTHER ...YOU BIG DUMMY!
YONEZA
K-CHAK☆
K-CHAK☆

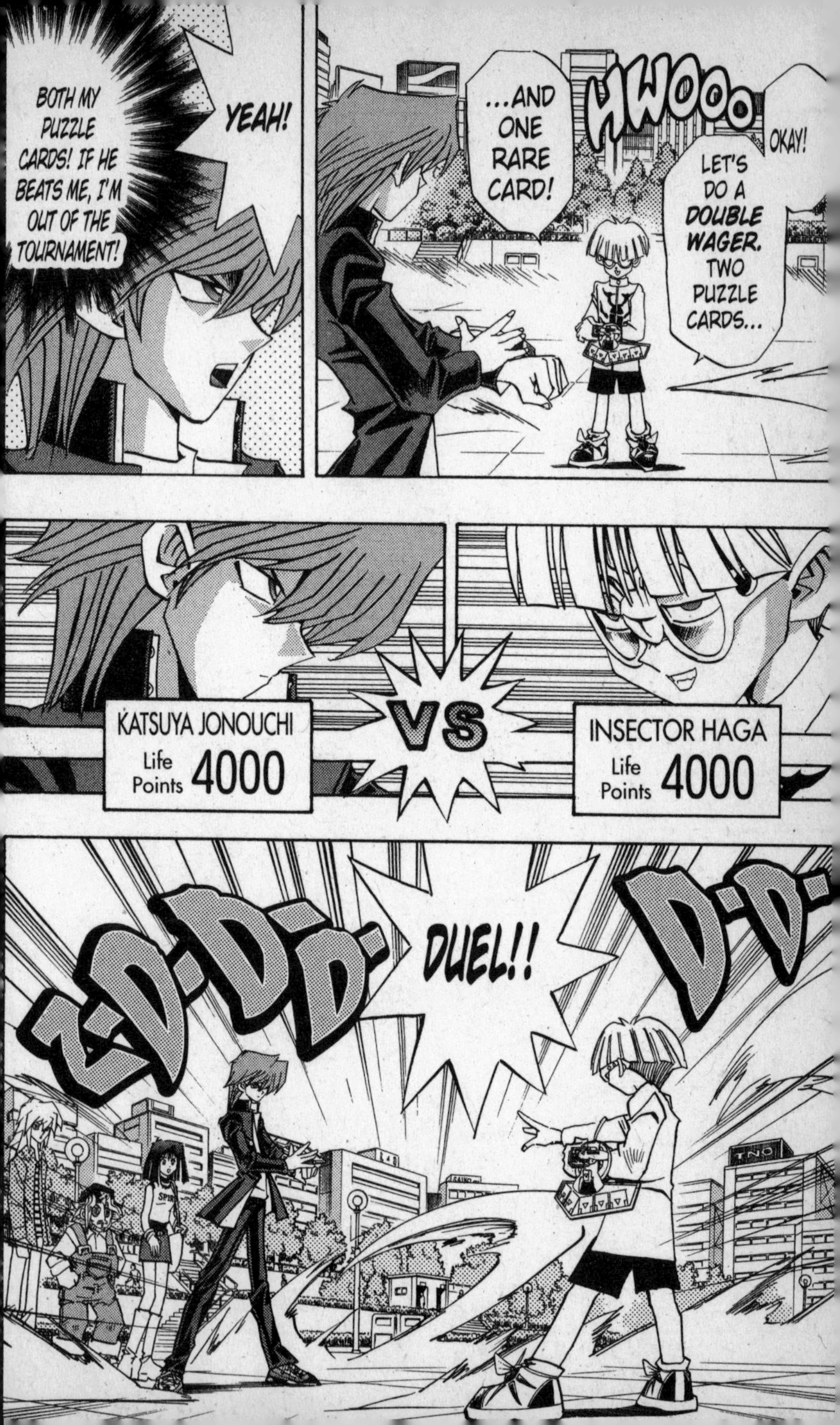
OKAY! LET'S DO A DOUBLE WAGER. TWO PUZZLE CARDS...
HWOOO
...AND ONE RARE CARD!
YEAH!
BOTH MY PUZZLE CARDS! IF HE BEATS ME, I'M OUT OF THE TOURNAMENT!
INSECTOR HAGA Life Points 4000
VS
KATSUYA JONOUCHI Life Points 4000
D-D-
D-D-D-
DUEL!!

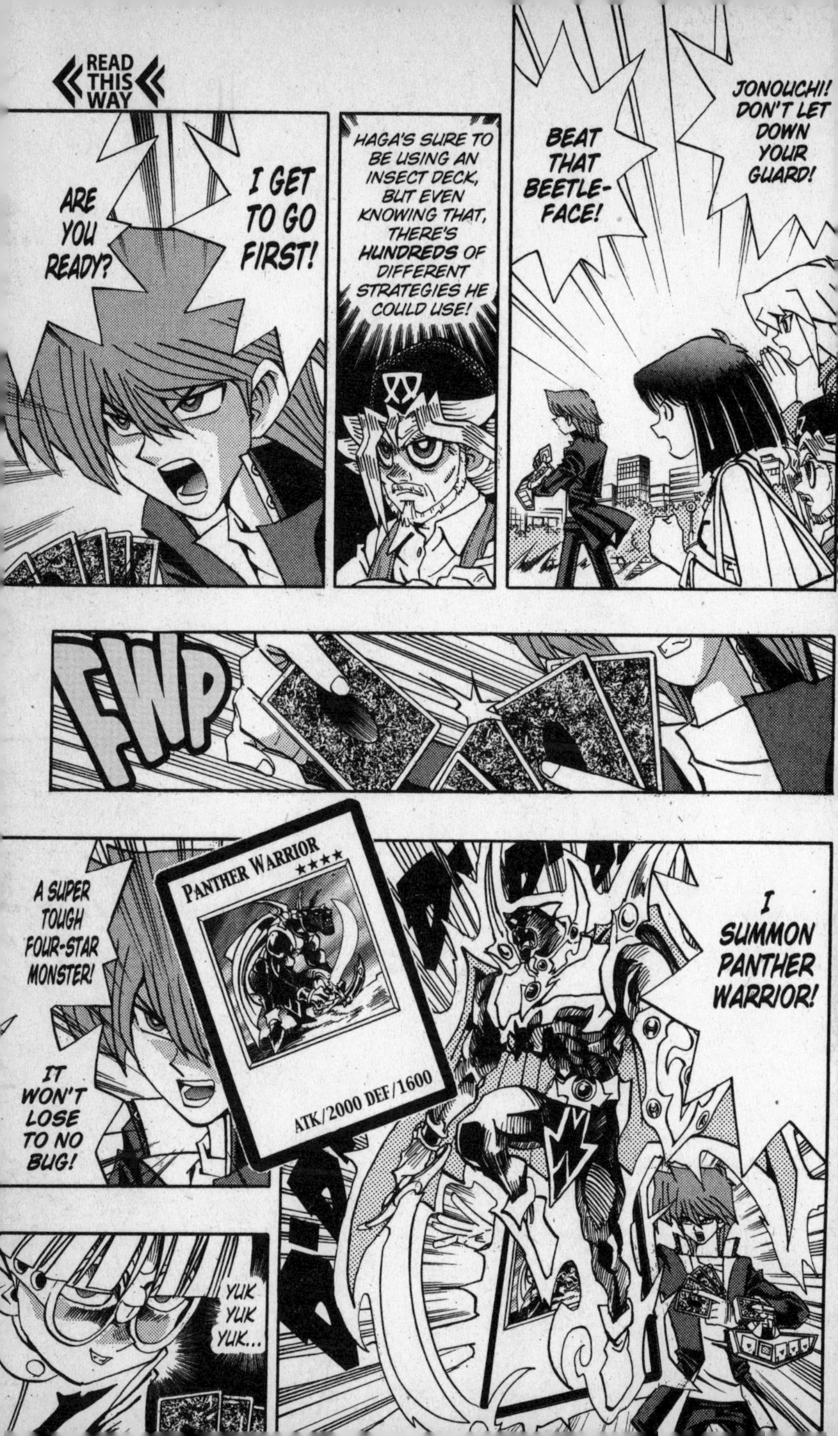
READ THIS WAY
JONOUCHI! DON'T LET DOWN YOUR GUARD!
BEAT THAT BEETLE-FACE!
HAGA'S SURE TO BE USING AN INSECT DECK, BUT EVEN KNOWING THAT, THERE'S HUNDREDS OF DIFFERENT STRATEGIES HE COULD USE!
I GET TO GO FIRST!
ARE YOU READY?
FWP
I SUMMON PANTHER WARRIOR!
PANTHER WARRIOR ★★★★
ATK/2000 DEF/1600
A SUPER TOUGH FOUR-STAR MONSTER!
IT WON'T LOSE TO NO BUG!
YUK YUK YUK...

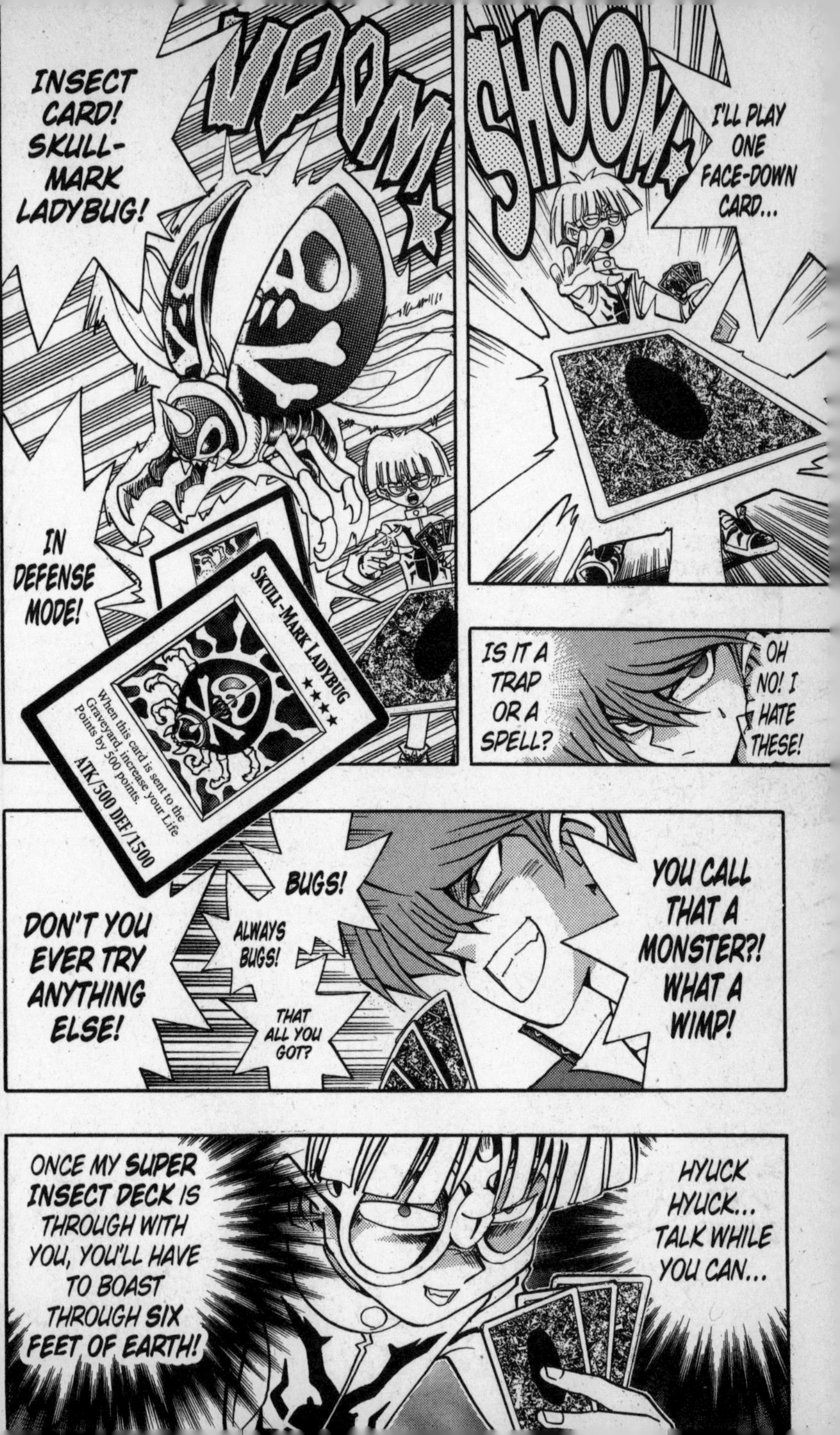
SHOOM
I'LL PLAY ONE FACE-DOWN CARD...
OH NO! I HATE THESE!
IS IT A TRAP OR A SPELL?
VOOM
INSECT CARD! SKULL-MARK LADYBUG!
IN DEFENSE MODE!
SKULL-MARK LADYBUG
When this card is sent to the Graveyard, increase your Life Points by 500 points.
ATK/500 DEF/1500
YOU CALL THAT A MONSTER?! WHAT A WIMP!
BUGS!
ALWAYS BUGS!
THAT ALL YOU GOT?
DON'T YOU EVER TRY ANYTHING ELSE!
HYUCK HYUCK... TALK WHILE YOU CAN...
ONCE MY SUPER INSECT DECK IS THROUGH WITH YOU, YOU'LL HAVE TO BOAST THROUGH SIX FEET OF EARTH!

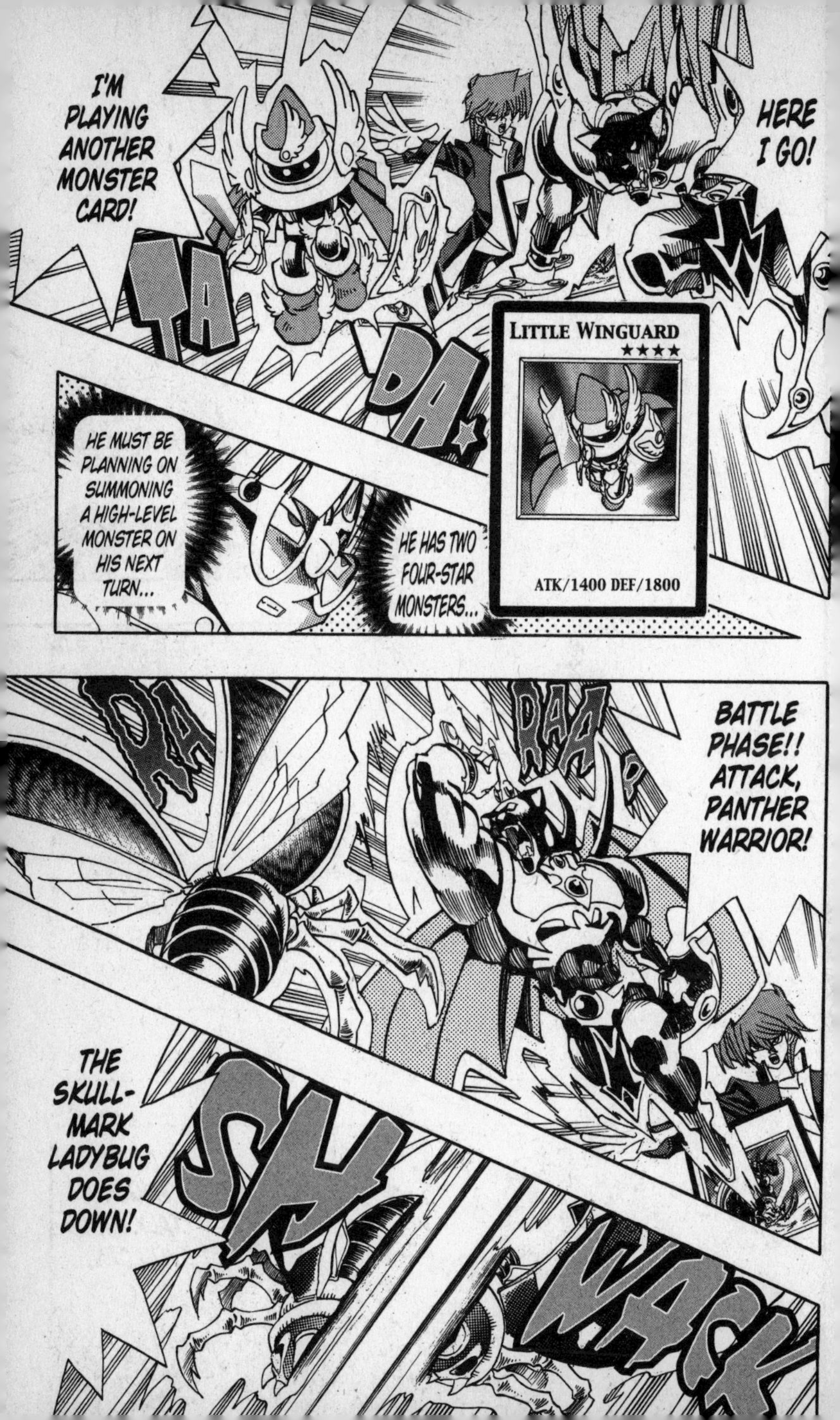

HERE I GO!
I'M PLAYING ANOTHER MONSTER CARD!
TA
DA
LITTLE WINGUARD
ATK/1400 DEF/1800
HE HAS TWO FOUR-STAR MONSTERS...
HE MUST BE PLANNING ON SUMMONING A HIGH-LEVEL MONSTER ON HIS NEXT TURN...
BATTLE PHASE!! ATTACK, PANTHER WARRIOR!
DAA
DA
THE SKULL-MARK LADYBUG DOES DOWN!
SH
WACK

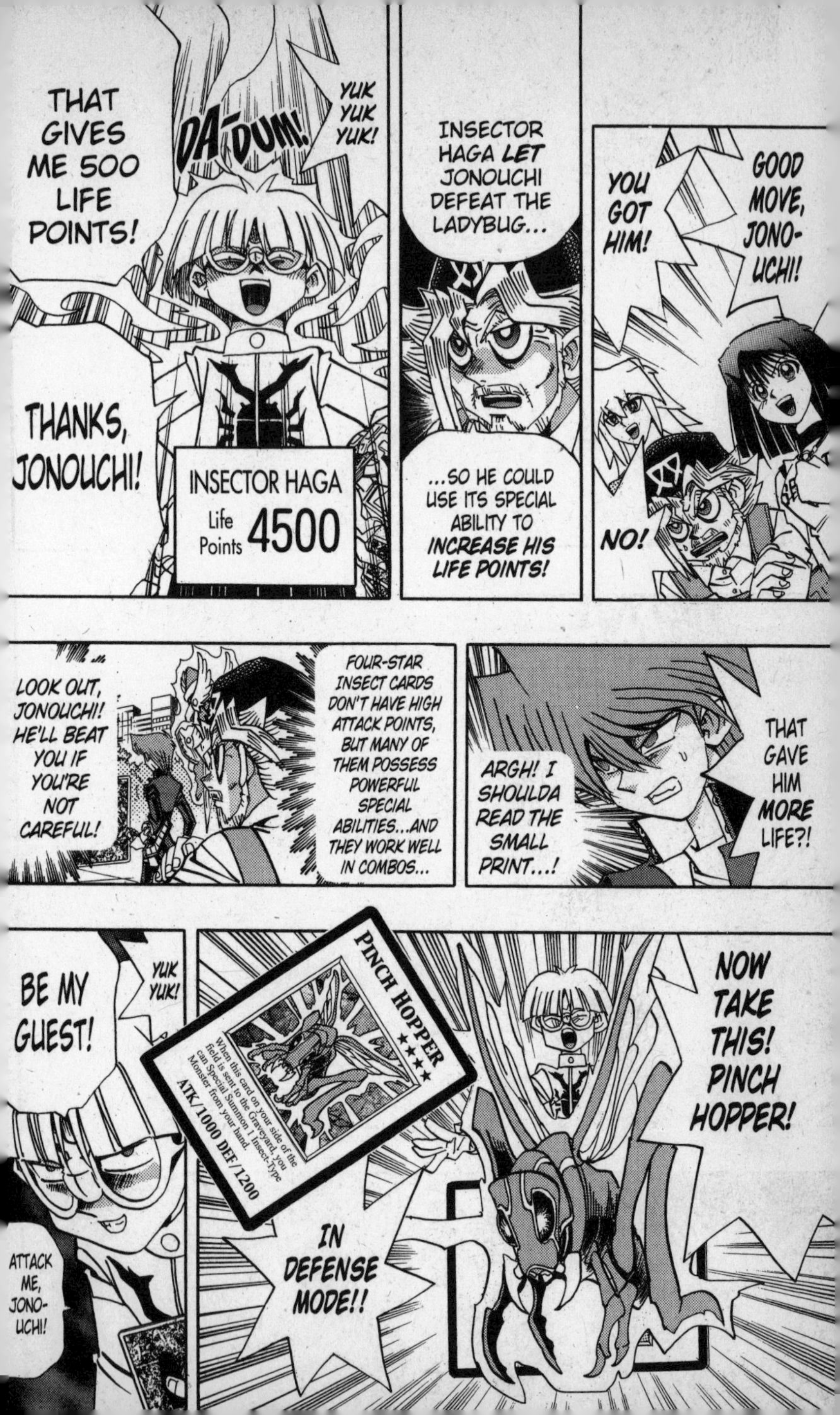
GOOD MOVE, JONO-UCHI!
YOU GOT HIM!
NO!
INSECTOR HAGA LET JONOUCHI DEFEAT THE LADYBUG...
...SO HE COULD USE ITS SPECIAL ABILITY TO INCREASE HIS LIFE POINTS!
YUK YUK YUK!
DA-DUM!
THAT GIVES ME 500 LIFE POINTS!
INSECTOR HAGA
Life Points 4500
THANKS, JONOUCHI!
THAT GAVE HIM MORE LIFE?!
ARGH! I SHOULDA READ THE SMALL PRINT...!
FOUR-STAR INSECT CARDS DON'T HAVE HIGH ATTACK POINTS, BUT MANY OF THEM POSSESS POWERFUL SPECIAL ABILITIES...AND THEY WORK WELL IN COMBOS...
LOOK OUT, JONOUCHI! HE'LL BEAT YOU IF YOU'RE NOT CAREFUL!
NOW TAKE THIS! PINCH HOPPER!
PINCH HOPPER
When this card on your side of the field is sent to the Graveyard, you can Special Summon 1 Insect-Type Monster from your hand
ATK/1000 DEF/1200
IN DEFENSE MODE!!
YUK YUK!
BE MY GUEST!
ATTACK ME, JONO-UCHI!

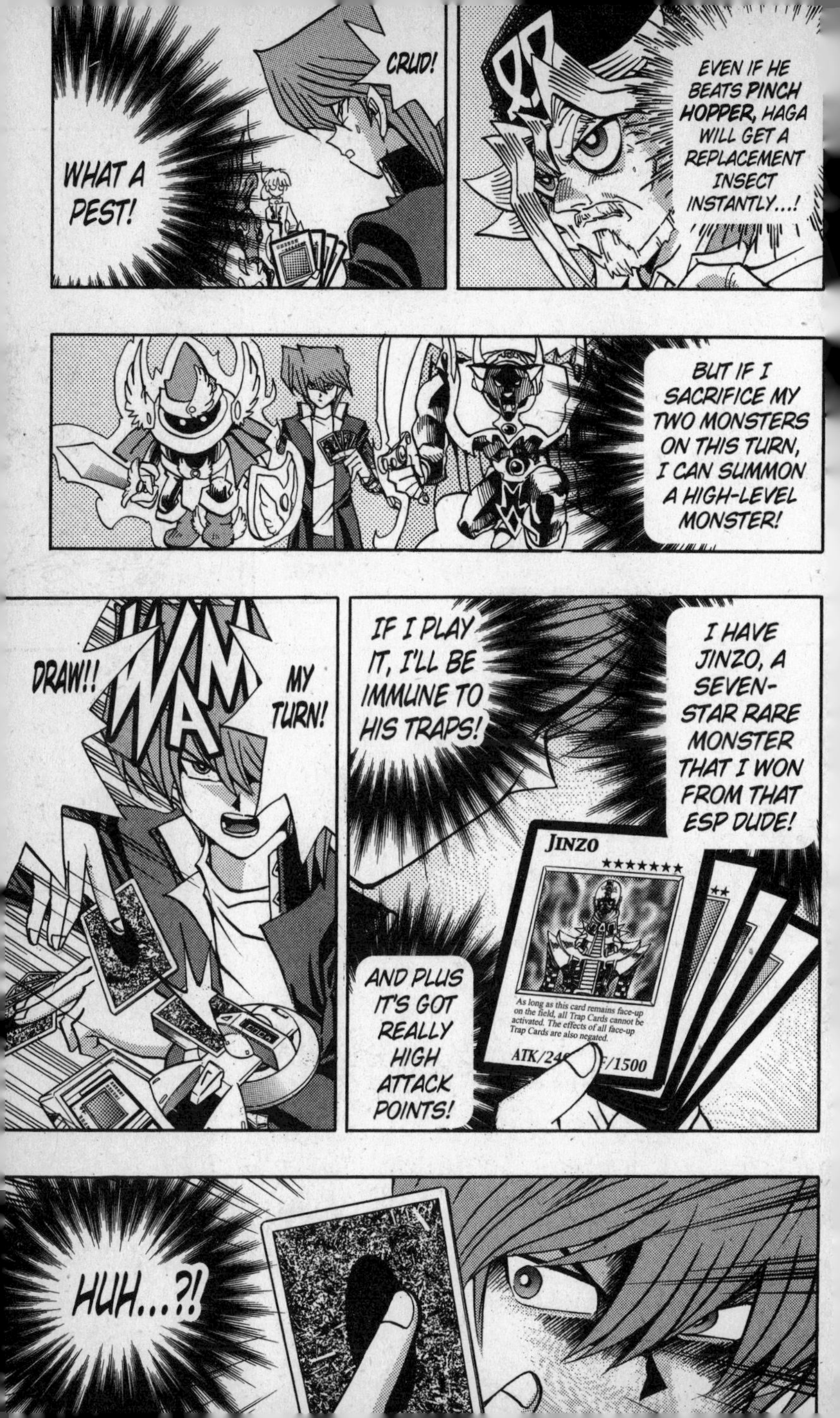
EVEN IF HE BEATS PINCH HOPPER, HAGA WILL GET A REPLACEMENT INSECT INSTANTLY...!
CRUD!
WHAT A PEST!
BUT IF I SACRIFICE MY TWO MONSTERS ON THIS TURN, I CAN SUMMON A HIGH-LEVEL MONSTER!
I HAVE JINZO, A SEVEN-STAR RARE MONSTER THAT I WON FROM THAT ESP DUDE!
IF I PLAY IT, I'LL BE IMMUNE TO HIS TRAPS!
JINZO
As long as this card remains face-up on the field, all Trap Cards cannot be activated. The effects of all face-up Trap Cards are also negated.
AND PLUS IT'S GOT REALLY HIGH ATTACK POINTS!
MY TURN!
DRAW!!
HUH...?!

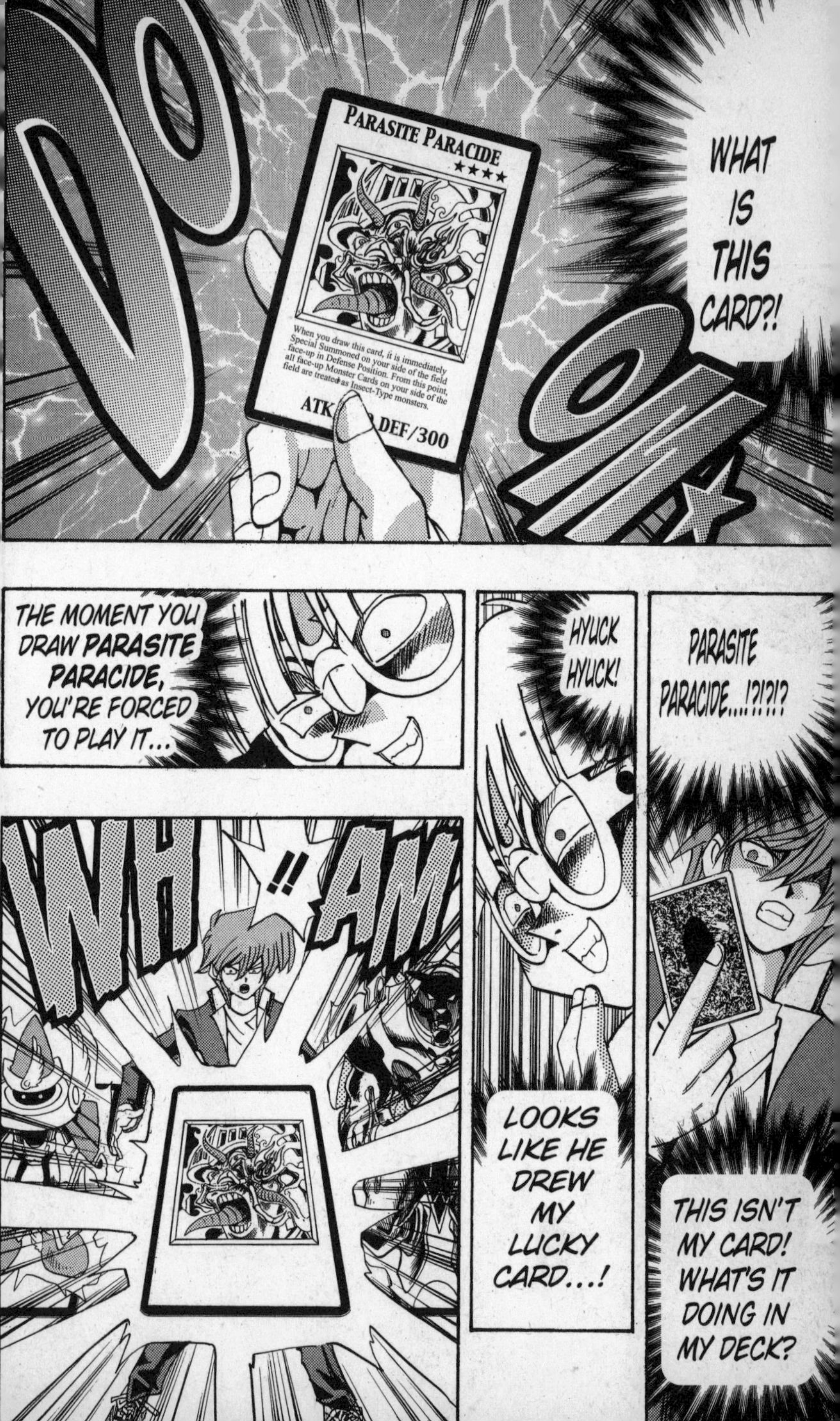
WHAT IS THIS CARD?!
PARASITE PARACIDE
When you draw this card, it is immediately Special Summoned on your side of the field face-up in Defense Position. From this point, all face-up Monster Cards on your side of the field are treated as Insect-Type monsters.
DEF/300
PARASITE PARACIDE...!?!?!?
THIS ISN'T MY CARD! WHAT'S IT DOING IN MY DECK?
HYUCK HYUCK!
LOOKS LIKE HE DREW MY LUCKY CARD...!
THE MOMENT YOU DRAW PARASITE PARACIDE, YOU'RE FORCED TO PLAY IT...
WH !! AM

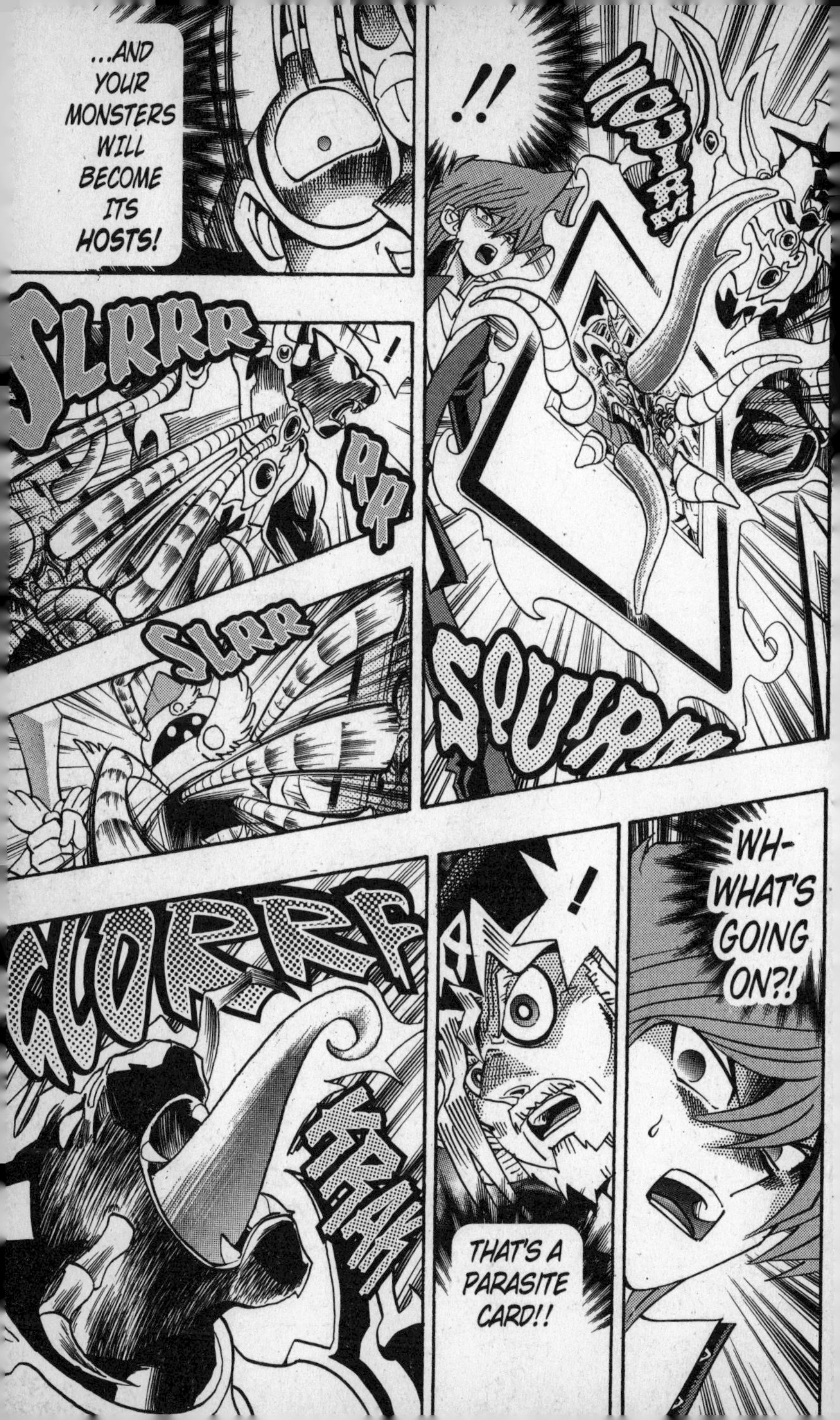
!!
SQUIRM
...AND YOUR MONSTERS WILL BECOME ITS HOSTS!
SLRRR
!
RR
SLRR
WH- WHAT'S GOING ON?!
!
THAT'S A PARASITE CARD!!
GLORRF

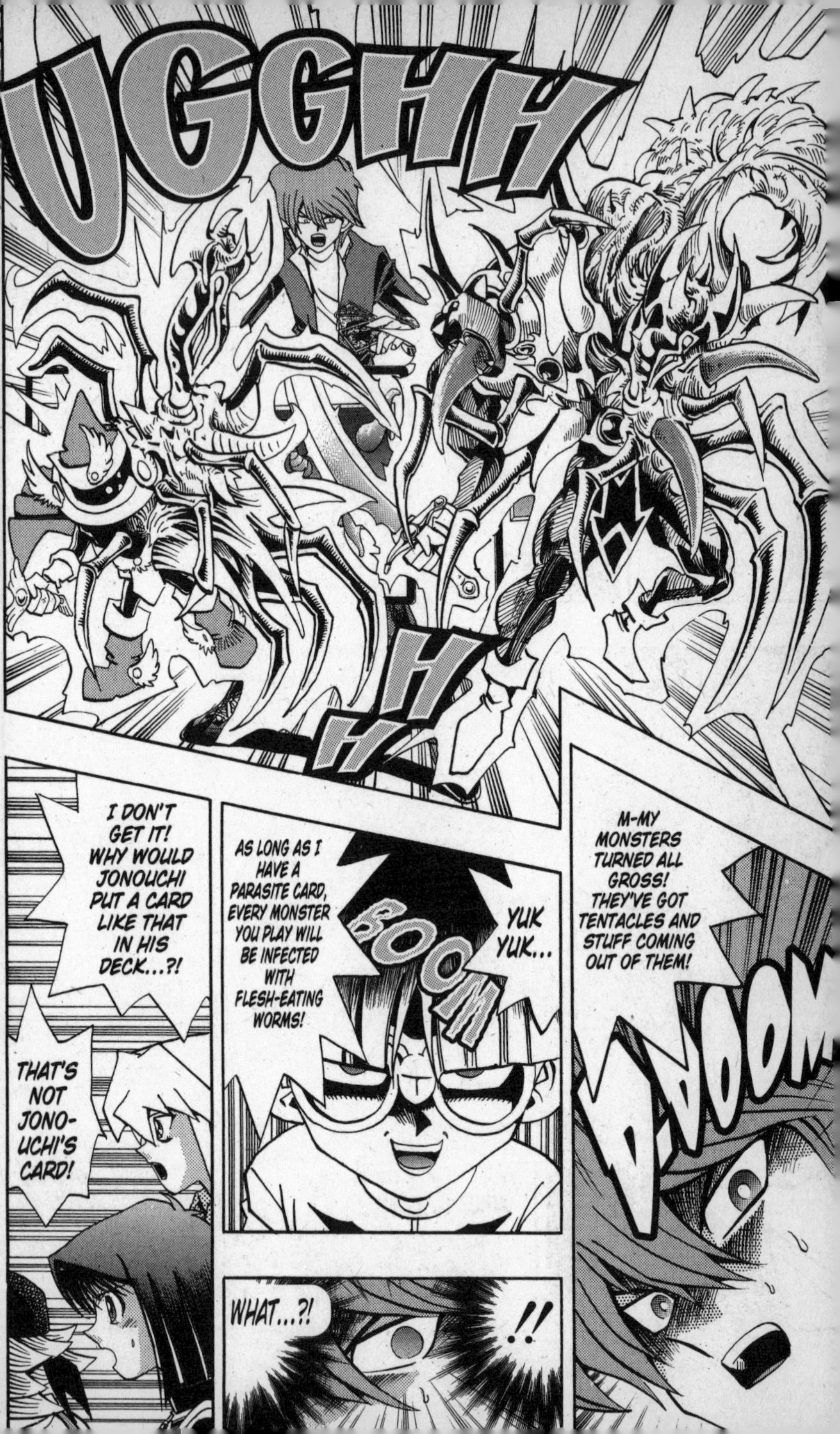
UGGHH
HHH
M-MY MONSTERS TURNED ALL GROSS! THEY'VE GOT TENTACLES AND STUFF COMING OUT OF THEM!
YUK YUK...
AS LONG AS I HAVE A PARASITE CARD, EVERY MONSTER YOU PLAY WILL BE INFECTED WITH FLESH-EATING WORMS!
BOOM
WHAT...?!
!!
I DON'T GET IT! WHY WOULD JONOUCHI PUT A CARD LIKE THAT IN HIS DECK...?!
THAT'S NOT JONOUCHI'S CARD!

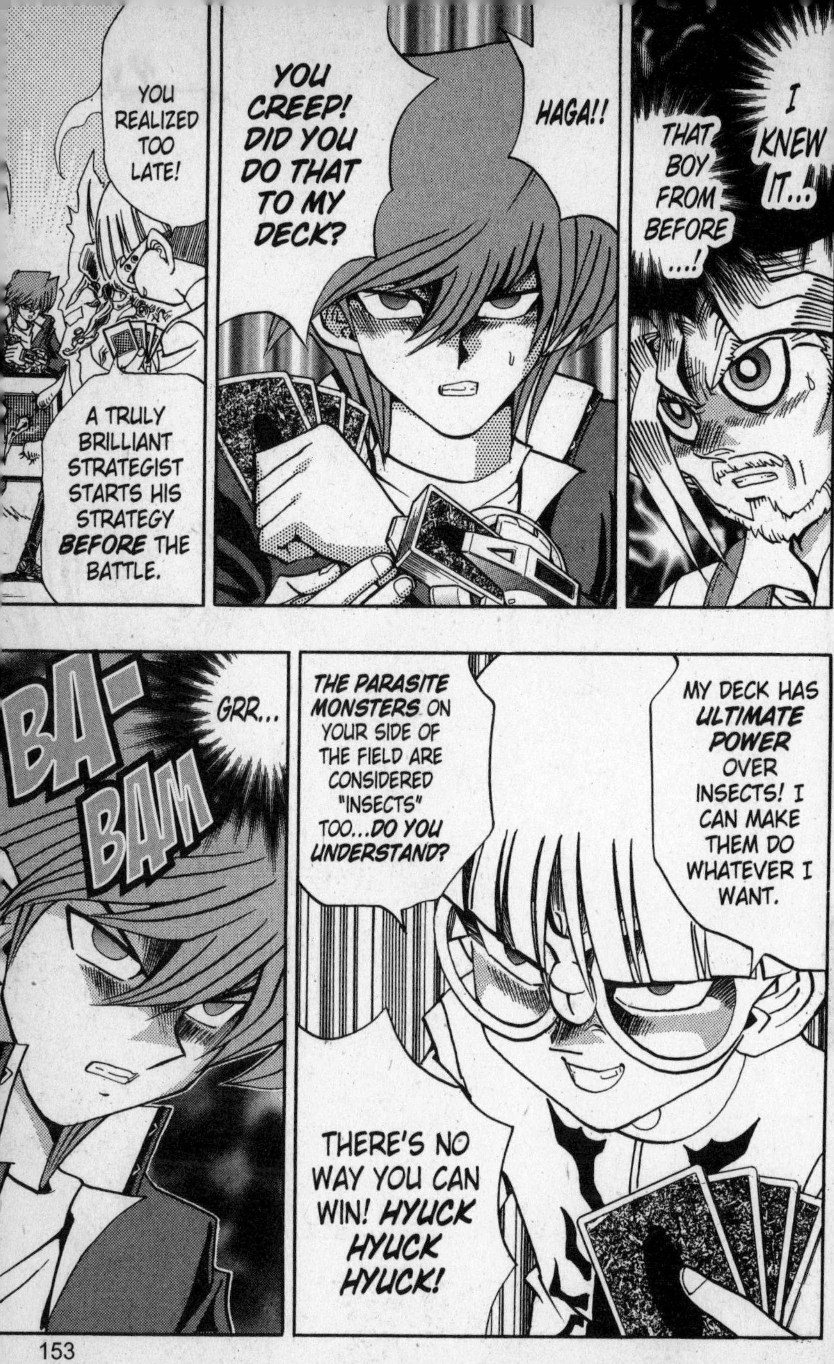
I KNEW IT...
THAT BOY FROM BEFORE ...!
HAGA!!
YOU CREEP! DID YOU DO THAT TO MY DECK?
YOU REALIZED TOO LATE!
A TRULY BRILLIANT STRATEGIST STARTS HIS STRATEGY BEFORE THE BATTLE.
MY DECK HAS ULTIMATE POWER OVER INSECTS! I CAN MAKE THEM DO WHATEVER I WANT.
THE PARASITE MONSTERS ON YOUR SIDE OF THE FIELD ARE CONSIDERED "INSECTS" TOO...DO YOU UNDERSTAND?
THERE'S NO WAY YOU CAN WIN! HYUCK HYUCK HYUCK!
BA-BAM
GRR...

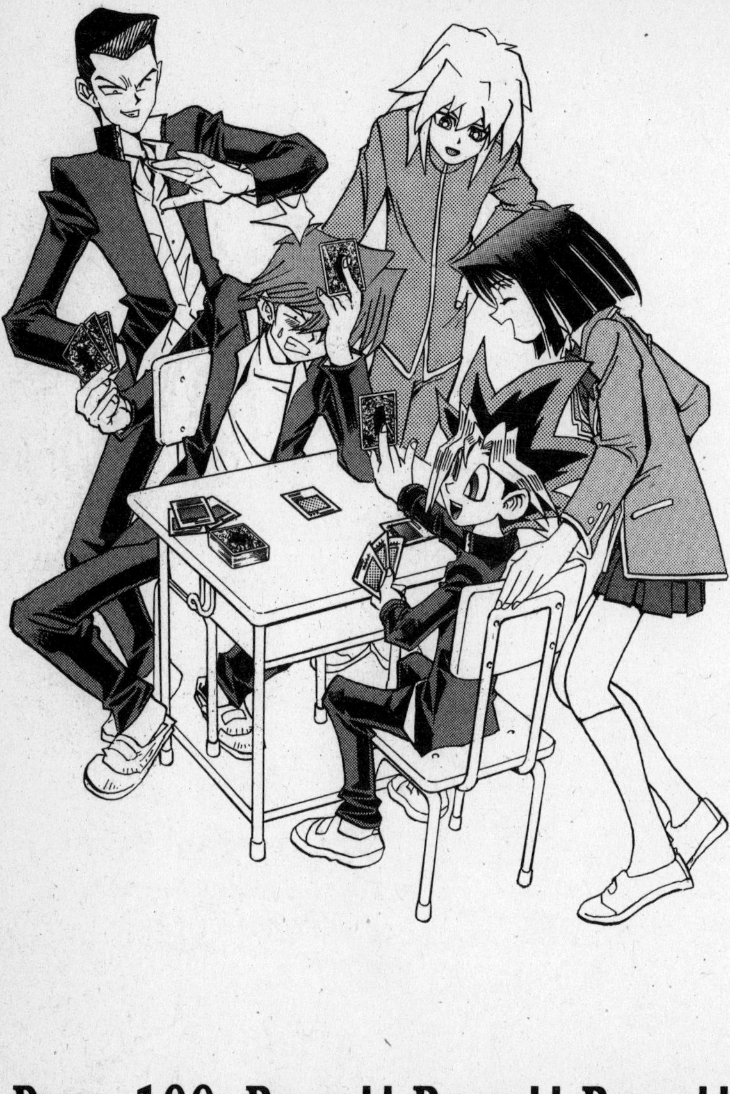

Duel 109: Bugs!! Bugs!! Bugs!!

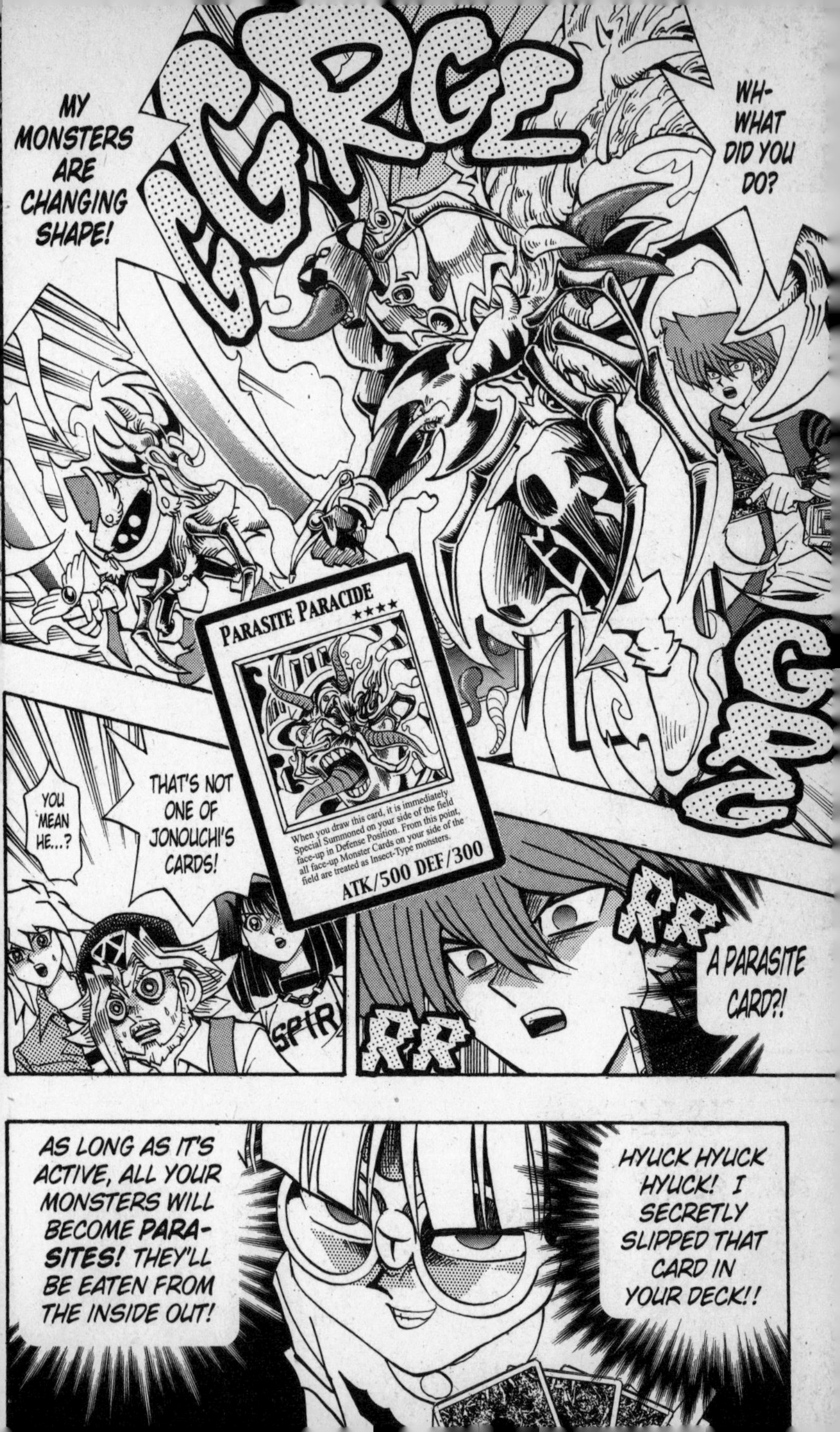
WH- WHAT DID YOU DO?
MY MONSTERS ARE CHANGING SHAPE!
PARASITE PARACIDE
When you draw this card, it is immediately Special Summoned on your side of the field face-up in Defense Position. From this point, all face-up Monster Cards on your side of the field are treated as Insect-Type monsters.
ATK/500 DEF/300
RR
A PARASITE CARD?!
RR
THAT'S NOT ONE OF JONOUCHI'S CARDS!
YOU MEAN HE...?
SPIR
HYUCK HYUCK HYUCK! I SECRETLY SLIPPED THAT CARD IN YOUR DECK!!
AS LONG AS IT'S ACTIVE, ALL YOUR MONSTERS WILL BECOME PARA-SITES! THEY'LL BE EATEN FROM THE INSIDE OUT!

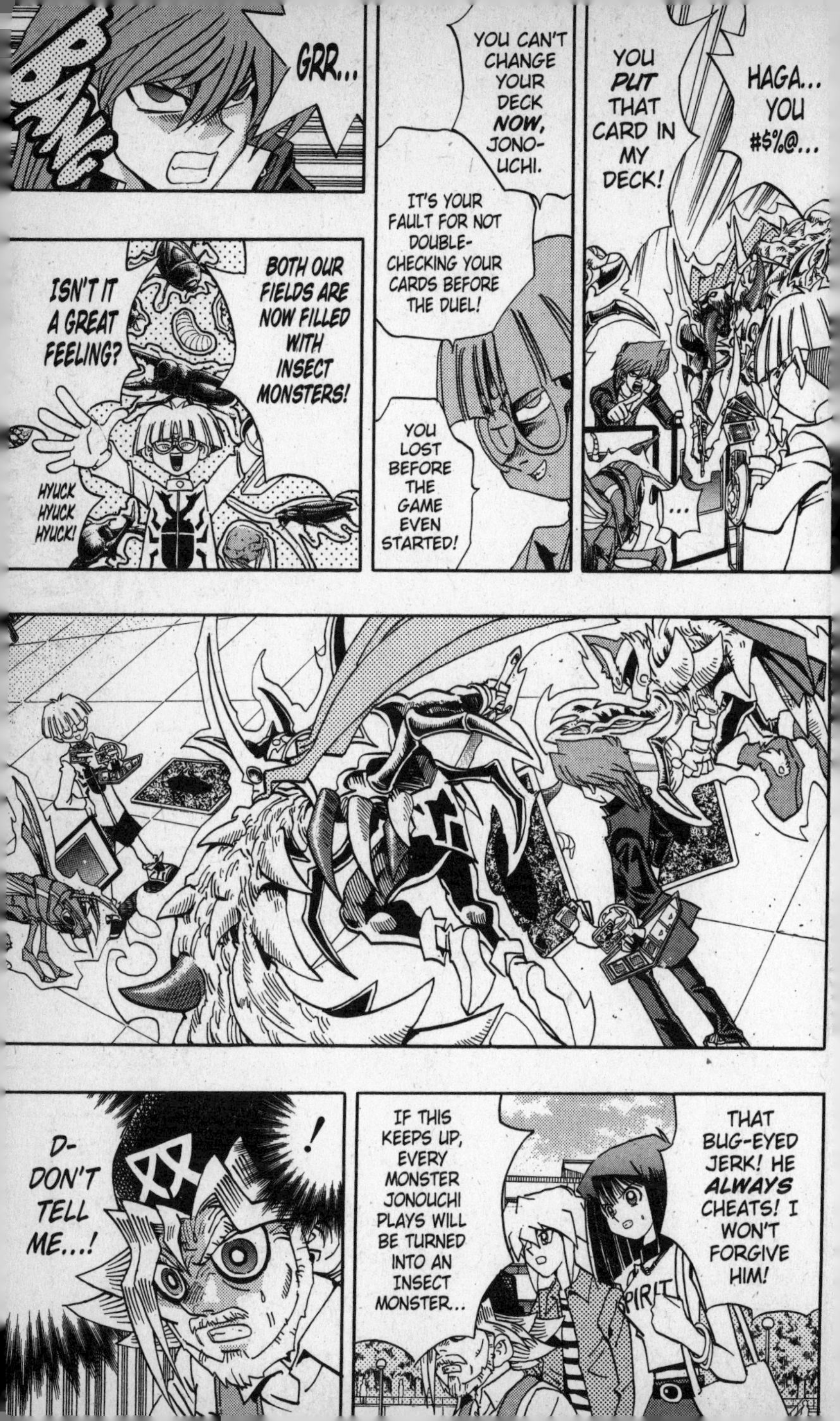
HAGA... YOU #$%@...
YOU PUT THAT CARD IN MY DECK!
...
YOU CAN'T CHANGE YOUR DECK NOW, JONOUCHI.
IT'S YOUR FAULT FOR NOT DOUBLE-CHECKING YOUR CARDS BEFORE THE DUEL!
YOU LOST BEFORE THE GAME EVEN STARTED!
GRR...
BRANG
BOTH OUR FIELDS ARE NOW FILLED WITH INSECT MONSTERS!
ISN'T IT A GREAT FEELING?
HYUCK HYUCK HYUCK!
THAT BUG-EYED JERK! HE ALWAYS CHEATS! I WON'T FORGIVE HIM!
IF THIS KEEPS UP, EVERY MONSTER JONOUCHI PLAYS WILL BE TURNED INTO AN INSECT MONSTER...
!
D-DON'T TELL ME...!

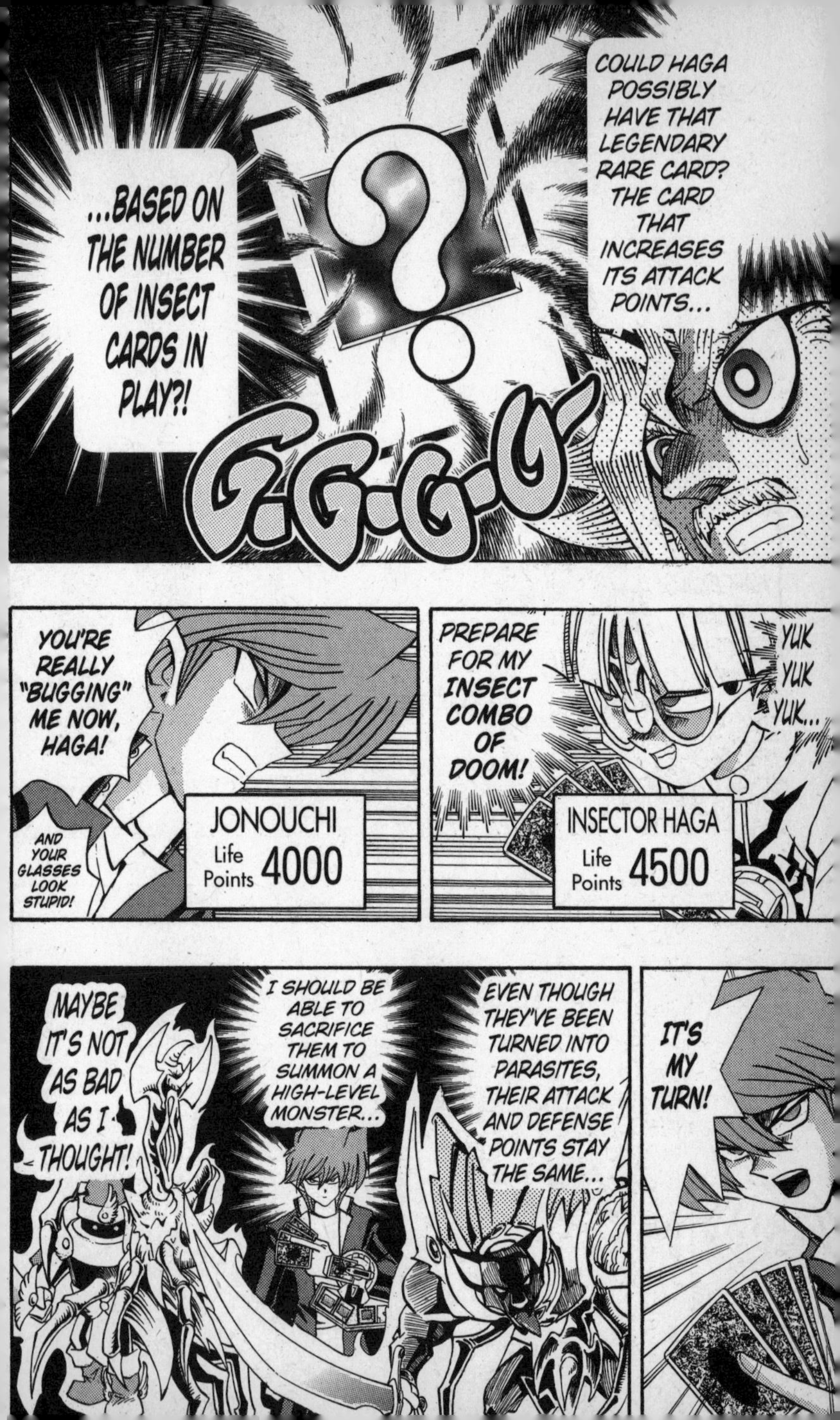

COULD HAGA POSSIBLY HAVE THAT LEGENDARY RARE CARD? THE CARD THAT INCREASES ITS ATTACK POINTS...
...BASED ON THE NUMBER OF INSECT CARDS IN PLAY?!
G-G-G-U
PREPARE FOR MY INSECT COMBO OF DOOM!
YUK YUK YUK...
INSECTOR HAGA Life Points 4500
YOU'RE REALLY "BUGGING" ME NOW, HAGA!
JONOUCHI Life Points 4000
AND YOUR GLASSES LOOK STUPID!
IT'S MY TURN!
EVEN THOUGH THEY'VE BEEN TURNED INTO PARASITES, THEIR ATTACK AND DEFENSE POINTS STAY THE SAME...
I SHOULD BE ABLE TO SACRIFICE THEM TO SUMMON A HIGH-LEVEL MONSTER...
MAYBE IT'S NOT AS BAD AS I THOUGHT!

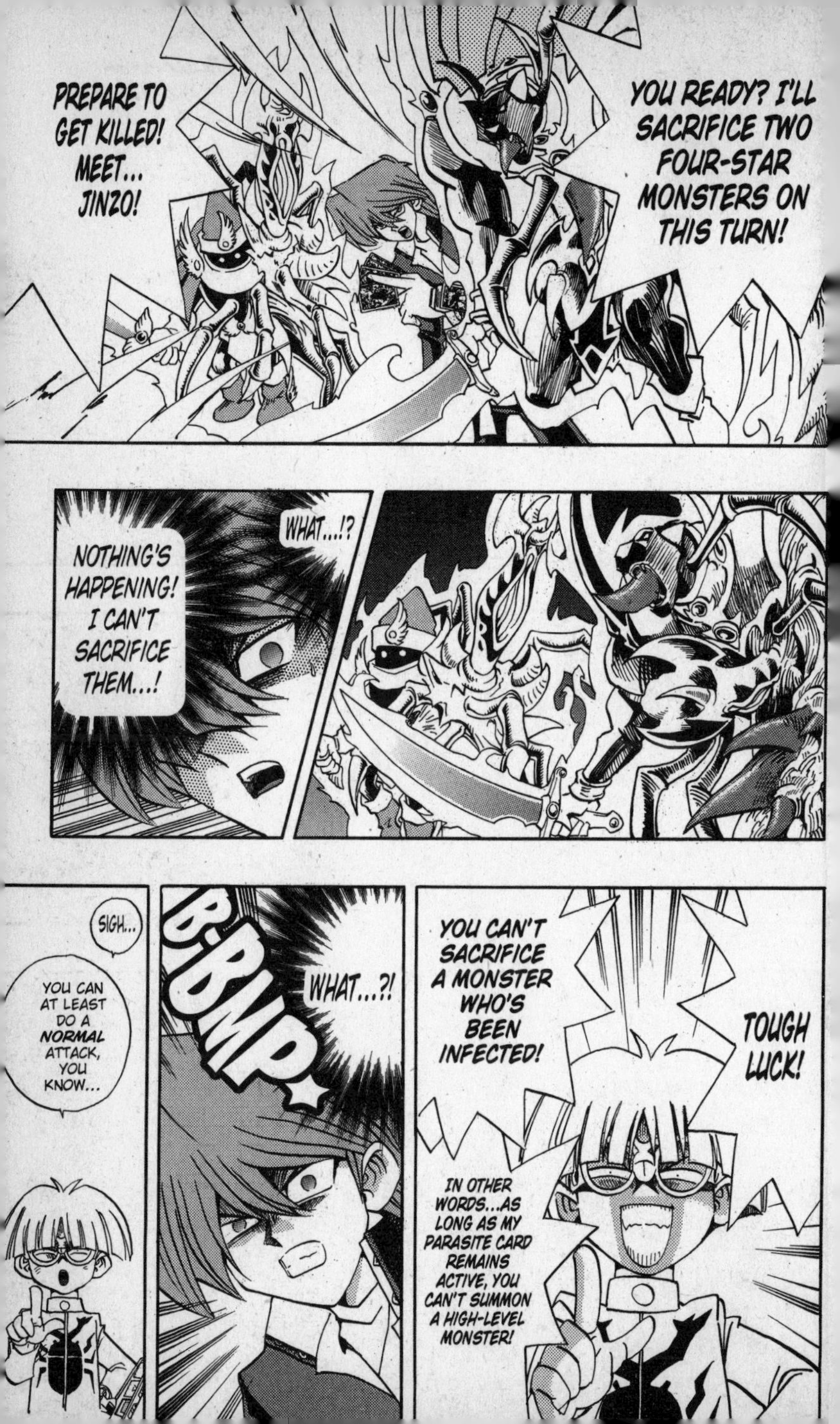
YOU READY? I'LL SACRIFICE TWO FOUR-STAR MONSTERS ON THIS TURN!
PREPARE TO GET KILLED! MEET... JINZO!
WHAT...!?
NOTHING'S HAPPENING! I CAN'T SACRIFICE THEM...!
TOUGH LUCK!
YOU CAN'T SACRIFICE A MONSTER WHO'S BEEN INFECTED!
IN OTHER WORDS...AS LONG AS MY PARASITE CARD REMAINS ACTIVE, YOU CAN'T SUMMON A HIGH-LEVEL MONSTER!
B-BMP
WHAT...?!
SIGH...
YOU CAN AT LEAST DO A NORMAL ATTACK, YOU KNOW...

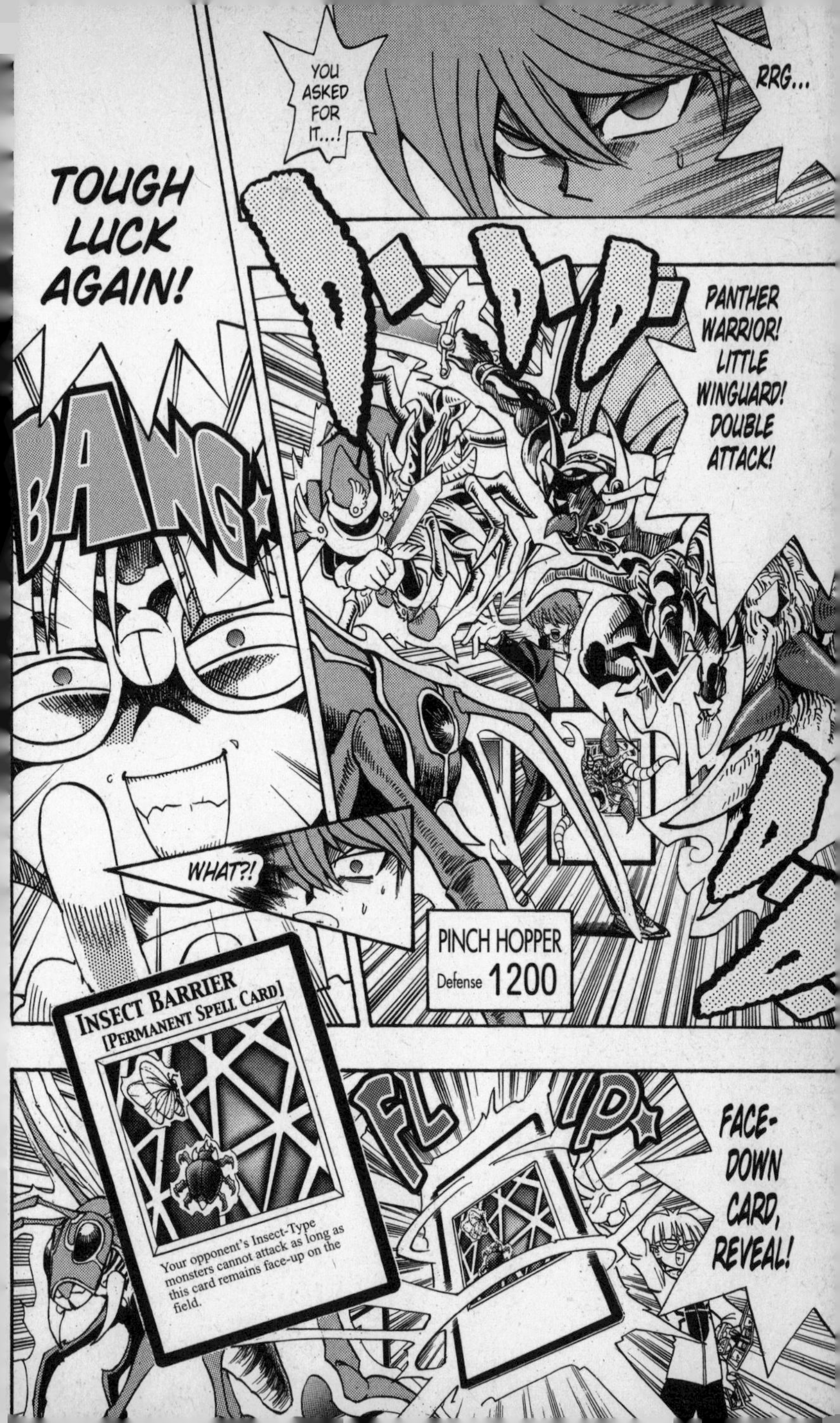

RRG...
YOU ASKED FOR IT...!
PANTHER WARRIOR! LITTLE WINGUARD! DOUBLE ATTACK!
TOUGH LUCK AGAIN!
BANG
WHAT?!
PINCH HOPPER
Defense 1200
FACE-DOWN CARD, REVEAL!
FLIP
INSECT BARRIER
[PERMANENT SPELL CARD]
Your opponent's Insect-Type monsters cannot attack as long as this card remains face-up on the field.

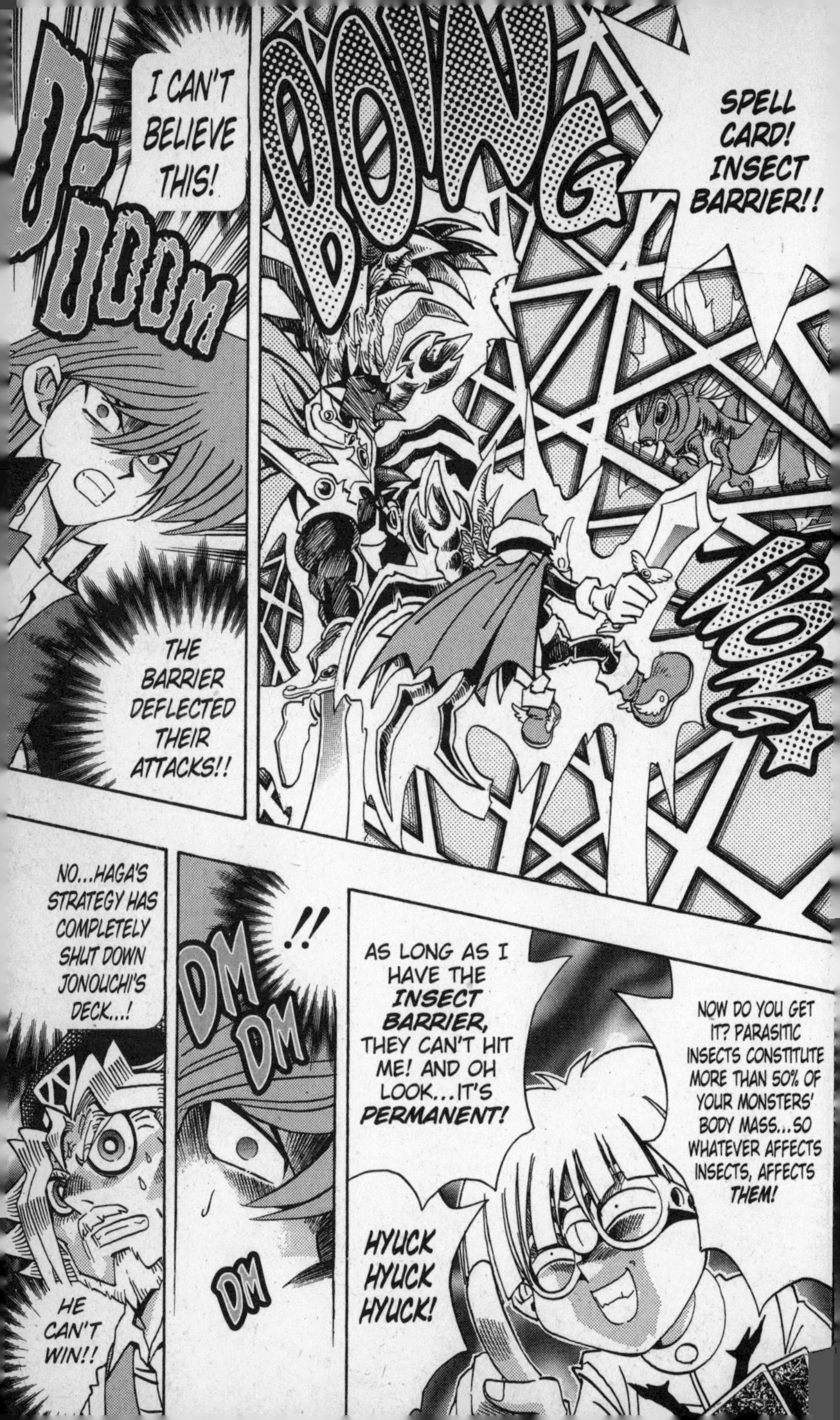
SPELL CARD! INSECT BARRIER!!
BOING
TWONG
D-DOOM
I CAN'T BELIEVE THIS!
THE BARRIER DEFLECTED THEIR ATTACKS!!
NOW DO YOU GET IT? PARASITIC INSECTS CONSTITUTE MORE THAN 50% OF YOUR MONSTERS' BODY MASS...SO WHATEVER AFFECTS INSECTS, AFFECTS *THEM!*
AS LONG AS I HAVE THE *INSECT BARRIER,* THEY CAN'T HIT ME! AND OH LOOK...IT'S *PERMANENT!*
HYUCK HYUCK HYUCK!
!!
DM DM
DM
NO...HAGA'S STRATEGY HAS COMPLETELY SHUT DOWN JONOUCHI'S DECK...!
HE CAN'T WIN!!

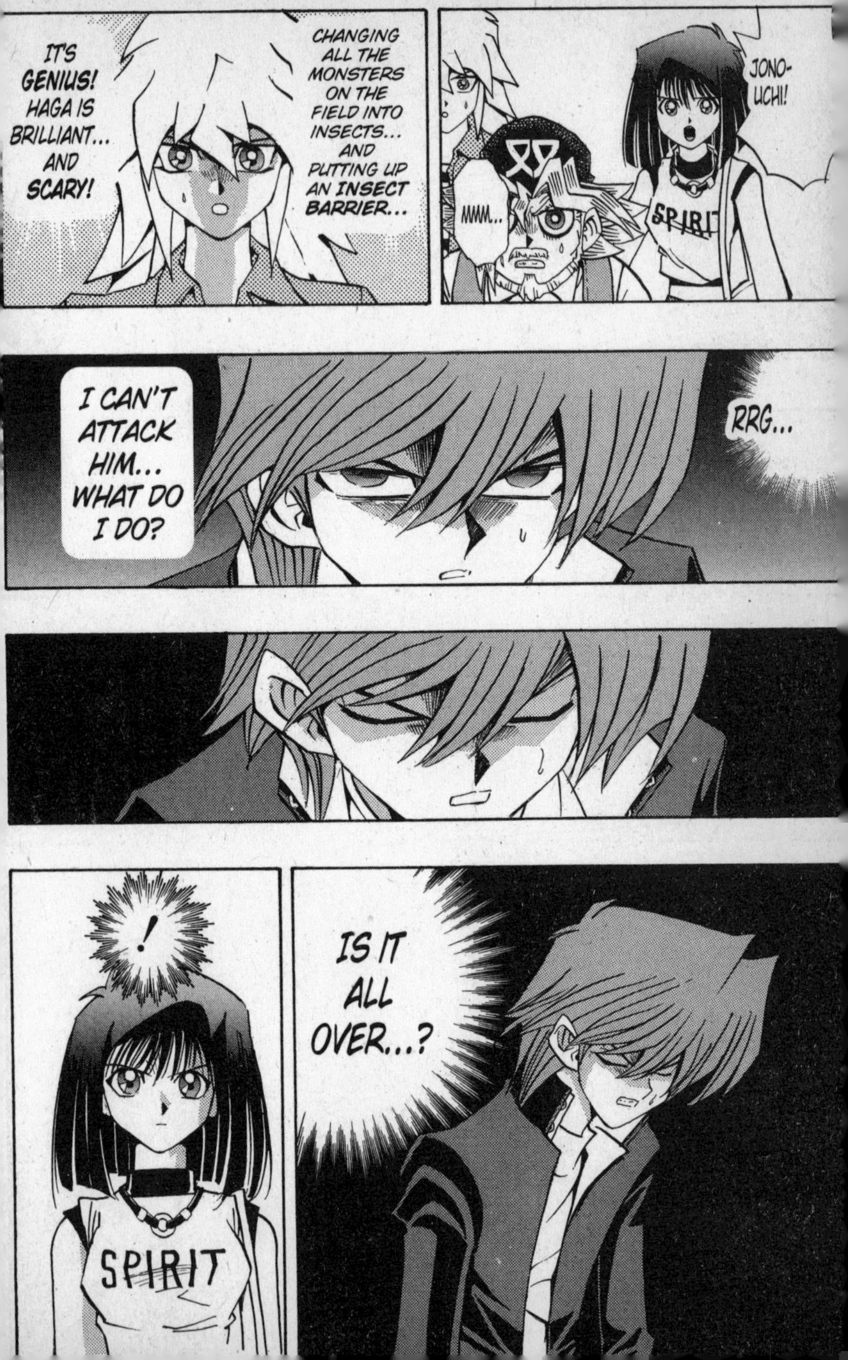
JONO-UCHI!
MMM...
CHANGING ALL THE MONSTERS ON THE FIELD INTO INSECTS... AND PUTTING UP AN INSECT BARRIER...
IT'S GENIUS! HAGA IS BRILLIANT... AND SCARY!
RRG...
I CAN'T ATTACK HIM... WHAT DO I DO?
IS IT ALL OVER...?
!

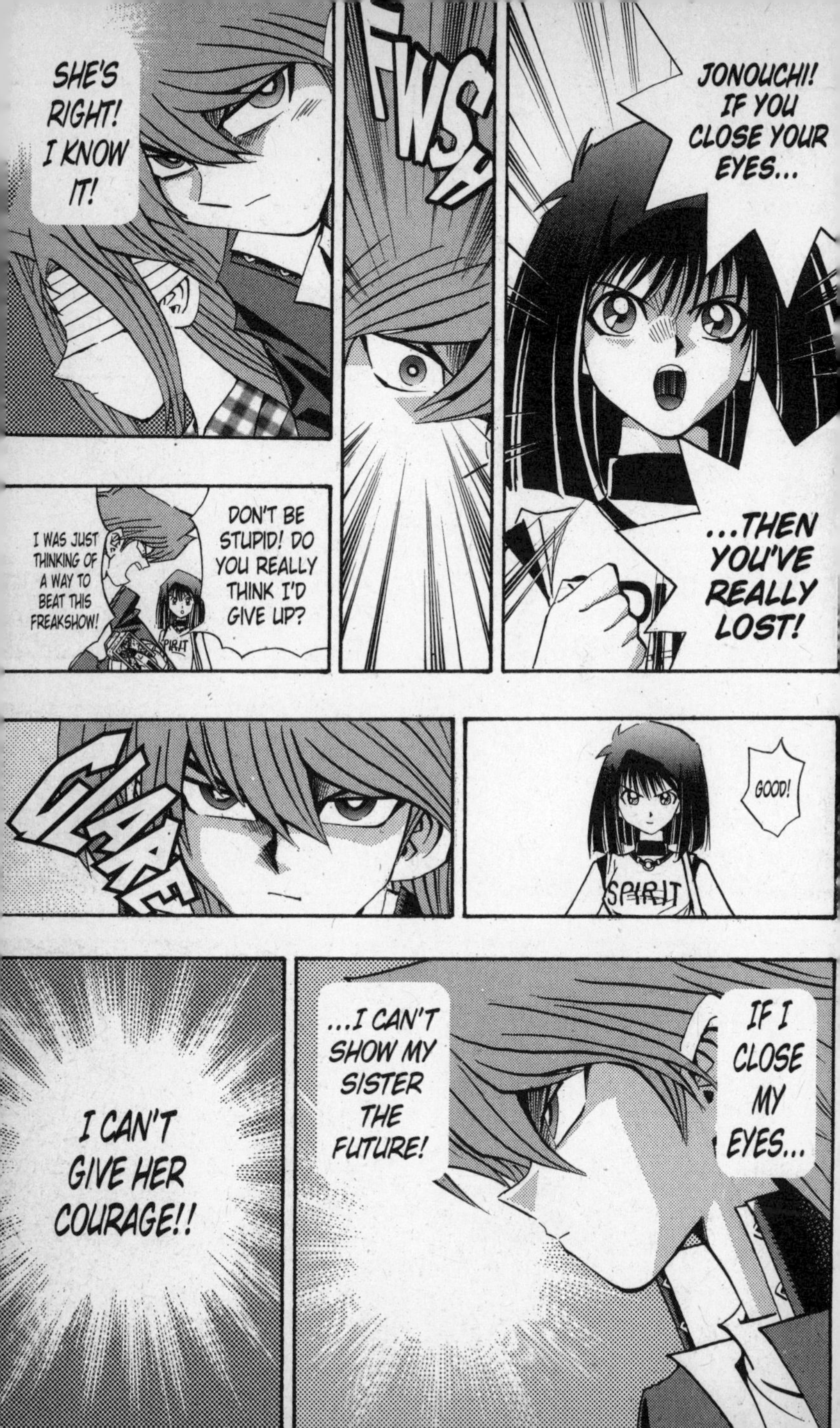
JONOUCHI! IF YOU CLOSE YOUR EYES...
...THEN YOU'VE REALLY LOST!
FWSH
SHE'S RIGHT! I KNOW IT!
DON'T BE STUPID! DO YOU REALLY THINK I'D GIVE UP?
I WAS JUST THINKING OF A WAY TO BEAT THIS FREAKSHOW!
GOOD!
GLARE
IF I CLOSE MY EYES...
...I CAN'T SHOW MY SISTER THE FUTURE!
I CAN'T GIVE HER COURAGE!!

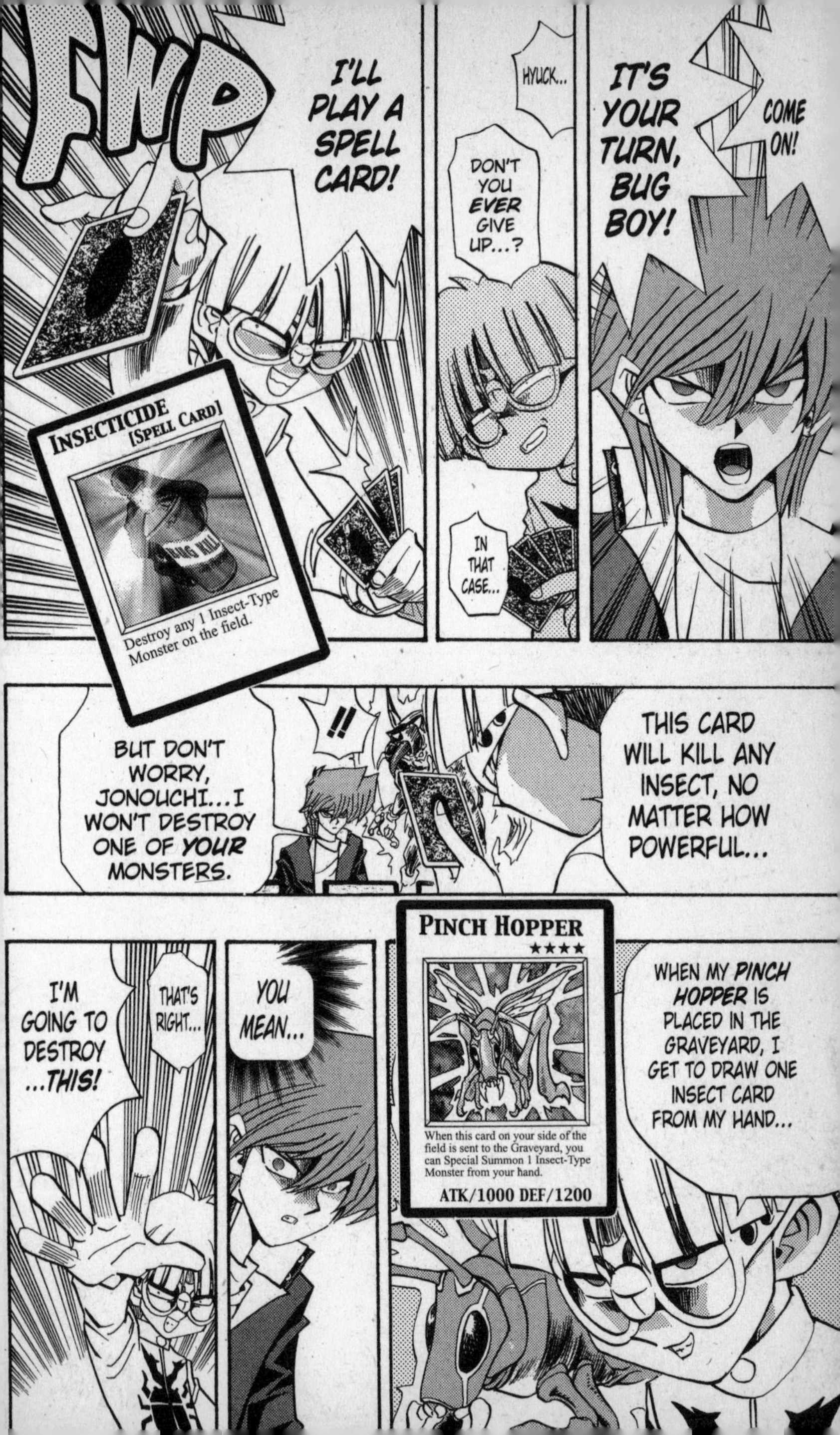
COME ON!
IT'S YOUR TURN, BUG BOY!
HYUCK...
DON'T YOU EVER GIVE UP...?
IN THAT CASE...
FWP
I'LL PLAY A SPELL CARD!
INSECTICIDE [SPELL CARD]
BUG KILL
Destroy any 1 Insect-Type Monster on the field.
THIS CARD WILL KILL ANY INSECT, NO MATTER HOW POWERFUL...
!!
BUT DON'T WORRY, JONOUCHI... I WON'T DESTROY ONE OF YOUR MONSTERS.
WHEN MY PINCH HOPPER IS PLACED IN THE GRAVEYARD, I GET TO DRAW ONE INSECT CARD FROM MY HAND...
PINCH HOPPER
★★★★
When this card on your side of the field is sent to the Graveyard, you can Special Summon 1 Insect-Type Monster from your hand.
ATK/1000 DEF/1200
YOU MEAN...
THAT'S RIGHT...
I'M GOING TO DESTROY ...THIS!

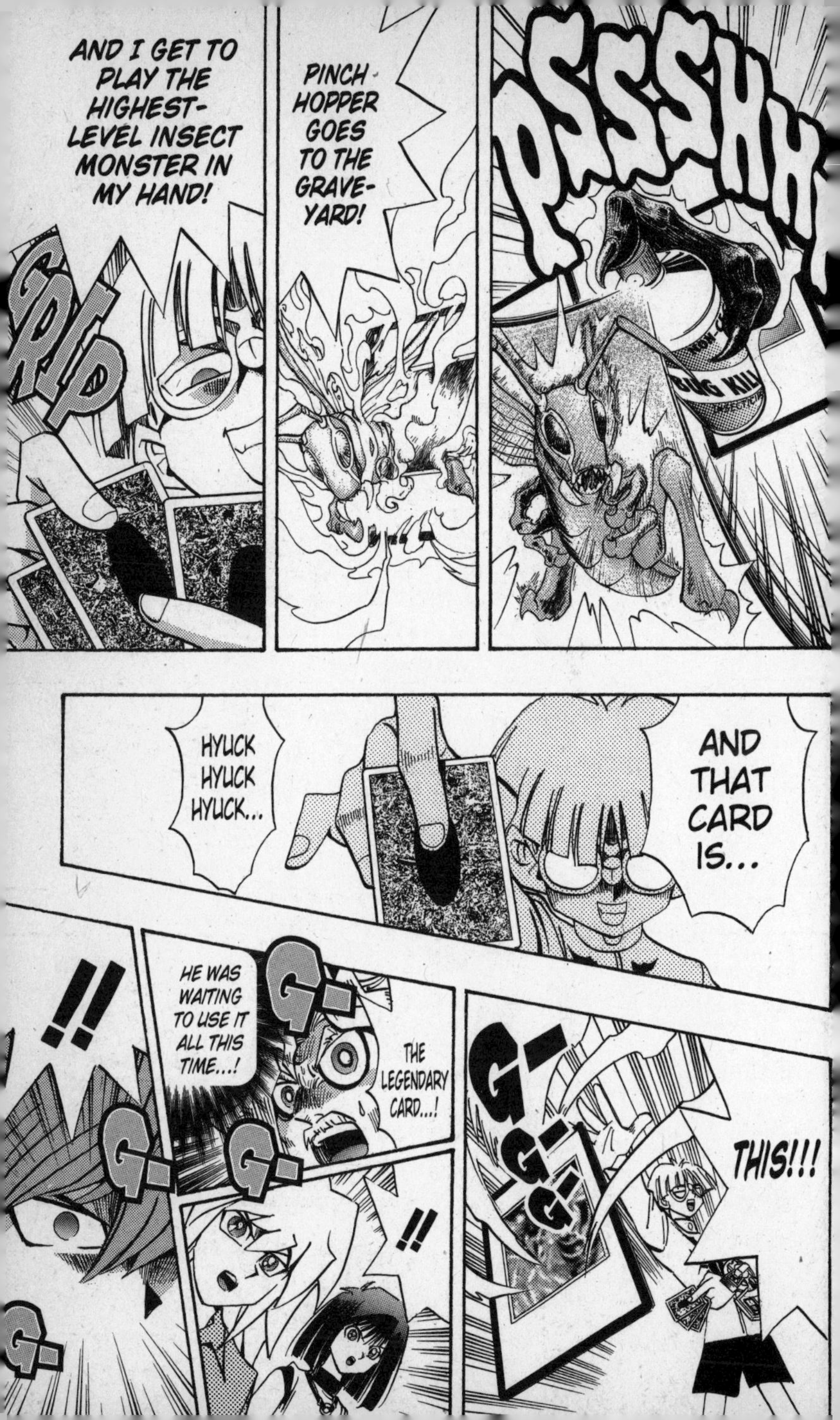
PSSSHH
BUG KILL
PINCH HOPPER GOES TO THE GRAVEYARD!
AND I GET TO PLAY THE HIGHEST-LEVEL INSECT MONSTER IN MY HAND!
GRIP
AND THAT CARD IS...
HYUCK HYUCK HYUCK...
THIS!!!
G-G-G-G-
THE LEGENDARY CARD...!
HE WAS WAITING TO USE IT ALL THIS TIME...!
G-
!!
G- G-
!!
G-

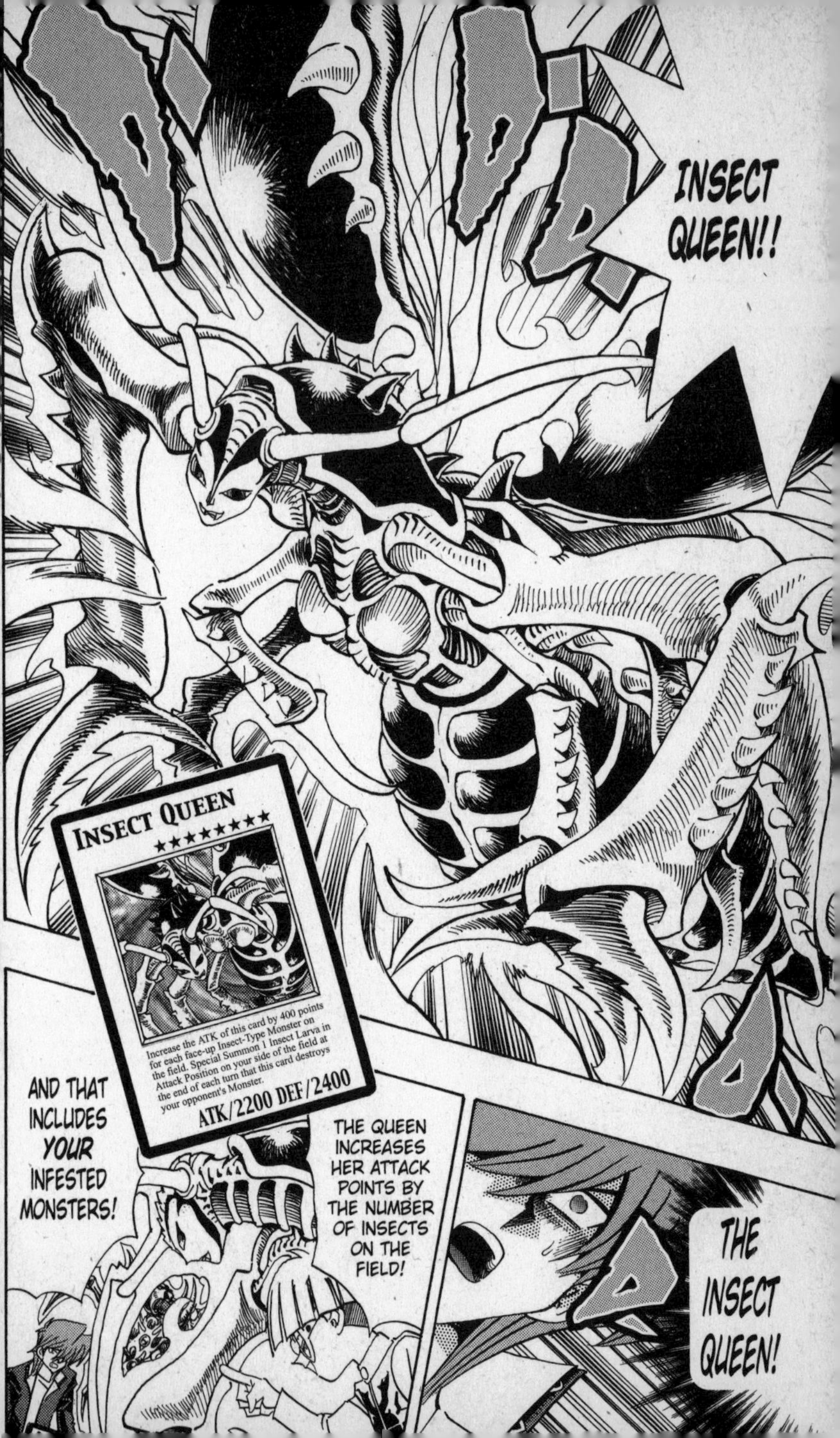
INSECT QUEEN!!
INSECT QUEEN
Increase the ATK of this card by 400 points for each face-up Insect-Type Monster on the field. Special Summon 1 Insect Larva in Attack Position on your side of the field at the end of each turn that this card destroys your opponent's Monster.
ATK/2200 DEF/2400
THE INSECT QUEEN!
THE QUEEN INCREASES HER ATTACK POINTS BY THE NUMBER OF INSECTS ON THE FIELD!
AND THAT INCLUDES YOUR INFESTED MONSTERS!

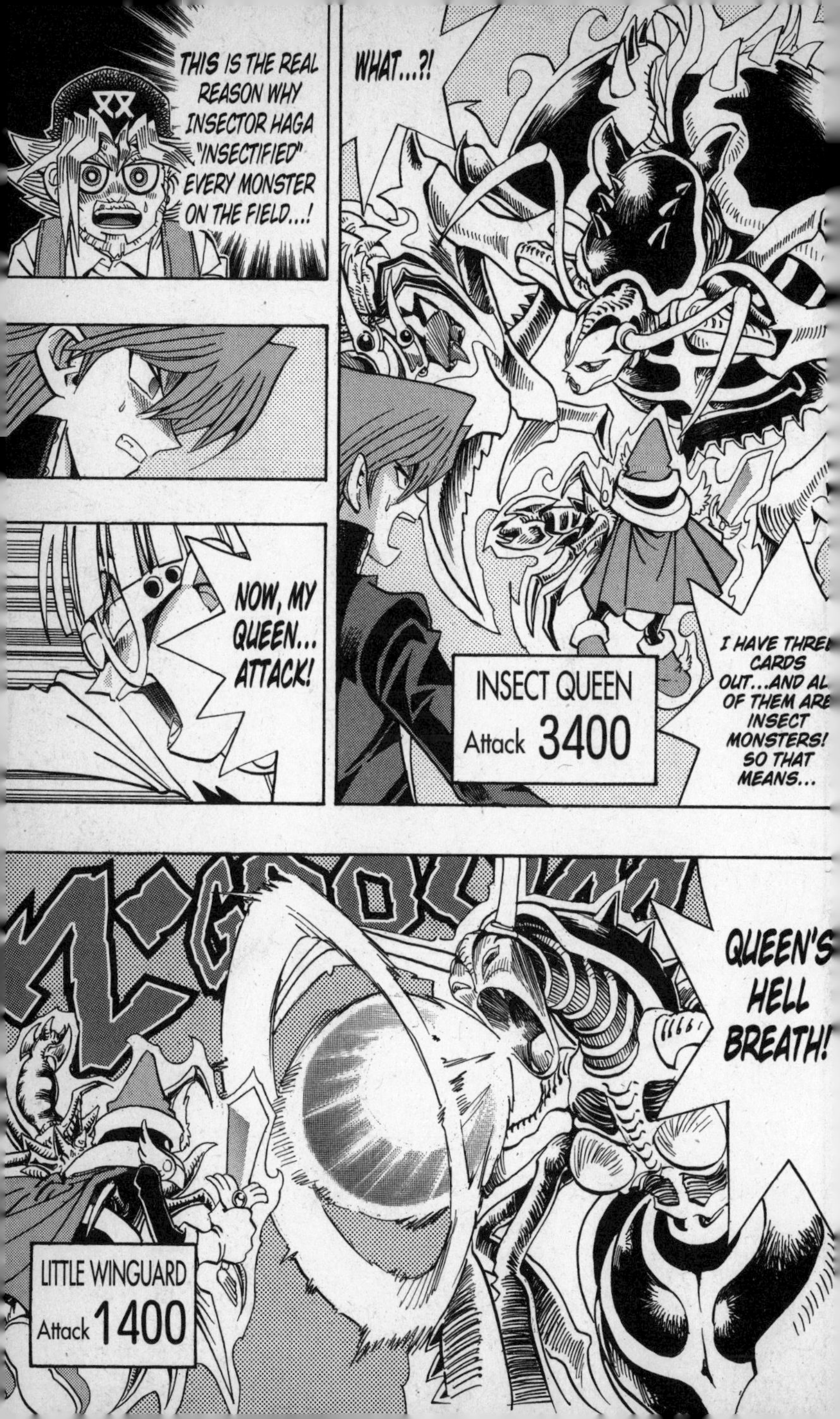
WHAT...?!
I HAVE THRE CARDS OUT...AND AL OF THEM ARE INSECT MONSTERS! SO THAT MEANS...
INSECT QUEEN Attack 3400
THIS IS THE REAL REASON WHY INSECTOR HAGA "INSECTIFIED" EVERY MONSTER ON THE FIELD...!
NOW, MY QUEEN... ATTACK!
QUEEN'S HELL BREATH!
LITTLE WINGUARD Attack 1400

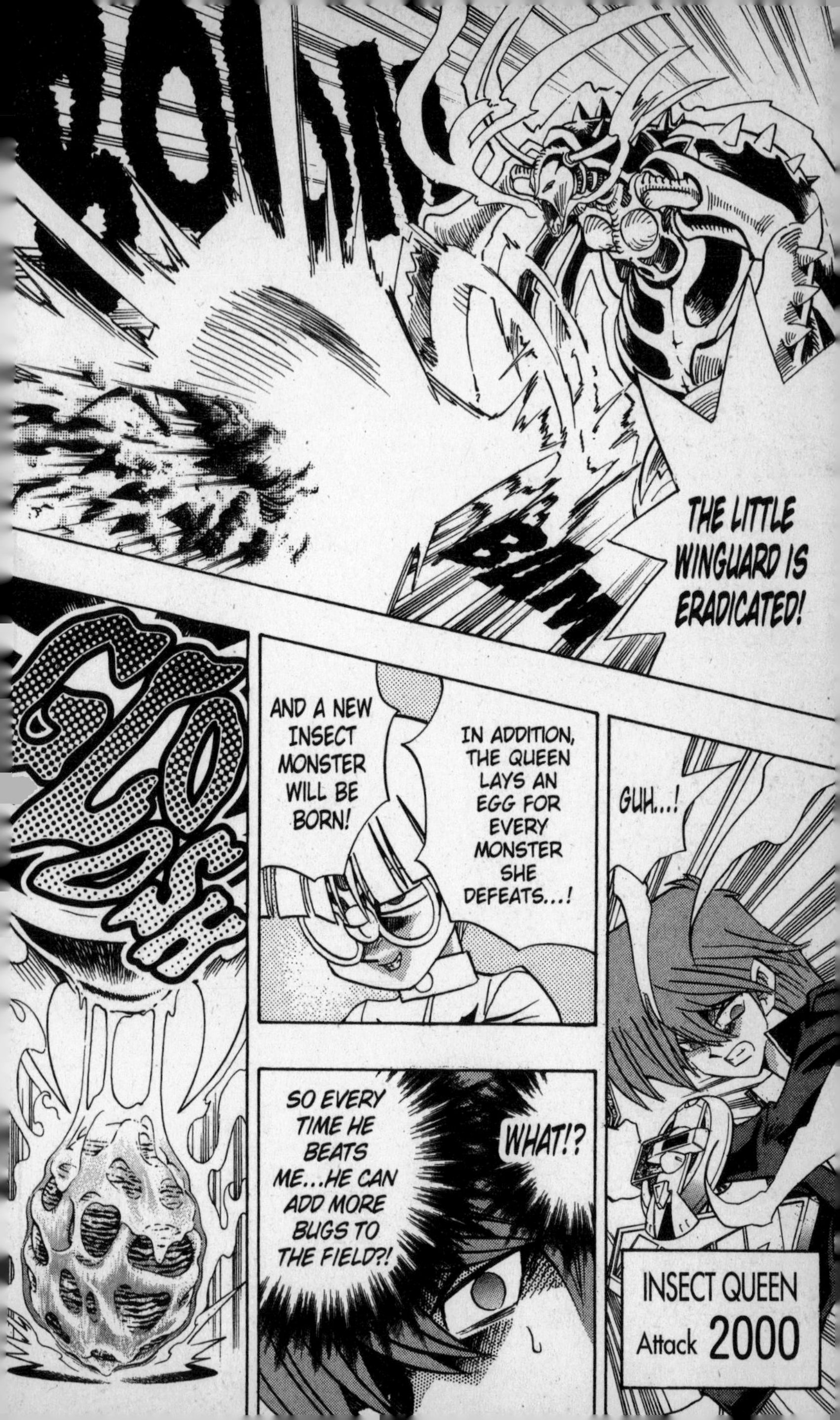
BAM
THE LITTLE WINGUARD IS ERADICATED!
GUH...!
INSECT QUEEN Attack 2000
IN ADDITION, THE QUEEN LAYS AN EGG FOR EVERY MONSTER SHE DEFEATS...!
AND A NEW INSECT MONSTER WILL BE BORN!
WHAT!?
SO EVERY TIME HE BEATS ME...HE CAN ADD MORE BUGS TO THE FIELD?!

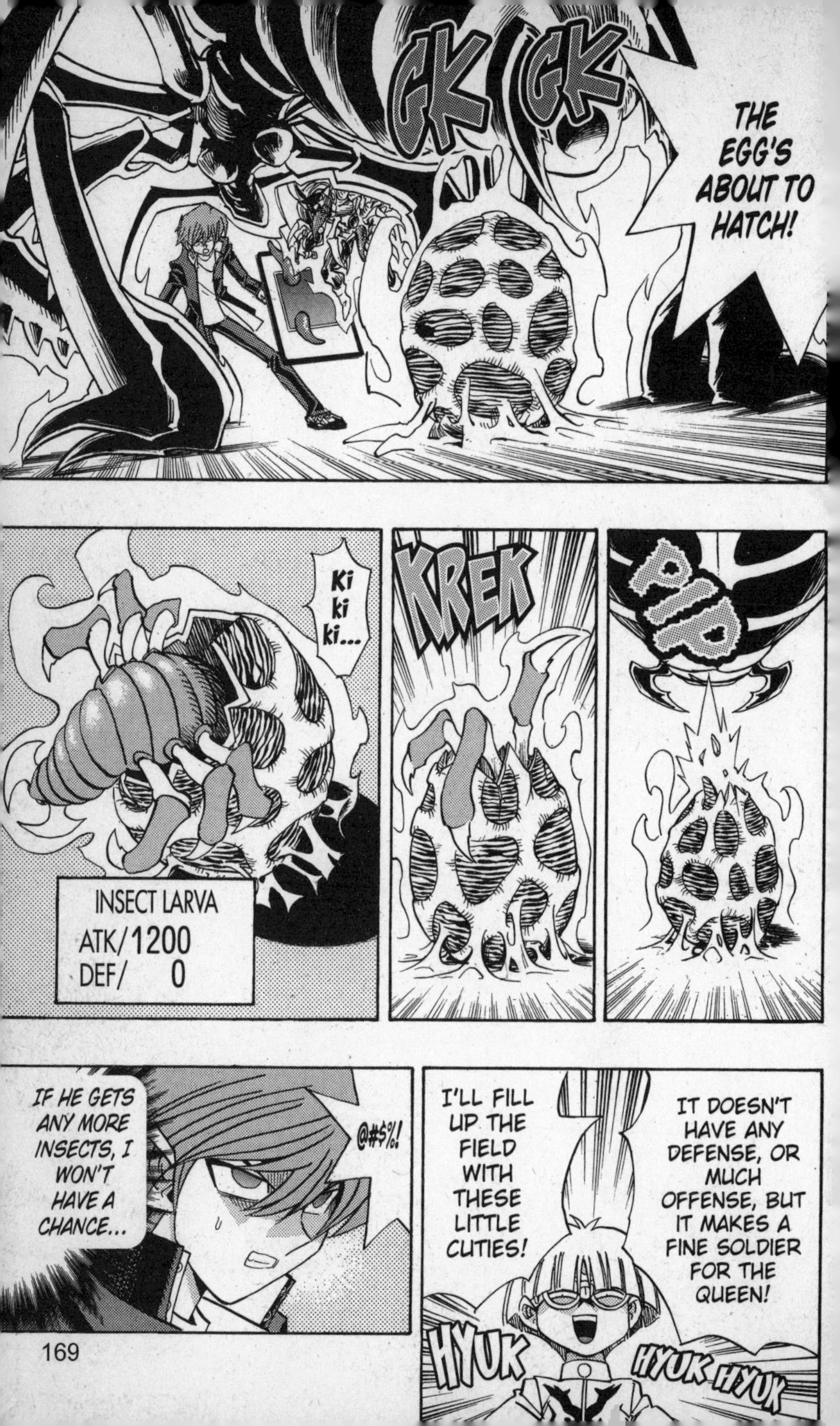
GK GK
THE EGG'S ABOUT TO HATCH!
RIP
KREK
Ki ki ki...
INSECT LARVA
ATK/1200
DEF/ 0
IT DOESN'T HAVE ANY DEFENSE, OR MUCH OFFENSE, BUT IT MAKES A FINE SOLDIER FOR THE QUEEN!
I'LL FILL UP THE FIELD WITH THESE LITTLE CUTIES!
HYUK HYUK HYUK
@#$%!
IF HE GETS ANY MORE INSECTS, I WON'T HAVE A CHANCE...

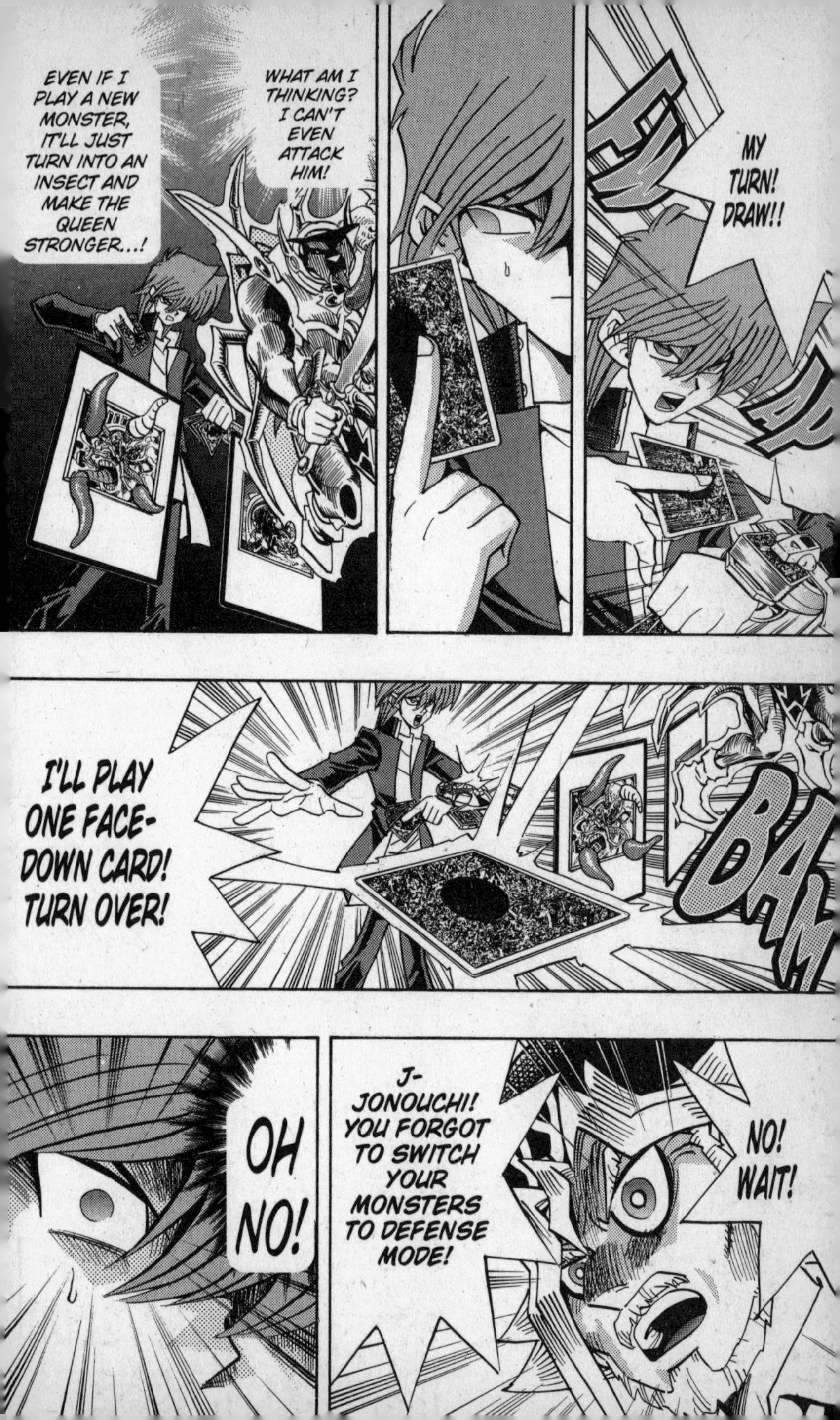
MY TURN! DRAW!!
WHAT AM I THINKING? I CAN'T EVEN ATTACK HIM!
EVEN IF I PLAY A NEW MONSTER, IT'LL JUST TURN INTO AN INSECT AND MAKE THE QUEEN STRONGER...!
I'LL PLAY ONE FACE-DOWN CARD! TURN OVER!
NO! WAIT!
J-JONOUCHI! YOU FORGOT TO SWITCH YOUR MONSTERS TO DEFENSE MODE!
OH NO!

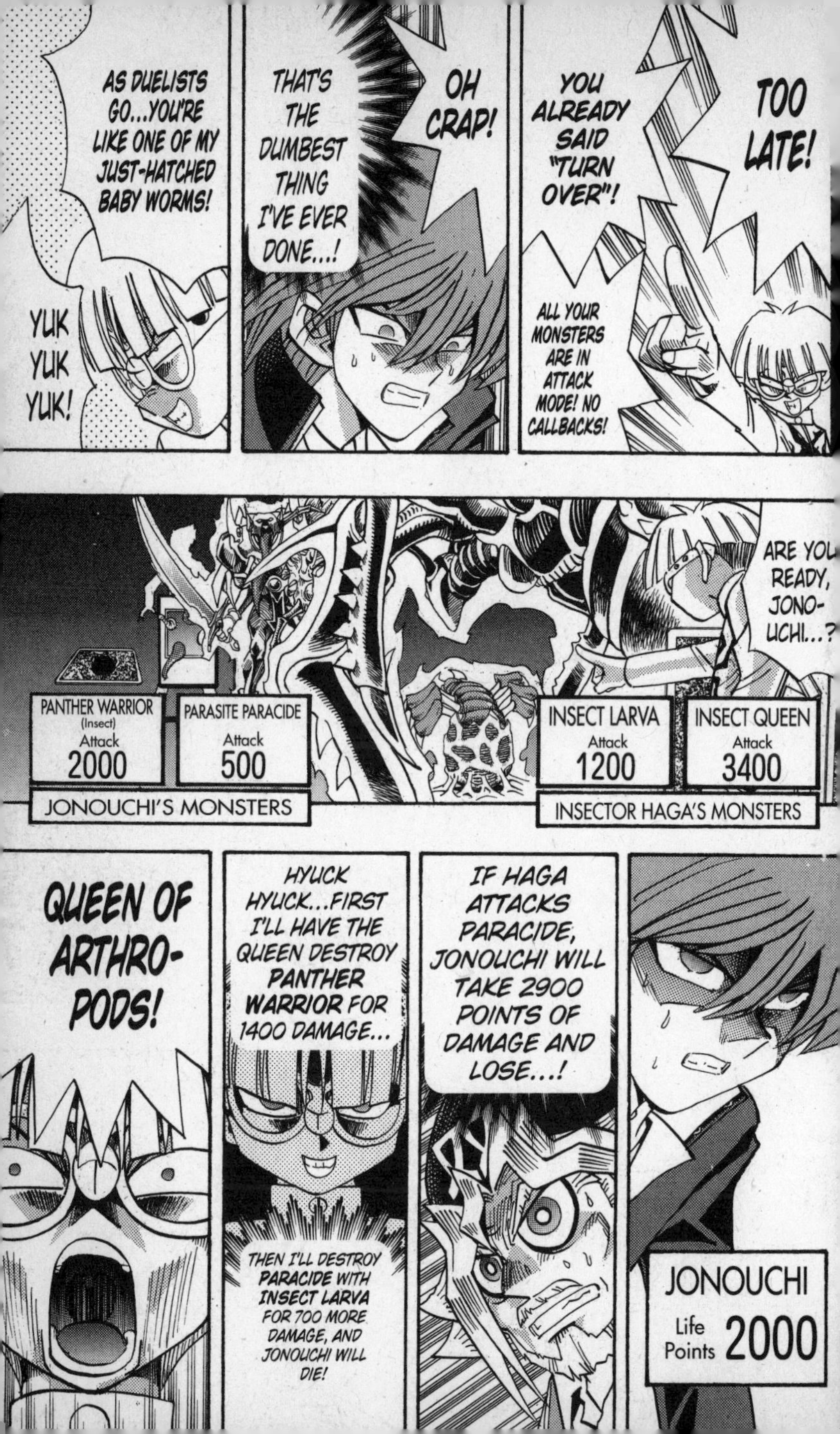
TOO LATE!
YOU ALREADY SAID "TURN OVER"!
ALL YOUR MONSTERS ARE IN ATTACK MODE! NO CALLBACKS!
OH CRAP!
THAT'S THE DUMBEST THING I'VE EVER DONE...!
AS DUELISTS GO...YOU'RE LIKE ONE OF MY JUST-HATCHED BABY WORMS!
YUK YUK YUK!
ARE YOU READY, JONOUCHI...?
INSECT QUEEN Attack 3400
INSECT LARVA Attack 1200
INSECTOR HAGA'S MONSTERS
PARASITE PARACIDE Attack 500
PANTHER WARRIOR (Insect) Attack 2000
JONOUCHI'S MONSTERS
JONOUCHI Life Points 2000
IF HAGA ATTACKS PARACIDE, JONOUCHI WILL TAKE 2900 POINTS OF DAMAGE AND LOSE...!
HYUCK HYUCK...FIRST I'LL HAVE THE QUEEN DESTROY PANTHER WARRIOR FOR 1400 DAMAGE...
THEN I'LL DESTROY PARACIDE WITH INSECT LARVA FOR 700 MORE DAMAGE, AND JONOUCHI WILL DIE!
QUEEN OF ARTHRO-PODS!

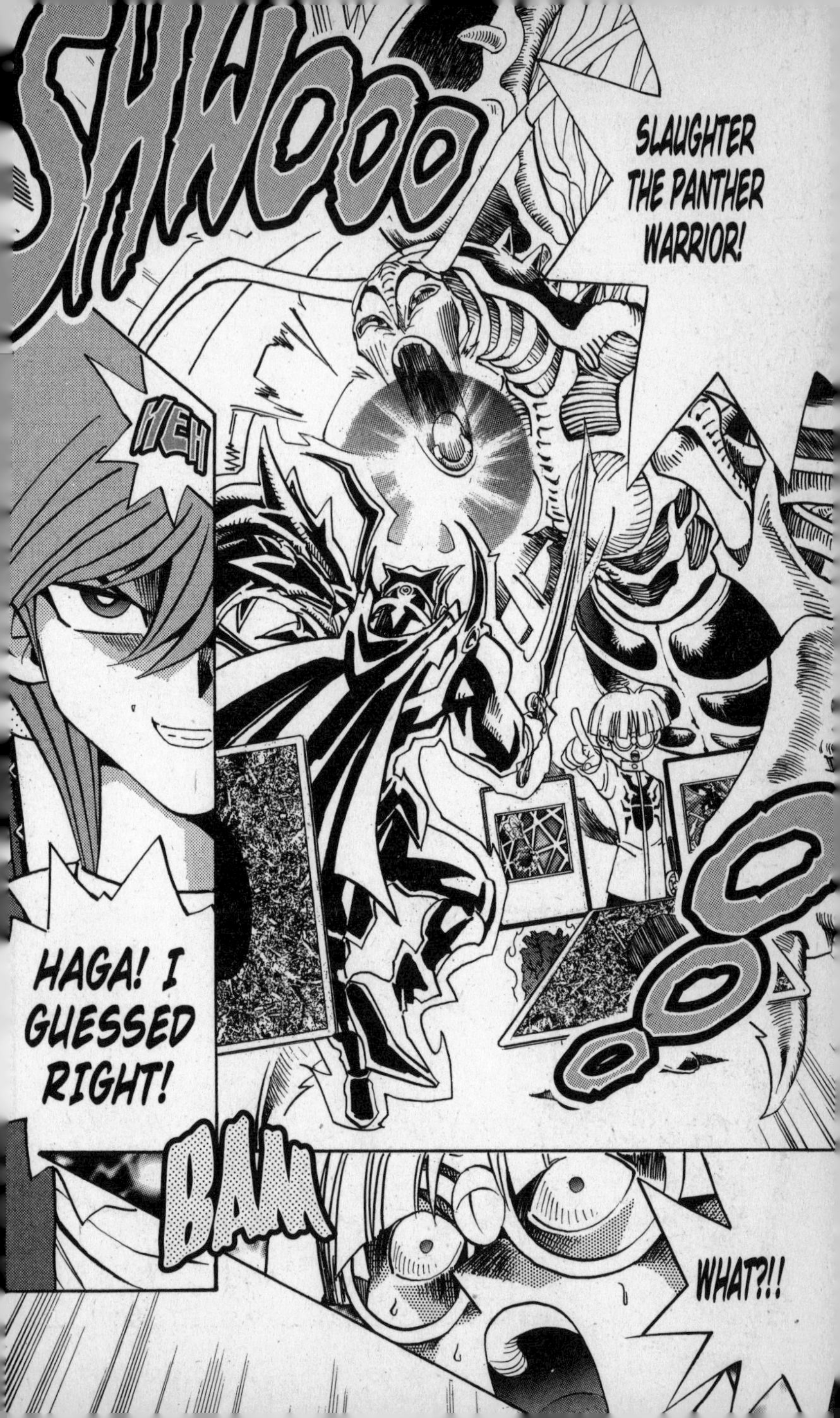
SLAUGHTER THE PANTHER WARRIOR!
SHWOOO
HEH
HAGA! I GUESSED RIGHT!
WHAT?!!
BAM

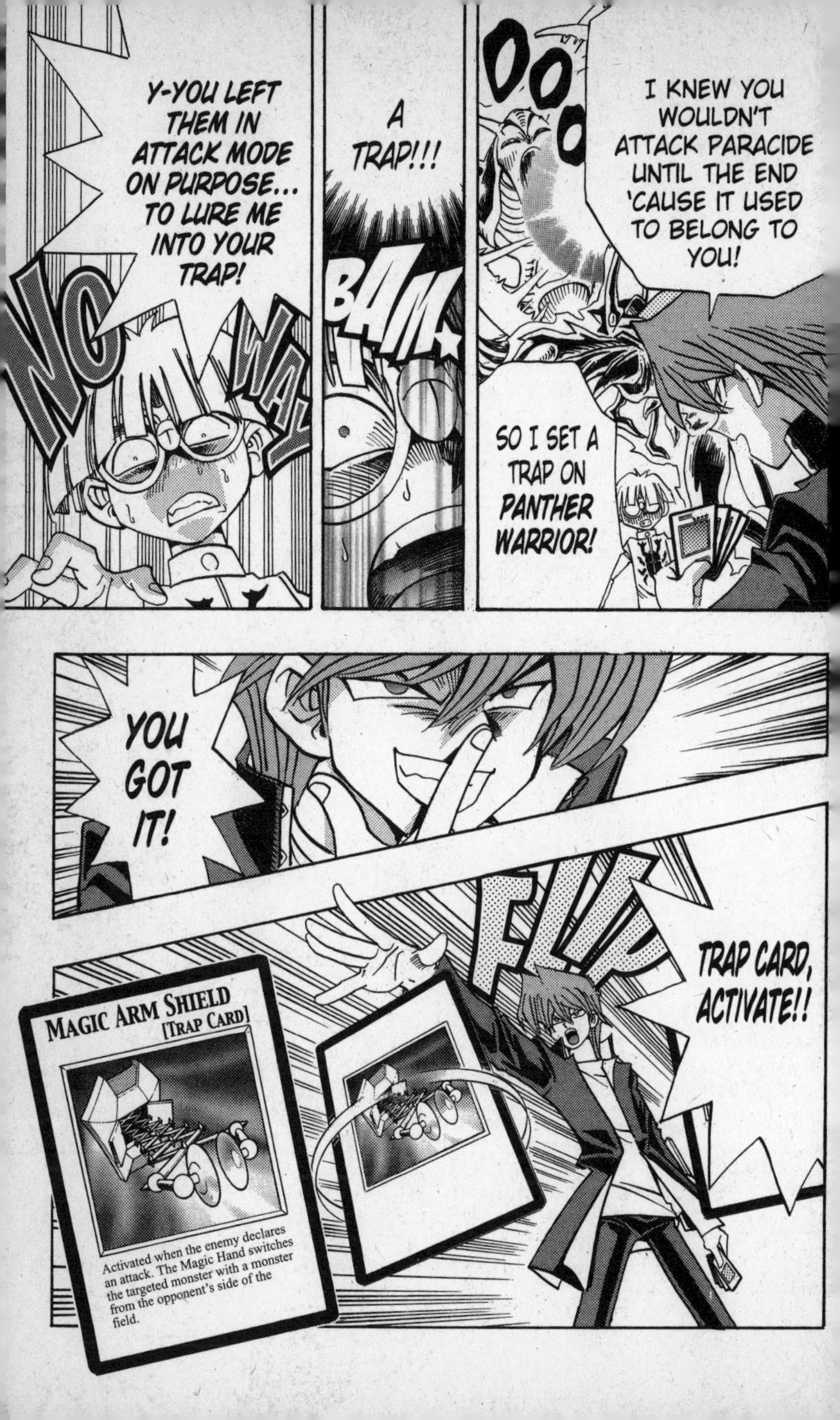
I KNEW YOU WOULDN'T ATTACK PARACIDE UNTIL THE END 'CAUSE IT USED TO BELONG TO YOU!
SO I SET A TRAP ON PANTHER WARRIOR!
A TRAP!!!
BAM
Y-YOU LEFT THEM IN ATTACK MODE ON PURPOSE... TO LURE ME INTO YOUR TRAP!
NO WAY
YOU GOT IT!
TRAP CARD, ACTIVATE!!
FLIP
MAGIC ARM SHIELD
[TRAP CARD]
Activated when the enemy declares an attack. The Magic Hand switches the targeted monster with a monster from the opponent's side of the field.

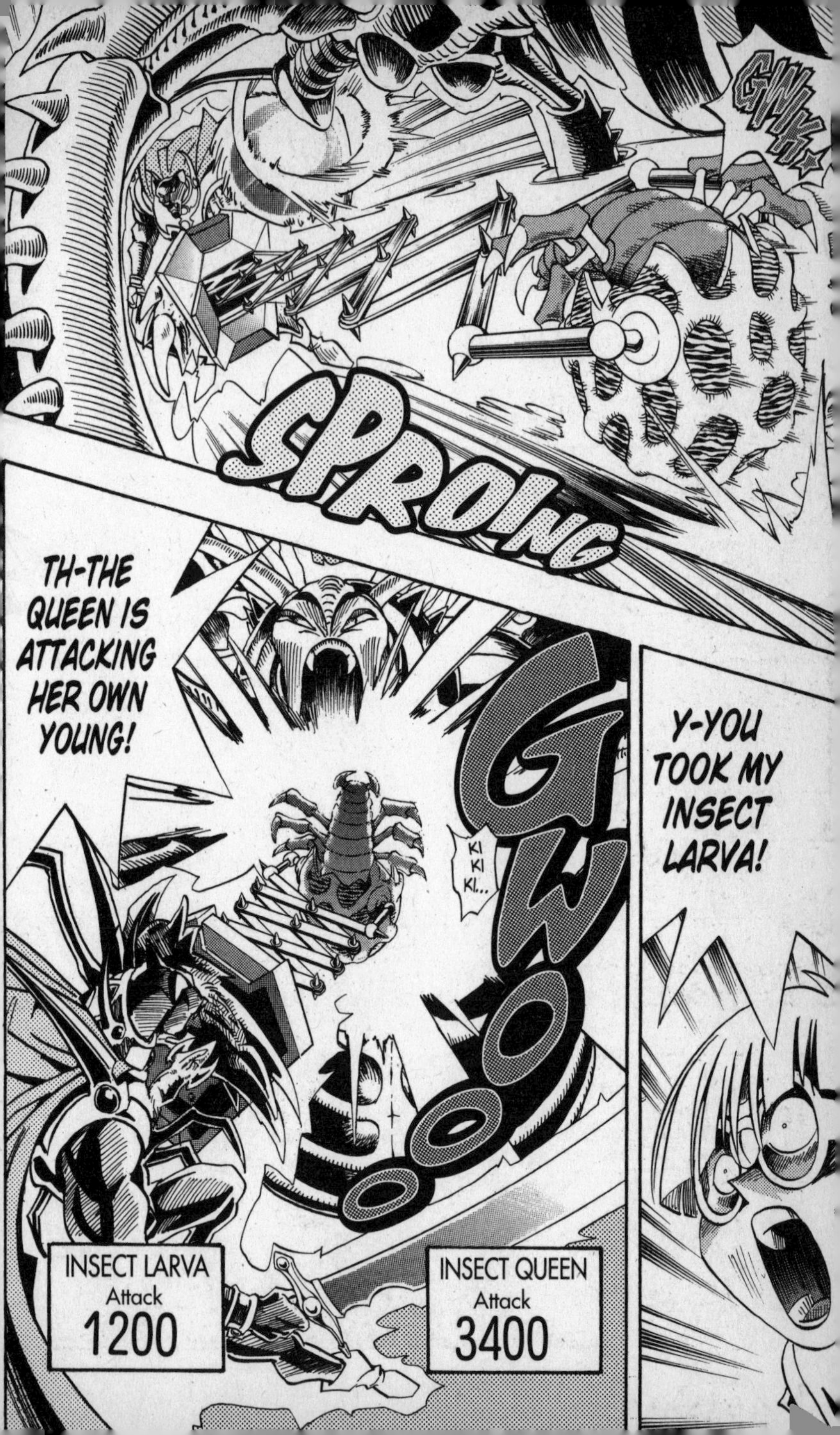
GWK
SPROING
Y-YOU TOOK MY INSECT LARVA!
TH-THE QUEEN IS ATTACKING HER OWN YOUNG!
KI KI KI...
GWOOOO
INSECT QUEEN Attack 3400
INSECT LARVA Attack 1200

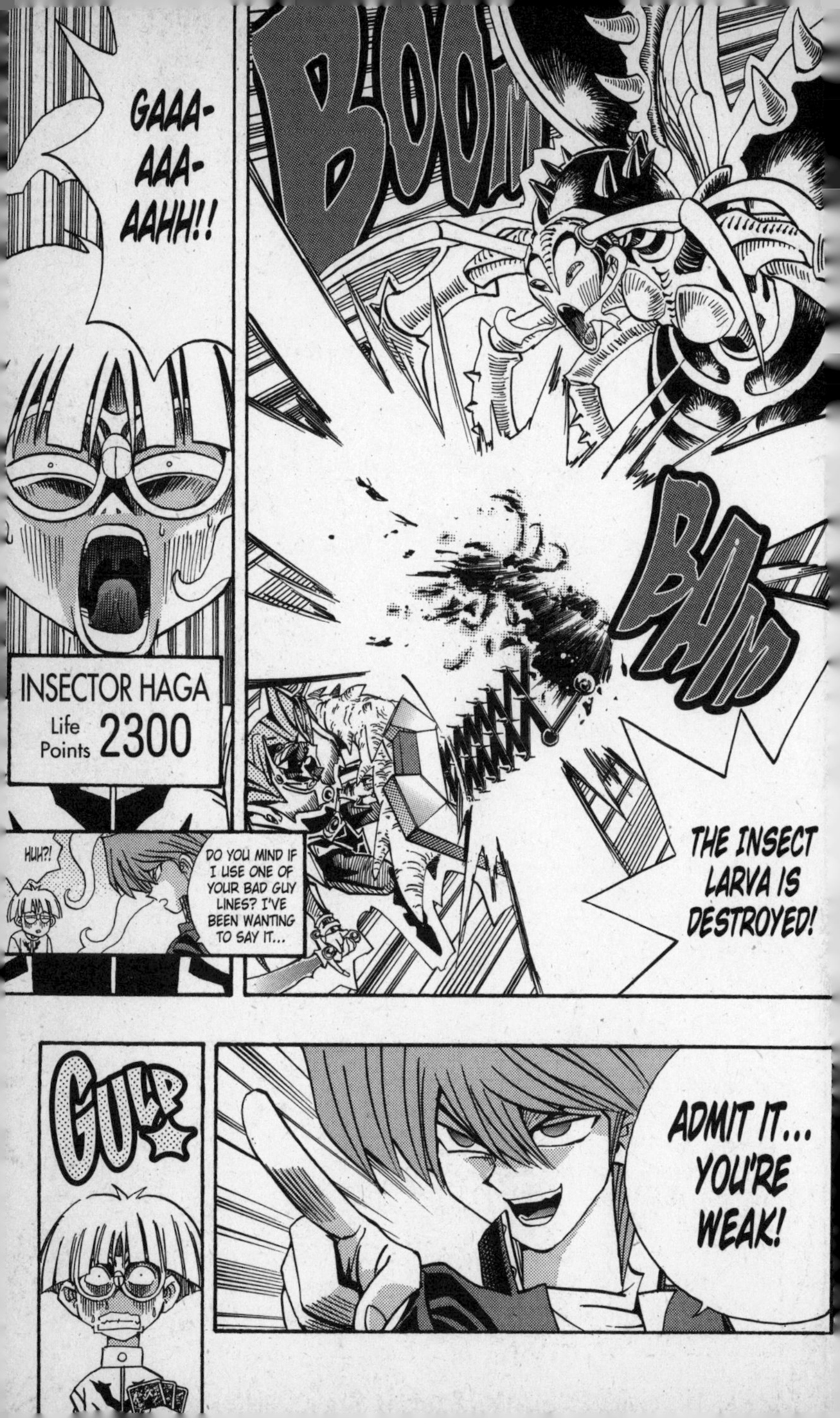
BOOM
BAM
THE INSECT LARVA IS DESTROYED!
GAAA-AAA-AAHH!!
INSECTOR HAGA
Life Points 2300
DO YOU MIND IF I USE ONE OF YOUR BAD GUY LINES? I'VE BEEN WANTING TO SAY IT...
HUH?!
ADMIT IT... YOU'RE WEAK!
GULP

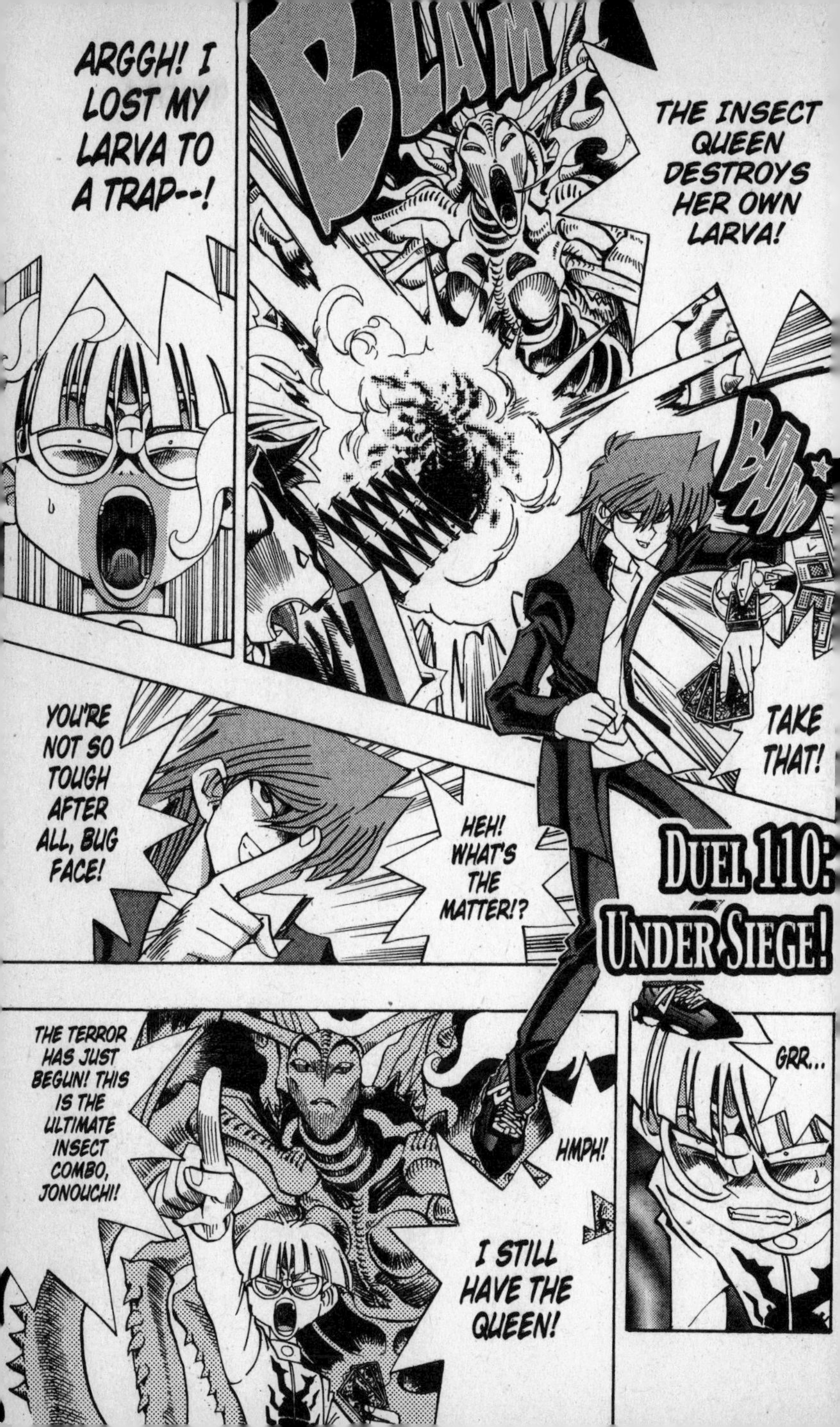
BLAM
THE INSECT QUEEN DESTROYS HER OWN LARVA!
BAM
TAKE THAT!
ARGGH! I LOST MY LARVA TO A TRAP--!
DUEL 110: UNDER SIEGE!
HEH! WHAT'S THE MATTER!?
YOU'RE NOT SO TOUGH AFTER ALL, BUG FACE!
GRR...
HMPH!
I STILL HAVE THE QUEEN!
THE TERROR HAS JUST BEGUN! THIS IS THE ULTIMATE INSECT COMBO, JONOUCHI!

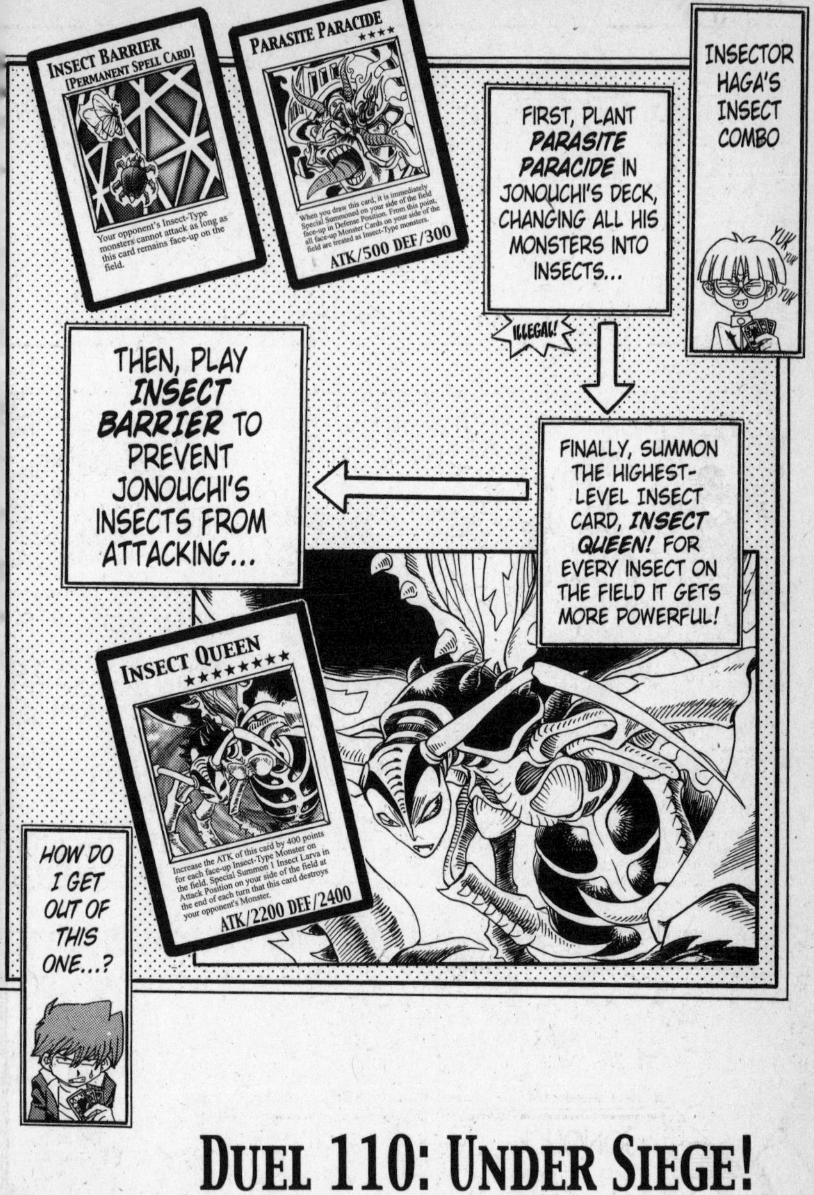
INSECTOR HAGA'S INSECT COMBO
YUK YUK YUK
FIRST, PLANT PARASITE PARACIDE IN JONOUCHI'S DECK, CHANGING ALL HIS MONSTERS INTO INSECTS...
ILLEGAL!
PARASITE PARACIDE ★★★★
When you draw this card, it is immediately Special Summoned on your side of the field face-up in Defense Position. From this point, all face-up Monster Cards on your side of the field are treated as Insect-Type monsters.
ATK/500 DEF/300
INSECT BARRIER [PERMANENT SPELL CARD]
Your opponent's Insect-Type monsters cannot attack as long as this card remains face-up on the field.
FINALLY, SUMMON THE HIGHEST-LEVEL INSECT CARD, INSECT QUEEN! FOR EVERY INSECT ON THE FIELD IT GETS MORE POWERFUL!
THEN, PLAY INSECT BARRIER TO PREVENT JONOUCHI'S INSECTS FROM ATTACKING...
INSECT QUEEN ★★★★★★★
Increase the ATK of this card by 400 points for each face-up Insect-Type Monster on the field. Special Summon 1 Insect Larva in Attack Position on your side of the field at the end of each turn that this card destroys your opponent's Monster.
ATK/2200 DEF/2400
HOW DO I GET OUT OF THIS ONE...?

Duel 110: Under Siege!

READ THIS WAY

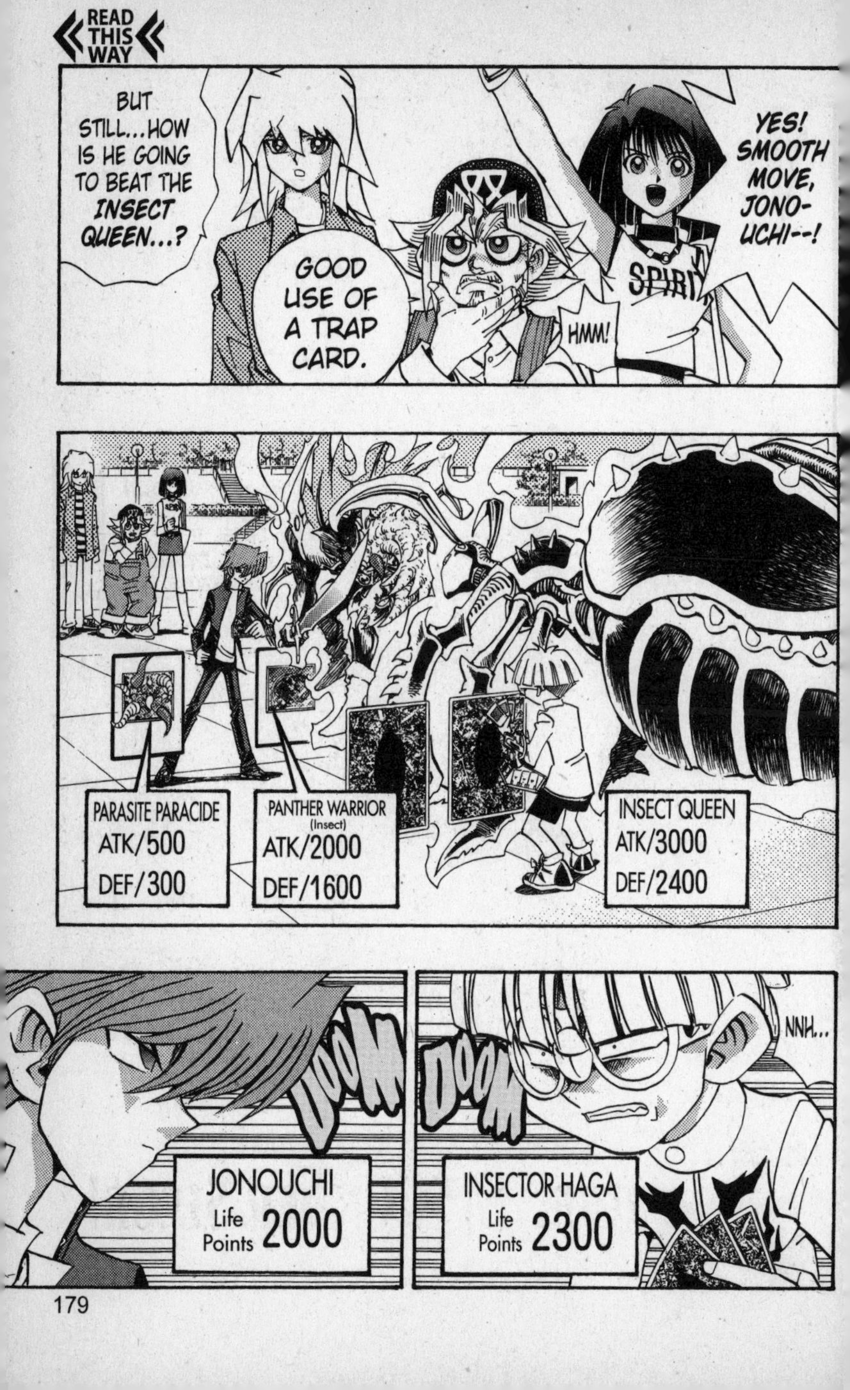

YES! SMOOTH MOVE, JONO-UCHI--!
HMM!
GOOD USE OF A TRAP CARD.
BUT STILL...HOW IS HE GOING TO BEAT THE INSECT QUEEN...?
INSECT QUEEN ATK/3000 DEF/2400
PANTHER WARRIOR (Insect) ATK/2000 DEF/1600
PARASITE PARACIDE ATK/500 DEF/300
NNH...
DOOM
INSECTOR HAGA Life Points 2300
DOOM
JONOUCHI Life Points 2000

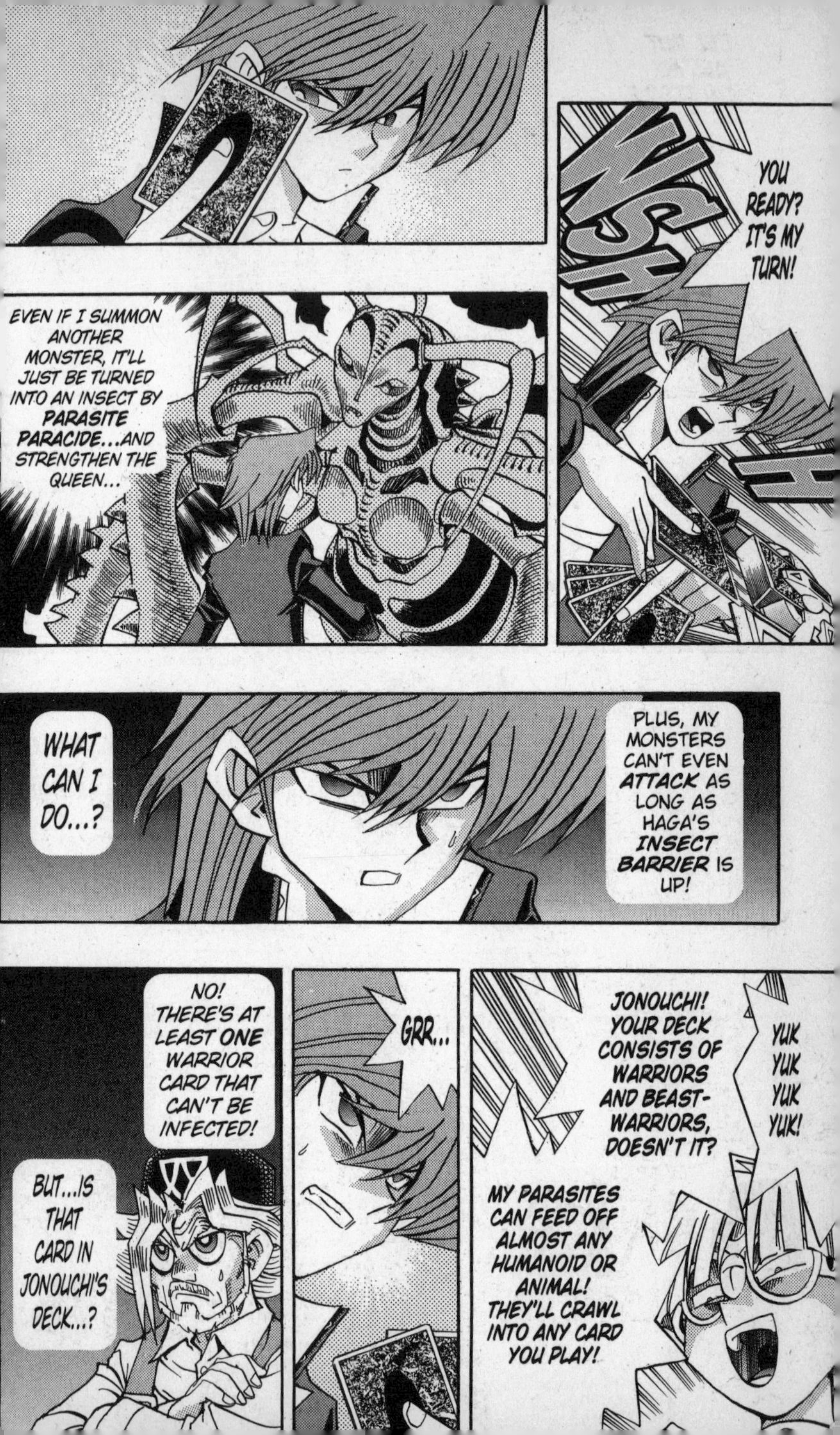
YOU READY? IT'S MY TURN!
EVEN IF I SUMMON ANOTHER MONSTER, IT'LL JUST BE TURNED INTO AN INSECT BY PARASITE PARACIDE...AND STRENGTHEN THE QUEEN...
PLUS, MY MONSTERS CAN'T EVEN ATTACK AS LONG AS HAGA'S INSECT BARRIER IS UP!
WHAT CAN I DO...?
YUK YUK YUK YUK!
JONOUCHI! YOUR DECK CONSISTS OF WARRIORS AND BEAST-WARRIORS, DOESN'T IT?
MY PARASITES CAN FEED OFF ALMOST ANY HUMANOID OR ANIMAL! THEY'LL CRAWL INTO ANY CARD YOU PLAY!
GRR...
NO! THERE'S AT LEAST ONE WARRIOR CARD THAT CAN'T BE INFECTED!
BUT...IS THAT CARD IN JONOUCHI'S DECK...?

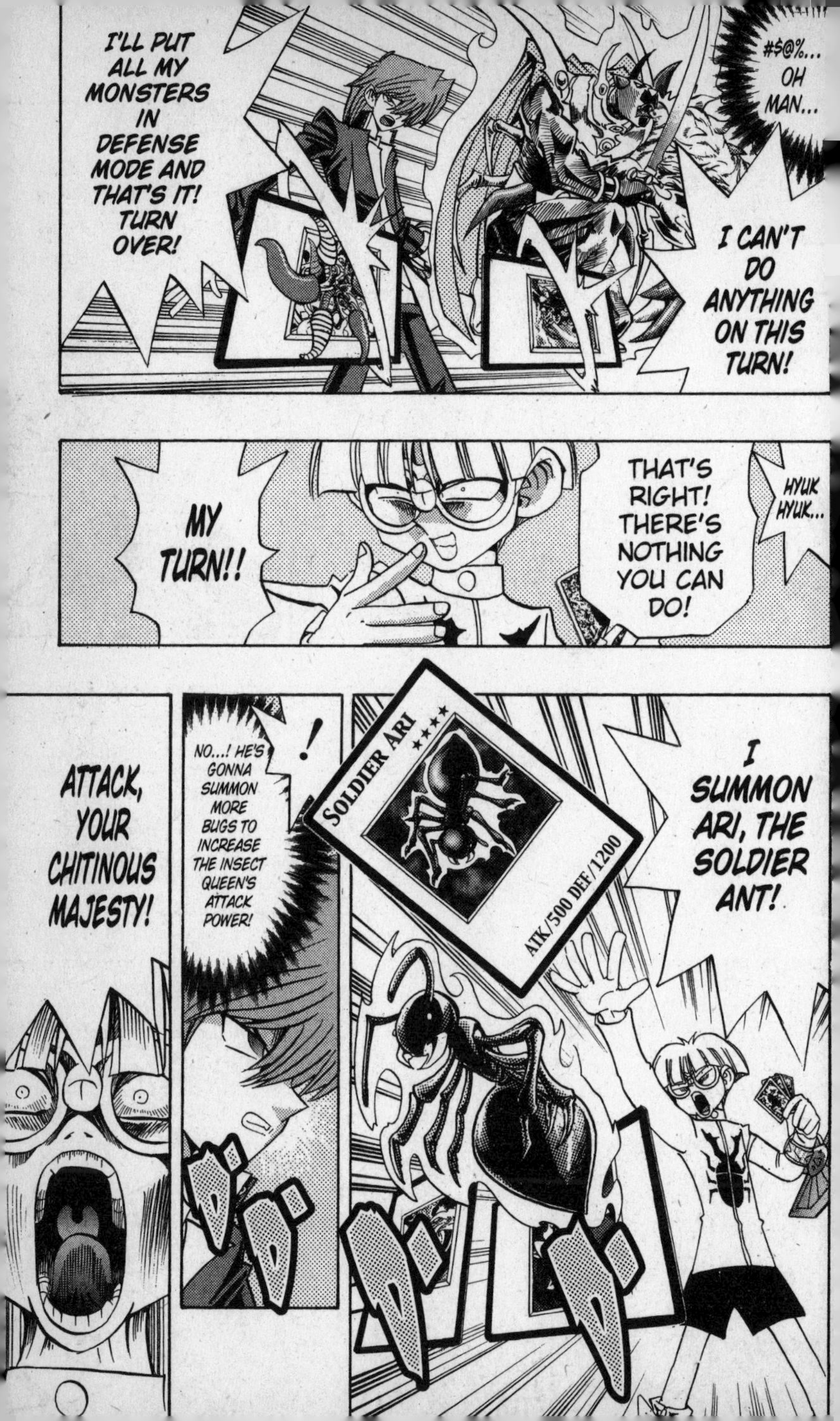
#$@%... OH MAN...
I CAN'T DO ANYTHING ON THIS TURN!
I'LL PUT ALL MY MONSTERS IN DEFENSE MODE AND THAT'S IT! TURN OVER!
HYUK HYUK...
THAT'S RIGHT! THERE'S NOTHING YOU CAN DO!
MY TURN!!
I SUMMON ARI, THE SOLDIER ANT!
SOLDIER ARI
ATK/500 DEF/1200
!
NO...! HE'S GONNA SUMMON MORE BUGS TO INCREASE THE INSECT QUEEN'S ATTACK POWER!
ATTACK, YOUR CHITINOUS MAJESTY!

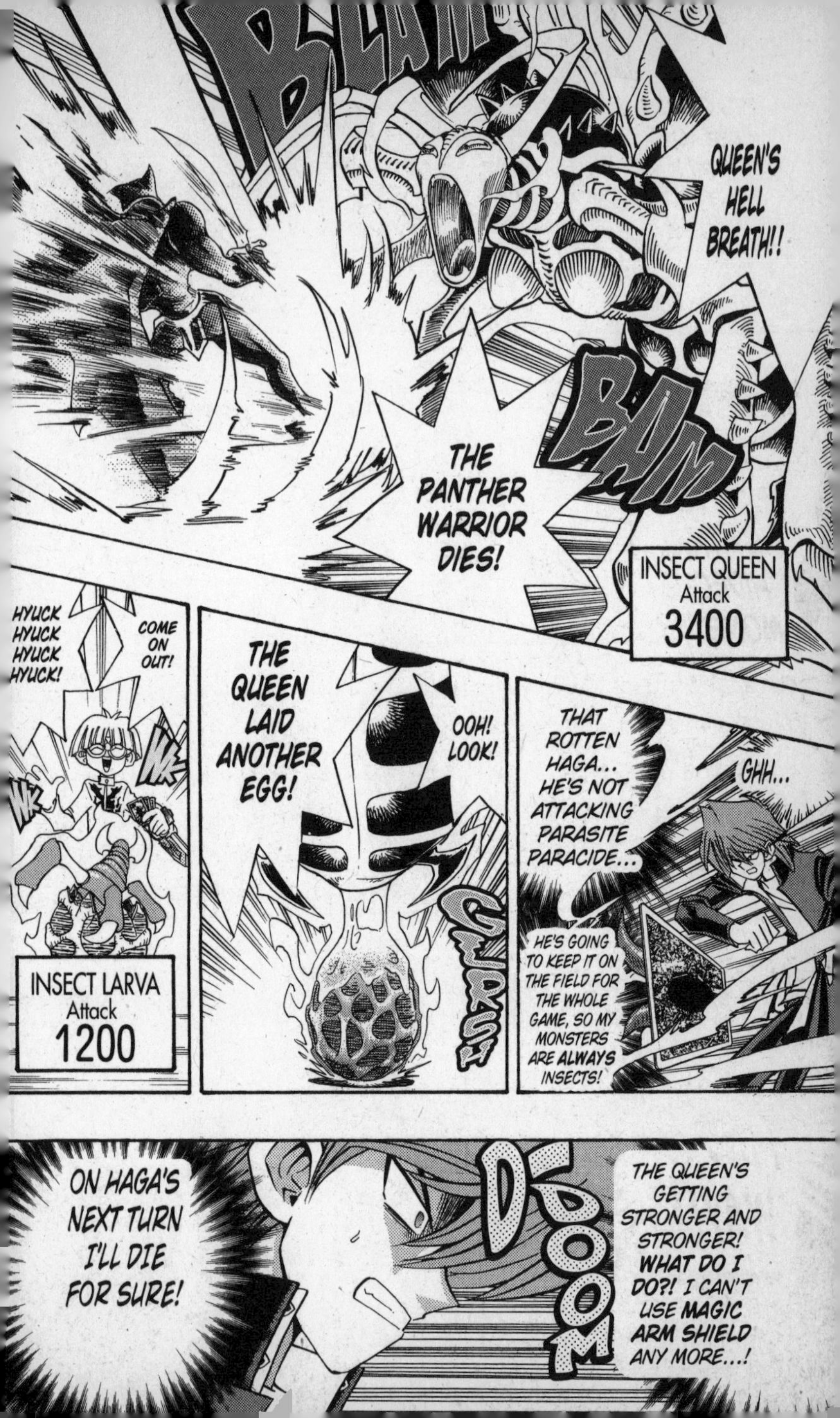
QUEEN'S HELL BREATH!!
BAM
THE PANTHER WARRIOR DIES!
INSECT QUEEN Attack 3400
THAT ROTTEN HAGA... HE'S NOT ATTACKING PARASITE PARACIDE...
GHH...
HE'S GOING TO KEEP IT ON THE FIELD FOR THE WHOLE GAME, SO MY MONSTERS ARE ALWAYS INSECTS!
OOH! LOOK!
THE QUEEN LAID ANOTHER EGG!
COME ON OUT!
HYUCK HYUCK HYUCK HYUCK!
WK
WK
INSECT LARVA Attack 1200
THE QUEEN'S GETTING STRONGER AND STRONGER! WHAT DO I DO?! I CAN'T USE MAGIC ARM SHIELD ANY MORE...!
DOOOM
ON HAGA'S NEXT TURN I'LL DIE FOR SURE!

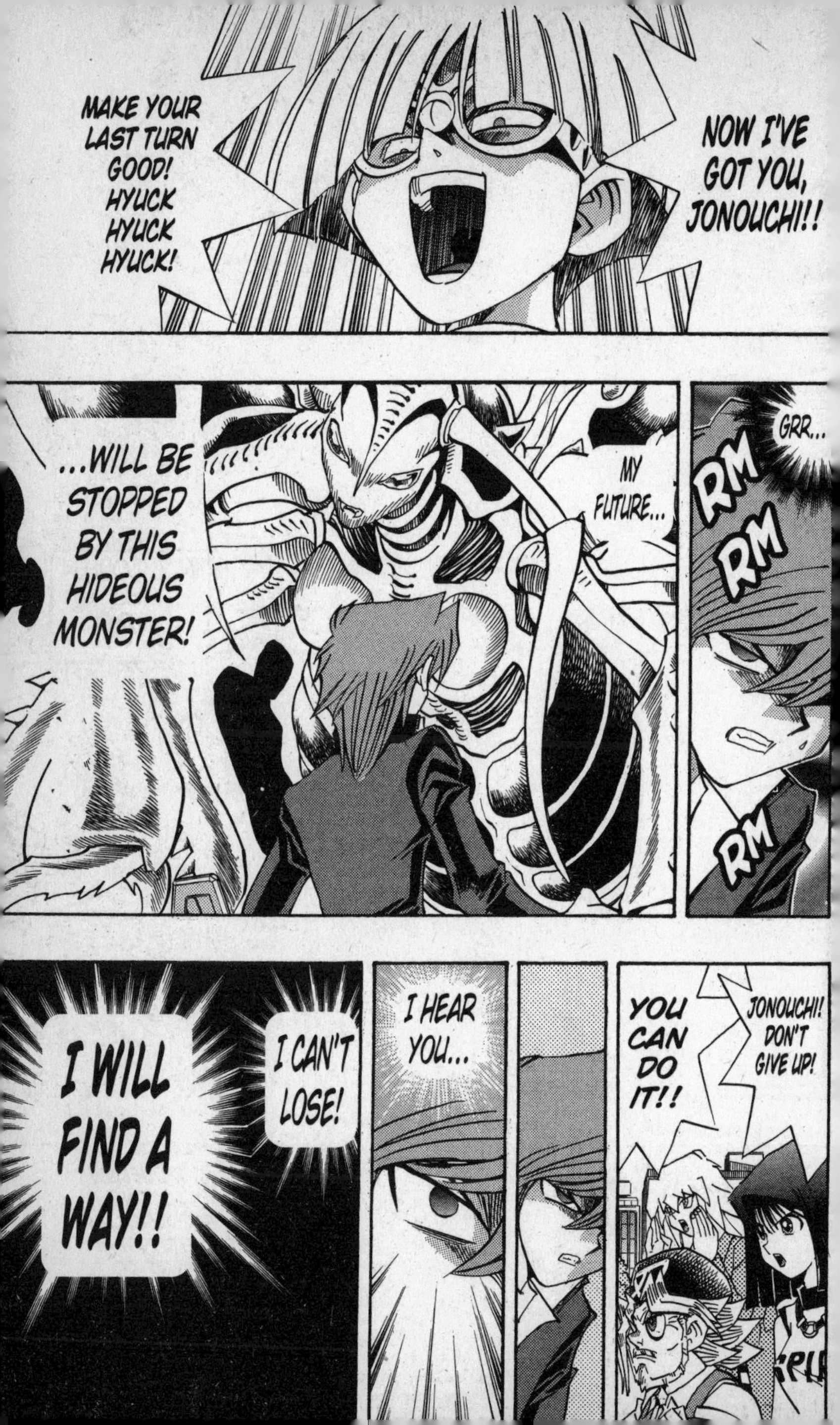
NOW I'VE GOT YOU, JONOUCHI!!
MAKE YOUR LAST TURN GOOD! HYUCK HYUCK HYUCK!
GRR...
RM RM
RM
MY FUTURE...
...WILL BE STOPPED BY THIS HIDEOUS MONSTER!
JONOUCHI! DON'T GIVE UP!
YOU CAN DO IT!!
I HEAR YOU...
I CAN'T LOSE!
I WILL FIND A WAY!!

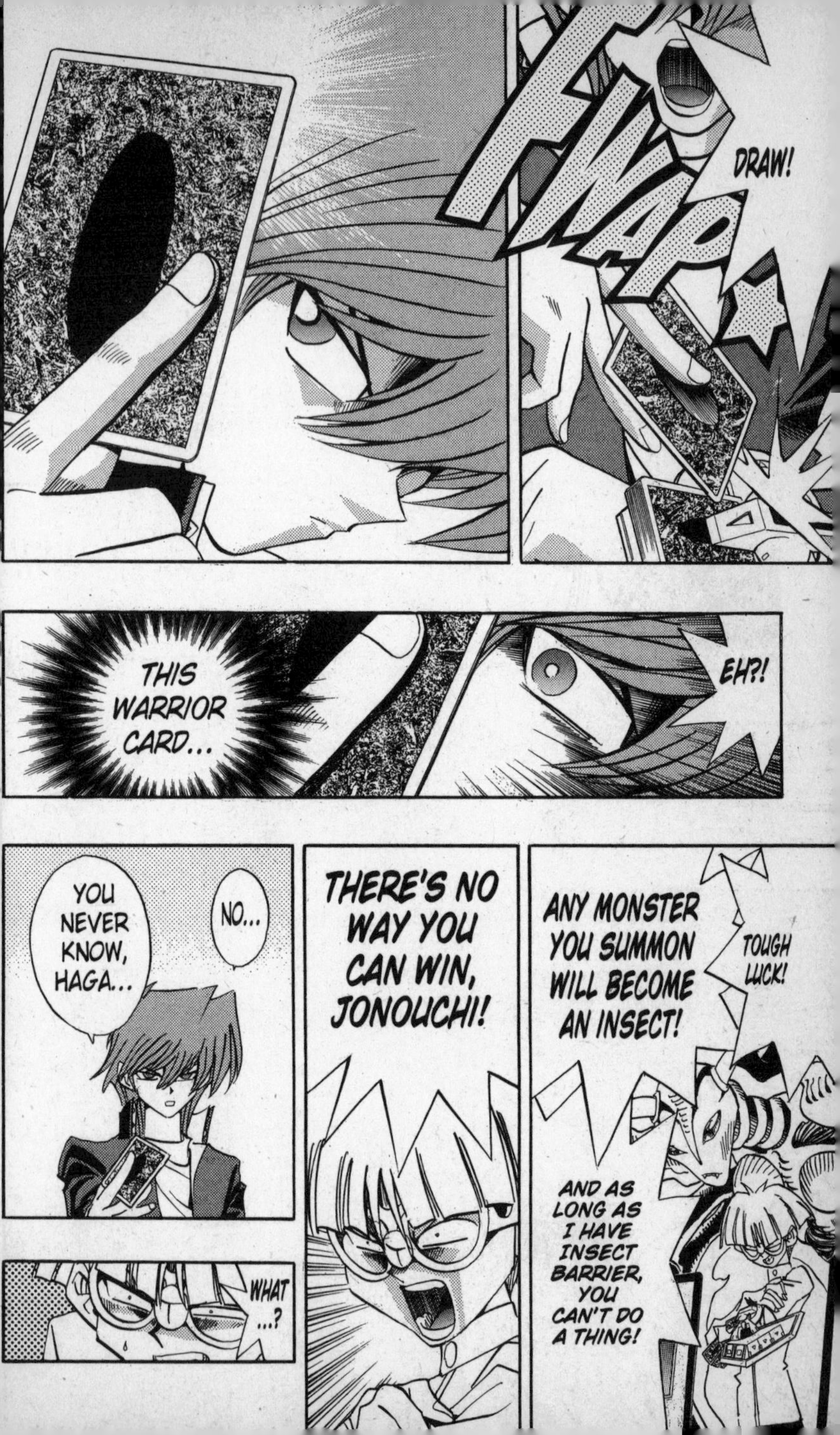
FWAP
DRAW!
EH?!
THIS WARRIOR CARD...
TOUGH LUCK!
ANY MONSTER YOU SUMMON WILL BECOME AN INSECT!
AND AS LONG AS I HAVE INSECT BARRIER, YOU CAN'T DO A THING!
THERE'S NO WAY YOU CAN WIN, JONOUCHI!
NO...
YOU NEVER KNOW, HAGA...
WHAT...?

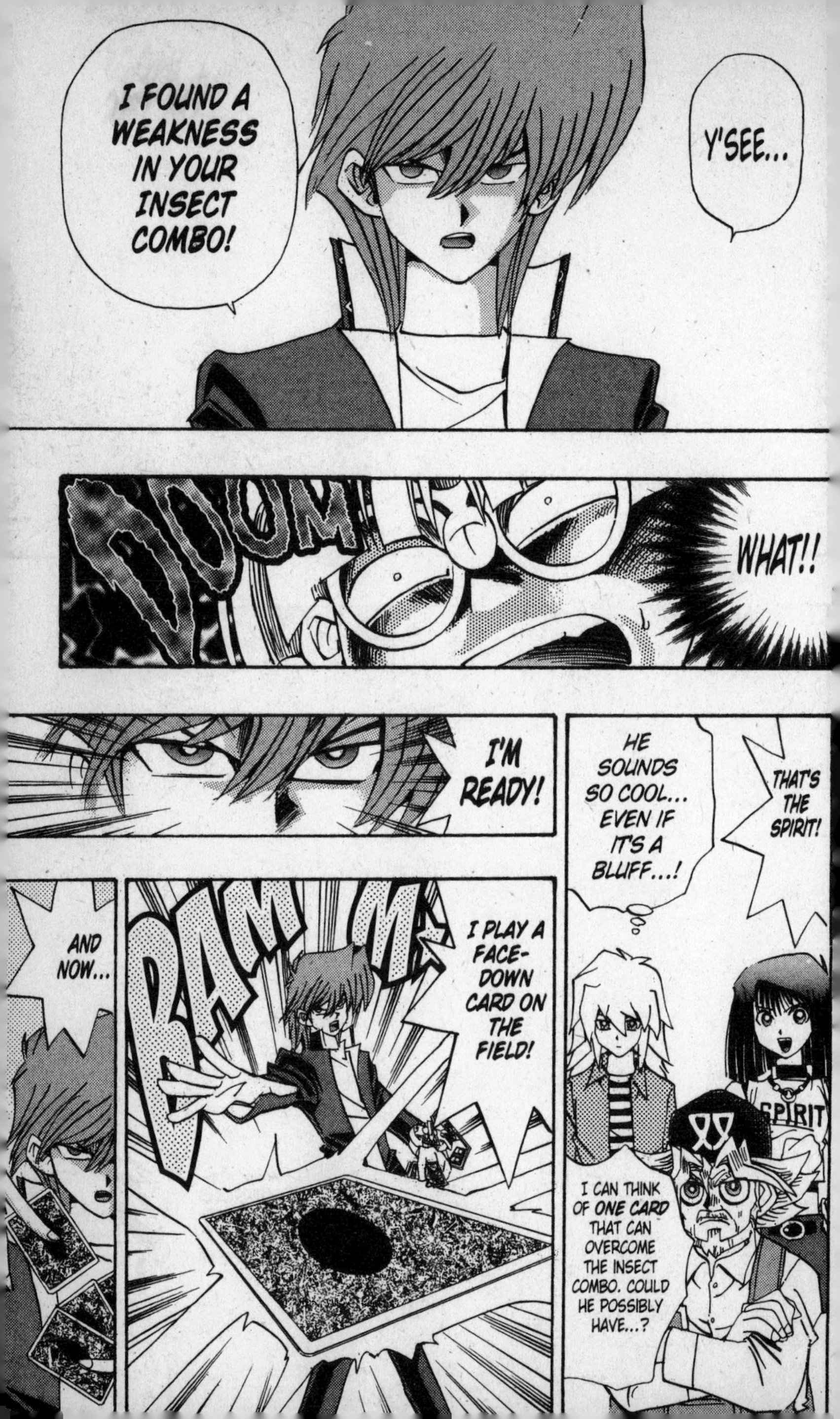
I FOUND A WEAKNESS IN YOUR INSECT COMBO!
Y'SEE...
DOOM
WHAT!!
I'M READY!
AND NOW...
BAMM
I PLAY A FACE-DOWN CARD ON THE FIELD!
HE SOUNDS SO COOL... EVEN IF IT'S A BLUFF...!
THAT'S THE SPIRIT!
SPIRIT
I CAN THINK OF ONE CARD THAT CAN OVERCOME THE INSECT COMBO. COULD HE POSSIBLY HAVE...?

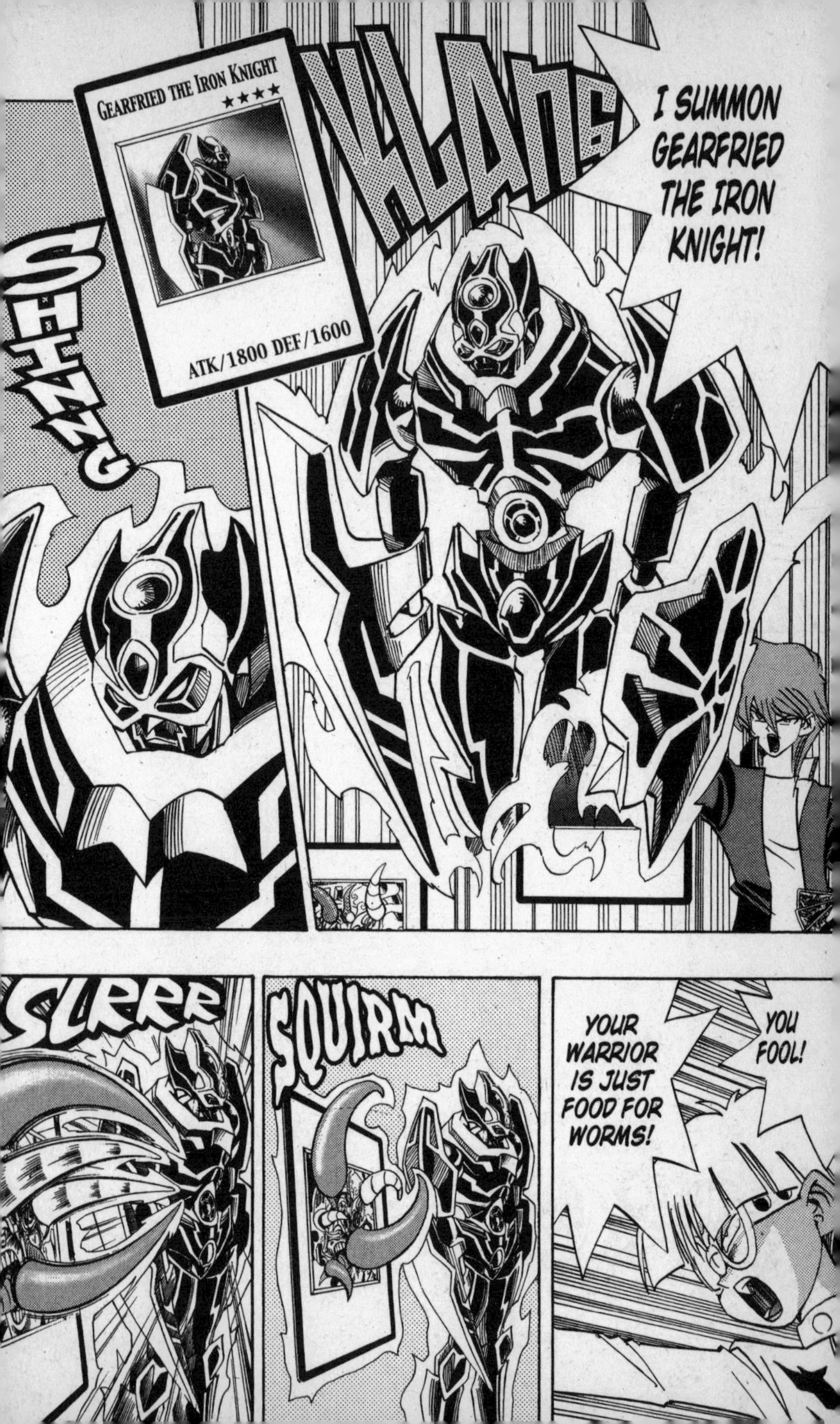
VLAM!
I SUMMON GEARFRIED THE IRON KNIGHT!
GEARFRIED THE IRON KNIGHT ★★★★
ATK/1800 DEF/1600
SHINNG
YOU FOOL!
YOUR WARRIOR IS JUST FOOD FOR WORMS!
SQUIRM
SLRRR

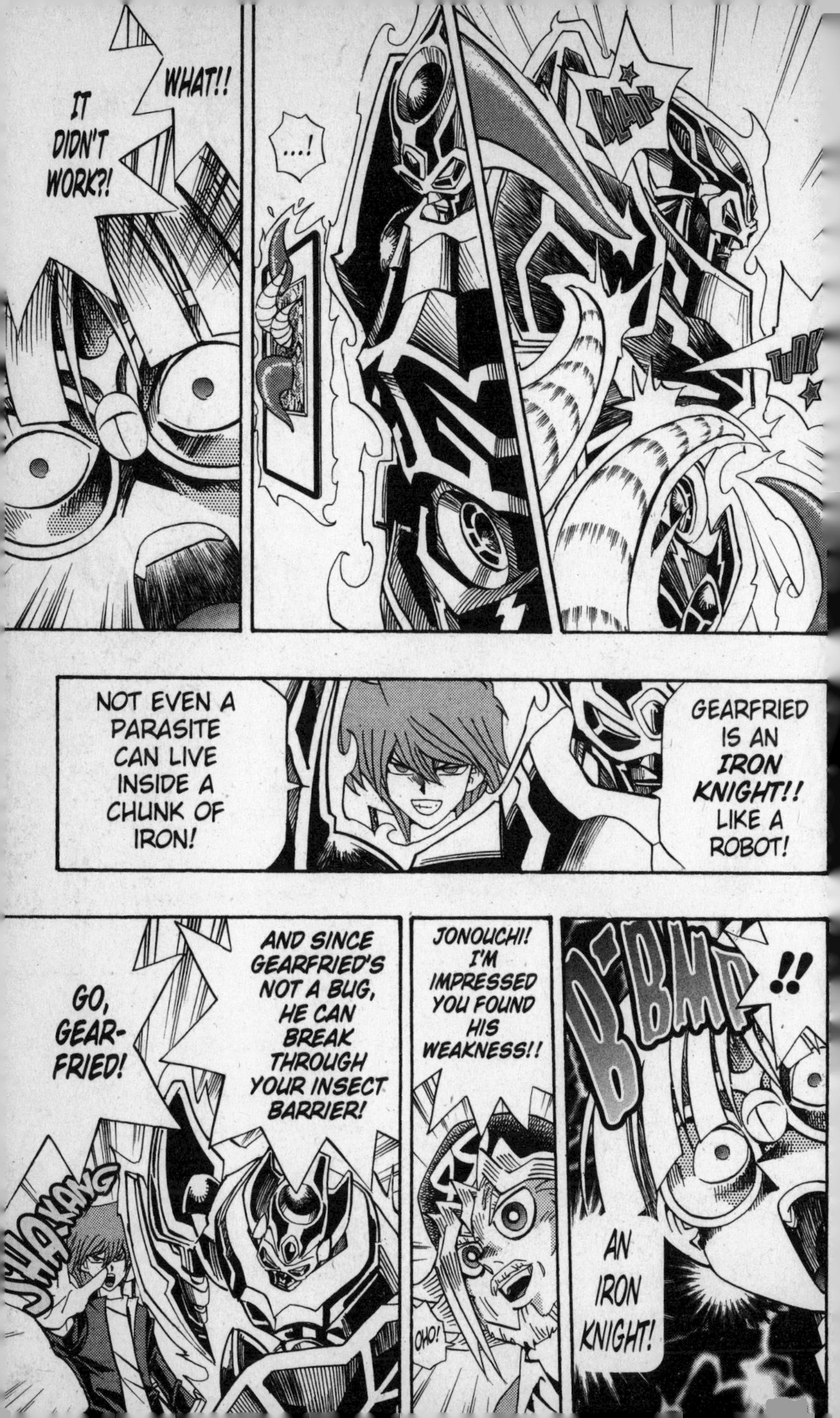
KLANK
TUNK
...!
WHAT!!
IT DIDN'T WORK?!
GEARFRIED IS AN IRON KNIGHT!! LIKE A ROBOT!
NOT EVEN A PARASITE CAN LIVE INSIDE A CHUNK OF IRON!
B'BMP!!
AN IRON KNIGHT!
JONOUCHI! I'M IMPRESSED YOU FOUND HIS WEAKNESS!!
OHO!
AND SINCE GEARFRIED'S NOT A BUG, HE CAN BREAK THROUGH YOUR INSECT BARRIER!
GO, GEAR-FRIED!
SHAKANG

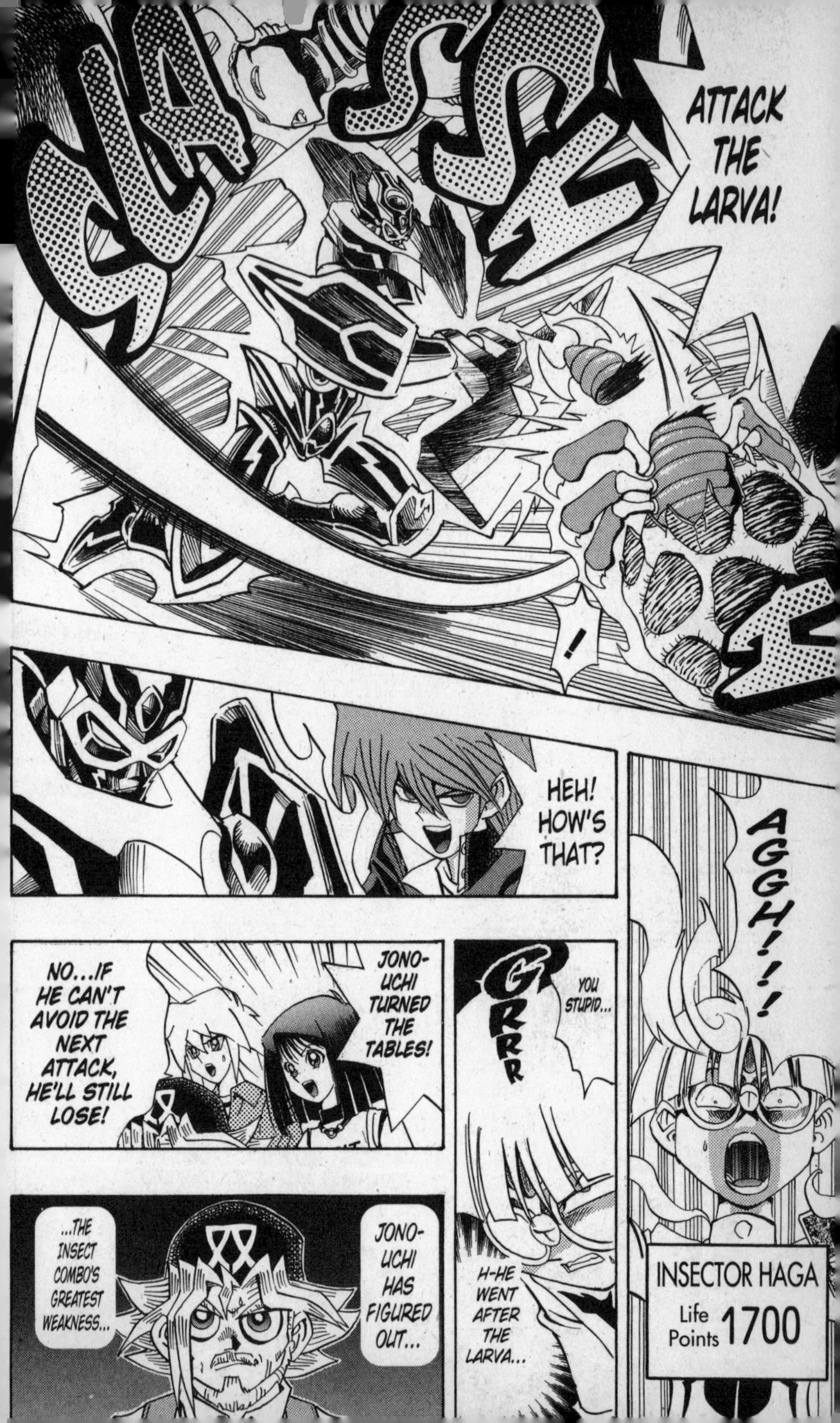
ATTACK THE LARVA!
!
AGGH!!!!
INSECTOR HAGA
Life Points 1700
HEH! HOW'S THAT?
GRRR
YOU STUPID...
H-HE WENT AFTER THE LARVA...
JONO-UCHI TURNED THE TABLES!
NO...IF HE CAN'T AVOID THE NEXT ATTACK, HE'LL STILL LOSE!
JONO-UCHI HAS FIGURED OUT...
...THE INSECT COMBO'S GREATEST WEAKNESS...

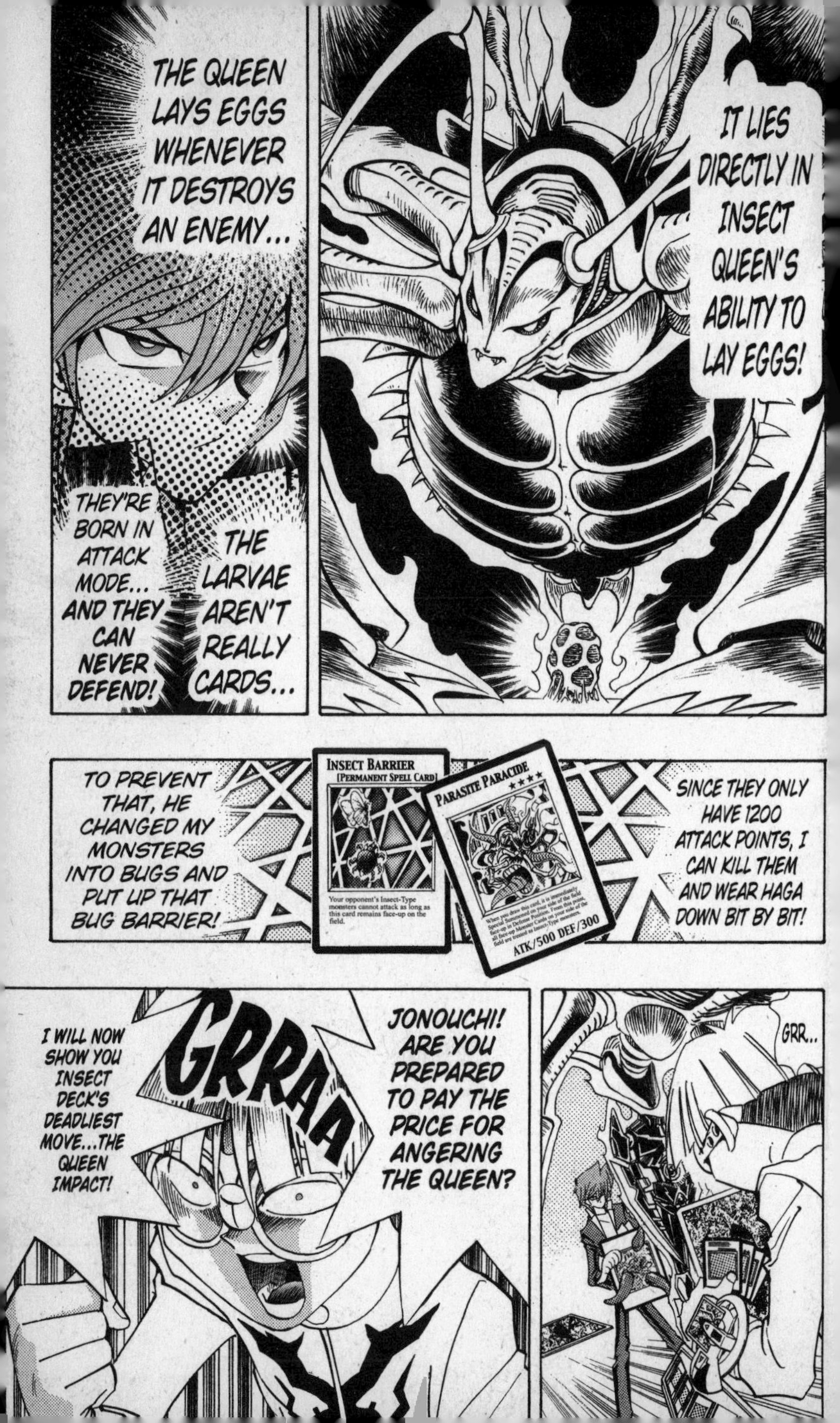
IT LIES DIRECTLY IN INSECT QUEEN'S ABILITY TO LAY EGGS!
THE QUEEN LAYS EGGS WHENEVER IT DESTROYS AN ENEMY...
THE LARVAE AREN'T REALLY CARDS...
THEY'RE BORN IN ATTACK MODE... AND THEY CAN NEVER DEFEND!
SINCE THEY ONLY HAVE 1200 ATTACK POINTS, I CAN KILL THEM AND WEAR HAGA DOWN BIT BY BIT!
PARASITE PARACIDE ★★★★
When you draw this card, it is immediately Special Summoned on your side of the field face-up in Defense Position. From this point, all face-up Monster Cards on your side of the field are treated as Insect-Type monsters.
ATK/500 DEF/300
INSECT BARRIER
[PERMANENT SPELL CARD]
Your opponent's Insect-Type monsters cannot attack as long as this card remains face-up on the field.
TO PREVENT THAT, HE CHANGED MY MONSTERS INTO BUGS AND PUT UP THAT BUG BARRIER!
GRR...
JONOUCHI! ARE YOU PREPARED TO PAY THE PRICE FOR ANGERING THE QUEEN?
GRRAA
I WILL NOW SHOW YOU INSECT DECK'S DEADLIEST MOVE...THE QUEEN IMPACT!

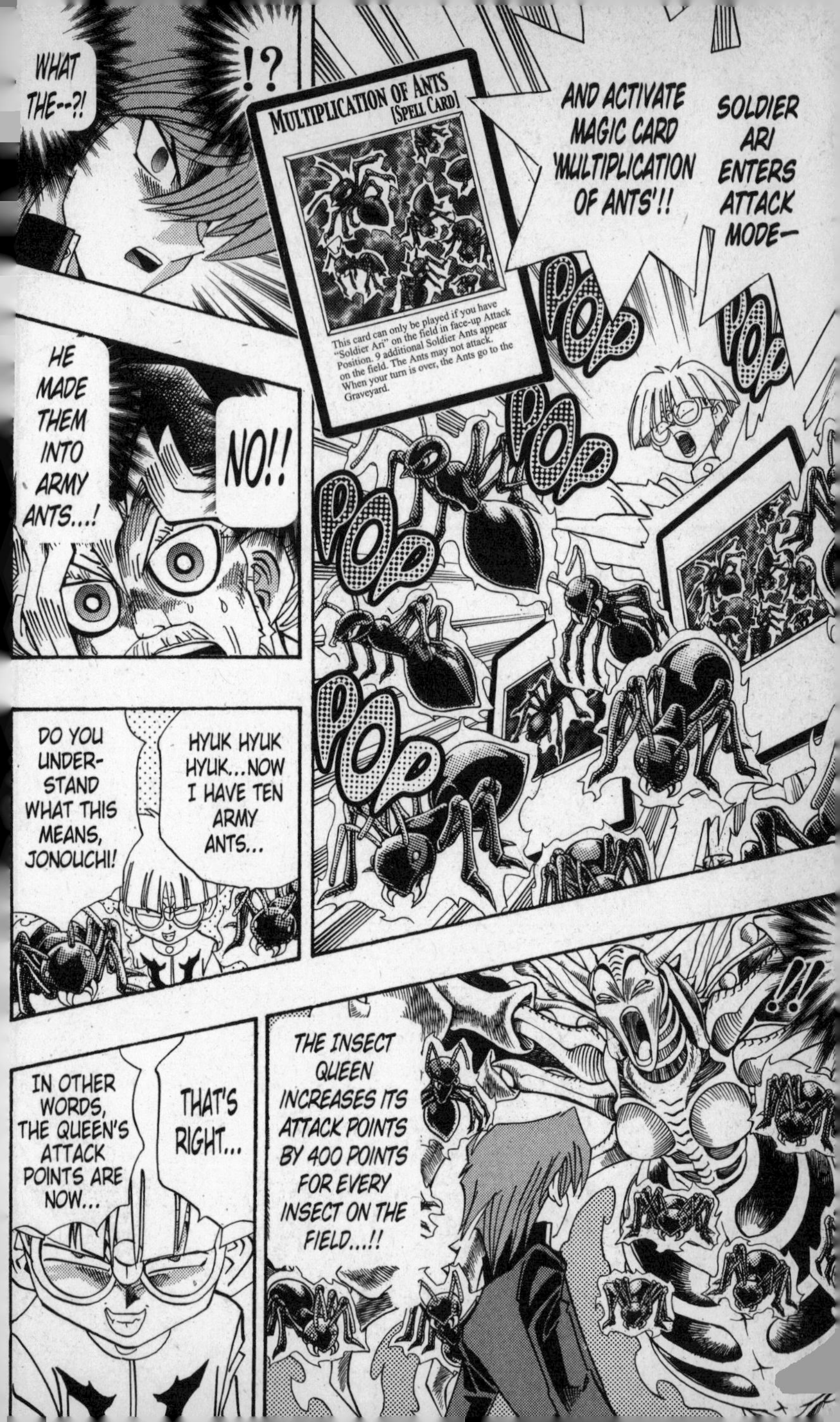
SOLDIER ARI ENTERS ATTACK MODE—
AND ACTIVATE MAGIC CARD 'MULTIPLICATION OF ANTS'!!
MULTIPLICATION OF ANTS
[SPELL CARD]
This card can only be played if you have "Soldier Ari" on the field in face-up Attack Position. 9 additional Soldier Ants appear on the field. The Ants may not attack. When your turn is over, the Ants go to the Graveyard.
POP
POP
POP
POP
POP
POP
!?
WHAT THE--?!
NO!!
HE MADE THEM INTO ARMY ANTS...!
HYUK HYUK HYUK...NOW I HAVE TEN ARMY ANTS...
DO YOU UNDERSTAND WHAT THIS MEANS, JONOUCHI!
!!
THE INSECT QUEEN INCREASES ITS ATTACK POINTS BY 400 POINTS FOR EVERY INSECT ON THE FIELD...!!
THAT'S RIGHT...
IN OTHER WORDS, THE QUEEN'S ATTACK POINTS ARE NOW...

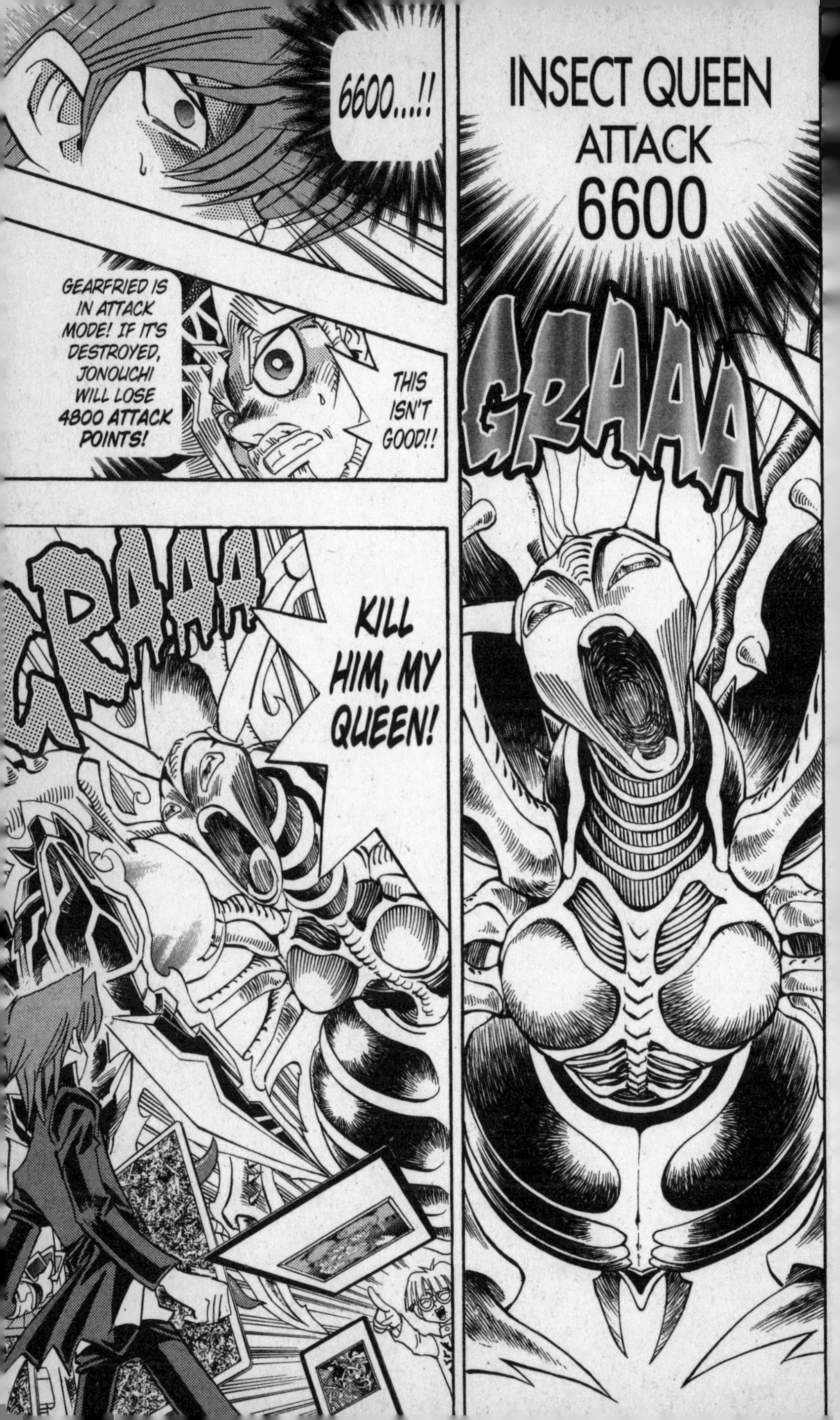
INSECT QUEEN ATTACK 6600
GRAAAA
6600...!!
THIS ISN'T GOOD!!
GEARFRIED IS IN ATTACK MODE! IF IT'S DESTROYED, JONOUCHI WILL LOSE 4800 ATTACK POINTS!
KILL HIM, MY QUEEN!
GRAAA

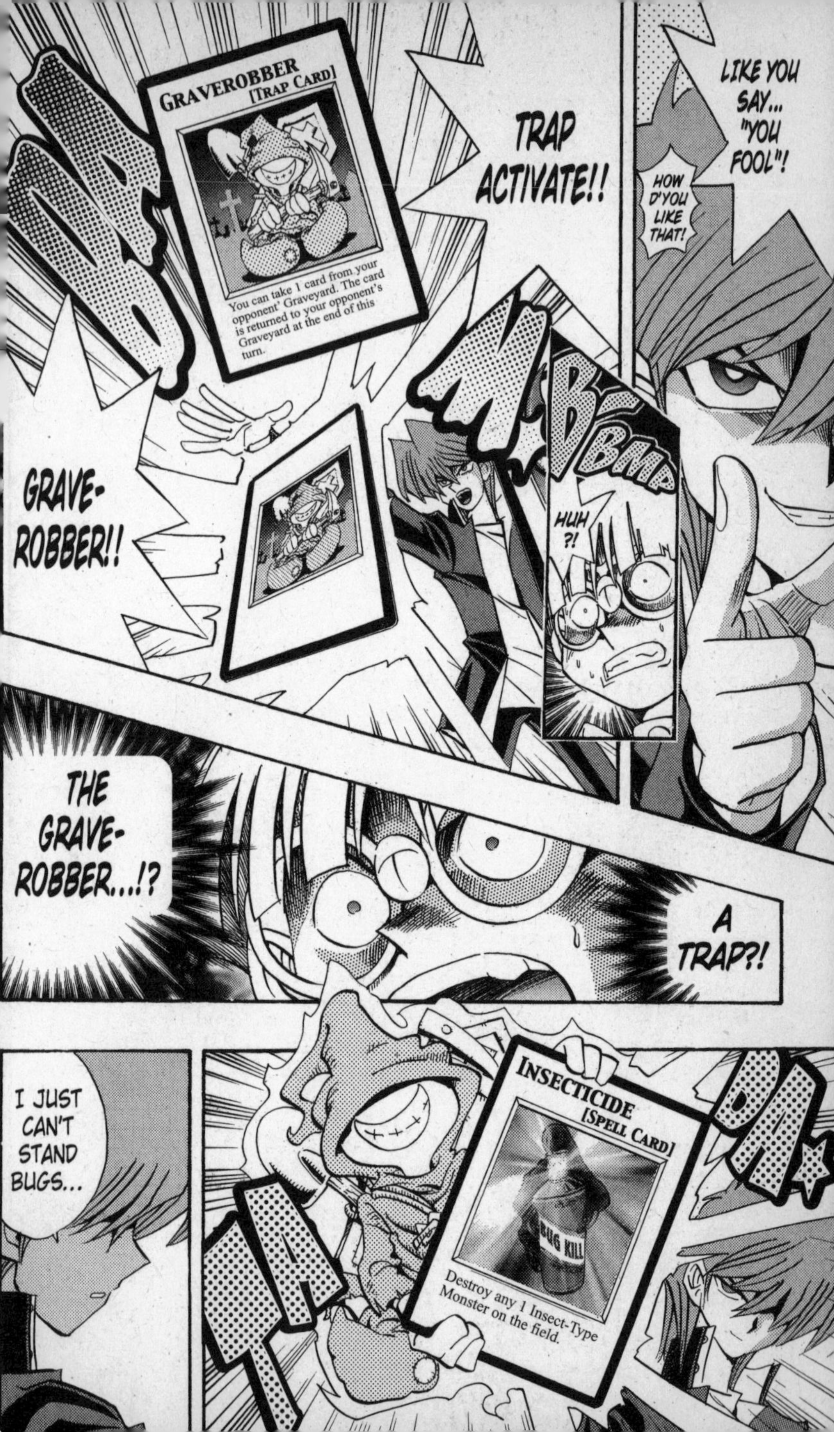
LIKE YOU SAY... "YOU FOOL"!
HOW D'YOU LIKE THAT!
TRAP ACTIVATE!!
GRAVEROBBER [TRAP CARD]
You can take 1 card from your opponent' Graveyard. The card is returned to your opponent's Graveyard at the end of this turn.
GRAVE-ROBBER!!
BMP
HUH ?!
A TRAP?!
THE GRAVE-ROBBER...!?
INSECTICIDE [SPELL CARD]
BUG KILL
Destroy any 1 Insect-Type Monster on the field.
I JUST CAN'T STAND BUGS...

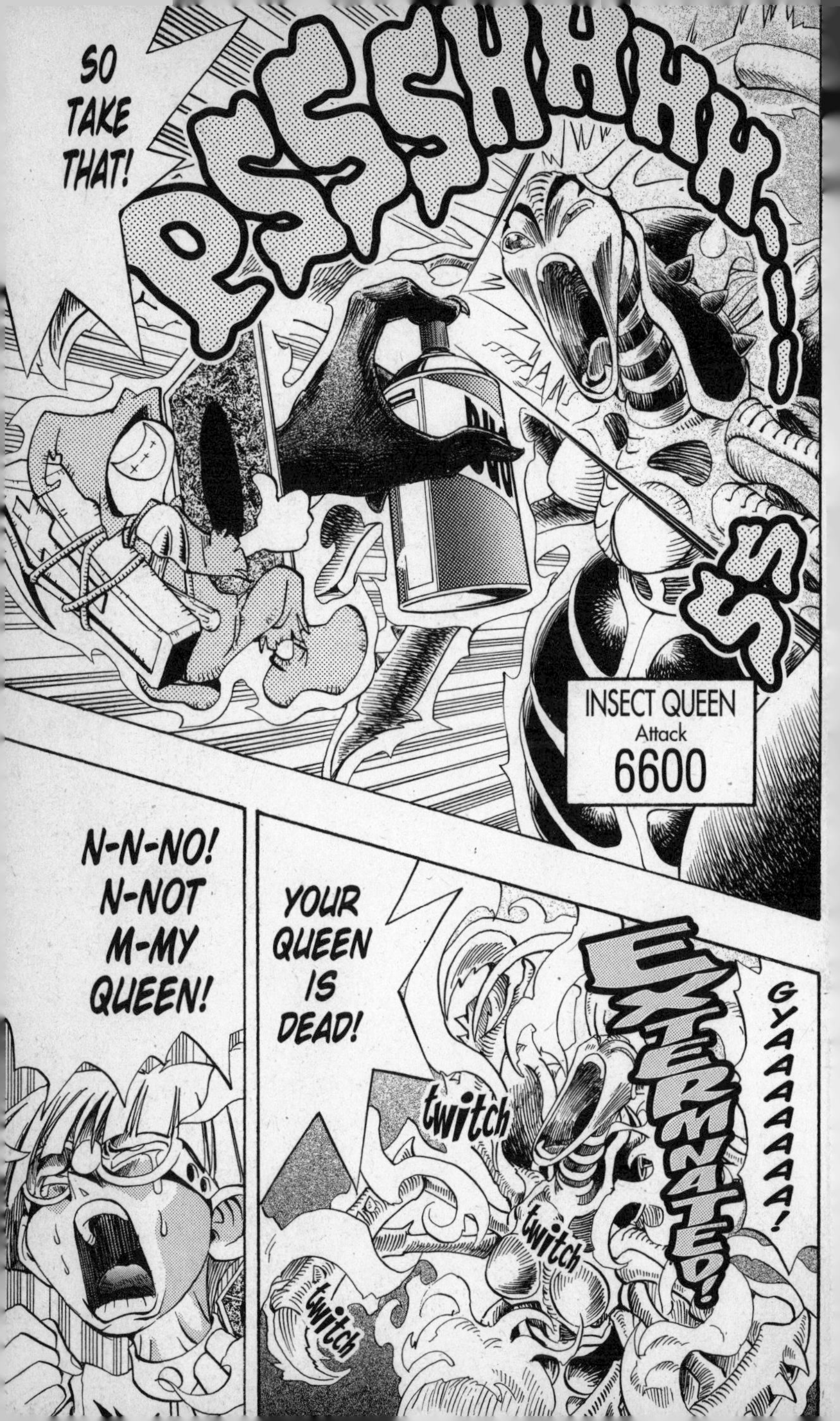

SO TAKE THAT!
INSECT QUEEN
Attack
6600
GYAAAAAAAAA!
EXTERMINATED!
YOUR QUEEN IS DEAD!
twitch
twitch
twitch
N-N-NO! N-NOT M-MY QUEEN!

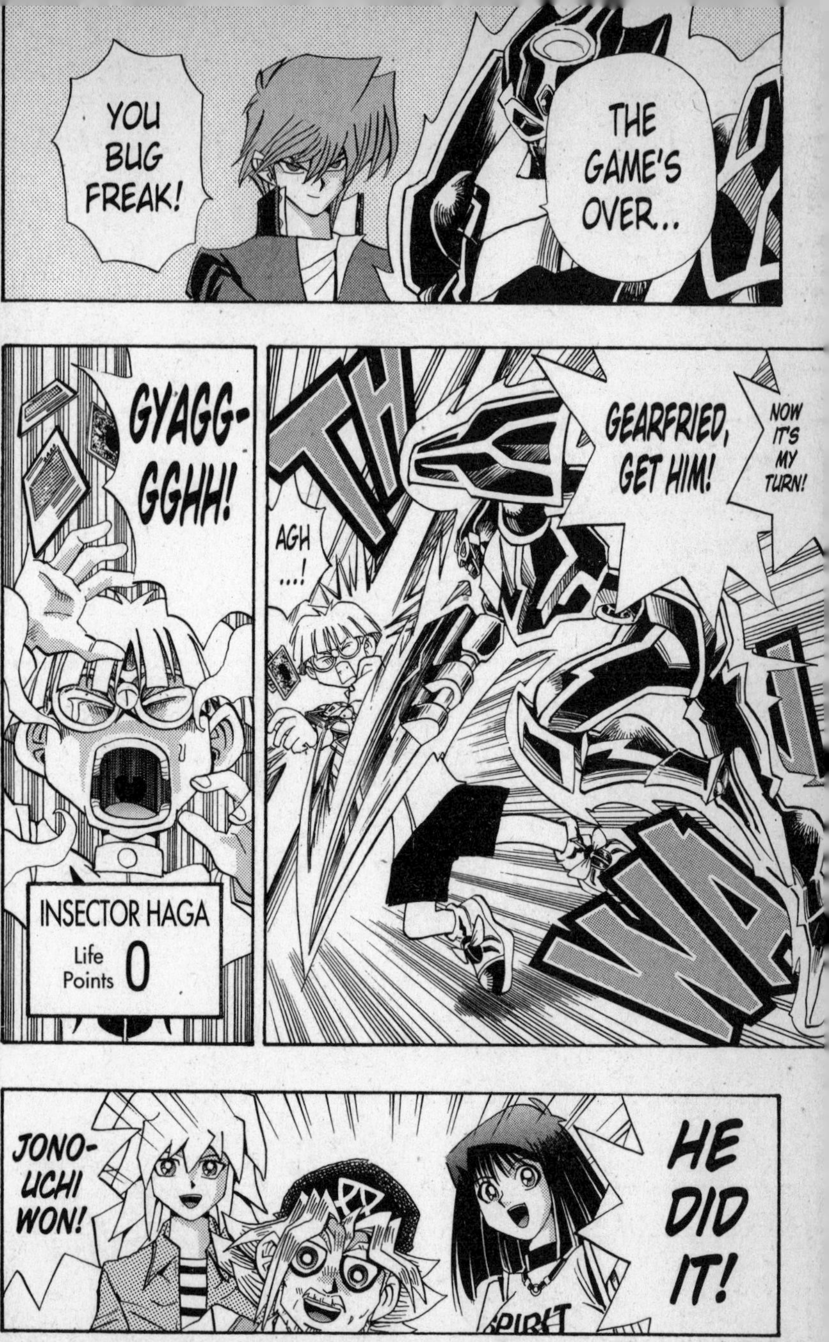
THE GAME'S OVER...
YOU BUG FREAK!
NOW IT'S MY TURN!
GEARFRIED, GET HIM!
AGH ...!
GYAGG-GGHH!
INSECTOR HAGA
Life Points 0
HE DID IT!
JONO-UCHI WON!
SPIRIT

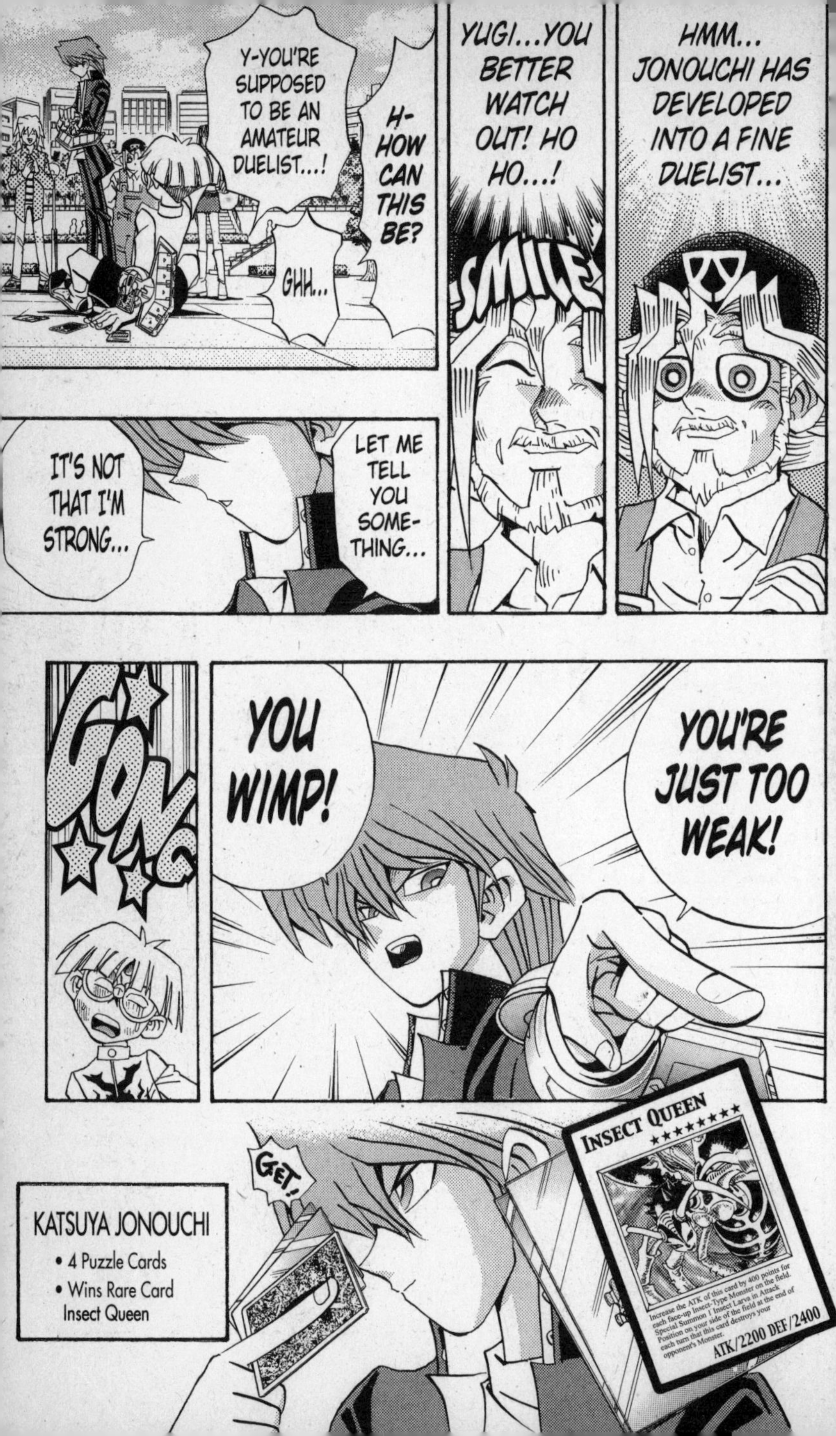
HMM... JONOUCHI HAS DEVELOPED INTO A FINE DUELIST...
YUGI...YOU BETTER WATCH OUT! HO HO...!
SMILE
H-HOW CAN THIS BE?
Y-YOU'RE SUPPOSED TO BE AN AMATEUR DUELIST...!
GHH...
LET ME TELL YOU SOMETHING...
IT'S NOT THAT I'M STRONG...
YOU'RE JUST TOO WEAK!
YOU WIMP!
GONG
GET!
INSECT QUEEN
Increase the ATK of this card by 400 points for each face-up Insect-Type Monster on the field. Special Summon 1 Insect Larva in Attack Position on your side of the field at the end of each turn that this card destroys your opponent's Monster.
ATK/2200 DEF/2400
KATSUYA JONOUCHI
• 4 Puzzle Cards
• Wins Rare Card Insect Queen

MASTER OF THE CARDS

The "Duel Monsters" card game first appeared in volume two of the original **Yu-Gi-Oh!** graphic novel series, but it's in **Yu-Gi-Oh!: Duelist** (originally printed in Japan as volumes 8-31 of **Yu-Gi-Oh!**) that it gets really important. As many fans know, some of the card names are different between the English and Japanese versions. In case you play the game, or you're interested in playing, here's a rundown of some of the cards in this graphic novel. Some cards only appear in the **Yu-Gi-Oh!** video games, not in the actual collectible card game.

FIRST APPEARANCE IN THIS VOLUME	JAPANESE CARD NAME	ENGLISH CARD NAME
p.7	*Black Magician*	Dark Magician
p.22	*Magnet Warrior Alpha*	Alpha the Magnet Warrior
p.22	*Kidôke Legion* (Demon/ Evil Clown Legion)	Legion the Fiend Jester (NOTE: Not a real game card.)
p.24	*Tefuda Massatsu* (Card Obliteration)	Card Destruction
p.26	*Sennô Brain Control* (Brainwashing/ Brain Control)	Brain Control

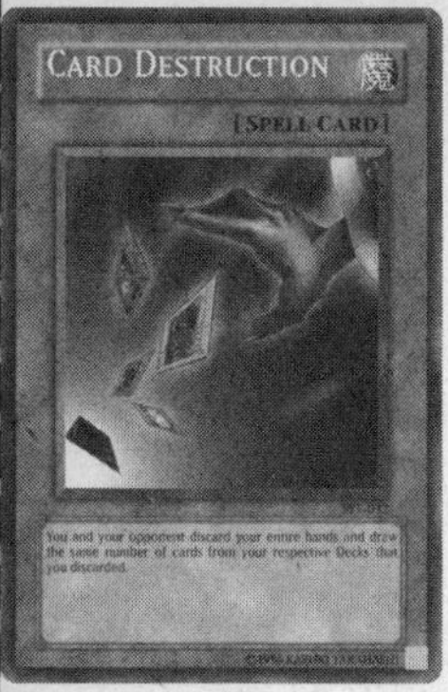
Card Destruction
魔
[SPELL CARD]
You and your opponent discard your entire hands and draw the same number of cards from your respective Decks that you discarded.
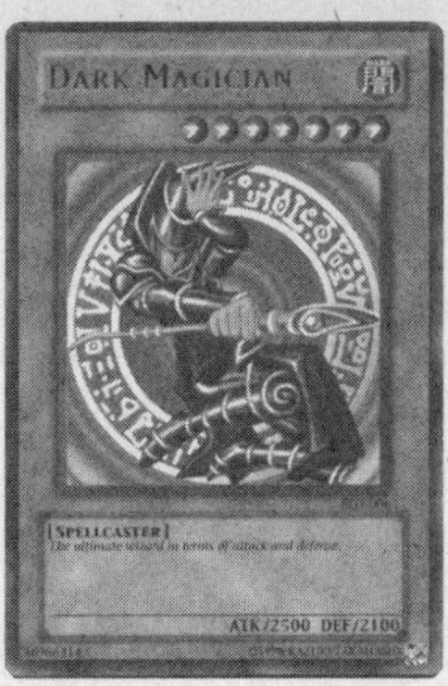
Dark Magician
闇
[SPELLCASTER]
The ultimate wizard in terms of attack and defense.
ATK/2500 DEF/2100
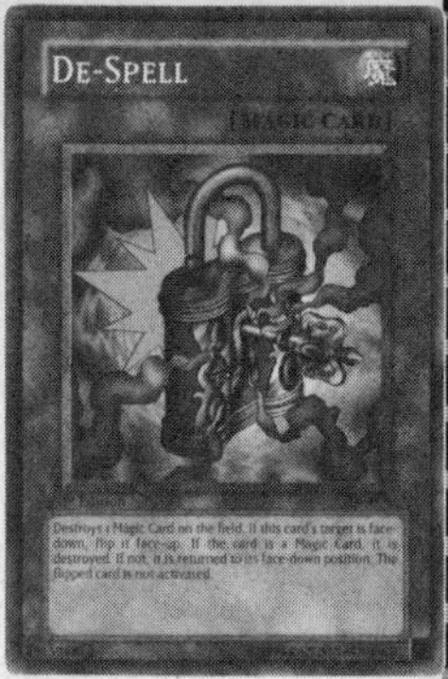
De-Spell
魔
[MAGIC CARD]
Destroys a Magic Card on the field. If this card's target is face-down, flip it face-up. If the card is a Magic Card, it is destroyed. If not, it is returned to its face-down position. The flipped card is not activated.

FIRST APPEARANCE IN THIS VOLUME	JAPANESE CARD NAME	ENGLISH CARD NAME
p.35	*Magnet Warrior Beta*	Beta the Magnet Warrior
p.36	*Kuromazoku Fukkatsu no Hitsugi* (Black Magic-Users' Coffin of Resurrection)	Coffin of Dark Resurrection (NOTE: Not a real game card. Called "Dark Renewal" in the anime.)
p.43	*Dantôdai no Sangeki* (Guillotine of Tragedy)	Mystic Guillotine (NOTE: Not a real game card)
p.44	*Magical Silk Hat*	Magical Hats
p.45	*Thousand Knife*	Thousand Knives
p.46	*Mahô Kaishô* (Magic Liquidation/Dissolution)	De-Spell
p.48	*Shisha Sosei* (Resurrection of the Dead)	Monster Reborn
p.54	*Yamie no Temaneki* (Beckoning to the Dark)	Beckon to the Dark (NOTE: Not a real game card. Called "Beckon of Darkness" in the video games.)

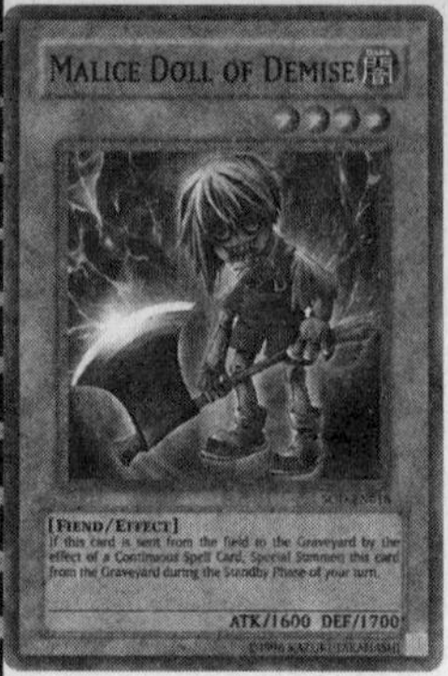
MALICE DOLL OF DEMISE
[FIEND/EFFECT]
ATK/1600 DEF/1700

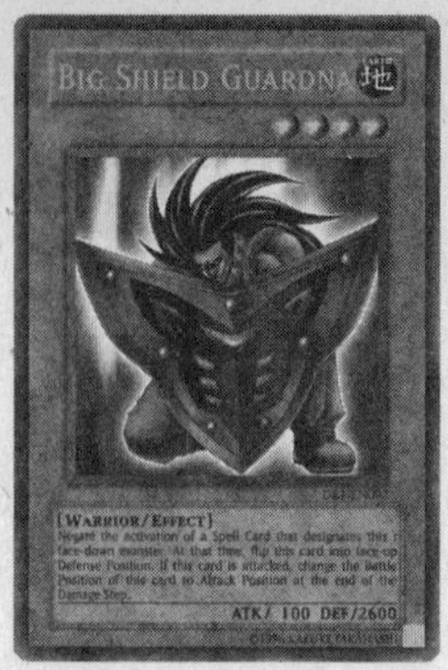
BIG SHIELD GUARDNA
[WARRIOR/EFFECT]
ATK/ 100 DEF/2600

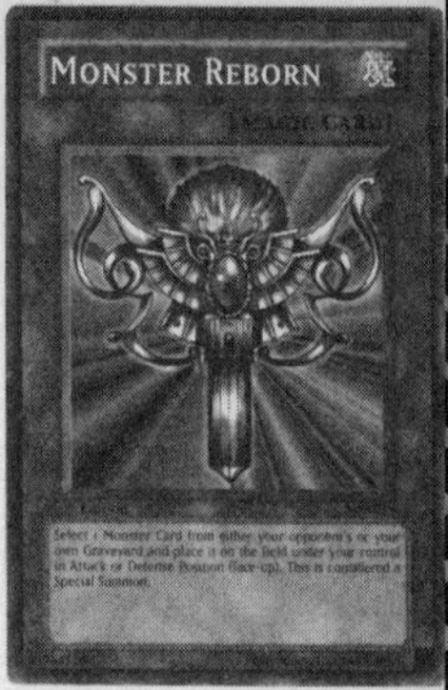
MONSTER REBORN

FIRST APPEARANCE IN THIS VOLUME	JAPANESE CARD NAME	ENGLISH CARD NAME
p.55	*Seirei no Kagami* (Spirit's Mirror)	Mystical Rift Panel (NOTE: Not a real game card.)
p.57	*Akumu no Jûjika* (Nightmare Cross)	Nightmare Chains (NOTE: Not a real game card. The art was changed for the English version.)
p.60	*Big Shield Guardna*	Big Shield Guardna
p.61	*Killer Doll*	Malice Doll of Demise
p.62	*Ectoplasmer*	Ectoplasmer
p.76	*Genjûô Gazelle* (Gazelle the Mythical Beast King)	Gazelle the King of Mythical Beasts
p.77	*Akuma no Tenbin* (Devil's Scales)	Devil's Scales (NOTE: Not a real game card. Called "Shadow Balance" in the anime.)
p.79	*Kuromajutsu no Curtain* (Curtain of Black Magic)	Dark Magic Curtain

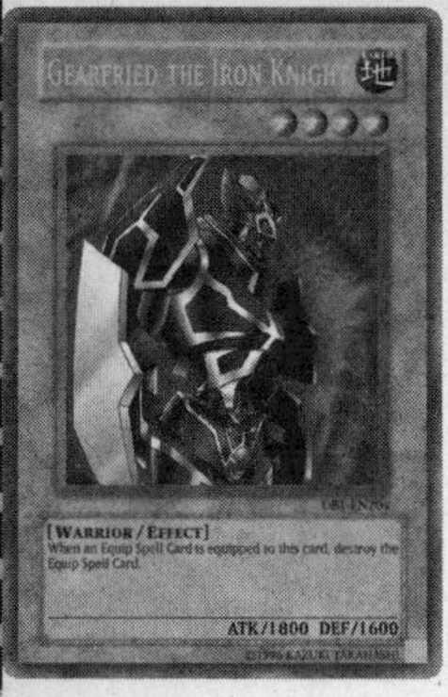
Gearfried the Iron Knight
[Warrior / Effect]
When an Equip Spell Card is equipped to this card, destroy the Equip Spell Card.
ATK/1800 DEF/1600
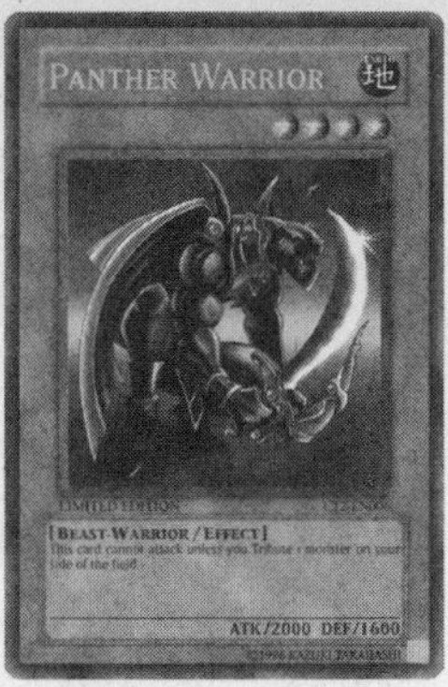
Panther Warrior
Limited Edition
[Beast-Warrior / Effect]
ATK/2000 DEF/1600
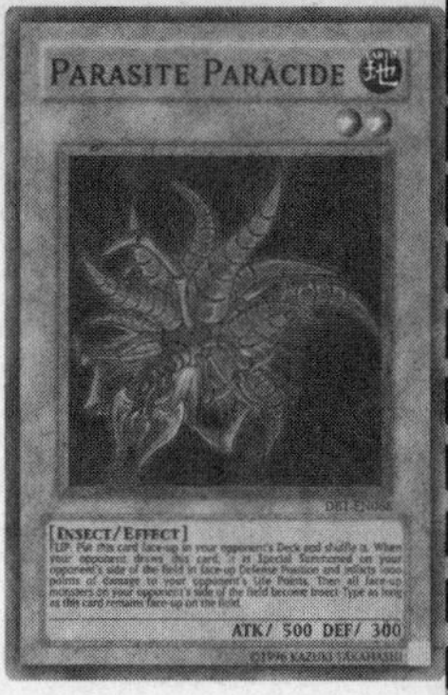
Parasite Paracide
[Insect/Effect]
ATK/ 500 DEF/ 300

FIRST APPEARANCE IN THIS VOLUME	JAPANESE CARD NAME	ENGLISH CARD NAME
p.82	*Fûma no Ya* (Arrows of Magic Sealing)	Anti-Magic Arrows (NOTE: Not a real game card)
p.86	*Black Magician Girl*	Dark Magician Girl
p.104	*Obelisk no Kyoshinhei* (Obelisk the Giant God Soldier)	The God of the Obelisk (NOTE: Called "Obelisk the Tormentor" in the English anime and card game.)
p.104	*Osiris no Tenkûryû* (Osiris the Heaven Dragon)	Slifer the Sky Dragon
p.104	*Ra no Yokushinryû* (Ra the Winged God Dragon) (NOTE: The kanji for "sun god" is written beside the kanji for "Ra.")	The Sun Dragon Ra (NOTE: Called "The Winged Dragon of Ra" in the English anime and card game.)
p.129	*Kiseichû Paracide* (Parasitic Insect Paracide)	Parasite Paracide

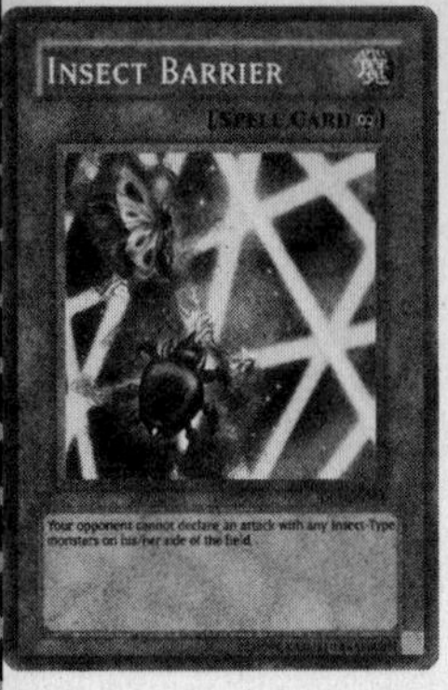
Insect Barrier
[Spell Card]
Your opponent cannot declare an attack with any Insect-Type monsters on his/her side of the field.
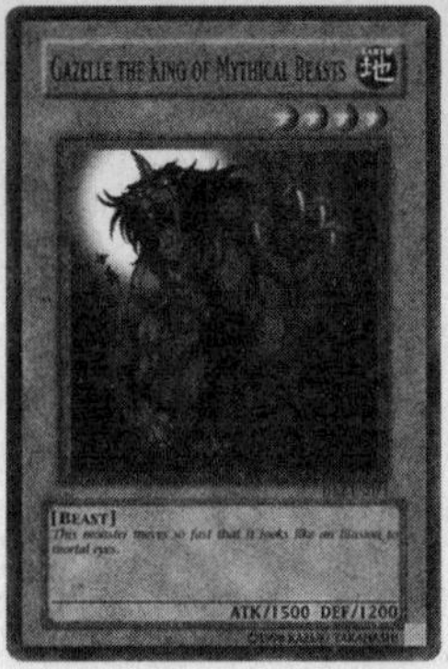
Gazelle the King of Mythical Beasts
[Beast]
This monster moves so fast that it looks like an illusion to mortal eyes.
ATK/1500 DEF/1200
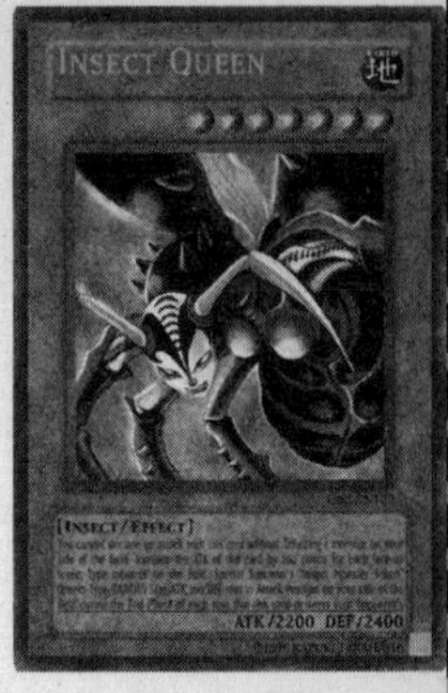
Insect Queen
[Insect/Effect]
ATK/2200 DEF/2400

FIRST APPEARANCE IN THIS VOLUME	JAPANESE CARD NAME	ENGLISH CARD NAME
p.129	*Gokiboru* (Roach Ball)	Pillroach (NOTE: Not a real game card. Called "Gokibore" in the video games.)
p.145	*Shikkoku no Hyôsenshi Panther Warrior* (Jet Black Panther Warrior)	Panther Warrior
p.146	*Dokurogan Ladybug* (Death's-Head/ Skull-Face Ladybug)	Skull-Mark Ladybug
p.147	*Little Winguard*	Little Winguard
p.148	*Daida Batta* (Pinch-hitting Batter/Locust) (NOTE: The word "batta" is a pun which could mean either "batter" or "locust")	Pinch Hopper
p.149	*Jinzô Ningen Psycho Shocker* (Android/Cyborg Psycho Shocker)	Jinzo

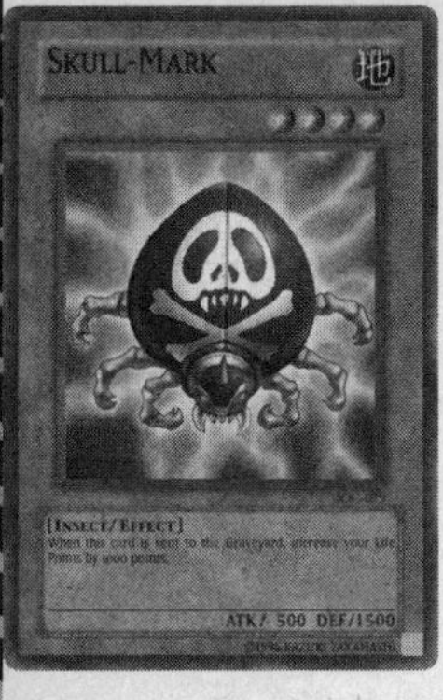
SKULL-MARK
[INSECT/EFFECT]
ATK/ 500 DEF/1500

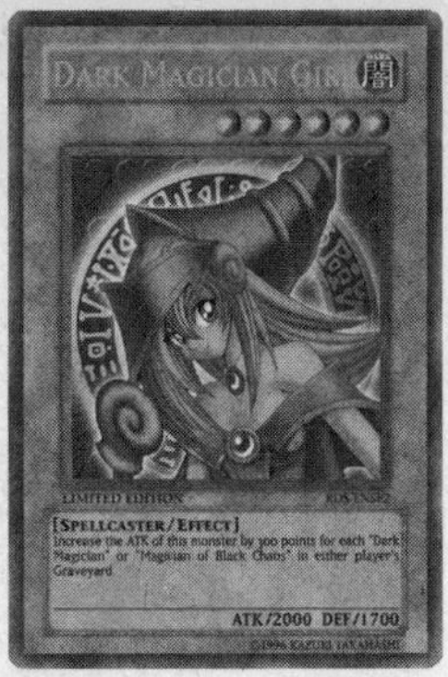
DARK MAGICIAN GIRL
[SPELLCASTER/EFFECT]
ATK/2000 DEF/1700

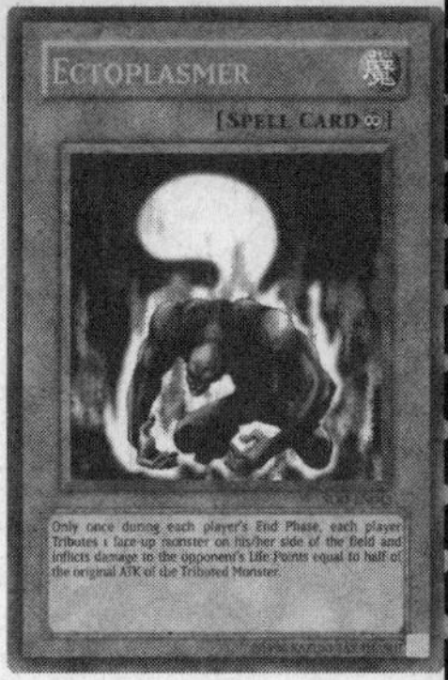
ECTOPLASMER
[SPELL CARD]

FIRST APPEARANCE IN THIS VOLUME	JAPANESE CARD NAME	ENGLISH CARD NAME
p.160	*Mushi yoke Barrier* (Insect Barrier)	Insect Barrier
p.164	*Sacchûzai* (Bug-killing Drug)	Insecticide (NOTE: Not a real game card. Called "Eradicating Aerosol" in the anime and video games.)
p.166	*Insect Queen*	Insect Queen
p.173	*Magic Arm Shield*	Magic Arm Shield
p.181	*Heitai Ari* (Soldier Ant)	Soldier Ari (NOTE: Not a real game card.)
p.186	*Tetsu no Kishi Gear Fried* (Iron Knight Gear Fried)	Gearfried the Iron Knight
p.190	*Ari no Zôshoku* (Ant Reproduction)	Multiplication of Ants
p.192	*Haka Arashi* (Graverobber)	Graverobber

IN THE NEXT VOLUME...

Marik arrives in Battle City, bringing the last of the Egyptian God Cards...and his murderous grudge! Using one of his brainwashed pawns to fight for him, the evil mastermind traps Yugi in a deadly cage match against one of the most powerful cards in the world... *Slifer the Sky Dragon!* Even with the dragon-fighting Buster Blader on his side, does Yugi have a chance?

COMING FEBRUARY 2006!

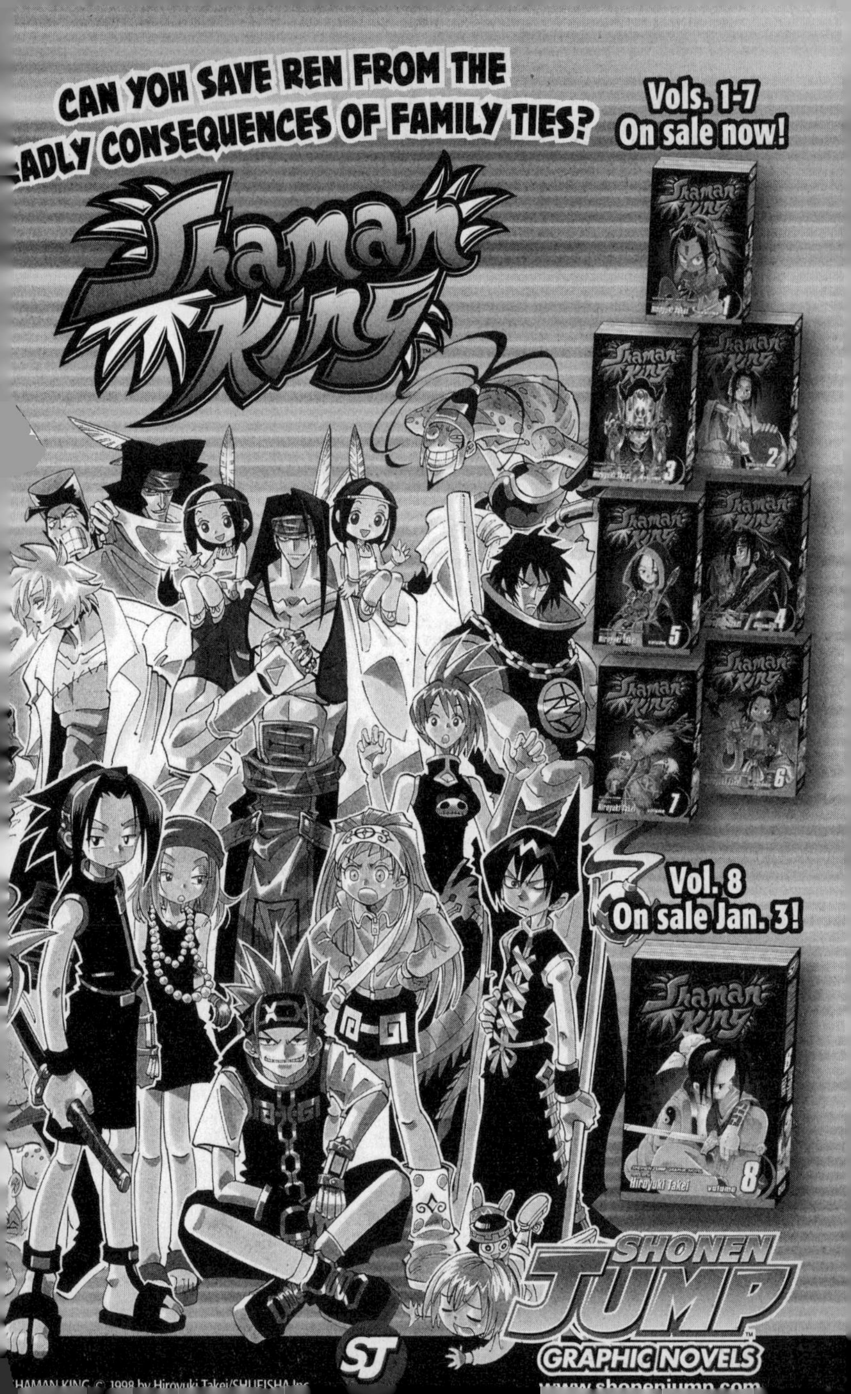
CAN YOH SAVE REN FROM THE
ADLY CONSEQUENCES OF FAMILY TIES?
Shaman King
Vols. 1-7
On sale now!
Vol. 8
On sale Jan. 3!
SHONEN JUMP
GRAPHIC NOVELS
HAMAN KING © 1998 by Hiroyuki Takei/SHUEISHA Inc.

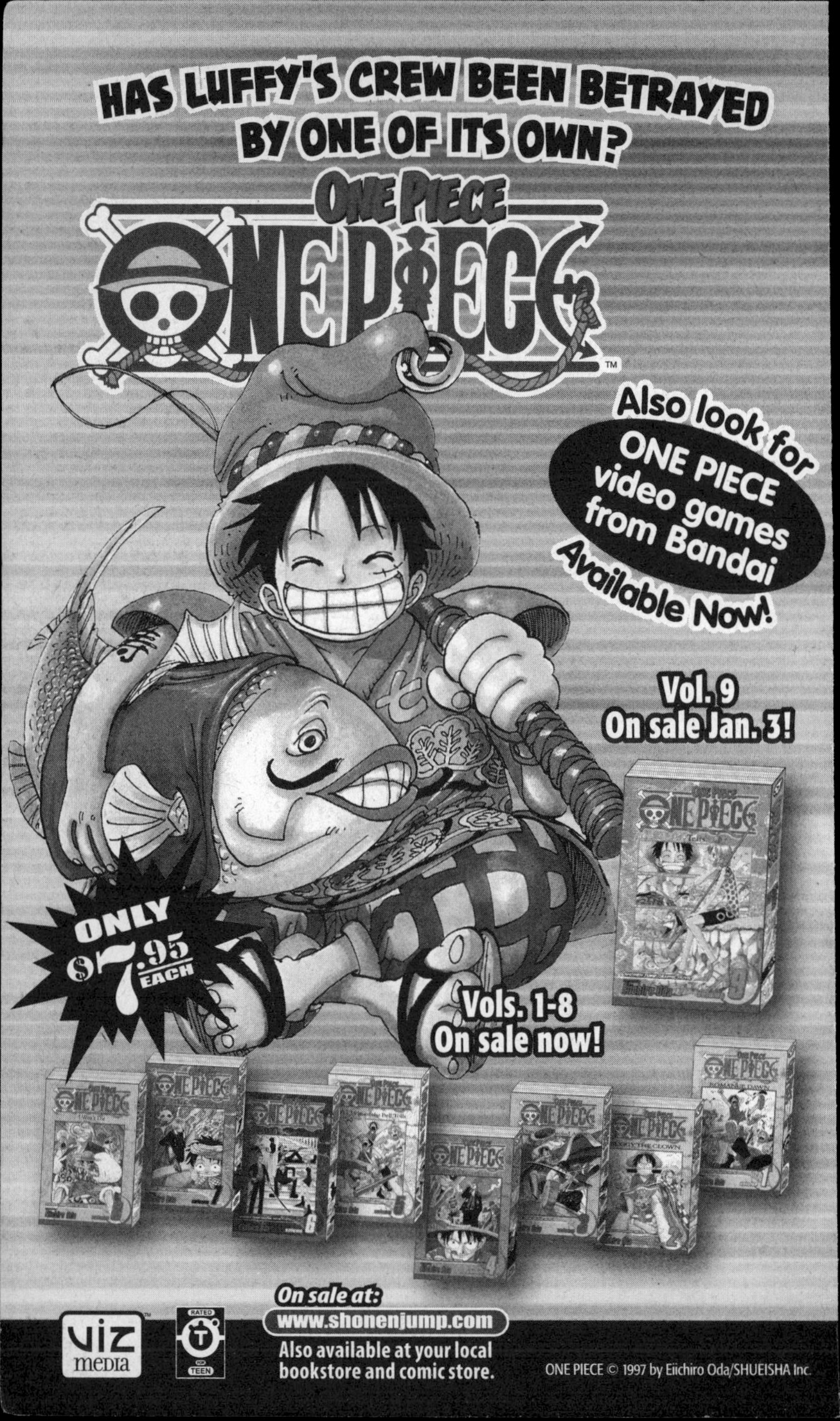
HAS LUFFY'S CREW BEEN BETRAYED BY ONE OF ITS OWN?
ONE PIECE
ONE PIECE
Also look for ONE PIECE video games from Bandai Available Now!
Vol. 9 On sale Jan. 3!
ONLY $7.95 EACH
Vols. 1-8 On sale now!
On sale at:
www.shonenjump.com
Also available at your local bookstore and comic store.
viz media
RATED T TEEN
ONE PIECE © 1997 by Eiichiro Oda/SHUEISHA Inc.

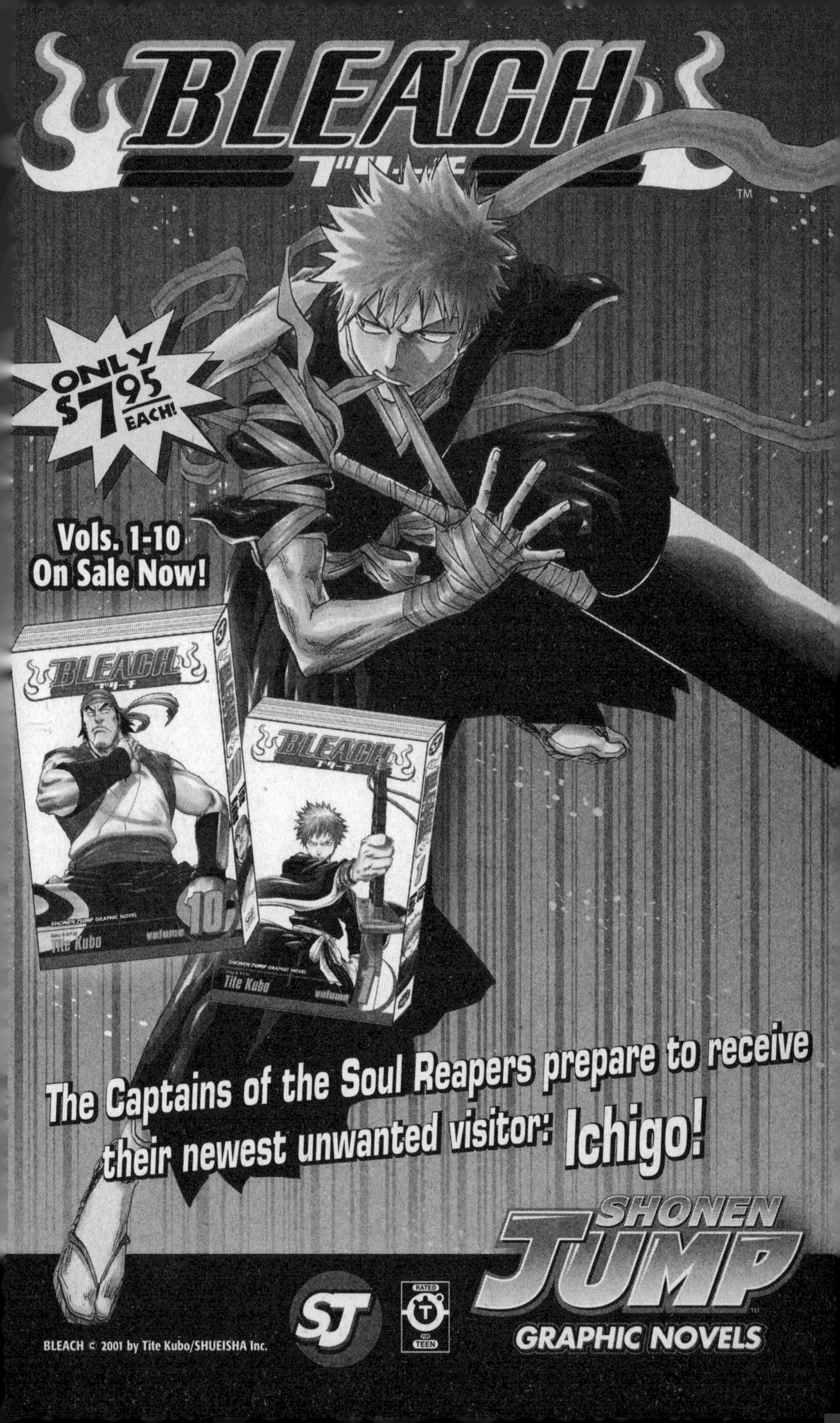
BLEACH
ONLY $7.95 EACH!
Vols. 1-10 On Sale Now!
The Captains of the Soul Reapers prepare to receive their newest unwanted visitor: Ichigo!
SHONEN JUMP GRAPHIC NOVELS
SJ
RATED T FOR TEEN
BLEACH © 2001 by Tite Kubo/SHUEISHA Inc.

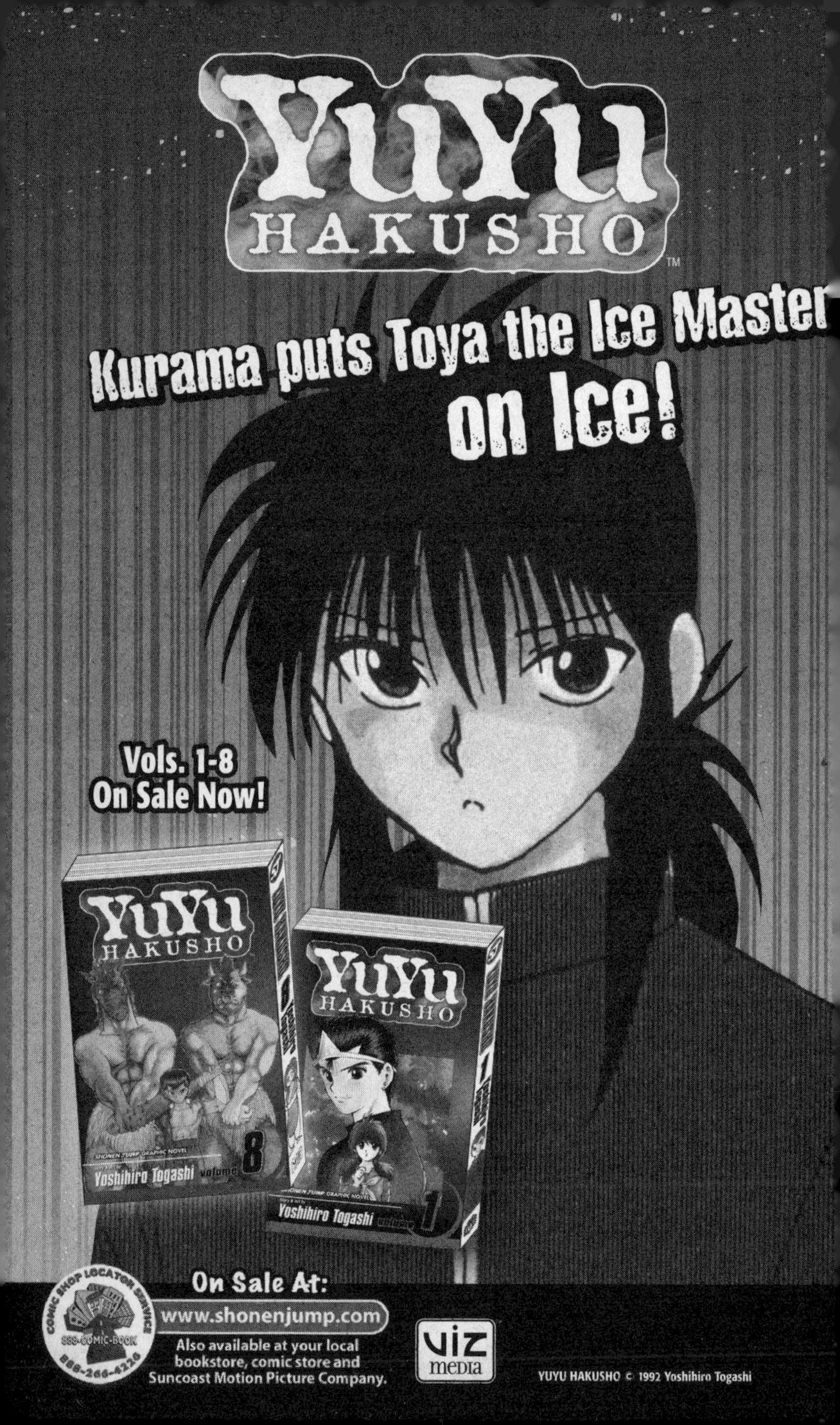
YuYu HAKUSHO™
Kurama puts Toya the Ice Master on Ice!
Vols. 1-8 On Sale Now!
YuYu HAKUSHO
Yoshihiro Togashi volume 8
YuYu HAKUSHO
Yoshihiro Togashi volume 1
On Sale At:
www.shonenjump.com
Also available at your local bookstore, comic store and Suncoast Motion Picture Company.
COMIC SHOP LOCATOR SERVICE
888-COMIC-BOOK
888-266-4226
viz media
YUYU HAKUSHO © 1992 Yoshihiro Togashi

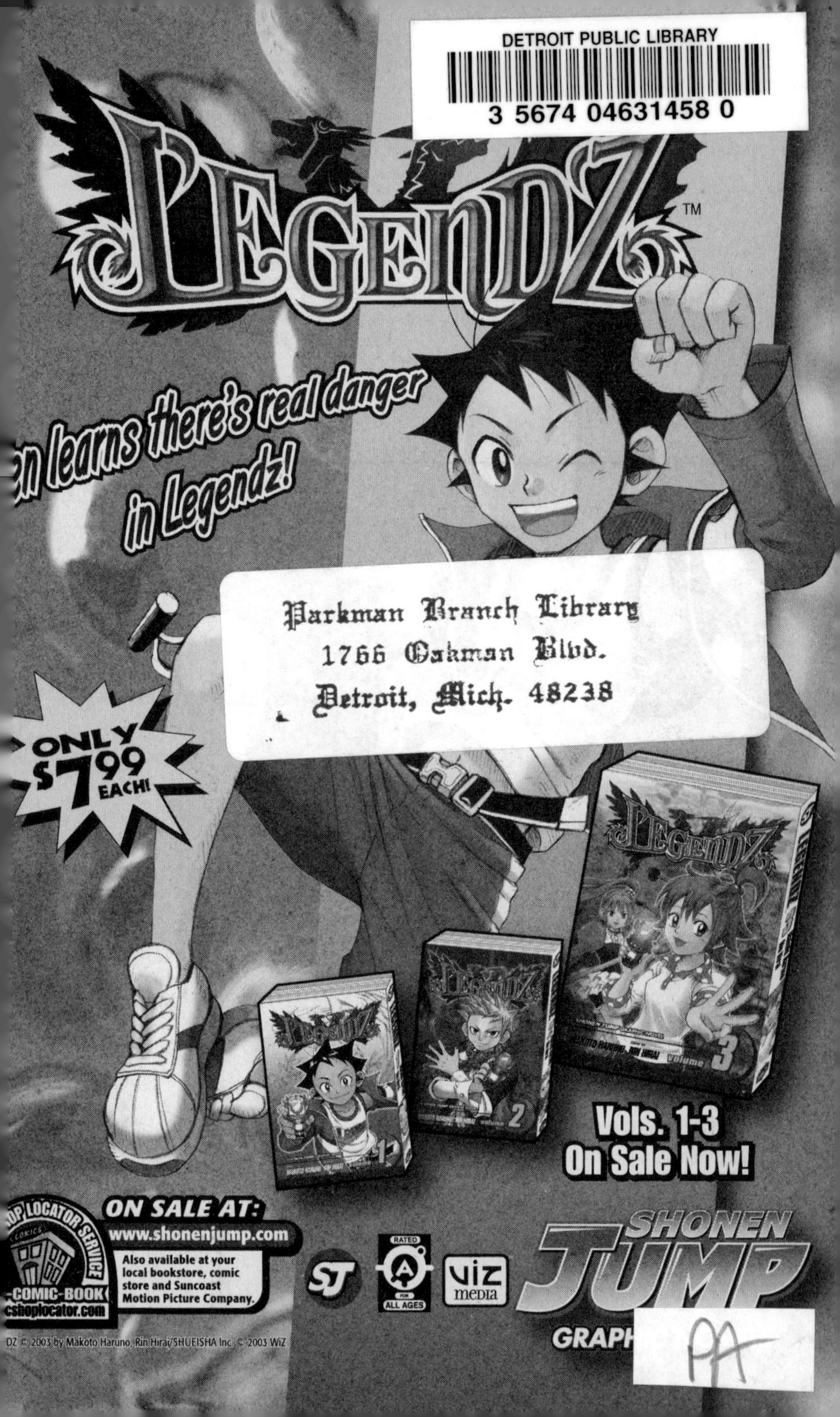

LEGENDZ™
en learns there's real danger in Legendz!
ONLY $7.99 EACH!
Vols. 1-3
On Sale Now!
ON SALE AT:
www.shonenjump.com
Also available at your local bookstore, comic store and Suncoast Motion Picture Company.
COMIC-BOOK
cshoplocator.com
SJ
RATED A FOR ALL AGES
VIZ media
SHONEN JUMP
GRAPH
DZ © 2003 by Makoto Haruno, Rin Hirai/SHUEISHA Inc. © 2003 VIZ